SURVIVED AGAINST ALL ODDS!

SURVIVED
AGAINST ALL ODDS!

MARY C S LIMA

XULON ELITE

Xulon Press Elite
2301 Lucien Way #415
Maitland, FL 32751
407.339.4217
www.xulonpress.com

Paperback ISBN-13: 978-1-66287-192-4
Ebook ISBN-13: 978-1-66287-193-1

CHAPTER 1

A Child that was Prayed for!

I was born in Portugal from a family of a mother and father and three older brothers that were set on protecting me …No way was I prepared for a journey of a lifetime!

My father and mother were also from Portugal but from two different locations, my father from Coimbra and my mother from the Island of Acores.

Acores is the 3rd island of 9 islands, known to be a volcanic island where the airfield "Lajes Field Air Base #4" is located. Discovered in the 1430's and named in the beginning after Jesus Christ was later re-named Terceira.

I loved their names! My mother had been named after Jesus Christ, so she was named "Jesuina", my father was named" Rogerio" but later to his friends and family was well known by the name of Roger...

My father went to serve in the army in the island of "Terceira", there he met my mother thru a friend, my mother used to joke that when she looked at my dad thru the door, she knew she was meeting the love of her life (I called it a match made in Heaven). Something else they also found out about each other when they got married was that they were born on the same day, same month and same year except in different cities! Something they joked about thru out their lives together, trying to find out who was born first was a joke between them! My mother had my brothers one year apart and she would later name them "a escadinha." "The staircase." Telmo was born on 05/01/1947, Jose Carlos was born on 04/16/1948 and Carlos Henrique was born on 11/10/1949. Her first pregnancy, so she told me later was her most difficult one! She had developed nausea that unfortunately was caused every time my father got close to her! In order to avoid throwing up in front of him, she would scratch the wall and sniff it! Fortunately for both this went away after a few months, otherwise it could have affected their relationship! My brother's loved to play in the beach nearby and loved to ride in our father's car! Many times, our cousin Victor would get in the car without anyone knowing to play with my brother's, from what my mother told me they played soccer together on the beach, Victor was notorious for hiding from his parents. They would send him to church all dressed up, he would change clothes and then go play with my brother's. My mother also made sure that my brothers were involved in Church activities from a very young age, my youngest brother Carlos Henrique was actually chosen to wear a crown at the festival of the "Bodos do Espirito Santo" a festival designed to honor the Holy Spirit. This festival was arranged every year in all the islands of Acores, my parents always took pictures whenever special events came around…

My father on the other hand had a taxi that he drove for a living, he gave rides even to prostitutes and when they didn't have the money to pay for the fare, they would offer my father (that was very handsome) free service! When it came to women my father was weak, he couldn't drink because it made him really sick…so, it was not like he could blame it on drinking! My mother unfortunately found out and so did some of our family, she told my father to leave and go back to Coimbra to stay with his mother. He stayed there for a while and she survived by sewing for people, she also received a letter from him asking her to come back and another from her mother-in-law asking her to give him another opportunity. I believe she probably had a few doubts about accepting him back so she wrote him back, told him she would accept him back with one condition and that was that he gave up the taxi service and tried finding work elsewhere. He accepted of course, when he came back he spent nights learning how to type and found work at the "Lajes Air Base". He would oversee the weight and the balance of airplanes to check if they were correct before taking off, he worked there for a while and enjoyed it but life for my father didn't really change until I was born! I was told by my mother that many times I would fall asleep with my father's hand in mine!

My mother had been told that she could not have any more children after Carlos Henrique, so I was the product of a miracle and named me after a saint (Santa Saosinha) that was very well known in the Islands, she was so happy with my birth that she bragged about me everywhere! Someone took a picture of my mother at a picnic holding me up in the air with a smile from ear to ear! My father on the other hand called me "Fofinha." In English this means "Cute." My parents were so protective of me that they got a female dog for our protection, her name was "Neca" she became my biggest protector! She would lay by my crib and growl at anyone that came by! My mother told me that one day as she held me in her arms that someone knocked on the door and she had to go to the bathroom at the same time! She placed me in Victor's arms and headed for the bathroom, she told me later on that the reason she got a hernia in her abdominal area was because she had waited too long to go to the bathroom and pushed too hard! Meanwhile by the time she came back to the kitchen I had peed all over Victor's pants (marking my ground)! My mother unfortunately was in pain after that... from that day on she had bouts when her hernia would get inflamed and she would have to lay down for a while. I believe that my parents started to suffer financially after a while because they arranged for passage on a ship for all of us to move from the Islands to the mainland...

CHAPTER 2

The Family Move to Coimbra.

I was just 3 years old when this took place and the whole family moved to Coimbra…. a move that proved to bring us all kind of problems! Because of our financial situation my brothers were not able to attend a private school in Coimbra instead they attended a local school.

My mother was working as a seamstress and money became very short but that did not stop my parents of trying to make life pleasant for us. My father for example took me on a trip that I never forgot to a miniature theme park called "Portugal dos Pequenitos" Portugal for the Little Ones, this park was designed for 5 years old it was like being in another world! Just like other children I loved to go in and out of doors to explore, open the windows and giggled with delight! We explored nearby parks and beaches and like any other family… had picnics and took pictures…

My father also found a job at a hotel, unfortunately short lived! One day after work as he was trying to cross the street to go home, he was hit by a motorcycle, fortunately the bike only damaged his foot and an ambulance was called. We were advised of the accident and by the time we got there we were told that my father was very lucky, only his foot had been broken! He had an extremely hard time when he got there because he had just eaten dinner and threw up everything in his stomach! It took time for him to recuperate, he was also advised that due to this accident every time the weather changed…. he would feel pain in his foot, we were just glad nothing more serious had happened, we could have lost him!

On the other hand, my brother Jose Carlos that was like a second dad to me, had become by his request my godfather as well, he would take me out sometimes while my mother was working for a walk. One day while I was out with him and holding his hand, we heard a big commotion by the train station…. when we looked at the train tracks, we saw what remained of someone's body! My brother immediately covered my eyes with his hands and told me not to look in that direction! Unfortunately, it was too late what I had seen would stay engraved in my mind forever more!

On the other hand, my other two brothers got into big trouble! The oldest and the youngest got involved with bad friends that talked them into stealing for fun! My parents were not informed until it was too late! One night we heard a knock on our door …when my father opened the door two policemen were standing there! My father and mother had a huge argument prior to this due to their disappearance, my father had told her that someone had spotted my brothers running away from the scene. He wanted to tell the police that he suspected that they were nearby…my mother threatened to leave him if he did!

I can just imagine how my father felt! On one hand he could face jail for hiding from the police that he knew where to find my brothers on the other hand he could lose my mother forever! It was not an easy decision!

I was just a little girl that loved her family and didn't want her parents to split up! I remembered how their arguments affect me!

The police were there to notify my parents that they had found my brothers and to arrest my father for harboring fugitives!

My brothers were arrested and taken to a Correction Facility since they were minors, my father was taken to a local prison and life totally changed for us!

The image of my father taken away in handcuffs would stay in my mind for years to come…for something that could have been avoided in the first place! I don't remember how long my father was in jail (we could not afford to pay the bail), I was either 5 or 6 years old when this happened but I do remember how hard life became after their arrest!

My mother continued to sew while my oldest brother Jose Carlos who had not been involved in the stealing with my other brothers left school and got a job to help support our family.

I continued to attend Primary school, my mother would take me and pick me up each day, unfortunately, teachers in Portugal at the time I was raised thought they had the same rights that parents do! One day while attending class I really had to go to the bathroom to have a bowel movement, I raised my hand and asked the teacher if I could go to the bathroom and she said out loud for all to hear "No, you can't …I know what all of you do in the bathroom, you hide there to avoid being in class, wait until break time." Unfortunately, I couldn't wait and when I sat back down the bowel movement had come out! I sat very still waiting for breaktime to go to the bathroom and clean myself up…. Of all things… the teacher called me to the board! As I walked in the middle of the aisle, I knew very well that everyone could smell it and I was so embarrassed! As soon as I reached the teacher, she saw what had happened and instead of being sympathetic she slapped me in front of everyone and my nose started to bleed!

I could hear gasps in the back of the class and she got scared! She made everyone take a break, took me in the back and cleaned me up… gave me cookies and milk and made me promise that I wouldn't tell my mother. I said yes so that she would not pick on me but when my mother picked me up, I told her…Not only because I was very humiliated but also because I did not want that teacher to do this to anybody else! My mother had a talk with her and told her she would contact the school board if this ever happened again… Of course, it didn't because she didn't want to lose her job…

I already felt less than other children by having to help my family in a way that was degrading to any child and incidents like these didn't help!

The money my mother and brother brought home wasn't enough to get by many times I had to knock at our neighbor's door to ask if they had anything they could give us as we were low on food …The visits to my father and my brothers were very sad! My brothers had been taken to a Correctional Facility for teenagers in "Sintra" and my father was taken to a local jail in Coimbra. When we set out to visit them it always had to be done on separate days since "Sintra" was quite far... On these visits all I could see was sadness on my mother's eyes and she always cried after we left!

As for my brother's all we could see in their eyes was regret and shame, they had a hard time looking at us and I could see a lot of sadness in both! Carlos Henrique asked my mother to tell Telmo to stop looking at him with reproach because he made him feel guilty! We knew that Carlos Henrique had been the one that had instigated the whole thing, but my mother decided not to say anything, she told me later "He needs to deal with his own conscience."

My father was another matter, my mother had to deal with her own conscience since it was because of her that my father was now in jail! She had not let him tell the authorities where my brothers were and he ended up being arrested! When we visited him, he hugged me and kissed me…. but he was cold towards my mother…there was also silent reproach in his eyes towards her...

Neither my father nor brothers had to be where they were if we had the money to pay good lawyers …the crime they had committed wasn't that serious (it wasn't murder) that money could not fix…

CHAPTER 3

Moving in with family
and our own place...

My mother (while my father was in jail) decided to move from Coimbra to Caxias, we would be moving in with my mother's sister ...we were living very poorly even with Jose Carlos help! On our way out of the city my mother cried and prayed afraid of what was to become of us and of leaving my father and brothers behind...

The driver of the moving van turned to my mother and said, "Pray to our patron saint "Rainha Santa Isabel" she is well known for doing miracles for those in despair." My Mother did just that, she promised her to go back one day, dress like her and attend a festival in her honor.

At last, we got moved in with my aunt and my cousins, a position I don't wish on anyone! There is an old Portuguese saying that goes like this "O convidado enjoa depois dos 3 dias." The guest starts to stink after 3 days" unfortunately, that applies even to family!

It didn't help that my uncle was very stingy! He watched the food we consumed and when I took baths, they had to be taken in the water my cousin had used to take her bath previously! The family meals were a torture for me! Deprived of good food like I had been... if I reached for a spoon to get a second helping, I would get a dirty look from my uncle and would give up on that attempt! My mother prayed continuously for a place of our own...When my father came back from prison,

8

we already had found a small house close to my aunt's house, we cleaned it and cleaned it and made it our home.... It didn't matter that there rats around or that there were snakes on top of the house via a garden that was out in the back! We were just glad to have our own little place!!

My father found a job at "Docapesca" (Port where ships docked to bring in all types of fish) in Lisbon, my father became an inspector for the company and my mother worked as a seamstress for anyone that needed alterations done....my father brought us home free fish every week and my mother had to really become inventive with our menu! There were many ways of making fish meals and out of one chicken, she would make 3 meals! One half baked, the other soup and even managed to make a rice dish with the chicken giblets!

My favorite past time was to make paper dolls (female and male) and made the outfits with the little tabs so that I could change the outfits often (you could tell that I took after my mother on this), I loved doing this while I sat on the floor, another past time of mine was to dress up my cat in doll clothes! While in my room upstairs, I would dress her up and she would run downstairs to the kitchen! My mother would see her and exclaim out loud "Saozinha, please leave the kitty alone, she doesn't like to have dresses on!" my cat however never scratched me and was very patient.... so, this habit continued until I outgrew it!

In our neighborhood we finally made a few friends including people that needed alterations done, right next to my aunt's house we developed a friendship with an older couple that had a dog named "Palhaco". They loved to watch a scary series on TV that fascinated me as much as it scared me! A nun dressed in total black would show up in people's lives when it was time for them to die! Since we didn't have a TV, we would watch these series with them and then walk home, for me this experience became a nightmare! I would get so scared after watching the program that I couldn't sleep! My parents finally noticed what an affect this was having on me and gave up watching the program.... We did keep the friendship because these people did not judge us instead treated us with respect and kindness!

Sometimes friends can become closer than family!

My father always made a point of spending time with me, he would take me to the zoo, to the nearby park and his favorite song that he sang to me was "O barquinho" (the little boat) …. He also made me little boats out of paper... these were memories that I would never be able to forget!

My brothers stayed in the Correctional Facility for a few years, we went to see them ever so often and directly from there they came home and later both were drafted to the army…. something my mother dreaded….

Telmo, my oldest brother developed a fear of being watched, his self-esteem was very low but of my two brothers he was the most kindhearted! Carlos Henrique the youngest, the most outgoing of the two decided to get a trade so he could use it after the army in the printing business.

CHAPTER 4

The Unconceivable Happened!

*B*oth my brothers were released and sent home and unfortunately Telmo did something unthinkable! He started to molest me…something I hid from everyone! He would grab me, take me to his bed and have me fondle him! He warned me not to tell our parents, it would be our secret! Victims no matter how young they are they always think they are also responsible, that day I stopped being a child! Many more days like these would follow…

I kept the secret more to protect him then to protect me! As I got older, he stayed away from me but of course the scars stayed… my parents saw him as my protector because he was 11 years older than me….

Attending middle school for me was something else! At that time, teachers had the power to act as parents and unfortunately, they didn't like special children! My mother had instructed me to tell my teacher that I had to be called "Saozinha" instead of my full name because of the promise she had made to the saint, so, when I was called to introduce myself, of course I gave my teacher my nickname! She immediately made a smart remark in front of everyone "In this school we don't go by nicknames, please give me your full name." I did just that but from that day on… she made a point of picking on me, one day when I was called to the board to finish a math problem because I was nervous…. I was not able to do it! She asked me to give her my right hand, got a big ruler out, held my hand in place and smacked it a few times!

The next time she did that to me I withdrew my hand quickly and she smacked her hand instead! She was extremely upset and complained about me to my parents, I had to explain to them what she had been doing, what we didn't know was that she was being watched and that other parents had been complaining about her! The school board got involved and eventually she was told to leave the school!

I finally made it to end of the school year, junior high was difficult for me because of math, I didn't like it but I was extremely good at writing and other subjects, I had done my finals and failed! My best friend and I decided to stop by the riverbank that was overflowing after recent rains and I told Candida that I was going to jump in! She looked at me and said, "Don't you dare do that! your parents love you and they know you can repeat the year!" I told her "I'm not going home, I don't want to disappoint them." she left me there looking at the river and walked to my house to get help, guess who came to get me? Telmo of course! He placed an arm around me and told me "Mom and Dad are not mad, you can always repeat the year, stop being silly and let's go home." As we walked home together, he placed his arm over my shoulder and tried to hide his laughter from me! In a way I was relieved that someone had stopped me! I happened to be really scared of the river!

By the time Telmo was in his 20's he was drafted to go to Guinee, Africa. When he left for Africa, he was depressed and I believe ashamed! His last words to us when he said goodbye was that he knew he would not be coming back! I would remember those words forever (I loved him even though I also feared him) …and I certainly didn't wish my brother dead!

After he left, we went back to our normal lives but there was a new sadness in our home that we tried to ignore…

CHAPTER 5

Life without a brother and Middle School…

*O*ur house was right in front of the beach, we could hear the waves in the morning and many winters we had flooding inside our humble home, but I loved the summers! That summer my father tried to teach me how to swim, he would hold on to me, then would let go and I would go straight to the bottom! I didn't want to become afraid of the water, so I told him I was going to try on my own! I learned how to swim hanging on to a rope on the beach holding with one arm and then letting go! I become a daredevil at the beach and even learned how to swim underwater! This experience taught me early in life how to become independent and how to respect currents and the ocean!

My father could not believe that I had done this on my own and found other ways to entertain me, many times, he would take me to my favorite park nearby and let me use the swings, he would take me to the local café and buy me "garoto" (coffee and milk) with a dessert. Our favorite place to eat was a small restaurant that served eggs and "salsichas" (sausages), these were memories never forgotten and treasured!

My youngest brother Carlos Henrique on the other hand left the army, got a woman pregnant and got a job at a printing company, if he carried any scars from jail, he didn't talk about it! He knew how to hide them…

I was attending middle school when I was invited to a field trip to Fatima with a group of students and nuns, I didn't like going myself but this trip was necessary to pass class, we traveled by bus and when we arrived there I was amazed by the size of the place! The chapels were beautiful! We visited the "Capelinha Cova de Iria" saw the tree where our Lady of Fatima appeared, the tombs where Jacinta, Francisco and Lucia were buried and finished by attending a huge mass held at the Chapel of Calvary that overlooked all of Fatima. The amount of people there was amazing! We were told to stay close to each other so that we wouldn't get separated…I don't how it happened but when I looked around, I didn't see anybody from my group and I was on my own! I got nervous because we would be leaving after the mass…I looked up at the image of Lady of Fatima and prayed that someone would find me because there was no way I could go and find anyone!

She wasn't known for the Lady of Miracles for nothing because not too long after that a nun from our group showed up and found me and my God! was, I relieved!!

I was so happy to be back at home! I shared this story with my mother, she said that she wasn't surprised that the nun came back for me because she had prayed for a safe trip for me! She also reminded me that she had made Lady of Fatima my godmother when I was born!

My childhood around our area wasn't that great! I had to deal with a bully that worked for my uncle and that would always wait for me after school! The last straw for me was when he destroyed a top my mother had sawn for me! That day I grabbed him, shoved him out of the way and told him that I would tell my uncle what he was doing and get him fired, actually, he should have been at school instead of delivering telegrams and packages to people! After that day he would see me coming from school and would walk the other way…

I also had a great protector, my brother Jose Carlos, he had found work in a Bakery and on his way home if he saw me playing outside among other kids, he would go home and ask my mother to make me go home! Most of the times that I was told to go home was because of my brothers, it was like having 3 fathers instead of one!

The area near our train station was well known.... right next to it was a very well-known restaurant by the name of Monaco... there was a rumor going around that the rabbit they served were local cats!

This was one place my family never went to because of their reputation and of their prices!

As a family we had the habit of taking walks to the train station, sit and observe people as they got out of the trains, this is how I became a people watcher... something that would help me to became very observant for the rest of my life! It was a harmless habit that proved to be very beneficial ...

I was attending Middle School when we had a huge bomb threat! We were picked up by soldiers and were sent to a plain field away from any housing, when I looked around all I saw was a huge number of strangers and soldiers! I started to panic a bit wondering where my parents where... from what I had been told by a soldier they also had soldiers going door to door warning people to evacuate in the housing community, we were told to remain at that spot until we were notified the danger was gone. Finally, we were told that it was a false alarm! We were taken back to the train station and told to go back home, I ran back home afraid that my parents were not there and was surprised to see my mother at home! After hugging her, she told me that she had decided not to leave our home and be there to wait for me! My father also came home from work worried about us, he had been told of the bomb threat and had wondered If we had been taken somewhere! We hugged each other, so happy that nothing had happened!

I often wondered why I matured so early in life, probably had to with all that happened to my father and to my brothers! I saw myself as my mother's protector and did anything that I could to help her, even after school, I would come home to do my homework and help her with dinner. I learned what dishes were my family favorites, with my brother Telmo it had been chocolate pudding and fried banana, with

Carlos Henrique dishes with linguica and with Jose Carlos the heads of the fish that my father brought home! Our routine at dinner time was to talk and often make plans for future meals…

My father also helped my mother in the kitchen, she was really good in alterations and always had quite a bit to do! We learned to enjoy my father's favorite dish that he had learned to make at the "Docapesca" and that was "Bacalhau a Bras" (cod dish made with shoestring potatoes and eggs) …This became one of our favorite dishes as well!

My brother Jose Carlos also had made a change in his life! He had gotten tired of working for the Bakery and found out that thru the Navy he could finish the education that he had not been able to finish, so he enrolled in the "Escola da Marinha" "Naval School" and graduated! We were all so proud of him! We attended his graduation and I knew my mother worried what would become of him! We were told that he would be sent to Acores.

CHAPTER 6

High School and Unbelievable News!

After middle school I was finally able to start High School in "Oeiras" and would have to take the train there back and forth and walk part of the way, I had found a group of girls to walk with and suddenly we were accosted by an older man that opened his raincoat and exposed himself!

We were too scared to keep it to ourselves and decided to confide in a teacher at school, she in turn notified the authorities! They were able to apprehend him and were called to testify in court, I wasn't scared because I had done nothing wrong, so when the judge called me up front to verify the man apprehended was the one, I very innocently looked at the man and exclaimed "Well I don't know! I wasn't looking at his face!" The judge and the people in court burst out laughing! I believe the case got dropped because the other girls that were with me were saying the same thing!

The good news was that this guy stopped showing up and the police kept an eye in the area for our safety.

On the other hand, my mother's father that had loved me dearly since the first day I was born was becoming quite ill and the whole family took turns caring for him (I was the apple of his eye) until he passed away. I had so many fond memories of my grandfather! When I was a little girl, he would pick me up at our home to take me for a walk and my mother always advise him "Father please remember, she has allergies, no chocolate, no eggs and no oranges." He would agree but when we would pass by a bakery…. I would start begging him for a chocolate and he couldn't say no! So, he would end up buying it and let me have it, by the time we came back home and knocked on my door I was already scratching myself, my mother would just shake her head at him! He ended up dying in my aunt's house, a place that I had visited quite often…After his death I got scared to go and visit my aunt and cousins…

Just as I thought my mother was recovering from his death…. we received a telegram from Africa informing us that Telmo had died while saving his Captain's life at the age of 23 on October of 1970! Attached was a letter from the captain, giving my parents his condolences and to let them know that not only did he have a very high regard for Telmo but also that he had died a hero…. saving his life!

Telmo according to his captain had pushed him out of harm's way and stepped on a mine that very well could have killed him… his body came down in pieces.! My brother many times in his letters to my mother had exclaimed of how many innocent people had died in vain, including women and children! He had almost died of "Malaria" and in the end he died to save someone's life! We were not allowed to view the casket when it came back from Africa, this made it very hard for us to believe that he was really dead… Especially for my mother! He was buried in a local cemetery by an organization called "Liga dos Combatentes" started after the Great War.

Jose Carlos was advised of his death while in a ship serving in the Navy and he was devastated! Because of his death he was not drafted to Guinee and ended up in the islands of Acores, got married and found himself a job thru the Navy, this job supplied him with housing nearby and he became well known in the community…

At this time in Portugal, we had a Dictator by the name of Salazar that was in power until 1968, he was succeeded by a Politian by the name of Marcelo Caetano that enforced a law that if a family lost one son in the war in Africa if they had other sons… they would be excluded from being drafted to Guinee. We were extremely relived that my other brothers would not have to be sent to Africa! It also helped us a bit that a close friend of my brother Telmo came to visit us one day from Guinee and shared with all of us that this in a way was better than having him come back without a limb or traumatized for life…

I didn't let his death affect our lives, I fought to bring my parents a bit of happiness every time I could, I learned how to cook by helping my mother in the kitchen and made homemade dishes, like "rissois de camarao" (stuffed dough with shrimp), "croquetes de carne" (meat croquetes) and even desserts. At Christmas time I went by the train station and found moss to use in our Nativity Scene, broken glass to use on the flooring to make it look like lakes and decorated our small little tree! I knew that if it wasn't for me my mother would have given up any celebrations, even her wedding anniversary! The telegram we received regarding Telmo's death was received the day before their wedding anniversary…a day they would remember forever!

We got used to taking daily walks by the ocean right after dinner, especially in good weather and talked along the way, I found out thru one of those talks that my mother as a young woman had been attacked by a dog and got traumatized by the experience! No wonder whenever she had to walk somewhere she would always ask for one of us to meet her somewhere!

Carlos Henrique on the other hand had kept a relationship with a woman and got her pregnant, she gave birth to a darling little girl, they named her Carla Andrea, my mother wondered why they had not made plans to get married, my brother told her once "I don't trust her mom, she has played around." It was a good thing because she made a pass at my father and once my brother found out he stopped seeing her! She would only come around to drop the baby for her to spend some time with us…

My brother Jose Carlos also decided to visit us one year with his new wife and right from the beginning I had the feeling that she didn't

like me! We were watching TV one night in our small living room....
all talking at the same time when my father looked at me and asked me
to turn off the TV. I got up and turned it off and out of the corner of my
eye I saw my sister-in-law speak to my brother, he got up and asked me
what gave me the right to turn off the TV without anyone's permission!

And for the first time in my life my brother/godfather slapped me
in front of our family! This was the first time one of my brothers had
lifted a hand towards me, I started to cry and told him "Our father asked
me to do it!" "Do you think I would do this without anyone's permission?" I was so upset that I left my family in the living room and went
to my room!

It goes to show you what kind of influence women can have in a
men's life!

Jose Carlos before he left for the Navy had been going out with a
girl that was a maid in someone's house, she loved him so much that
she decided to go back to school to get a degree so she could live up to
his standards! Maria was extremely kind and loved our family but no
matter how much she tried he couldn't love her the way she deserved....
probably the reason that he had decided to stay in the Navy and go live
in Acores...They left and in a way, I was glad that she was not going to
be around us.... we women can always tell who like us from the heart
and those who fake it!

CHAPTER 7

Learning to live without a brother...

My Mother survived and lived because of us otherwise she would have let herself die! Telmo was her firstborn child and she had been extremely close to him...

For years after she looked everywhere for him.... even on train stations, hoping to see him somewhere.... hoping that it was all a big mistake!

She looked older, constantly were a black scarf around her face, black clothing and was obsessed with Telmo's death! One day walking back from school I was stopped by the priest of our church he knew our family very well and asked me how we were all doing. I shared with him that our home was now a very sad place to live and that my mother still wore black from head to toe and couldn't stop crying!

He looked at me very seriously and told me to give her a message from him, he said "Tell her that she has to change things as soon as possible at home! Let you listen to music, laugh and tell her to stop wearing so much black because this way he will never be able to rest in peace." I thanked him and went home to share with my mother what I had been told, she took it seriously and went about to change things in our home. Unfortunately, my mother also lived with resentment towards my aunt Mathilde, something that I couldn't stop her from doing! Before Telmo was drafted he had spoken to our mother about visiting and staying in Bethel, Ohio with our aunt for a while to avoid being drafted, my mother had written to her sister and she had replied back that my uncle didn't think this was a great idea! In my mother's own words "If they had given him a chance to live there for a while, he would still be alive!" It would take her many years before she let go of this resentment…

What I didn't share with my mother and the priest was that I lived with the guilt of thinking that he had died because of me…maybe he couldn't live with himself and could care less if he lived or died! I even thought that God had punished him because of what he had done to me!

My mother suffered from depression for a long time, not only from the death of her father but especially from the death of her son, it didn't help that my aunt Carmen came to see us one day and told my mother that she had seen Telmo passing thru her bedrooms! My mother had told me that even as a child my aunt Carmen had been prone of seeing spirits and had told my grandmother about it…. this was something she hated and feared!

My mother asked her if he had given her message and she responded "No, but I told him that I didn't want to be afraid of my own home and if this happened again, I would stop praying for him." She later told us that he didn't show up again and that she was extremely relieved!

His death had affected all of us in a different way! My father that loved to take me to see movies now had to be careful and choose the movies carefully that we saw together…. if it happened to be a war movie…. I would walk out! It would take many years before I was able to see a movie about war…

My mother dealt not only with grief but also with past resentments, she had forgiven my father his past infidelities but had not forgotten them! Her own family had criticized her because she had chosen to forgive my father and kept her marriage together, I became her confidante and by the time I was 13 or 14 years old I already didn't trust men…

Being the only daughter also meant having overprotective parents and when my mother sent me to neighbor's houses to deliver alterations, my father would stay outside and wait for me, one evening while delivering a skirt for my mother I was grabbed behind by an older guy and started to scream! My father heard me and came after the guy with fits blazing! I thought he was going to kill him! I ran home and got my mother, both of us started pleading with my dad to let him go… He set him free but I'm sure the man learned a valuable lesson that day!

My father also had a bit of bad news that year…. his mother had fallen, broken her hip and never made it out of the hospital, she passed away and we took a trip to Coimbra for the funeral. On this trip I found out how my grandfather had died! According to my dad he had suffered from depression because he wasn't appreciated at home (my dad was a young man at the time), he had tried speaking to my grandmother but had been ignored so the only way out he saw was to jump in front of a train! From that day on my father's brother Fausto became the head of household, he made life very difficult for my father forcing him to join the army and that's how he met my mother! I loved Coimbra but my mother and father had nothing but bad memories from that place, after the funeral we came home and my father said to us "There is nothing left here any longer, let's go home."

Once at home I had to deal with school and had a tough time there! I didn't feel like I fitted in anywhere, I compared my life to other teenagers around me including my cousins next door and their lives seemed so much happier!

For years I had suffered from insults at school for being short-sighted…they called me "zarolha"…that's worse that being short-sighted! It's a slang word referring to someone that's blind in one eye, I wore glasses from a young age and as a teenager and kept on losing them on purpose to fit in (something that unfortunately cost my parents money). My school was full of groups of young women with parents well off…I was not one of them!

My mother made my clothes from materials and clothing from clothes donated to us from relatives that lived in the US, from a dress we received from America my mother made my dress for my brother's wedding! I was probably 13 at the time still wearing glasses, starting to mature and I loved my brother dearly! Carlos Henrique had met another woman and married her in a local church, they were surrounded by family and friends that day, for the first time in my life, I got to dance the Tango with a friend of our family and truly enjoyed it!

They moved into our home and stayed in the room next to mine… something funny happened one night! I woke up with Rosa crying out "I think we have a hole in the ceiling and it's raining." when she looked at my brother laying next to her…. he was asleep and peeing up!

We all teased him the next day but that turned out to be one of many incidents that he couldn't explain! My sister-in-law found him one night peeing in a drawer and still asleep!

It got better with time, one good thing about having them around was that they took me to "Feiras" (Fairs) and dances and my parents trusted them to be my chaperones…. otherwise, I would have a hard time going anywhere!

My mother and I on the other hand had no secrets from each other! When I doubts about something, or my heart was broken it was her that I went to… I had learned early in life in whom I could trust! All my life I had seen my mother pray in her room (even the rosary) and one day I asked her "Mama, why do you pray every day without fail?" She told me something that would stick with me for the rest of my life "That a house that is prayed for is a house protected by God and that she had learned this from her mother." I believed her because she had always been faithful in her love for God, I had seen her pray even when most people would have given up on Him!

She worried a lot about me because I developed early at 14 years old, I acted and looked older.! I dropped the glasses; my mother highlighted my hair weekly with a homemade mixture I knew nothing about but still liked the effect…this change of course made guys take a second look at me way too early and that made my parents keep a tight grip on me….

They always made sure that one of my brothers met me at the train station and walked with me home after school…On one occasion I was heading back home in the train, inside the cabin was my teacher for religious studies and a couple of students from the same class. When the train stopped, I got off the train, my youngest brother Carlos Henrique placed his arm around my shoulder and asked me how my day was… We walked home together and that same week my mother received a note from my teacher asking her to go and see her! My mother asked me if I had done anything wrong and I told her "Of course not…. I would remember." My mother went to see her and actually cracked up! My teacher asked her who was the young men waiting for me at the train station, before she had a chance to reply… she immediately told my mother that I was too young to be dating!

My mother pulled out the picture of Carlos Henrique and asked her if that was the young man she saw with me? She said "Well, yes!" My mother didn't miss a beat and told her "That happens to be her youngest brother, we always have one of her brother's waiting for her at the station and walk with her home… so you see, you don't have anything to worry about!" Of course, my teacher was embarrassed and probably learned not to mettle in people's lives! When my mother got home, she hugged me and I just shook my head!

Getting my mother to drop the black clothing completely because of my brother's death was something we couldn't talk her into! Even just walking to my aunt's house she would place a black scarf on her head before heading out! She came back home one afternoon very upset because she had been visiting with her sister when she was asked to leave by using the back door! My mother looked at her questionably and my aunt simply told her "My youngest daughter's boyfriend is coming to see her … I would prefer that you are not here." I hated this type of discrimination especially if it was directed towards my parents and when my mother told me about it, I told her to keep away for a while. My mother because this was the only family we had nearby asked me to keep this from my father and ignore it, she knew my cousin

Saozinha liked taking me places with them and she didn't want bad feelings between us!

My uncle was another issue! He had just bought a Volkswagen; he loved this car so much that he preferred to place sandbags on the back of the car (to keep it level) than asking his family to ride in the car! Most of the times we waited for him to be in a good mood to take us out to one of their favorite places and have coffee at the cafes in Cascais, this coastline was absolutely beautiful and was well known as the "Linha de Estoril" (Estoril coastline) … they would sit and have coffee and a treat… admire the ocean view for a while and shop at the local shops…

Chapter 8

Maturing early and getting your heart broken…

$\mathcal{B}$esides my cousins I also went to trips with my sister-in-law Rosa, her mother lived in "Aveiras de Cima" and she asked me to take a trip to see her. Her mother's house was a very poor home and the bathroom was an outhouse (the first one I had ever seen) but her food and hospitality made up for it! She made the best homemade stew I had ever tasted! Rosa also wanted me to go with her to a private birthday party and I accepted, when we got there the music was already playing!

It wasn't too long before I got approached by a very attractive guy (probably in his 30's) that made a huge pass at me and gave me my first French kiss! I pushed him away because I could feel that he was becoming aroused and I didn't want to become embarrassed in front of other people!

Unfortunately, his friend offered us a ride back home so that we wouldn't have to take the bus back, this same guy tried to take advantage of me in the back seat but I put a stop to it and pushed him away! Rosa and I fortunately were able to get home safely that night and relieved that this party was over!

Once they left us by the house, he grabbed my hand and told me that he would like to see me again, I told him that I would think about it to get rid of him. My sister-in-law once inside the house told me that she thought he was married and of course way too old for me! Before we left that weekend, I asked Rosa to get his address so that I could send him a letter and she agreed. Once at home she gave me his address and I wrote him a letter, I told him that if I ever visited "Aveiras" again, if he approached me that I would contact his wife personally to let her know what he was doing behind her back!

I hated men like him because I knew how my own mother had suffered with my father's infidelities...

That same year I also got my first experience regarding discrimination due to lack of money and social status from Jose a guy at school, my first real crush! My mother did alterations for his family and in school he hung around a group of people that had money, I hang out with them, we went swimming together, cooked and even had small parties at their family homes, I think they felt sorry for me and that's why they asked me to come along… When Jose started to pay attention to me, I couldn't believe it!

The daughter of the woman that my mother did alterations for confronted me one day by telling me "Don't place your hopes in Jose, his father has money and they will never accept you." I told her "He was the one that pursued me so he must be interested, you may be feeling a bit of jealously, am I right?"

Of course, she denied it but I kept away from her as much as possible since I didn't want to affect my mother's job, Jose confided in me that his father owned a jewelry store in town and that he suspected that he was cheating on his mother! When I asked him if she had confronted him about it, he said "No, she is way too comfortable with her lifestyle to rock the boat."

We started dating a bit and one day he broke my heart by telling me that he could not see me anymore otherwise his allowance would be taken away from him and his father would disown him! In another words I wasn't rich enough to fit in! From that day forward I avoided the gatherings because it hurt me too much to see him flirting with other girls while he looked at me every chance he got!

I usually met my mother after school.... walked to where she was working so that we could go back home together but after this experience I refused to go inside the house and would wait outside for her....

I had another experience that thru me off guard completely! I had been friends with a friend that lived nearby.... we both had our eyes on the guys across the street, when we moved to our home I had noticed a big building that housed young men that I believed were being prepared for the Navy, they would march right in front of my window, many times I would stand by the window to see them march together while attempting to do homework!

My girlfriend Susana had her eyes on a particular guy with green eyes, so I was very surprised one day when she took me to her home (her family wasn't in) and made a move on me!

This was my first time being approached by another woman! I looked at her and said "Susana, you know I like guys, please don't try this with me! You really embarrassed me today!" I left right after that and decided to let go of the friendship, I was so embarrassed that when my mother asked me later on why I wasn't friends with Susana any longer I told her that she knew I liked a certain guy and went after him anyway...

Experimenting is very natural in teens but I was very different from other young girls and had a religious family to answer too....

This experience plus the one with Jose made me very weary of girl-friends! My mother became my best friend and confidante, she told me to write my feelings down especially regarding Jose on a fake letter and then throw it away. I read it to her and then destroyed it... but the hurt never left! He was probably my first love! Those are never forgotten!

Rosa and I took frequent trips to "Aveiras de Cima" to see her mother... this was a place that I really liked! Thru Rosa's friends I met another guy by the name of Max that lived nearby, he was a "Forcado" (group of men that challenge a bull in a bullfight) something he really liked. He was so taken with me that he took trips to Caxias (by train) quite often to see me and even asked to meet my parents! I liked him very much but he would not introduce me to his family for some reason!

My 15th birthday was coming up and my parents decided to throw me a party and I had invited Max…. he accepted and then on the day of my party he didn't show up! Big mistake here!

The day after he showed up! I asked him what happened and after seeing me upset he finally said "My parents don't want me to see you anymore because they think women from Lisbon are loose, they also think that I'm wasting my time with someone that would not make me a good wife… so we have to quit this relationship." I just looked at him and told him "You could have at least told me that you were not coming! You actually met my parents! Please make sure you don't come around here anymore." I left pretty upset…

Again discrimination! I was fed up with it!

CHAPTER 9

Invitation to visit the US.

*S*o, when we received a letter from my aunt Mathilde inviting me to visit them in Bethel…. I pleaded with my parents to let me go on vacation there since my aunt and uncle would be paying for the trip, a golden opportunity to take time off away from school and from the stupid guys that I had met!

My father took me to the Portuguese Council in Lisbon… arranged for my passport and got my vaccines up to date, I found out he was a bit skeptical about this trip but he knew that this was an opportunity for me to have a good vacation and to meet my mother's side of the family…

However, before I left, I was warned by my parents and my brothers that they didn't want me to sacrifice myself in anyway …they wanted me to come back and continue my education… but I also knew that their biggest wish was to have a better life in the US (Including my brother that had passed away).

This was my first trip on a plane… alone and at the age of 15! It turned out to be a long flight! From Lisbon to New York and then another flight to Cincinnati Ohio…. by the time I was picked up by my aunt and my cousins I knew what jet leg was all about!

I loved meeting all my cousins (all 6 of them) and immediately took a liking to my aunt Mathilde! They all wanted to talk to me, unfortunately because of jet leg all I wanted to do was sleep! I also ended up taking Pepto Bismol for an upset stomach! It would take a couple of days to adjust to another time zone!

They all laughed when I told them to please keep fish away from me because of our diet at home and they told me of all the wonderful foods around...

I also found out that my aunt and my cousins had a little match-making in mind with someone the family knew very well (the whole thing was also to get my family in the US) and that they hoped I ended up liking….

My uncle took a liking to me right away and introduced me to country music and homemade breakfast (Tennessee style), I loved waking up in the morning and smell the wonderful smell of fresh cut grass thru my window! This was totally different from Ocean breezes!

Uncle Larry also took all of us fishing and laughed when I started to sing along ...Fishy ...Fishy and started to get fish! It was a coincidence, believe me!

My aunt took me everywhere while her kids were at school… her hairdresser, grocery shopping, etc.… we ate out and cooked Portuguese dishes that I knew how to cook from home. I traded clothes with one of my cousins and got to spend time with my grandma that was also living with my aunt…. the best part!

On the weekends we spent time exploring places for me to visit, one of them Kings Island… my first experience with an amusement park! Like most teenagers I loved the experience!

I also learned how to ride a bike and play baseball!

My uncle insisted on a trip to Tennessee to visit his family… there was much beauty to see…. including beautiful farms along the way! I was amazed how much the women of the family cooked! They spent most of the day in the kitchen making homemade meals for breakfast, lunch and dinner! All made by scratch!

For the first time in my life I saw someone spit on a spittoon while chewing tobacco from a distance like it was some kind of contest!

By the time we got back home I had gained 5 pounds but it was an experience I wouldn't have missed for the world! People from Tennessee were the most hospitable people I had ever met!

I loved this family right from the start and I wished with all my heart that I would have been born into a big family like this! They were loving people and they treated me with so much love and respect that I didn't even miss home!

The young man I meet was very taken with me! He asked me to marry him and promised me that he would find a way to bring my whole family to the US! I was very tempted and tried to connect with him but I couldn't even tolerate his arms around me!

I remembered my family's words to me before I left and I knew I could not marry someone that I didn't even feel an attraction towards, imagine a lifetime with someone that you don't love! The hardest thing I had to do was to explain to this young man how I felt! He was really determined to find a bride and I explained to him that it would be to his benefit to find someone that could love him and not just tolerate him!

I was introduced to another young man that was a friend of the family, I did like him quite a lot but unfortunately, I found that he drunk too much! I didn't want to be involved with someone with that kind of addiction…

Meanwhile my mother's brother found out I was in Bethel on vacation and not only wanted to meet me but wanted me to meet his oldest son …in my country marriage between cousins was common and I had never met that side of my family…I was skeptical, so was my aunt …Victor and I started talking on the phone and the attraction was immediate…

Frankie my youngest cousin was very funny! When he found out that I could possibly be flying to California to meet Victor told all of us "If Sao really needs someone to marry her for her to stay in the US, I will marry her myself!"

We all started laughing because Frankie was 3 years younger than me!

My aunt also made a point of contacting her family doctor to check if a marriage between cousins was safe… in case we decided to have kids, we were assured that everything would be fine and if we ended up wanting to get married, we should get blood work done and then decide if we wanted kids….

Chapter 10

Meeting other family in CA and first meeting with Victor.

My uncle flew to Ohio to come and get me and take me to meet his family. On the plane he asked me to become a little closer to my cousin Gina because she was a little heavier and her self-esteem was lower compared to my other cousin, Maria was very outgoing and had quite a lot of friends…of course I agreed but I was a bit worried about his request!

My first glimpse of San Francisco captivated me! It was like looking at Lisbon at night! Even the Golden Gate Bridge looked like our Vasco da Gama bridge over the ocean! I found out that just like Lisbon, San Francisco had an older and a newer part and had also been devasted by earthquakes!

The whole family was at the San Francisco airport to meet me including Victor …he leaned over to give me a kiss on the cheek and I knew immediately that there was something there!

He was 23 and I was 15 but it didn't matter…I was very mature for my age (had ditched the glasses and highlighted my hair at my aunt's house) and I wanted to give him a chance…. what I felt for him was totally different than anybody else I had ever met!

I stayed at their home and observed his family, Victor's parents had lots of problems and fought very often…. very different from my home!

I was however very attracted to Victor! While I was there, I had misgivings very often about staying in California, I was already dealing with jealousy from my cousins…by being closer to the oldest the younger felt that was doing this on purpose and complained to Victor's mother… in turn she became angry at me…

Besides family conflicts Victor's ex-wife kept on calling him (out of jealously) trying to get him back and wanting to meet me (I had no intention of doing that). He had married her when he was just 18 years old because she got pregnant, he claimed he never loved her and that she got pregnant on purpose to trap him into marriage…unfortunately their baby died with a brain tumor 3 years after and Victor and Joan got divorced.

I did try to back out…. but Victor and his dad convinced me that sense there was already a big attraction between us that we should try to make it work, this would allow my parents to come to the US…they also reminded me that my Visa was about to expire! Victor's dad absolutely wanted his son to marry a Portuguese girl after his last relationship with an American girl… especially because I had come directly from Portugal and had not become modernized.

Victor asked me to marry him and I accepted, we started to get the papers ready…. One of them was to get my parents' consent in writing, we also had our blood work done and were told that if we had any children that there would not be any problem...

We went everywhere together always chaperoned by my sisters-in-laws, he knew that I missed the beach and took me to one in Alameda… as soon as I saw the water… I ran to go swimming and as soon as my feet touched the water I cringed and backed out! Victor laughed at me and said, "I forgot to tell you that the ocean here is much colder than the ocean in Portugal but if you miss swimming, we can also find pools around this area." We ended up swimming most of the time in indoors pools but I still found the coast side in California absolutely beautiful!

I was also introduced to a different lifestyle, Victor practiced soccer twice a week and played on the weekends and I attended all of them…

his friends and their families got to know me very well and they placed bets of how long our marriage would last!

With my parents' consent we finally went to the courthouse (I did insist that once my parents were here that we would get married by church) and got married... When we got home, they had a cake waiting for us and Victor took me to spend our first night at a Motel...I was extremely nervous due to the sexual abuse I had experienced as a child and was worried that I might not be a virgin...also afraid that his family or him would send me back home!

Many years ago, in many cultures if a woman was not a virgin on their wedding night they would stone her to death... in my culture if you were from a catholic background and from a decent family you were expected to be a virgin. My mother had explained that to me when I was in my early teens, I believe to keep me away from sex at an early age, I had tried for so many years to block the sexual abuse out of my mind... but I found out that the images of child abuse stay engraved in your mind forever!

I was however surprised to find out that I was still a virgin! For me that first night was something I did not enjoy, it was a painful experience and I wondered if I was ever going to enjoy lovemaking!

The next morning because I had been so tense... I was sore everywhere! Little did I know what kind of sexual education I was going to be exposed to!

We went back to his house the next day after breakfast and I moved my stuff to Victor's room upstairs, from the first day I did not like that room (way too stuffy and very small) but I was assured by him that sooner or later we would move to on own apartment...

Things only got worse at home...no matter what I did I could not get close to my cousins! Victor's youngest brother was the only one that seemed to like me, I tried to get close to my mother-in-law but she also resented the fact that I knew how to clean and cook! The compliments I got from my father-in-law made the living situation around us much worse and I was too young to know how to handle all of this....

My mother- in- law on the other end made me afraid of the house! She told me that she found out that the previous owner was a drunk that had died in the house and abused his wife! She was a religious woman that would bless the house backwards with a rosary in her hands as a form of protection (she believed) from evil… Even included our room upstairs!

I corresponded with my parents by mail and hid the truth how miserable and scared I was not to worry them! I loved them too much to place this burden on them… I had however shared what I was going thru over the phone with my aunt Mathilde that posed a very important question "How are you? Are you happy?" I paused long enough for her to insist "Tell me what's wrong." I had no one to share what I was feeling because I knew no one in California so I told her how I felt and asked her to keep it to herself… I told her that sooner or later we would be moving out and that I was willing to work on our marriage, she agreed but told me that she expected me to keep in touch with her and didn't want me isolated while going thru all of this!

My father-in-law started the paperwork to get my parents in the US, one day he approached Victor and told him "The paperwork is ready for her parents to come here, things around our place have not improved so it's for your benefit and hers as well that you both move to an apartment… also for them to have a place to stay."

If my father-in-law had not had that conversation with Victor and convinced him to move out I would of probably ran away from their home…I saw my mother-in-law one time in a fit of anger throw an ashtray at my father-in-law and almost got him! That day I got out of the house and went for a walk in the neighborhood…scared to death!

CHAPTER 11

Finally a place of our own for us and for my parents!

$\mathcal{S}$ince Victor worked in a company in San Pablo called Myers Container... we found a two-bedroom apartment nearby with hardly any furniture ...slept on the floor for a little while and little by little got the apartment furnished, I really didn't care if it was furnished or not ...all I wanted was peace!

In January of 1974 my parents finally arrived from Portugal and moved in with us with the understanding that they would stay until my father found himself a job and then they would find themselves a place of their own...

My father found himself a job at Noll Manufacturing in Richmond and my mother found herself doing alterations for a dry-cleaning shop nearby...

I finally found out what had made my parents give up their home and join me so soon! One day they cornered me in the kitchen and asked me outright "Why were you going thru so much with Victor's family and you never wrote to us about it?" I told them "Because both of you were very far and I didn't want to worry you about it! How did you find out?" My mother turned to me and said "Your aunt Mathilde wrote to us and told us all about it and the day we received her letter we both cried! Your father had it made in his job but he was so upset that he immediately said for us to pack and get ready to leave for the US." She also told me that my cousin Saozinha had come over and told her "Why did you give your permission for Sao (my nickname) to get married to a man that has been married before? She is way too young to get married in the first place!"

My mom had to explain that it had been my wish, they made sure of that before giving their permission and that they had kept this from her so that she didn't worry about me...

Now I knew that the sacrifice they had made had been for me!

Meanwhile our marriage was not an easy one right from the beginning! Every time we fought, Victor went to see his family and he would tell them all about it (resentment set in) ...they would give him advise and he would come home and use that advise to what he thought was for our benefit! Most of the times it only made matters worse! Sometimes we had plans to go somewhere and if his family did not agree with those plans, they would be cancelled!

One trip they were not able to mess with was our first trip to Disneyland, I was fascinated by the place...I had never seen a place like this in Portugal! We saw all kinds of shows, went in almost all the rides and ate some really awesome food! Victor had stopped to pay for a beer somewhere and I was waiting for him in the middle of a plaza when something strange happened to me! I looked to the right and saw a carriage with horses coming down the road and suddenly it was like time stood still and I had my first experience with déjà vu...it was like I had lived here before and I think what brought this on was the carriage and the horses!

I shared this with Victor but he just shrugged his shoulders and told me we still had much to see! That night I saw the most beautiful parade of lights I had ever seen and after that a beautiful display of fireworks!

On the way home we stopped to see some friends of Victor that lived in Chino, very nice people that treated me with a lot of respect and were very happy that Victor had found a Portuguese bride...

I went thru quite a bit of confusion! Quite a few people that knew Victor liked him (especially Portuguese) … others like a woman that I befriended at our apartment complex we lived in for some reason took a dislike to him!

Sue actually advised me to leave the marriage before children showed up! Of course, that was a decision I was not about to make because I wanted the marriage to work…we stayed friends anyway and unfortunately, she proved to be right in believing that he was not that trustworthy!

I had joined a small gym nearby and Victor very often dropped me off to work out, one day he saw this good-looking woman getting ready to go in the gym and he just sat there in car drooling over this woman as she passed by our car! I turned to him and told him "You could at least try to hide it from me, you know this actually hurts me quite deeply!" His answer was "There is no harm in looking!" I told him "Yes there is, it all depends how you look at another woman…. especially in front of your wife."

I left him there to think about what I had said and went inside the gym…

As I entered the locker room, the woman was there and I could not believe what she did! She turned to me and said, "You know honey, men like yours never change, once a womanizer always a womanizer and you are too young to go thru that the rest of your life." I was so embarrassed! Too young to know how to respond to this but afraid that what she said was true! I had never seen either my father or my brothers look at women the way that he did…

We visited some of his friends and went to Portuguese functions, people would look at me with pity sometimes …probably because they knew of his reputation!

In a way he was very proud of the girl he had married, he made a point of introducing me to close friends… including a Portuguese family that he knew. As soon as we entered the door we were asked if we wanted to have dinner with them (I was too embarrassed) and Victor accepted, I went home hungry that night and asked him if he would take me to McDonalds on the way home. He could not believe that I had not accepted dinner, I told him "In Portugal people usually ask you 3 times before you can accept it, they asked me once." He laughed at me and told me "That was years ago in Portugal and now you are in the US."

I learned a valuable lesson that night and another when he asked me out to eat Pizza with him! That was one meal I learned to eat fast! Otherwise, I would end up eating one slice...

He loved his Friday night's out with his buddies (something we both agreed on), they played dominoes and "sueca" (card game) drank and socialized, I on the other hand learned to really like TV, while waiting for him to come home I became a big fan of the "Sonny and Cher Show." Watching TV helped me to improve my English! What we learned at school in Portugal was a more refined English than the US used, they used a less formal version... something I couldn't have not learned in my country!

Victor was also involved in a soccer league, of course I went to all the games, practices and developed friendships...

CHAPTER 12

Learning to be a good wife…

$\mathcal{A}$bove all I wanted to be a good wife, so I learned to socialize with his buddies, went fishing with him and even learned how to hook the bait without cringing! Quite often we would go to Stinson Beach …drove up the cliffs …parked up on top and walked down the cliff to fish on the rocks below…most of the times we did this I came home with poison ivy! But we always managed to come back with a big bag of fish that Victor would fix and I ended up making great fish dishes including fish stew…

We also took many trips to Berryessa Lake on hot weekends to go swimming, we used a rubber raft that we had and one weekend on a very hot day, Victor decided to drink and teach me how to maneuver the rubber raft at the same time! I did manage for a while but the stupid thing decided to go down on one side!

I started to get upset and all Victor could do was laugh! We managed to get the raft to shore and walked the rest of the way… I fell and bruised my knees! When I got home, I could not believe what I saw!

I was all sunburned and couldn't lay down without cringing …Life with Victor was never boring!

I was also taught by him about lovemaking and learned to love it (some of it made me embarrassed) that was also a way of trying to keep my marriage strong…he had told me when we got married "You keep me happy sexually and I will never stray". I took this to heart because my father had strayed and with prostitutes! I had the suspicion that my mother had not satisfied my father in bed…but he never looked at women when my mother was around…

Victor unfortunately had a couple of habits my father did not possess, one was a roving eye and an obsession with Porn! When I turned 16, he took me to a movie theater to watch a porno that shocked me but once again I would do anything to keep him happy sexually…. he also bought pornos for us to watch at home, I had to put my foot down when he tried to have sex with me while watching these movies, I told him "When you do this it makes me feel like you want to have sex with those women, not with me."

As a form of birth control, I was placed on the Birth Control pill but it did not agree with me! I started to gain weight and getting headaches…after a while Victor convinced me that he knew how to withdraw just on time so that I would not get pregnant unless we both planned on it, since I did not feel right, I decided to trust him and got off the pill…

At 16 I also tried to work, I wanted to be productive, applied and was hired at a Taco Factory, I oversaw the stacking of taco shells and unfortunately this would be done in between open doors that had a huge draft! I got a terrific cold because of it and one day woke up without being able to breathe!

Victor took me to the nearest Hospital and I was diagnosed with bronchitis! My parents and Victor immediately requested that I give up this job, in their point of view, it didn't pay enough and every time I got home from work, I smelled of tacos and would have to take a bath to be able to be near them...

They were right, my health was more important than any job that didn't even pay enough for all the work they requested! I also tried going to Richmond High to take a few classes, especially to improve my English and was amazed how much racism was going on in that place! The first week I was there I got hit behind with a stack of books and laughed at! Very different from the environment that I had come from! Schools in Portugal were very strict!

I decided to study English on my own and didn't go back...

As far as Victor and me we had quite a few arguments because of family disputes and of Victor's drinking! When he got drunk, he sometimes would forget that he was married! ...my mother always advised me to have patience that as he grew older, he might get over his obsession with other women...

CHAPTER 13

Moving back to San Leandro, CA.

*M*y parents moved to a Duplex in San Pablo near where my father worked and my grandmother as soon as she heard that they now had a place of their own requested to come and live with them.

As far as work we had decided for me to wait until I was 18 and we also decided since my parents were settled to move back to San Leandro, Victor had found an apartment near his parents that he really liked with a pool and he was set on teaching me how to drive. We had a Mazda with a stick shift and fortunately because Victor only made me nervous when he was trying to teach me I had a girlfriend show me how to drive in an automatic...

A couple of friends of ours also were taking a trip to Tijuana on a Saturday to see the bullfights and had invited us to come along, I was very excited because I had never been to Mexico (even Spain that was so close to Portugal) but I was quite disappointed, there was so much poverty all around us! Young children begging for money and prostitutes coming straight to men even with their spouses next to them!

The plaza for the bullfights that afternoon was pretty full! There were vendors all over the place selling tacos, drinks and while they were preparing the tacos (with not so clean hands) they were also giving out the change! Something I decided not to touch! I told Victor that I would eat after the bullfight and it was a good thing because what I saw made me sick of my stomach!

In Portugal we do not kill the bulls! They tantalize them and put on a show but the bulls in the end are enticed to leave the plaza by the cows that come to get them out, at this plaza the playing with the bull was not over until the bull was down and the matador finished the job with his sword! All around you all you heard was the agonizing cries of the animal and the cheers of the crowd! From there I was told the bulls were taken to the butchers…

Once the show was over and we left, I told Victor "Never again! This is very hard to watch if you love animals! From now on if you want me to go with you only to Portuguese Bull fights." He agreed! We shopped around a bit and Victor was approached by a prostitute and he actually told her "No, thanks! I have my wife with me!" We finally managed to grab a bite to eat in a cleaner place and drove back home the same day!

So much for our weekend trip! We enjoyed ourselves a lot more around the bay, very often we took drives up and down the coast because Victor knew that I missed the ocean! Many times, ended up in Santa Cruz (our favorite place) …I loved Santa Cruz on site and the ocean wasn't so cold that you could not swim on a hot day!

The foods were awesome, the shops, etc.… and for the first time in my life, I saw a young man collapse in front of me and have a seizure! There were people all around him and they called an ambulance, it was a sad thing to see, unfortunately this young man suffered from seizures especially if he was stressed or got too tired!

Incidents like this made you appreciate that you were healthy! We went back home that same night and took caution because the road back home was full of curves! Mother nature all around us was a beautiful sight to see!

We socialized quite often and for us soccer was always there as well as tournaments, Victor and I had decided to put money away so that one day we could buy a house. He had promised me to stop betting money on card games and tightened the belt but on one tournament we had to attend he went back on his word! We checked in at a Motel for the weekend, the soccer tournaments were in the morning and our evenings we were free…

I had gone to the grocery store nearby and when I came back Victor was sitting playing cards with his buddies and money was on the table! My blood was boiling! I hated lies! I approached the table carefully, pretended that I was cleaning up and he said, "That's nice of you honey! look guys… don't I have a nice wife?"

Once I got all the glasses and ashtrays out of the table, I grabbed the table with the money and cards and threw it across the room! They all stood there open mouthed looking at me! I looked straight at Victor and said, "This should teach you to never make promises to me that you don't intent to keep! You promised me… no more gambling so that one day we can buy a house."

I left the room and went walking… when I came back Victor was swimming in the pool by himself and his friends were gone….

I went inside our room, he came after me and tried to kiss me, I pushed him away and he finally realized that I was very serious and promised me once again that he if he played cards, it would be without gambling. I hoped that he was serious about his promise and of course we kissed and made up. Later when he shared this with his father, he laughed at him and applauded me for what I had done, he also wanted us to have a place of our own…

Once back at home we had made plans to go see a movie that everyone was excited about, we picked up Victor's brother and went to see the Exorcist!

My first experience going out to see a movie had been in Portugal with my father "Gone with the Wind" I had loved the movie! No way was I prepared for this one! It was frightening and after 3 days of not being able to sleep I was forced to get sleeping pills for the first time in my life! I told Victor "No more movies like this ever again!"

As the New Year's approached, I made the mistake of trying to get a new look, had my hair cut and permed (something I didn't need) and came home brokenhearted! We already had reservations for a New Year's celebration with a bunch of friends at a Bowling Alley and I didn't want to look like this! My mother had made my dress for this occasion and a shirt to match for Victor, he looked at me, left for a while and came back with a long blonde wig! This would be my first experience wearing a wig! I soon learned that I didn't like them at all!

We went out for the celebration all dressed up but I was extremely warm that night because of the wig! I definitely learned to be careful with hairdressers!

Just like any young woman I loved to experiment with new products and ideas, another one was false eyelashes, even that proved to be a waste of money and gave me a scary experience instead! I was out having dinner with Victor one night and we started by having soup, suddenly when I looked down, I saw a black spider in my soup, I told Victor "Can you believe there is a spider on my soup?" He looked at it and said, "That doesn't really look like a spider to me!" I looked at it a bit closer and realized that my right eyelash had fallen on the soup!

I was so embarrassed! I immediately took the left one out! Victor just sat there cracking up at me! It would take me years to be able to give up on the eyelashes… but I did learn to carry the glue with me everywhere…

CHAPTER 14

Turning 18 and family conflicts!

*M*y mother that still loved to make my clothes was making me a special outfit for my 18th birthday and we would also be celebrating that I had just received my driver's license! My parents joined us at our apartment along with Victor's family and I took a very special picture with my dad that day!

My mother on the other hand surprised me by giving me a gold ring with a blue stone! There was a story behind this ring… my father had given it to my mother years ago, one day because they needed money to pay the rent he took it to a Pawn Shop, my mother found out and went back later on to buy it back from the Pawn Shop!

She flat out told him to never again take the ring anywhere because she wanted to give it to me when I grew older, I treasured the ring for years to come! It was my mother's birthstone and something given to me from the heart!

I was happy that my parents also got to experience the Portuguese Community in the US, they joined us at Portuguese Festivals and "Soupas" (Portuguese soups) and I could tell that they were happy in the US… especially because they were near me! What they wanted changed for me was how Victor's family treated me and that unfortunately they could not do!

My mother was very smart and could tell that there was friction between my sisters-in-laws and me…. many times, I asked my mother not to interfere because I knew it would only make matters worse! Out of love for me she would hold her tongue when she witnessed something she didn't like…

There were times my parents also got excluded from invitations for the Holidays because of the friction that was going on between our families and those were horrible times for me! Having to leave my parents and grandmother behind eating TV Dinners for Thanksgiving wasn't something I had dreamed of!!

I couldn't rely on Victor to take my side on anything, his answer was always the same "If I take your side, they will be offended and if I take their side, you will be offended, so I have to stay out of it."

He didn't know but this hurt me quite deeply! My father had always been my mother's biggest defender and he wouldn't allow anyone to hurt her or me!

Victor was also getting very tired of the commute back and forth to work (it would take him 30 minutes each way) on slow days, one day he came home after speaking to a friend of his at work and told me that he had a small house for sale in San Pablo near my parents' duplex. He asked me what I thought about it and I told him that I wanted to see it, on the way there the next day he told me that his friend being the owner would allow us to make monthly payments, instead of making payments to an apartment complex we would be making payments on our own home!

Victor and I went by the house, it was small but had a huge backyard! When I looked at this house I really didn't care if it was an older home, I looked at the backyard and knew we could make it bigger (the house only cost us at the time $16,000) … I knew that if we did not make this move my chances of having a home of my own would be very slim…

We also decided to move temporarily with my parents, this would make it a lot more convenient for Victor and me to clean it, paint it and have carpets delivered…. we slept in their sofa bed and this was quite an adjustment! We would wake up quite often either because of their cuckoo clock that sang a different song every hour or to the sound of my parents snoring!

In the morning my father always made his coffee before going to work and would stir it and stir it and stir it! This would wake us up because the kitchen was right next to the living room, he would finally enjoy it and go off to work!

After a while we adjusted! We were just so happy that we were preparing our own home to live in that nothing was worth complaining about!

CHAPTER 15

Moving to our new Home!

We finally got to move to our home and set out to decorate it as best as we could, being careful in not spending too much, this for us was a labor of love!

Of course, this purchase did not agree with my father-in-law and I was the one that had to tell him to look at the backyard and see the possibilities… he made fun of the house instead! We made all kinds of improvements to the house and added rooms and he exclaimed that he could not believe what the house looked like before and after we finished with it!

What I didn't agree with was that Victor refused to get a permit to add rooms to the house and somehow I knew that this would cause us problems later on…

We were both young but one thing we had in common was that we liked making new friends, even if they were older than us. Across from our home we made friends with an older couple, Harold and Arlene, they had a saint Bernard that scarred me to death! They invited us over for coffee and to chat and we didn't mind at all!

One day Arlene told me to meet her in the back yard because she had some leftovers for us to try, when I told her that I was afraid of the dog, she told me he was a loving dog and not be afraid, I opened the gate carefully and met head on with the saint Bernard, he placed his paws on my shoulders and stared me down! All I could do was gulp big time! Arlene came to my rescue and told me "Well, look at that! He actually likes you!"

Eventually I learned not to be afraid of him and we became quite close to this couple to the point they even asked us to babysit their home on one weekend…that weekend we had a huge laugh! I had never tried a waterbed before and Victor insisted that we try it together! As he reached out to get fresh with me, I was thrown off the bed and landed on the carpet! I told him "No more waterbeds! Not unless you want to get me sick and throw up all over the place." We laughed together, fed the dog and went back to our place…we kept this experience to ourselves!

My parents themselves also made some Portuguese friends that they visited quite often… Salome and Francisco loved me dearly and wished more than anything that their only son Francisco would meet someone like me and get married. Unfortunately, they had raised their son to believe that women were expensive mistresses, just like cars and he became leery of women! Except for me! They called me "Menina Sao" Little girl and my nickname! This was a sign of respect! The problem with their son was that he didn't socialize outside of their home and for him to find a Portuguese girl he would have to attend dances, festivals and go to our Catholic Church…something he refused to do… so he remained single and unfortunately a loner!

What I liked about our home was that I was close to my parents duplex and was able to walk back and forth since it was within walking distance…

That year we had a huge flood in San Pablo that left us all stranded! It took days for my father's car to get dry completely, he had bought an orange Chevrolet that he absolutely loved! It was his baby, he washed it and polished it many times a week, one day he called me all stressed out that someone had stolen all his tires and left his car on top of cement blocks!

We couldn't believe it! I asked Victor to help him and they bought new tires, this was a car that my father would cherish for years to come!

Guys sometimes do stupid things and Victor did a big one! He didn't like having health problems and kept from me that he had a yeast infection! Because he had waited too long to tell me about it, he ended up burning quite badly, took matters into his hands and used underarm spray to stop the burning! When I asked him why in the world had he resorted to using underarm spray he said, "Because it has talcum powder!"

I just shook my head and called the advice nurse at Kaiser that just laughed at me! After she stopped laughing, she told me to stop by the Kaiser pharmacy and pick up a couple of vaginal creams, one for Victor and one for me, so that I wouldn't end up getting it as well! Victor learned a valuable lesson that day, I'm sure!

This Kaiser nurse also shared something with me that I didn't know about males and that was that men that are not circumcised are more prone to yeast infections and even sexual diseases, unfortunately Victor was not circumcised, this information was essential if we ever conceived a son in the near future….

In front of my parents duplex I had met a woman by the name of Sylvia that turned out to be a good friend to have, she was married to a man that was an acholic and also worked for Myers (where Victor worked). She worried about my happiness, we had interesting discussions about men… she had decided to stay married to Dale even though she knew he would never change, her excuse was "He only drinks after work." Dale ended up dying of liver decease and she stayed at that same house for many years…

My mother on the other hand made laugh one day by telling me that she had an eye on a window that lived across the street that developed a crush on my dad! She would show up and talk to him every time she saw him park the car…. when I shared this bit of information with Sylvia, she took matters into her own hands, went to speak to the woman and told her to stay away from my dad because he was married!

This was something my mother would have done herself if she spoke English… I couldn't blame the woman my dad was still a very handsome man in his 50's.!

That same year we a got a visit from my aunt Mathilde and my uncle (she wanted to see her mother and her sister) and I could hardly wait! I loved them dearly and they decided to stay with us while they were visiting, it was wonderful to see these two sisters together!

My grandma also loved all the attention she was getting! My aunt asked me to ask Victor not to offer beer to my uncle since he was trying to give up that habit and I certainly complied with her request, we set out to spend a Saturday together at Great America and were prepared to have a great day and it did start out that way… We saw many shows together, did a few rides and ate some great food!

Victor and my uncle asked that we split for a while and then meet at a certain location, this would give us the opportunity to shop at the souvenir shops and chat, after a while we caught up to them and we could tell that they were both drunk!

My aunt was furious! She turned to me and said, "Is there any way that we can leave them here by themselves and go back to your house." I told her "Of course we can, I have the keys to the car, let's leave them and find a way to get home." They tried to stop us… but we left anyway! I drove us back home and it was quite late by the time they got back! None too happy but we just ignored them… My aunt and I were very similar in this respect, never make a promise to me that you don't intend to keep! My uncle Larry learned the hard way that weekend!

I also knew that he wouldn't hold it against me because after all I had done this at my aunt's request, when they left, they had already made up, they really loved each other and my uncle also respect her. I was glad that by the time they left these two guys knew they were married to two very strong women that they couldn't play with!

Unfortunately drinking was also a problem with Victor that caused problems in our marriage for a long time, one habit that would take many years to break!

CHAPTER 16

Breakups!

W̄e had been living in our home a few years when we went thru a series of break ups, mostly because of his family interference and his drinking, Victor also had the habit of every time we had an argument about anything he would share it with his family …This did not help my relationship with them and of course they always believed his side…

He would stay at our house and I would stay at my parents' duplex, I really tried to make it on my own but it was hard to get away from him! He called me one night from a San Leandro nightclub very drunk to tell me that if I didn't meet him there, he was going to kill himself! I was young and naïve and believed him!

I told my parents that I was driving to San Leandro and the reason why… drove scared and met him at the club, he was of course drunk and alive and all over me when I got there! In his own words "Let's get back together, there is no one else like you." We ended up making up… but it wouldn't last …

Shortly after we had another breakup and I was actually embarrassed to even ask my parents to take me in! It helped that they loved me and they knew what I was up against… but they also knew that we loved each other. My mother never, ever told me to leave Victor but she didn't want me to go anyplace else…

I found a position in a nearby Portuguese restaurant as a cashier, hostess, server, etc. and liked working there, "A Bit of Portugal" was mostly frequented by American people and the owner needed someone that spoke both languages, I ate my meals there and advised the owner to let me speak to people as much as possible, he was quite rude to customers and they actually avoided him as much as possible.!

Victor would come by my parents duplex and spy on me to check if I was dating someone, my father had actually found out from a friend of his! All I wanted was to have some peace in my life, dating was the furthest thing from my mind!

I started a friendship with a Brazilian girl that had a baby and we became close friends, I visited her quite often, stayed for dinner and listened to Brazilian music. My mother would see me leave the house and thought that I was dating someone and prayed and prayed for me!

My friendship ended with her when she introduced me to a friend of hers that was very interested in me and once in car with me… exposed himself! Of course, I told him off! When I told her about this experience, she laughed about it, I didn't find it funny because I could have been forced into a sexual act that I didn't want!

Unfortunately, Victor could not make up his mind if he wanted to stay married or single! He asked me to meet him after work at a nearby park so that we could talk our problems thru and we started meeting there, one day I actually brought him a cheeseburger from the restaurant that I worked at, gave it to him and he had the audacity to ask me to taste it first! I looked at him and said, "Can you explain where this request comes from?" he said, "My mother believes that the reason that I cannot get over you is because you have placed some kind of spell on me and told me not to accept anything from you."

I looked straight at him and told him "You fool, can it be that we just love each other too much and can't stay away from one another?" I tasted the cheeseburger right in front of him and got ready to leave, he stopped me and said "We can get back together but first because I have been talking too much about you…. you will have to speak to my father, he doesn't want us together, if you can convince him then we will start over."

At first, I didn't want to do it but I also knew my mother wanted us together so I told him that I would go and speak to his father that same weekend. I drove there by myself without telling my parents, entered the house that I feared and met with my father-in-law.

He sat in the chair like a king presiding over a kingdom, after I told him that Victor and I wanted to give our marriage another try, he leaned over and said "I don't agree! You guys have been separated quite a few times and keep trying and it doesn't seem to be working, just give it up." I told him that we loved each other and what we needed was for the family to stop interfering in our lives, let us make mistakes and be happy and then left…...

I got in the car and Victor came over, leaned over the window and said, "See he doesn't agree but that doesn't mean that we cannot see each other." I looked at him very seriously and told him "Victor if I'm not good enough to be your wife, I'm not good enough to be your mistress, this relationship is over and don't come and see me anymore." I drove back extremely humiliated by this experience and when I got home, I asked my parents to come and sit down in the living room so that we could have a conversation.

Finally, I was able to put my mother's mind at ease that I was not seeing anyone, that when she had seen me leave the house and go somewhere it was to meet with Victor but that this would not be happening any longer. I told them what happened at the park about my meeting with my father-in-law that morning and they were both extremely upset! My mother looked at me and said, "You did more than I would have done after being asked to taste the food that you wanted to share with him! I would not have gone to meet with his father today… he is not man enough to make his own decisions.?"

They were both very proud of me after I told them what I had said to him "Not good enough to be wife, not good enough to be a mistress" My father always the quiet one… simply looked at me and said,

"I just want for you what makes you happy… in the long run it's your life not theirs."

I hugged them both and told them "From now on mom and dad please trust me a little bit! I'm not about to go from a relationship to another, you raised a woman with principals and morals", they both agreed and smiled… I placed this very unpleasant episode behind me and went back to work the next Monday…

My job helped quite a bit! I lost quite a bit of weight… became really good at it and made a few friends. They totally depended on me for everything in this restaurant, unfortunately the owner didn't listen to my advice and continued to be rude to the few customers we had! He also had not listened when I suggested he publicized on the radio about his place and ended up closing the restaurant….

Since Victor had decided to listen to his father instead of his heart and had not contacted me, I decided to file for divorce and restart my life….

My parents also agreed that I should leave Victor alone and let him live his life as he wished…

CHAPTER 17

Trying to re-start a new life
and not succeeding…

*M*y aunt Mathilde heard about the breakup and called me to invite me to come and see them and take a much-needed vacation, I stayed close to 3 months but did not have the heart to stay permanently because my parents were living in California …otherwise I probably would have stayed. I loved being around my cousins! I also needed the rest! I took the time to sit outdoors and sunbathe, we sat outside on a bench after dinner to chat and even went to see Jerry Lee Lewis at a concert!

I actually saw the guy they had introduced me to before but he was still drinking too much and I didn't want another relationship that would result in a heartbreak!

On the way home I had the worst flight ever! I sat next to a man that was not feeling well… we experienced so much turbulence that the poor man had a heart attack on the flight! They kept him on oxygen until we were able to land and all I did on the way to the San Francisco Airport was to pray that we would make it safely home…

My parents were surprised how tanned and slimmer I looked… my mother told me that Victor had been asking for me quite a lot and wanted to talk to me asap, I was dreading it but my mother convinced me to hear him out (she was a true believer in marriage and did not want a divorce for me) ...I knocked at the door and of course Victor was full of excuses and promises!

He knelt by me, grabbed my hands and told me that things were going to be different! I looked at him and said, "Are you sure you are not going to need your father's approval before we get back together?" He apologized and said "Sorry about that! You were right, it was the love that we have for each other that would not allow us to be apart, nothing else."

I decided to give him another chance and go back home, more for my mother than for me but willing to give it another try, he had hurt me deeply this time! He also asked me to call the lawyer and stop the divorce and I did.

It was funny because when he finally convinced me to go visit his family together, his mother actually said to me "We are going to stop paying attention to Victor when he complains about you when you have an argument because in the long run, you love each other and we need to butt out." I was surprised by her comment and hoped that things would now change between all of us so that we could become a normal family...

What I didn't share with anyone was that I also had taken a risk of going back to him! Victor whenever we split up, his answer to the problem was to go to nightclubs and have one-night stands! I on the other hand refused to go to bed to anyone unless there was something there, I had been approached before by a guy that flat-out told me while he was dancing with me that he just wanted to take me to bed! I said to him "Looking in the wrong place buddy" and left him on the dance floor...

Because of Victor's one night stands I contracted crabs' lice and we both had to be treated... all of our clothing including all of our bedding had to be truly cleaned or thrown away!

That summer we were invited to his youngest sister's wedding (she had moved to Ohio to study there) and of course this meant that once again I would be staying with my aunt Mathilde but this time with Victor as well…

Maria ended up not wanting me in her wedding because of something really stupid that happened between her sister and myself that escalated into a big argument! Prior to the wedding we were spending the day outside in a park nearby and my sister-in-law Gina forgot her bathing suit and asked me to borrow mine (I was smaller than her). I told her in a nice way that I thought my bathing suit may not fit her, immediately she got offended and said that I was calling fat!

That day even my in-laws got involved and I got called a bitch! I told my aunt about this episode when I got home and told her "I wasn't raised to insult people and what I said was simply the truth", I also knew that whatever I said was always twisted around because to put it simply I was not liked from day one…simply tolerated!

Victor because of the pressure my aunt placed on him decided not to go to the wedding and was not very nice to me either (he had witnessed the incident at the park) and stayed silent instead of coming to my defense! Something my aunt wanted him to do! I started to pack my bags to go back home to California and my aunt stopped me …before we got ready to go back home my uncle and my aunt had a few words with my in-laws requesting that they cut out the insults towards me….

We went back home together and my father-in-law convinced is son that maybe having a child together might help our marriage (something I did not know until later) so I was not prepared to get pregnant! I thought that my husband was still withdrawing is seed…of course I got pregnant but I was almost 3 and half months when I started to miscarriage!

Victor was out on that Friday night playing cards with his buddies at a local Portuguese club when I started to bleed, I got in my car and went to get him to tell him that I was losing the baby…his answer was "Why don't you have your father take you to the hospital? I'm playing cards and very soon they are going to cook rabbit for dinner." I looked at him and told him "Victor this is not my father's child it's your child and for your information I'm bleeding and in pain." I believe he took me to the hospital out of shame, by the time I got to Kaiser in Oakland the baby was halfway out, had a DNC and was told to go home and rest for a few days…

Victor took me home and we picked up my mother at the duplex so that she could keep me company, once home…he came to our room and said, "Since your mother is here, I'm going back to the club and eat some rabbit." I just looked at my mother without saying a word!

So much for wanting a child!

I managed to get over this! Since this child was conceived out of deceit I was not overwhelmed with grief, I took care of myself after this experience and Victor also promised me that whenever we decided to have a child it would be when we decided to have one… instead he got himself involved in raising Fleming Giant Rabbits, Cornish Hens and even got me to go with him to a farm to get a Billy Goat!

The way he convinced me to buy the older goat was by explaining that we needed the Billy Goat to clean up the backyard that was full of weeds. He told the owner the same thing but never explained however how he would get rid of the goat! He showed up at my kitchen one day with the goat all cut up in pieces and asked me to cook it!

I looked at him and said, "Are you crazy?" He told me "He did his job and goat meat is very good, just try it!" So, he convinced me to cook it, after 3 hours of trying to cook it on a regular pot I finally switched to a pressure cooker and told him "Never again! You try the darn thing! It's probably as old as Moses." He also had me cook rabbit and the kids refused to eat it…

Rabbits I had cooked in Portugal and liked and Cornish Hens but what I didn't like was that he would make money on the side and would hide it from me! I used to joke with my family and friends that I wouldn't be surprised if he brought home an Elephant and expect me to cook it!

He even tried to do a "Mantanca de Porco", this was a Portuguese tradition! The pig was killed, cleaned and roasted in the backyard and friends and family got invited for the event, this turned out to be a lot of work for everyone and expensive, so we didn't do it very often. Also, some of our best New Year's Parties were done in a huge shack we had in our backyard with family and close friends…

CHAPTER 18

Getting married at our local church and facing doubts!

*I*n a way we did love each other so he finally agreed to get married by Church …something I wanted to do right from the beginning but had waited for my parents to be in the US, we did the wedding ourselves and invited family and friends. My mother had been against a white dress because we had already been married for 3 years, so I went to the mall, got myself a pink dress and my mother placed a really pretty trim on the neckline. It wasn't what I wanted, I actually thought that I deserved a white dress…

We were all so tired! Arranging, cooking and decorating the hall for our wedding ourselves was a big job but we were also saving money, so it was worth it!

On the day of the wedding, I went to my parents duplex to get dressed there and my dad came in the living room to tell me how pretty I looked, I looked at him and said "Daddy, I'm not sure I want to go thru with this! What do I do?" He grabbed my hand and was honest with me "Now it's a bit too late! We have a whole bunch of friends and family coming! In the long run you and Victor love each other, give it a try." For some reason my father said something to me that I needed to hear! I felt a bit calmer! We left for the church together, my father walked me to the altar and placed my hand in Victor's, he gave him the look "You better not hurt my daughter." Victor nodded… smiled and we did our vows before God….

My in laws for some reason did not arrive until the ceremony was over! They claimed they got stuck in traffic! I didn't want to create a scene on my wedding day, so I kept silent…. Victor and I proceed to the reception followed by the family, we had rented a small hall that we had decorated the night before, when we got there a few friends of mine were already there making sure all the food was laid out including the wedding cake.

We included a Portuguese couple on our invitations that we knew thru my father (he was my father's supervisor), we choose Isaura and Joe to be our godparents, they were fun loving people with children of their own…

I had the feeling that my godfather would not live long! He, just like my mother suffered from angina! He had the bad habit of placing his pill underneath his tongue and then drink a glass of wine afterwards! I told him that my mother had been warned to avoid alcohol while taking her medication…he said he would try to remember that but winked at me instead! Typical Portuguese guy! Very stubborn!

My godparents had lost a son due to a heart attack at the age of 23! My godfather because he didn't listen to anyone regarding his health ended up losing his life! It seemed to me that my culture was a very stubborn culture!!

On our wedding day we did end up having fun, socialized with everyone, ate some really good food and danced! The bad part about arranging your own wedding is the cleaning up! After everyone left, we did some of it and the next day my mother went with me to finish the rest…

After our wedding I found a job close to where we lived, this company specialized in jewelry that was set in molds using gold leaf "Pounded Gold Jewelry" was well known for designing jewelry for customers by request. While there I actually made a belt buckle for Victor that he absolutely loved!

We had set a date to go see Tom Jones one weekend and he wore the belt to the event, I like most women was gaga over Tom Jones and had never been to one of his concerts. I was amazed that he had women throw underwear at him! Since there was no way that I was going to throw my underwear at him I turned around to Victor and asked him to let me have his belt, he was pretty upset and said "No way! Do you expect me to just hand over my belt to him.?"

I replied "Common, I promise that I will make you another." Of course, he didn't and I didn't get a chance to get close to Tom Jones… but he was well worth watching! He had an unforgettable voice!

It was while at this company that I first observed the way that a woman's mind can work when dealing with men! Michelle was a striking woman, long black hair, nice eyes, tall and totally drawn to wrong guys! She confided in me that she only went out with married men, her excuse was "Nobody treats you as good as a married man!" She didn't care that she could be destroying a marriage, she only cared about what she could get from that relationship, this was one woman I made sure to keep away from Victor because I knew she was very dangerous to have around! I was glad that this job didn't last long… It was very hard to sell this type of jewelry and they ended up closing the shop.

I kept working on my marriage and in order to keep our relationship strong, I made sure we had a date night. We had an agreement, he would have his night out with his friends to play cards and we had one night to go out by ourselves. Most of the time I waited for him at my parents duplex and we watched their favorite shows like He-Haw and The Lawrence Welk Show, my favorite was always the Lawrence Welk because of the dancing….

After work on a particular Friday, I was waiting for Victor at my mother's house for us to go out to dinner and he was late and didn't call me! Hour after hour passed and finally was close to 11PM when he knocked on the door totally drunk! He said "Common, let's go out." I looked at him and said, "I'm not going anywhere with you on that condition, let's go home instead."

I drove home and when we got there, he tried to hug me! I acted really cool and told him "Let's get you cleaned and sober up." He was surprised that I was not acting upset but I had something in mind! I helped him undress, got him in the shower and turned the cold shower full power on him, he cried out and said, "I knew you were up to something!" I told him "I told you before not to make me any promises you don't intend to keep, please don't even think of approaching me tonight."

He was little by little learning that I was not someone you can play with… Things like this he unfortunately shared with his father which prompted him to pay a visit to my parents to visit his mother. He made a comment to my mother at the door before he left "I wish that your daughter was more like you, then their marriage would work." My mother turned around and told him "If she was like me, she would not be married to your son! I would never put up with what she has put up so far!" He left and that was the last time he made a smart remark about me to my mother…

I was very different than Victor! I believe that most women if they make a mistake, they learn from it and don't repeat it, men on the other hand it may take a few times before they get it!

For example, I learned a valuable lesson one night out with Victor at a nightclub! He introduced me to a "Long Island Iced Tea" which I loved right away and he told me "Go slowly on this one!" I took a few sips because you couldn't taste the alcohol on it and he asked me to dance, I got up, starting dancing with him and the next thing I knew I was down on one knee on the floor! That's when I knew that this wonderful drink had really gotten to me! Victor cracked up at me and after a couple of attempts at dancing, we gave up and went home!

From that day on whenever we had this drink, I knew better how to drink it!

Like most relationships we had good and bad times, formed lasting and not so lasting friendships and found some friendships that gave us examples of what to avoid or what to imitate…

One of the friendships that I formed thru my parents was with a Portuguese family that was totally sad to see! The whole family suffered from diabetes, the mother was going blind, the father had already lost half of a leg due to diabetes and both daughters suffered from it… I became closer to the oldest daughter, even being as young as I was, I couldn't believe how they ate being that sick and relied on insulin to survive!

We continued our relationship with the whole family but one thing I learned about my culture is that they tend to be very stubborn and set on their ways! Most of their family perished and I also lost touch with the oldest daughter…

Because my parents had health issues, I had insisted that my mother kept me informed if something was going on with their health because they relied on me for doctor appointments. She was worried that my father was not sleeping well, he was snoring loudly and would wake up very often not breathing correctly! I spoke to his doctor about it and he recommended that he get tested for sleep Apnea (sleep disorder), he would have to sleep overnight at a local hospital and the results would be given to us in a few days' time. A few days later we were given the results and the confirmation that he did have sleep Apnea, the doctor immediately recommended that he lose the extra weight that he was carrying and suggested the use of a double pillow to elevate his head. I spoke very seriously with my father about what he had to do because like my mother often said, "He doesn't listen to anyone but you." Unfortunately…not always!

CHAPTER 19

Women versus men and dealing with weight issues...

*A*s for me I paid attention to my body and listened when someone gave me good advice, one of the things I had to give up and that actually was not good for me was tampons! I used them to go swimming and also because they were less messy. A report came out that year (1980) that quite a few women had gotten sick and died due to Toxic Shock Syndrome and I switched to pads instead, I was quite pleased that I had heard this because I found that they left me quite dry inside and it was hard to get the natural lubrification back....

That same year we received a letter from my brother Jose Carlos to let us know that Terceira had suffered a great earthquake and that his oldest son had been so frightened that he had started to stutter out of freight! Because of the building structure in all the islands there had been a lot of damage! It would take a long time to rebuild homes and for his son to be able to speak without stuttering...

I also managed to get a job at Kmart and met a Portuguese girl that became my closest friend.... Lia was also married to a Portuguese man that had his own business, we got close and our husband's met and become friends. Strange... this was the first time my mother advised me to be careful with a friendship!

She didn't believe that Lia had my best interest at heart and many times we had arguments over this but this was a friendship that was hard to break, our husbands had become good friends and I also felt sorry for her because I knew she was not happy...

People at Kmart were something else! I actually worked in a couple departments, one was the Layaway Dept, the other one cashiering out front. Sometimes I would help out our Customer Service Dept where I was surprised by a woman that wanted to return underwear that you could tell had been worn already!

One day while cashiering out front two women placed their stuff they were buying on the belt and one woman turned to the other and said in Portuguese, "Repara nesta rapariga e ve quanto maquilhagem ela usa!" this meant "Look at this girl and see how much makeup she is using!" The other woman agreed and made another nasty comment, they continued to talk about me in my language and I choose not to say a word until I was finished with their transaction, then very sweetly turned to them and said "Obrigado, tenha um bom dia." "Thank you and have a good day!"

They both looked at me very startled and couldn't believe that I was Portuguese! Of course, they both apologized for their comments... I just said, "This goes to show you that you never know who can actually speak your language, right? I also don't look like your typical Portuguese woman and to tell you the truth my mother doesn't either, she has dark blonde hair and blue eyes. My father however has dark hair and dark eyes." They left smiling but I believe they also learned a valuable lesson that day!

Lia and I were set one Saturday morning to go out to lunch, while I was taking a shower the phone rang in the kitchen... instead of letting it ring, I got out of the shower and ran to get the phone! Unfortunately, because my feet were wet, I slipped on the floor that had a cement foundation and hit the back of my head! I was dazed and confused for a few seconds and since I didn't feel like myself, I drove to the nearest hospital. They examined me and I was told that I had a slight concussion!

I was also advised to keep awake and to rest that day, I called Lia and cancelled our lunch, drove to my parents' house and my mother made sure I didn't fall asleep that afternoon. That day I got to experience what football players experience many times and it was definitely a scary feeling!!

My friendship continued with Lia and her husband, we would go to their house often to eat and invite them to our family gatherings...

Unfortunately, when you keep on being invited everywhere it makes it extremely difficult to keep your weight under control and Victor and I struggled to keep our weight down… we both loved to eat! It seemed to me that when I got serious and lost the weight, he would jeopardize it by bringing home food and make smart remarks like "Hey baby, you are losing too much weight! I can't find you in bed!"

One particular time we had been invited to Lia's house for dinner and she asked me to bring a dessert, I stopped by Nations to buy a lemon pie and went to pick up Victor at home. While he was driving, he looked at what I had on my lap and started to give me smart remarks "How are going to lose weight if you keep eating desserts? Are you serious or not?" and so on…I turned around and told him "Victor, Lia asked me to bring a dessert, I bought a lemon pie because it's not my favorite."

He annoyed me so much on the way there, that while on the freeway when we approached a hillside, I opened the window of the car and threw the pie out the window! I looked at him and said, "Happy now?" He shook his head and I told him "Now, when we get to Lia's house make sure and explain why we didn't bring the dessert." He did just that and they all laughed about it, except for me because I didn't want anyone to put that amount of pressure on me to lose weight…

People in general cannot be pressured to lose weight and reminded how to do it on a daily basis, most will rebel and jeopardize their efforts, in the long run the person will lose the weight when they are ready to do it…

So, I rebelled and decided that I was going to accept a heavier me! I decided to attend a fashion show with a friend of mine that was targeted towards the heavier woman, it was great because I already had the knack to put outfits together but also saw for myself how heavier women could make themselves more attractive…

With Victor's family, that was a totally different story! I couldn't develop a close relationship with them and they could care less if I was heavy or slim, I was tolerated not loved! I always tried to never talk back when I was accused of something or insulted, biting your tongue can be a lot harder than speaking out! It takes a bigger person!!

Chapter 20

Childbirth and my father gets seriously ill!

Victor and I had finally decided to have our first child and informed the family.

When Carlos was placed in my arms, I decided that this roller coaster of a marriage was going to stop and so would the mistreatment I had been suffering for years! I became a much stronger person from that day forward... I was 23 years old and had been suffering for 7 years of verbal abuse from his family... On the day Carlos was born, 07/22/1981 I realized that my mother had been right about having a child! I had shared with her years prior that I thought that I was not cut out to be a mother and she told me "Wait until your baby is placed in your arms after you give birth." She was absolutely right! Immediately I felt the bond between us and the overwhelming feeling to protect this child!

My parents and Victor came by the Hospital to visit us both and we left with our first son to start our new lives as brand-new parents...

On the day my son got Baptized we had a reception at our home and the whole family plus friends were invited to attend...we had not finished renovating our home and the windows on my dining room were closed (I had the drapes closed) because I was embarrassed, they were very old windows.

My father-in-law walked in and made a comment about our house looking like a Mexican house with windows shut! I had enough! I looked straight at him (in front of my husband) and said, "If this house is so displeasing to you the door is right behind you." This was the first time I had spoken to him that way but from that day forward he started to have a little more respect for me...

We ended up having a good time regardless and took plenty of pictures!

Unfortunately, sometimes we can also hear stupid remarks from other people when you least expect it! Victor and I received an invitation for a Portuguese function that unfortunately we could not refuse to go to! This one was just a couple of months after I gave birth to Carlos and I was still pretty heavy, I found a pretty dress... did my hair different but I was not looking forward to being there!

As we entered the place everyone of course turned in our direction... most of these people knew us and an older man that knew me very well in front of everyone asked me out loud "My goodness what happened to you, how come you are so fat?" I looked straight at him and said out loud "I don't know! I woke up one day, looked in the mirror and suddenly this fat was there!" He looked at me surprised that I was speaking to him that way and I finished it "For your information I just gave birth to a baby, what's your excuse?" He sat down while people all around us burst out laughing!

I was the type of person that would never make a comment to anyone regarding how they looked but unfortunately not everyone was like me...

I made myself a promise that night and told Victor about it ...No more Portuguese functions unless I managed to lose this extra weight, I was not about to be embarrassed by anyone! This incident made me so self-conscious that I went to buy a full body girdle, something that I would use for many years to come...

My mother called me one afternoon to talk to me about my father and she asked me to come by their home, I walked in and my mother told me that my father was having problems with his eyes, when I asked her what type of problems, she said "He said that when he looks in the mirror his vision is not the same."

I told her that I was going to contact his doctor and called him from their home, I was advised to tell my father to clean his glasses regularly and also to have him buy some eye drops from the pharmacy! That same day I bought him the eye drops but unfortunately that didn't help much!

Carlos was 6 months old when my father had a major stroke at the age of 61years old that left him paralyzed on his right side! I had for a year been asking my dad to watch his coffee intake and to watch his blood pressure!

A year before the stroke he had a heart attack at work, was taken to the Hospital and hid it from all of us! He went back to work right after, we only found out about the heart attack from his private Doctor a few weeks later! My mother and I were then informed about the heart attack! I found out later that eye problems are quite often an early sign of a pending stroke…

When I told my mother about the heart attack that my father had at work and how he hid it from both of us, she was not surprised… she told me that in Portugal my father had tried to hide from her that he had boils in his skin that produced pus and pain! He didn't want to tell her not to worry her… it was only when the pain became too much for him to bear that he finally confided in her and a treatment was started… Maybe an early sign that something was wrong with his immune system?

The night my father had a stroke I walked into their home and as I started to talk to my father, I noticed his slurred speech and that he was a bit wobbly. Immediately I told him that I was going to take him to Kaiser, of course my father started to refuse but I also refused to budge until he got in the car with me, we got to Kaiser and they kept it him overnight…the next morning when I got to the Hospital I could hardly recognize him! He was all swollen up! Unable to speak and paralyzed on the right side!

I was told by his doctor that in order for him to recuperate it would take a change of lifestyle and quite a bit of physical therapy ...he also told me that if I had not brought him to the Hospital the night before he might have not made it! I looked at my father laying on the Hospital bed and decided at that precise moment that I was going to help him recuperate from the stroke and I told my mother "Mom, we are not going to speak negatively in front of dad, you hear me? We both are going to learn how to help him heal, ok?" She knew I was very serious and agreed…

As soon as I knew what would take for my father to recuperate from the stroke from his doctor, I started to do research on strokes and the human body. When we visited my father in the Hospital I reenforced to my father that he would recuperate from the stroke and asked him to try to work with me and the doctors to recover faster. We were placed on a waiting list for my father to be transferred to a Physical Therapy Center in Vallejo where they would work with him until he was ready to come home. There were many people waiting to get to that Physical Therapy Center, so he had to be temporally moved to a Nursing Home, my mother and I along with my baby made a point of visiting my father at the Nursing Home every day…one day we walked into his room my father was sitting in his wheelchair covered in spaghetti and smelling of urine…. When he looked at me, he started to cry!

I was so angry!! I looked at my mother and told her "I will be right back mom". I went up to the front desk and asked to speak to the head nurse…in front of everyone and in a clear voice I told her "How in the world do you expect a person that just had a stroke to feed himself when the stroke affected his right side and how dare you leave a man smelling of urine all morning?" She looked at me and apologized but I told her that this better not happen again, or I was going to report the Nursing Home for neglect. I told her that having a stroke for a man like my father that used to have such a strong personality was already degrading enough besides having his wife and daughter see him in that state!

From that day on I watched those nurses and how they treated my father until the day he got transferred to the Therapy Center…thank goodness my father had us to watch over him…others were not so lucky!

I promised myself that no other family member of mine would ever be placed in a Nursing Home…

My father was finally transferred to the Physical Therapy Center and stayed at the center for about 2 months…what I saw there was heartbreaking!

People of all ages recovering from strokes, cancer, car accidents, etc…

How he was treated there was quite different …it made a world of difference in his recuperation!

Finally, he was sent home with a diet to follow… I was given instructions how to work with him with the physical therapy…it made it easier for me that my parents lived only a few blocks away. I took over my father's role as a caregiver, took care of their bills, my bills, their grocery shopping and mine in between doctor's appointments and while raising Carlos! Sure, I was tired, but I loved my father too much to care how tired I was! I was also the only girl in our family so there was no other choice!

My father became my hero! Right in front of my eyes I saw him get off the wheelchair, use a walker and then a cane… Watched him flex and slap his right hand to practice writing, he was even able to drive locally!

He learned to take daily walks, we got him a stationary bike and his speech also came back little by little!

I found on my own something we all have to learn to accept… A person that has a major stroke will never be completely the same, he had laughing spells for no reason, cried sometimes for no reason and his memory was affected! I became his right arm and his biggest protector!

He would go out for daily walks with his bone cap and his cane… This was part of his physical therapy and he came back a few times with urine down his pants, my mother and I would help him to clean up and change his pants…at times like this he would cry and would get extremely embarrassed! Our love for him never diminished! I looked at my dad and told him "Daddy, look how far you have gotten so far! Don't let accidents like this affect you! We are here to support and love you no matter what!"

What I didn't tell my father was that I missed the father that he once was! He had been the type of man that would walk into a room and people would notice and pay attention when he spoke, he had a great personality and was now a shell of the man that he once was.…

I knew taking care of my father would take both of us, my mother wasn't feeling well physically because of her diabetes and angina, I took on the task of cleaning their bathroom once a week because my mother couldn't not bend down without getting dizzy!

Many times, I would have to hold my breath while cleaning it because the bathroom would smell of urine, unfortunately, this was the result of my father missing the toilet while aiming and my grandmother that could not see and missed the toilet as well. I didn't mind believe me! I just wanted to have a clean environment around them, they trusted me so much that they even asked me to cut their hair!

Every time I went to the hairdresser, I watch them cut hair and then practice on my family! I found out that I had a knack for it… even Victor asked me to give him haircuts!

I'm sure my father was seen by many people sometimes walking by himself sometimes with Carlos holding his hand, God knows how much I worried about him taking those walks by himself but this also would bring his independence and self-esteem back…

CHAPTER 21

My father's recovery and a new job for me!

*I*t took 2 years for him to be able to take care of his household and I was finally able to start taking care of myself a little better...

We also got news that made us all happy! We found out that my youngest brother Carlos Henrique and his wife Rosa were coming to the US to try making a living here! I was about 14 when I last saw them, when they got married in Portugal...of all my three brothers he was my favorite (he would take me places that my parents did not take me, like dances and act like my chaperone) and he was also the most affectionate one...

He got himself a job at "Capwell's" in the El Cerrito Plaza as of head of the Janitorial Team, Rosa also worked with him there for a few years until she setup her own janitorial team and left "Capwell's"

Since Victor loved to go fishing he took my brother to Stinson Beach on a weekend, we drove up there, the guys took their fishing gear to the rocks nearby... Rosa and I stayed behind and decided to go swimming, neither one of us had swimming suits on and once in the water she dared me to take my bra off!

I was one you could not dare! So, I took it off and swirled it around and we both laughed out loud! We went home after that with plenty of fish and while the guys cleaned the fish...Rosa and I took a shower to get rid of the salt water, she took a shower first and while I was getting my clothes ready I happened to look up and saw her naked in front of me, when I looked down she laughed at me and said "eu chamo a isto a mata da cerreta." I call this "Cerreta Forest." I knew very well what she was referring to and we both burst out laughing!

Once we were done with our showers, we joined the guys in the kitchen and prepared a great fish stew! Fried some perch that we had caught and our fishing experience turned out to be something we would remember forever!

Meanwhile when things settled a bit with my father, I started searching for something for me, I had a lot a talent for different things but I didn't know which direction to take! I loved to write, to cook, to cut hair…etc… So, on impulse I looked into a Hair Cutting School nearby and was in training for a week when I decided to call it quits!

We had to practice on each other, the person that would be doing my hair had just finished with someone that had very greasy hair and proceed to use the same comb on me! I said, "Are you actually going to use the same comb on me?" She said, "We all do it, it's ok it save us time." I held her hand with mine and said "Not on my hair! That's not sanitary!" After what I had seen at that place in the space of a week I left and gave up on a hairstyling profession…

I looked for work instead and found a position at Mechanics Bank, the Bank manager that interviewed me knew I didn't have any experience in this field but I told her that I could learn anything…given the opportunity, she told me that she believed me and I started working for the Customer Service Dept in Richmond.

This job gave me the confidence I needed to start on a diet and exercise routine, unfortunately, I found out that excepting myself the way I was didn't last long! The weight didn't stay the same, it kept going up and I noticed it thru my clothes! I did it the wrong way in the beginning, I would starve myself during the week and then splurge on the weekends! After a while I realized that this was becoming a vicious cycle because I was gaining back the weight that I had lost during the week!

I decided to become serious about this diet and started to lose the weight and keeping it off! This also meant having a serious conversation with Victor about cooperating with me instead of jeopardizing my efforts...

When I got this job one of the hardest things I found I had to do was to leave my child in someone's care and go to work! I did some looking around and found a daycare for Carlos, I didn't want to ask my mother because she was still helping my dad and the first day I left him at the Daycare I cried! It didn't help me at all to see Carlos little face full of tears by the front window crying for me!! I took that picture with me to work....

That same week I went by the place a little earlier to pick up my son and saw children neglected, including Carlos sitting in a corner by himself! He had been crying and had peed on himself! When he looked at me there was so much hurt in his eyes that I grabbed him and left! I stopped by my parents and told them what I had seen and immediately my mother said, "No more of that Day Care! Leave him with us from now on! We will make do so that you don't have to go to work worried about him." I was so happy! I knew my mother was doing this for me but there is nothing like having family taking care of small children!

There are people taking care of kids that do it for the money not because they love the little ones!

It helped that Carlos loved them dearly (especially close to my dad) and there were times that Carlos and I stayed with them (Friday nights of course) and watched Don Francisco's show on TV, this became a habit with us and also allowed me to stay close to my parents and grandma and check on their needs.

With my mother it was very hard to get her to admit how she felt! She didn't want to bother me and ask me to take her to the doctor! She had been suffering with pain in what she thought came from her uterus and finally became bad enough for her to tell me about it, I called Dr.Stevens, made an appointment and took her to see him, she was scared to find out what it was of course but we found out she had a small cyst in her cervix, the doctor had it removed by using a laser, she was also given antibiotics to prevent infection…

That day I rebuked her by telling her "Mom, don't wait until the last minute to tell me if there is something bothering you or dad, please! It's not good to wait around for things to get better on their own!" She understood me and from that day on she became a lot more open with me regarding their health issues…

My mother always tried to place herself last but I did not allow her to do it…

Victor and I scheduled our first vacation after the birth of our son to Los Angeles, CA, we would be stopping in Disneyland, Universal Studios and The Wax Museum. Unfortunately, our son that was still recuperating from an ear infection threw up quite a bit on the way there! We stayed at a Motel and took pictures everywhere! When we entered The Wax Museum at the door, we were greeted by a guy that I could have sworn was Burt Reynolds! I immediately asked him if he was indeed Burt and he said "No, but I have done quite a few stunts for him in a few movies." I asked him if he mind taking a picture with me and he said "Of course not! It would be my pleasure!"

These experiences I wished with all my heart my parents had been there to share them with us! Unfortunately, because of their health problems and having to watch over my grandmother made it impossible for them to go anywhere!

Universal Studios was by far one of my favorite places because I loved the movies and while there we took plenty of pictures to share with our family!

Once back home, the next day I stopped by my parents duplex and showed them all the pictures we had taken and told them all about our vacation.…

My parents and I discussed everything together even people that I had met and many times my mother would give me her input on situations! For example…a woman that I had met at work that totally amazed me! She had become my friend but she was running her life and her husband's life! He was Mexican, she was American and she was having an affair with his brother! She would actually use her lunch hour to meet him at a motel and then come back to work smelling of men's cologne and brag about it!

Totally addicted to Coke, she couldn't go one day without it! I told her one day "Liz, you know I read somewhere that it takes 3 weeks to give up a bad habit and 3 weeks to develop a new one! Try it! It works! That goes for the Coke and for being unfaithful to someone! These 2 brothers you are messing with will lose their relationship with each other because of you!"

Later that year I saw her at a grocery store, she had left her husband for his brother and like I predicted they had a huge fight, their relationship was lost and their children got separated as well...

Sometimes when we help people it's up to them if they listen or not, even family sometimes will listen.... sometimes not!

From the Customer Service Dept I was promoted to the Bookkeeping Dept, stayed there for a while and was promoted to the General Ledger Dept at the Hilltop Branch, at this branch I made incredible friendships! Two women became quite close to me and would become my greatest allies, Victor and I were invited very often to their homes... Judy was a very fun-loving person that got involved with a Portuguese man but refused to marry him... Teresa (my supervisor) got married to a wonderful man that unfortunately contracted cancer from asbestos exposure and left her a widow!

These two friends of mine and I would become friends for years to come! Thru my job we also did Pre-Christmas celebrations, one of them was a dinner at a Moroccan restaurant, my first experience with Moroccan food, sitting on the floor and eating with your hands was an amazing experience! This had been a girl's night out that I would never forget!

That year we also had a visit from a cousin of mine, Frankie and his wife Kim, we decided to take a weekend trip to Vegas, Kim was amazed that her allergies got better when we got to Vegas! We went sightseeing and stopped to gamble at a casino on the strip, I got really excited and told Victor to look towards the poker tables (his favorite place to gamble) and there sat Red Foxx!

We had been watching re-runs from Stanford and Son for years and absolutely loved this guy! I told Victor "I'm going to get his autograph!" Victor tried to stop me but I was determined and headed towards his table, the guy by the dealer stopped me and I told him "I really admire Mr.Foxx and I would love to get his autograph."

He told me "Please wait a bit, he is playing right now and he is not in a really good mood (I guess he was losing)." I waited a bit, when he was done, I approached him a bit nervous and said "Mr. Foxx, my husband and I really admire your work and we watch Stanford and Son every week, do you mind signing an autograph for us.?"

He got a picture of himself from a stack on the table, signed it and threw it across the table for me to grab it! I grabbed the picture and said, "Thank you." and left…I was so disappointed with his attitude that I told Victor "I'm not watching this guy on TV any longer, you can have the picture." We played for a while, ate at the Buffet, shopped and left once again for California…this experience taught me to lay low of celebrities, what we see on TV is not actually how people are!

My parents had kept an eye on Carlos that weekend and when we arrived the following day, I told them about this experience with Mr.Foxx… they also watched his program and they were disappointed in him just like me…

I made a point of keeping an eye on my parents even while working and took time off to take them to their doctor's appointments and even Social Services appointments, my mother also worried me because of her health, she refused to change their eating habits and her hernia many times would take her to bed. I did some research and found out that many people had better lives after having surgery to remove hernias but because she was afraid of surgeries, she preferred to avoid them… She would let the inflammation go down and then resume her lifestyle, I loved and respected my parents enough to know what I could or could not change…

Because of how much my parents relied on me they were always willing to help me in anyway… every Christmas my mother always made sure I had a warm coat and my grandma always gave me the money to buy a new dress for New Year's Eve.

My grandmother was something else! Every time we gave her money back from her social security check… she would hide it in her closet… she was almost blind due to macular degeneration, when she tried to look for it, she couldn't find it and then she would ask for me! She would tell my mother that someone had taken her money! It would take me looking in her closet and count her money for her to relax! Then she would smile and kiss me! My mother would just shake her head!

We loved her dearly and because she was getting older she constantly needed our reassurance! Every day she would tell us that she wouldn't be with us for very long and one day I reminded her "Avozinha, you are not leaving this world when you want but when your time comes, I bet you still have quite a few years left in you'" She would smile at me but she was very well known for her stubbornness! She refused to wear her dentures because they hurt her gums too much and for the rest of her life she had to eat soft foods!

Many times, I would find her in her room praying the rosary…a picture that would stay engraved in my mind forever!

I had finally lost quite a bit of weight and had cut my hair, that was how my youngest brother loved to see me…Victor and I were celebrating our wedding anniversary and he was taking me out to our favorite restaurant… Skates by the Bay in Berkeley! We loved the view and most of the time right after dinner we would take a walk on the pier (this was also one of his favorite places to fish on the weekends), we went by my parents duplex to leave Carlos with them and my brother happened to be there, he liked what I was wearing that day and for some reason grabbed me and kissed me on the cheek! My mother got the camera and took a picture of both of us…Treasured memories!

Carlos Henrique's daughter, Carla had flown to California to get to know her father for a bit, she had been living with her mother in Portugal and was also curious about living life in the US. Unfortunately, she was not accepted by my sister-in-law in the beginning and developed a close relationship with me instead…

I felt sorry for her (I had first met her as a baby at our house in Portugal) and kept on telling my sister-in-law to be patient with her because she was a teen and it takes time for a teen to mature, she eventually decided to go back to Portugal! She confided in me that she did not want to get in between her father and Rosa! Something I found strange! She called me occasionally but refused to come back…

Just before Christmas that year I took my son Carlos to see Santa and this child of mine absolutely freaked out! He was so cute that people always stopped me to ask me how old she was (because of his curly hair) and I would have to correct them and say "He, not she!" they would laugh and apologize!

In order to get a picture of him with Santa I actually had to sit on Santa's lap myself first and then had our pictures taken!

CHAPTER 22

Oldest brother moves to the US and a serious breakup!

W̶e also received news that Jose Carlos my oldest brother, his wife and 3 kids had decided to move to the US to see if they could make a living here, we got together and found them an apartment, furnished it with used furniture donated by friends and family and my husband found a job for him in his company, for my brother this was quite an adjustment! His previous position was a prestigious one without so much physical work with a free place to live and good pay…he was mainly doing this move to give his kids a better future…

I also helped my sister-in-law by teaching her how to drive and become independent and the kids were placed in local schools, for fun we had barbecues together that summer, attended Portuguese functions and played cards in the winter!

Unfortunately, quite often conflicts happen in families and also jealousy and the family started to split apart! Victor did something really stupid and took my two brothers to single bars! Once this came out it created a big issue! My sisters-in-laws blamed me and Victor!

I actually split from my husband and went to live in a Mobile Park with Carlos and my cat Foxy! Victor also had been neglecting me, he was never around, probably because he had met someone at one of those bars and I got tired of trying to get his attention!

Many times, while Victor was watching TV, he would become so observed that when I tried to talk to him he wouldn't even respond, so I would get in front of the TV raise my arms up in the air waive them around and say "Hello there, Victor! Your wife here is trying to get your attention and we have something to discuss", then he would look at me say "What? Do you have something to ask me?" Typical male!!

My moving out was mostly because of what he had done with my brothers and because of the suspicion I had that he had someone on the side…

I moved to the Mobile Home Park and I felt so at peace in that place! Victor unfortunately made a point of stopping by unannounced and tried to get me into bed with him! I told him to stop by my mother's house to see our son (I knew Victor was still doing the bar scene) to avoid having him come around. I had the feeling that my suspicion was correct about him having an affair…

I loved to fix my meals and sit in front of the TV with a glass of wine and relax before going to sleep, many nights I would open my front door to hear the crickets outside… I also loved Carlos room and my biggest struggle was getting him potty trained! Most mornings before I went to work, I would have to change all the bedding before I got him ready to be dropped off at grandma's house and still make it on time to work…

The only one that had the hardest time adjusting to our new place was my kitty! We couldn't find her one morning and I finally gave up and proceeded to my car since I didn't want to be late for work, when I started my car suddenly, I heard meow! meow! and didn't know where that came from! To my surprise when I opened the hood of my car, Foxy was there meowing all over the place! I grabbed her and left her in my kitchen… relieved that she was unharmed!

Victor would not stop coming by using any excuse to see me and one night grabbed me and we ended up in bed after a few drinks! …when we were done he looked at me and said "I got to go, my buddy and I are going to try a new club tonight." I told him "You got to be kidding …am I a one-night stand to you?"

He left anyway and for the first time in my life I felt like a prostitute! I called my brother Jose Carlos the next day and told him what happened the previous night and he was very upset, he asked what I wanted him to do, I asked him to tell Victor to stay away from me and to see his son at my mother's house…

My brother did more than that I'm sure because Victor came back the next day to talk to me about going back to him and was even willing to stay at the Mobile Home for a while! I was very skeptical but my family also wanted me to give him another chance for Carlos's sake…

I noticed a change in him however… he was colder than usual (like he was doing me a favor) probably because he had been pressured by my brother! I wrote him a letter and left it where he could see it on top of the table before I went to work, that letter stated that unless he made a true effort to make our relationship work, I didn't want him back and I meant it!

We were apart a whole 3 weeks but long enough to do us damage …the trust would have to be rebuilt even with my brothers, I certainly did not want Victor going to bars and taking my brothers with him! That had created huge problems with my sisters-in-laws!

I got in my car and went to speak to Carlos Henrique and Rosa, told them that I had no idea of where Victor had taken them and that if I had known I would have put a stop to it! Rosa knew me well enough to believe me because she knew I didn't believe in open marriages! Rosa also told me that Carlos Henrique had shared something with her that she wanted to tell me "Carlos Henrique saw Victor after quite a few drinks rub himself against a woman while dancing! Carlos Henrique and Jose Carlos did not like that all! That was a lack of respect for you and for them! After all they are your brothers!" This was why I couldn't trust Victor completely! He would have to change his behavior towards women if he ever expected to regain my trust again! I kept this information to myself because I didn't want to create a conflict between Victor and my brothers.!

Unfortunately, conflict happened not between my brothers and Victor but between two brothers that had always been very close!

Problems developed between my two brothers that got really serious! They stopped speaking to each other, it was something I promised myself I would keep secret to protect their families (some things are better off not being shared for the sake of others) and to avoid future confrontations...

Jose Carlos was also extremely tired of having to work so hard and according to him having problems in his marriage... something he had confided in me...

He finally decided to take his family back home to Portugal and go back to his prior position, when he left, I was very sad! I loved him dearly and I knew he was also breaking my mother's heart...

After my brother left, I was informed by a neighbor that they had seen my father sitting in his car smoking a cigarette ...something I had warned my father not to do after his stroke! I had done my research and found out that that the immune system is left much weaker than normal once someone has a stroke, therefore if another illness attacks the body your chances of survival are much lowered...

I spoke to him about it, he promised me that he would try not to smoke for my sake and I told him "Not for my sake dad! For yours! You could end up getting another illness on top of a stroke.!

CHAPTER 23

Learning to accept a husband as he is and another child prayed for!

Victor and I decided to go back home and sell the Mobile Home to my father-in-law and start our relationship anew… There were good days and bad days but we were determined to make it work, our family was glad because after all we had a child to think about …My in-laws came to see us many times and I was amazed how unhappy my mother-in-law was sometimes! She would confide in me and I finally had to give her the same advise that my mother had given me regarding my relationship with Victor "If you cannot change him, then accept him for who he is and try to make the relationship work." She listened but I could see doubt in her eyes, I totally understood because my father-in-law could be very difficult …

Victor also asked me to help him quit smoking, he took the cigarettes out of his pocket and handed them over to me and said "No more smoking, that was my last pack!" He totally amazed me by quitting cold turkey! I was extremely happy because we had Carlos and I didn't like him smoking in the house.

You cannot make a person give up everything at once, most of the time one bad habit can lead to another! The other one was sleeping in the nude, I found it embarrassing! One night we woke up with noise in the backyard and I told him "Victor, please go look thru the glass door."

He got up and went to look in the backyard without putting clothes on! We found out that it was probably a critter of some kind but that prompt him to get a gun for our house and a dog for our protection, of course the habit of sleeping nude stayed for quite a while…so did other habits… But nobody is perfect!

We were together for about a year when we started to talk about another child (I was afraid to have an only one child because of what happened to my oldest brother) and my mother was extremely happy because she really wanted me to have a girl, like she said, "To take care of you when you get older!"

I had been promoted to work at Hilltop Mall Mechanics Bank and truly enjoyed my work and my friends but for some reason I started experiencing anxiety and panic attacks just about every day! I went for a checkup at Kaiser to check if something was wrong physically and the doctor told me that what I was going thru was a lot of stress…he also told me that I was too young to be placed on medication and that due to my high stress level it would be unlikely that I would be able to get pregnant!

Instead of getting discouraged I prayed for a miracle baby like my mother had prayed for me! A doctor had told my mother the same thing many years before and she had prayed and gotten pregnant …believe it or not I got pregnant and even managed to enjoy my pregnancy.!

I got pretty big…the baby was feet down and did not want to move in the right position and I also knew that Victor wasn't as thrilled as I was! He wasn't really what you call father material and he also managed to make me feel very unattractive, I caught him one night masturbating while watching a porno…I walked away and didn't tell him anything …too embarrassed to let him know I had seen him!

Suddenly I started to have contractions in my lower back a month before the baby was due to arrive and we end up in the hospital….

Much was going to be revealed there! No way was I prepared for what was told to me that day!

The Doctor came in and told my husband to leave! I was afraid this might be bad news about the baby but was very surprised when the doctor asked me straight out if either my husband or I had any previous sexual relationships outside of our marriage! I knew I hadn't but I knew he had a year ago when we had been separated, I asked the doctor if a sexual disease could survive in a body for a year! She told me that yes it could and if left untreated, trichomoniasis **could lead to severe health problems**. Trichomonas infection is closely tied to co-infection with HIV, easing transmission of the virus that causes AIDS, I was so angry I didn't know how to react!

She informed me that Victor and I would have to be treated immediately after our son's birth. Danny thanks to God was not infected with this infection… in a way it was good thing that he had to be delivered thru a Caesarian! Doctors had tried with their hands to move the baby's position to be born naturally but he would move halfway and then go back to the same position!

He weighed 8 pounds 7oz and I was just happy that he was healthy! Coming out of the delivery room I had the worst shakes I ever experienced in my life! They placed me in a room and I had to confront Victor with what the doctor had told me. At first, he refused to admit that he had contracted this illness thru a relationship he had a year prior but then he finally admitted that he had symptoms he should have told me about! …He also knew that he had to be treated …this was very serious! He could not keep on denying that he had given me this sexual infection when I had contracted crabs before from him and we both had to be treated at that time…

I was finally released from the Hospital and had to find a way to not only heal but to forgive as well!

Worried that my husband might have AIDS kept me away from him! I forgave him because of our kids but I was upset that this man that I loved refused to use condoms while he was having flings all over the place! So, I told him that I would not let him touch me unless he got tested for AIDS …he started to argue with me but I stopped him by letting him know how serious I was and volunteered to have the test as well, I had never slept with anyone but him but now I worried that I might of have contracted something from him!

It took 2 weeks of pure hell to get the results! Keeping him away from me was not easy! To our relief we both tested negative! Rebuilding trust after this ordeal would be very difficult but I was determined to make the effort…

CHAPTER 24

Family crisis in a big way!

*A*nother difficult crisis arouse within my family… my mother's angina got worse, the medication she was taking wasn't strong enough and she was extremely stressed! My parents also had been advised that their rent was going to be doubled and they couldn't afford it!

Their income came from Social Security and from whatever my mother could get from sewing and that was not enough! My mother and I started to look for a place for them to move but every place we found was either too expensive or too far from me so that I could keep an eye on them…

They also lived in a place that was not very safe, I always worried about someone messing with my father while he was out there walking with a cane, instead I received a call from Food Max to come and get my parents since something had happened… when I got there my mother was trembling and my father was clearly shaken! I found out that they had been mugged by a man that took my mother's purse and had pushed my father to the ground! (Cane included) …I was extremely upset! I never knew such people existed!

They didn't have much money with them but I did have to replace some of their documents with Social Security, I told my parents that from that day forward I would do the groceries for them and take my mother with me...

I went home one day very worried about the rent increase my parents were facing and about what happened at Food Max and discussed the situation with Victor, he came up with a plan of building two extra rooms in the back of our house and have all 3 of them move in... Of course, also according to him charge them a small amount of rent and extra for expenses, I was very surprised by his offer since I knew he didn't care that much about my mother, but he explained that this would be good for me and for them. They would be closer to me so that I could watch over them and in the long run we would all benefit from this change! So, the renovation started in our house to get them ready to move in….

I also had decided to quit working for a while, I had no one that I trusted to take care of Danny and I knew that my mother (that wasn't feeling very well) was going to need me…

She tried to hide it from me as much as possible but she forgot how observant I was! She loved to go with me and the kids to Hilltop Mall, have a cup of coffee and look around and see people, I noticed as I walked in front of her that she was having a hard time keeping up with me on a simple walk and was out of breath! Of course, she blamed it on the angina but I had the feeling there was much more than that!

This move of my parents to our home caused a controversy between our families! My father-in-law showed up and had a conversation with Victor out on our front yard…thru the window I heard the conversation and it made me sick that my mother's brother was telling his son "Do not let these people take advantage of you, you hear me?" I had to stop myself from going outside and remind him "Do you know, who else is moving in? Your own mother, you fool!"

I had Danny in August of 1989 and my parents and grandmother moved in December of 1989…. that same month my mother was taken to Brookside Hospital with chest pains! She was admitted and got scheduled to go thru a balloon procedure to unclog her arteries, I almost lost her! In the waiting room I prayed and prayed for my mother and best friend to make it! She stopped breathing and they found a way for her to come back! When I finally had a meeting with Doctor Stern, I was informed that this would allow her to be able to breathe better for about 6 months but eventually she would have to go thru a heart bypass!!

She was able to come home for Christmas! I was so happy that she was alive and that we would be able to have a family get together for the Holidays! Unfortunately, after the Holidays were over things changed dramatically! One day as I walked into the dining room my father was sitting in a chair with a handkerchief in his hand… when I looked at it, he looked at me very sad and my heart sunk! He had spit up blood and I noticed how pale he was! I didn't want to tell him but deep down I had the suspicion of what it was…I took him to a specialist that same week, they ran some tests and in February of 1990 my father who I loved with all my heart was diagnosed with lung cancer!

Before I had time to digest this information the Doctor was already scheduling radiation treatments for him! I immediately asked him if surgery was an option, he informed me that his lungs wouldn't survive it! How in the world would I find the words to tell my mother that the love of her life had lung cancer.!

I had to convince her that the radiation treatments would give him a chance of survival but deep down I knew my father's days were counted… I prayed, she prayed and we hid our feelings from him! What we went thru with my father's illness was heartbreaking!

The radiation treatments left him very weak and affected his appetite and it seemed that a new side effect showed up every day…including depression. One of the worse days for me was when were given a wheel-chair for my father! We brought it home and Victor had to build a ramp on our front door so that we had an easier way to get my father in and out of the car for doctors' appointments, I wondered what my father thought of having to use it…Every day I made a point of telling my dad that I loved him and he always responded back "I love you too" There were times when I closed myself in my room and just let the tears go…

My father and I had an extreme bad day, we were once again in the hospital for a radiation treatment when my father had to go the bathroom (I knew he always needed help with that) and there was not a soul around to help! He needed to go really bad, so I took him to the men's bathroom and unzipped his pants. My father's cancer had spread to his hip, so he had limited motion on his right side, I told him to hold on to my shoulders and he started to lose his balance! I thought he was going to fall and held on to him almost crying because I knew if he fell…. I would not be able to lift him up by myself!

When I finally got him close to the toilet, he had urine allover his pants, I told him "Never mind daddy clothes can be washed." By the way he looked at me I knew he was extremely embarrassed and there was so much sadness in his eyes that it was overwhelming!

We got back to the waiting room to be seen by his doctor, I looked at him and he was very silent, I asked him "Daddy please speak to me" What's wrong?"

He replied, "I'm just tired of suffering."

I felt awful at that moment! When you love someone, you don't want them to suffer but even in our love we can be a bit selfish by hanging on to dear life to someone you love dearly!

Each day got worse not better to the point he could not taste food any longer and had lost quite a bit of weight!

I believe that if he had seen improvement depression would have not been there…even the conversations I had with my father's doctor were away from him….so that he would not get discouraged….

CHAPTER 25

Almost losing my mother!

*O*n the other hand, my mother's heart problems got worse and one day it got so bad that I had to take her to Brookside Hospital once again! I was told by her doctor that if she didn't have a heart bypass asap... she would not survive another angina attack!

So, they got her ready for surgery and she was so calm that I wondered if she was putting up a front for my benefit! I was advised to take her the night before to intensive care to show her where she would be placed after surgery so she would be better prepared, she refused time and time again and her words to me was "I trust in God, let His will be done."

The next morning, she had the surgery (they replaced arteries in her heart with arteries from her legs), major surgery for someone with diabetes! When she woke up from the surgery and saw herself hooked up to all kinds of tubes she totally freaked out! She started to pull on them and they finally sedated her so that she would not hurt herself...

The first night she spent at the Hospital after the surgery was terrible! I had gone home to get some sleep when I received a call from a nurse at ICU asking me to please come by! She would not let them come close to give her medicine, she cried and screamed to the point they had to call me! When I approached her, I held her hand and told her "Mama eu estou aqui." ...in English "Mama I'm here." She thought they were trying to kill her and started to see things due to all the medications they had given her, I could only imagine how frightened she was!

It wasn't the only night I spent with her, she trusted only me and was afraid to go to sleep! I finally had a discussion with her doctor and told him about the situation at home with my father and my kids… I also told him that I could not bear seeing my mother this way! He finally explained to me that she had developed a condition called Sundowner… a fear that some older patients get after surgery, I asked him what we could do to help her get over this…his answer was for us to have lots of patience, lots of love and eventually she would go back to normal…... But it would take some time…

Her doctor also decided to move her to a regular room to help her with the fears she was experiencing, it did help somewhat but most of my time was spent at the hospital back and forth between taking Carlos to school, checking on my father, grandmother and have Victor take care of the kids a bit in the evening until I got home.

I was exhausted and stressed to the limit but still determined to help my parents no matter what!

Unfortunately, my brother Carlos Henrique did not believe Sundowner existed and believed my mother was doing all of this for attention!

I asked him since he lived nearby for him to watch over her a few times so that I could get some rest and give Victor a rest from the kids, he flat out refused and told me that it was my duty as her daughter to take care of her! He didn't surprise me much with his answer since he also had tried to convince me to admit our father to a nursing home! Something I refused to do!

It's funny how you can get free advice from anyone but not help when you needed it the most…

That day my brother broke my heart!

He told me that since I was the girl in the family it was my duty to take care of them! Also, since Victor and I had taken the responsibility of moving our parents to our home we should be able to take the good with the bad! He also brought up that he knew they were helping us with expenses, I was pretty upset and told him " I didn't bring our parents to my home to get help from them financially, I brought them to my home because I didn't have no other choice, they are both sick and I didn't have no one else to ask for help…but if you and Rosa are interested in helping them by all means build an extra room in your home and take them to live with you… they will be able to help you instead." I looked straight at him and told him "We are a family after all, for your information I'm exhausted otherwise I wouldn't have asked for help."

He got quiet and told me that he would talk to with his wife but of course I didn't get an answer, knowing him the way I did I imagine how he felt afterwards when he had a chance to reflect on what we had discussed…

My mother came home but it would take a while for her to recuperate physically and mentally from her surgery! My brother come to me one day and apologized in my kitchen, he came up behind me to hug me but it would take at least a good year for me to able to look at him the same way…

I tried to make my father feel that life was as usual and when we received his social security check… I went to their room, showed it to my dad and asked him "Daddy, can you please let me know how much cash you need back before I take it to the Bank?" He looked down, since I was holding it in my hand and shook his head! When I looked at him, he looked at me like he didn't even know what I was holding! At that point I knew something had changed for the worst and just told him "Don't worry daddy, I will take care of it." Now I knew I that I would have to take care of their finances by myself, this was something that I couldn't even share with my mother…

I was right about my father, he developed gout and even singles from his lung cancer… even worse when I took him to his doctor, I found out that his cancer had spread from his hip to his lymph nodes and possibly to his brain! At the doctor's office when he looked at me wondering what had been said to me, I just told him "The tests are coming out the same daddy, at least you are not getting worse!" He would have given up if I had told him the truth!

As sick as he was, he was also concerned about my mother's mental health and I reassured him that the doctor had said that she would get better with time, I was also hiding from my mother the fact that my father was getting worse! I was so afraid of her getting sick after her surgery from the stress we were all going thru...

Another problem was that my mother was a very stubborn woman and refused to follow the doctor's orders to walk everyday (with a pillow pressed against the breast area), I told her that I would walk with her... but I couldn't persuade her even after telling her that the doctor had said that after her surgery it was essential for her to walk! He also advised me that if she changed her eating habits and started a walking routine that her life could be extended as much as 10 years or longer!

A Portuguese friend of ours had the same surgery and decided to follow the doctors' orders... but my mother was not willing to change! One of the greatest things that someone told me while I was going thru all these things was that I was very observant and to use this gift for my benefit ... that was told to me by my mother's heart surgeon! He trusted me so much with her care that I was instructed how to take care of an open wound that she had developed on one of her legs when they had taken an artery out to replace one on her heart. Due to her diabetes this wound became impossible to heal… I had to learn to clean it and disinfect it daily until it closed completely...

Victor also had to do something that he probably never thought he would have to do and that was to place a urinary catheter on my father (we didn't have a nurse around) ...I hid in bathroom hearing my father scream in pain with tears running down my face! I wondered if our lives would ever change for the better!!

My father woke up one night with trouble breathing and I had to call an ambulance, they took him to Brookside Hospital and he was seen by a very unsympathetic doctor that flat out told me "Of course you know he is dying, so what do you want me to do about it?"

I wanted to tell him to go to Hell…instead I told him that I had 2 kids at home, my mother recovering from heart surgery and I didn't want them to see my father die in front of their eyes. I looked in my father's direction and he was looking straight at me with so much pain and sadness in his eyes that I could hardly breathe! The doctor cleared his throat and told me that he would see what he could do… he found a way for my father to get admitted and they actually found a room for him….

I was at the hospital every day, my mother would come with me whenever she felt strong enough, we would feed him, talk to him an encourage him as much as we could, I knew we were losing him, but I refused to give him up to death!

CHAPTER 26

Facing my father's death
and losing my grandmother…

$\mathcal{H}$e had been in the hospital for about 3 weeks when one day as I looked up from reading a paper, I heard my mother once again plead with my father "Rogerio come por favor." Of course, she was trying to get him to eat and as I looked at my dear father, he looked so tired! It looked like his eyes were pleading with me to let him go!!

I felt so selfish at that moment!

I got up…. left the room and went to the waiting room by myself and spoke to God… I asked Him to forgive me for being selfish in my love and to please stop his suffering! I also told Him that if He had to take him to please do it quickly before I lost my courage!

I went home that night with a heavy feeling in my heart and while I was giving a bath to Danny, I felt this compulsion to call the Hospital and check on my father but hesitated afraid to find out! Just as I was drying my son, I got a call from the Hospital to inform us that my father didn't have much time left….

My mother and I rushed to the Hospital and my father had already passed away and gone with him a piece of me had left as well! I was totally devoted to him! I had changed him and he had changed me…

My brother Carlos Henrique showed up at the Hospital as well to pay his respects and as I looked at my dad, I looked at him and told him

"Carlos Henrique… if you don't quit smoking you could end up like our dad, this should give you the motivation to quit." He answered me right away "Please don't compare me with dad, he is much older than me, I'm too young." I told him "It's not how old you are is how long you have been smoking and you have been smoking since you were 11 years old." I knew he would not listen to me… but I loved him too much not to try…

I tried to let go of my father but my grief was overwhelming! We held a service at our Church that was filled with friends and family… and as I stood there looking at my father's coffin, tears flowing with a big ache in my heart, I felt this strange urge to look to the right side of me and felt his presence!

It didn't give me any comfort what happened there! I even hid from my mother how much I was suffering because I had to be strong for both of us! I wore black and white as it's common in my country and went to Church to find comfort… nothing helped…

One night I had this dream of my father sitting on top of his grave! As I stood there looking at him, he looked straight at me inserted his hand in the soil and I asked him "What are you doing daddy?" He looked straight at me and said, "I cannot rest because you won't let me go." This dream was so real to me that the next morning I went to my closet and got rid of my black & white clothes, went to talk to my mother, told her about the dream and advised her to do the same! We had to stop loving and missing him so much in a way that would stop him from getting the peace that he deserved!

Thru our church I had met a wonderful priest that had blessed our home and knew our family very well…. Father Ignatius loved to garden and we all knew that he only had half of a lung! One Sunday after mass I saw him out gardening with a cigarette in his hand! I spoke to him from the heart "Father Ignatius please get rid of that habit! I just lost my father to lung cancer… he couldn't even have his lung removed but you have another chance at life…don't waist it! Life is too precious!" He smiled and said that he would try! Unfortunately, I found out much later that he had lost his life to cancer and that the cigarettes had won!

Life had to continue no matter what… I still had two women that I loved to take care of besides my husband and my children and somehow, I found the strength!

My father-in-law made a point every so often to come by to see his mother and he always managed to get on my nerves! You would think that his appreciation for what Victor and I were doing would have made his attitude change but every time he visited, he always had smart remarks!

A few months after my father's death my grandmother started to get ill!

To my grandmother I was everything, she called me "minha querida netinha" (my dearest granddaughter), she relied on me to keep her updated how the family was doing and I was the only one that she allowed to give her showers even when she fell in the bathtub one day! She had gotten blind little by little, a condition that I had refused to accept! I had taken her to a specialist to get a confirmation that this condition was not reversable… unfortunately he confirmed it…her eyes had closed little by little! Never once did I ever hear her say anything about her condition!

I like my grandmother was a chameleon (I adapted and blended in any place I lived) because of my grandfather's business (grocery store owner) my grandma had to move very often especially when business got slow or people were not paying their bills…

She had a tumor removed from her breast without anesthesia when she was younger and was well known for being a strong woman! She had developed a habit of saying that she was going to die soon! When I went to talk to her in her room, she would hold on to my hands and I would reassure her that she was a strong woman and that she would get better!

She also suffered from anxiety, her whole body would shake and her hands would freeze up to the point we would have to soak them in warm water so that she would be able to move them once again…

We had just lost my father and we could not face another death… but we don't have the power over life or death! She told me before she was taken to the Hospital that she had seen my grandfather and my dad by her bed! I believed her…how could I not?

My mother and I watched her slip away from us little by little on a cold fall day in the Hospital room, my mother holding on to one of her hands and I holding the other hand! My only consolation was that my grandmother had not died of cancer and she had not died alone….

She didn't deserve that! My grandma had never known who her real mother was! As a baby she had been left on a wheel in a Church in Acores designed for babies that needed to be adopted, the story I heard was that she had been adopted later on by a widow…

My grandmother didn't know how to read and write but she knew how to love unconditionally!

Losing both her husband and her mother left my mother in a state of depression and exhaustion that was hard to witness! I reminded her that we still had each other and I decided that the rest of my mother's life was going to be a much happier one if I had anything to do it!

She also had to cope with living with diabetes, from pills they placed her on Insulin… I had changed the way my family ate when they came to live with me but my mother would miss her own Portuguese foods and would cook her Portuguese dishes. When I spoke with her about her food habits, she would answer me "Don't worry about it I have my medicine." Too stubborn to listen! In the end I was the one that had to learn how to give her insulin shots in her abdominal area and take her blood count… many times her fingers would bleed from being tested everyday…

Chapter 27

Life after two major deaths!

*I*n between taking care of her I took care of my husband's and my kid's needs!

Danny's pre-school also called me that they wanted to speak to me… I met with his teacher and she advised me to take Danny to speech therapy because she noticed he stuttered! I told her "Sorry, that is not true, Danny becomes excited when he wants someone's attention and with all that has happened in our family sometimes our attention has been elsewhere." I explained a bit of what we had been thru as a family and asked her to be patient with him and also to do what I been doing with him at home…. that was to stop what I was doing when he wanted to speak to me and pay attention to what he was saying. That worked at home, she looked skeptical but agreed to try it…

I also started to go on field trips with my kids to show them that they could still count on their mother to be there for them…

There are habits as parents that we try not repeat with our own children, one of them was something that truly irritated me about my mother and that was her habit of talking to herself after I left the room after we had a discussion … I told her "Mama when you have something to discuss with me, please say it to my face, I can take it! I don't like to hear you griping after I leave the room." She did get better once she saw that I was serious about it…

There was another habit that she had brought with her from Acores and that was superstition! She would tell me not to take garbage out at night because it was bad for the family, another one was to place a broom upside down when you got company in case you wanted visitors out of the house asap! Black cats crossing the street meant someone close to you was going to die, etc... I would ignore her many times and told her "Mom, I cannot live that way! I don't believe in all those old superstitions! You were passed down old sayings from grandma and I refuse to believe in them."

She really tried but this was an old habit and old habits are hard to break! Another one was sniffing tobacco! Another bad habit that she had learned from my grandmother! Many times, my mother would have me go buy the tobacco... I hated to go to a store and be seen buying that product! I had done enough research regarding smoking to know that it wasn't just smoking that caused cancer but also sniffing or chewing tobacco...

But my mother also was full of good advice! I had a bad habit of my own and that was worrying about things before they happened and she gave me great advise "Don't worry about things before they happen, this way you suffer twice and sometimes what you worry about does not happen anyway!" Sometimes we do have a reason to worry! One for me was being out of the house while Victor was out back in the Avery, he was the type of person that got easily distracted and when he tried to multi-task he would forget things! He had the bad habit of trying to take care of his birds and leave something frying in the frying pan! That resulted in a fire in our kitchen that unfortunately caused quite an expense and caused us to have to remodel the kitchen!

We also started to take my mother to camping trips with us... I had convinced Victor to buy a used RV, we had been using an open and close trailer that was a pain in the butt to get ready! We had taken that small little trailer everywhere, but we very tired of all the work it took to get it ready to leave and to put things away once we got home! We loved exploring new towns and cooking meals outside!

One of our favorite places became Pismo Beach (my mother absolutely loved this town), Victor would go fishing at the pier and we walked around the beach, barbecued outside and at night cooked marshmallows over the fire! Just like any other mom I would make pancakes for my son's even shaped like mickey mouse! Something Danny never forgot!

One afternoon while Victor was out fishing, I went shopping and found on a store near a restaurant, chocolate covered make believe cigarettes! When I got back to the motor home I sat on our little sofa and placed one in my mouth. When Danny saw me with the make-believe cigarette in my mouth…he started to cry! When I asked him why he was crying so hard… he told me because he didn't want me smoking! I hugged him really hard and explained to him that they were not real cigarettes but chocolate sticks…. even after I explained that to him, he didn't want to try them and I ended up throwing them away! Somehow Danny had figured out that we had lost my father due to cigarette smoking! It goes to show how observant kids can be!

CHAPTER 28

Family trips and recuperating together...

*W*e took camping trips everywhere with our little RV... went as far as Casa de Fruta! Another place we loved and had an experience I never forgot!

We were quite far from home and Victor's back went out! Carlos had to go back to school on Monday... my husband looked at me very seriously and said, "You will have to drive us home because I will have to lay down on the floor on the way home." I was pretty nervous but I knew when his back went out it would take a few days for him to recover! So, I got behind the wheel and put up with his backseat driving until I got fed up! I told him that he just had to trust me otherwise we would have to park somewhere until he got better...that closed his mouth! I was able to drive us home, park the darn thing on my driveway and gave myself a high five!

As a family we made sure we also took our kids to amusement parks including Great America... my kids favorite! I had done something outrageous and had my hair permed the week before (wanted a natural look) and because my hair was already naturally curly it got out of hand! While at the park, Carlos looked at me and said "Mom, please go to the bathroom." I looked at him kind of wondering what he was up to and told him "Sorry, kiddo, I don't have to go right now!" He laughed and said, "You need to go and look at your hair!"

When I got to the bathroom and looked at myself in the mirror I gasped! I looked like a French poodle! Some of the ladies in the bathroom laughed at me as I poured water and water on my hair to get a controlled look! I was given good advice by one woman to get a straightener and she promised me that would tame my hair! That same week I got the straightener and swore off perms!

That same year I joined a gym to get into shape and my mother and I started sewing together... she taught me everything she knew and we made great outfits that looked great on me since I had lost quite a bit of weight. She would do most of the sewing by hand and I would use the sewing machine to finish the outfits. Due to her diabetes her vision had gotten pretty bad but sewing was something she absolutely loved!

Her favorite past time was gardening, she planted in our front yard, roses, daisies and her favorites calla lilies that came back year after year!

That love of gardening also brought her a small problem that could have been much worse if it had not been found at an early stage, I looked at my mother's face one day and saw a small spot that worried me and told her "Mom, that spot has been there for quite a while, I'm going to call a Dermatologist in our area and have him check it out." She knew better than argue with me! I called around, found a good doctor and I was right! She had the beginning of skin cancer and he used a laser to burn it off... She was also advised to watch out for too much sun exposure because of being so fair and watch for future spots...

Cooking was something else she and I loved to do together, I had made a deal with her to have her try some of my healthy meals and in turn occasionally give in and fix everybody some of my recipes they loved so much, that included some of her own favorite recipes. I really tried to help with her diet not only because of her diabetes but also because she suffered quite a bit from constipation and used Correctol just about every day. Unfortunately, when she didn't have a good bowel movement she refused to eat and that didn't help her either! I could tell when she did have a good one! There was such a change on her, even her mood would improve!

I saw that change in her one day when I was cleaning the house and Carlos was cleaning his room! She come out of her room and found an excuse to start chasing us around the kitchen, we were all giggling like little kids!

With my kids it was a constant struggle to get them to eat correctly, school and close friends were a big influence in their lives! They constantly craved foods that they knew I knew how to cook or buy foods in school…

One day Carlos actually told on his brother, came to me and said, "Mom have you noticed that Danny's room smells?" We went to check it out together and looked everywhere, under the bed and inside his drawers and found Nutella sandwiches in baggies! I was extremely angry! No wonder the room smelled!

I had spoken to Danny before about stopping the Nutella sandwiches and he told me that he wouldn't eat anything else, I wanted to make him healthier lunches but I was afraid he would throw them away... when I asked him "So my son what are you eating for lunch?" he finally told me the truth "Sorry mom! I save whatever money I get from you, grandma or dad and buy lunch at school." From that day forward I made him a different lunch every day and forbade anyone in the house of giving him money...

That year, my mother and I prepared a feast for Thanksgiving with the traditional Portuguese Stuffing, mashed potatoes, corn souffle (my kids favorite dish) and desserts! We ended up not being able to eat any of it because we all got the flu! Instead… we made a quick soup and watched Mr. Bean on TV! Once better we had plenty of leftovers to enjoy!

Balancing a marriage and motherhood took ingenuity! On one hand I tried to keep Victor as happy as I could, spent time with my mother as much as I could and spent quality time with my kids! In order to spend time with my mother we started watching a Spanish "novela" (soap opera) in the evenings together. Spending time with the kids meant to stop cleaning house, help them with homework and even learning how to play video games! The last one helped me to under-stand where the addiction to those games came from! Once I started playing especially if the games were games that I really liked, it was very hard to walk away and go back to what I was doing!

Many times, I would have to get tough with them if I had com-plaints from their teachers about their grades and would hide their games for a while until the grades improved. They didn't like it one bit but I wanted to make sure my kids had a great education and I had to teach them priorities ...

One of the things I learned as a parent was also to listen to kids if they kept on complaining about something! For example, I liked to dress them alike when they were smaller (especially around the Holidays) and found out as they grew a bit older that they didn't like wearing the same outfits! That made me go buy individual ones and learned to ask their opinion if they liked what they had on that day!

One tradition they never gave up on or complained about was the gift for Santa Claus on Christmas Eve of a couple of cookies and a glass of milk left by the fireplace! I stayed up until they went to bed, ate the cookie, drank some milk and then placed their gifts from Santa by the fireplace, much later they told me that they knew all along that Santa was not for real! But of course, they didn't want the gifts from Santa to stop! My kids were no fools!!

I didn't want this tradition to stop either but eventually we had to give this up!

My mother was a great help with the kids, she would keep an eye on them if Victor and I decided to go out at night dancing, watch a movie or attend a Portuguese function. I found help from a couple that had moved next door…they were both from Mexico, Chela proved to be a great help to my mother, even with Danny and in keeping her company! I really felt sorry for this young woman! She was married to a young man that was wheelchair bound due to a car accident and both proved to be great friends to have around!

Many Friday nights were spent at the Benfica club! We usually had dinner there and played cards (sueca) with different partners...also became close friends with an older couple that had been married for years and with an older gentleman by the name of Cesar that had a pacemaker placed in his heart, we both treasured the time and laughs we spent together with our friends...

Much later I attended the funeral for the older couple that died I believe one year after the other.... sometimes it happens with older couples...

CHAPTER 29

Balancing family life and dealing with a flirt!

*S*pending time with Victor was essential! He was a bit insecure, he would deny it if I brought it up but would get upset if he wanted to go someplace with me and I gave him an excuse (like spending time with our kids or my mother). He loved flea markets! He had made many friends there while buying birds and supplies, many times, we would just go for a quick stop to the flea market in Oakland or go for a longer ride to the San Jose Flea market…

Dancing was one thing that Victor and I loved but what I disliked about dancing with him was to be placed on display! I loved dancing because I got lost in the music and had natural rhythm but for Victor it was more like a show! I felt like he was looking around him and saying "Look at me! Look who I have on my arm!" I told him one day "Please Victor don't flash me around like I'm your trophy, I'm your wife not a possession!" He would just laugh it off and say, "Let them look!"

We were regulars at the WPLJ's in Concord and at the Saddle Rack in San Jose and people loved to see us dancing together! Sometimes they would stop us and ask us if we were professional dancers!

Our favorite club Familia Portuguesa was about 30 minutes from our home and we liked it so much that we became members, many New Year's Eve parties would be spent there with our friends! The only problem I had driving to San Leandro was that Victor loved to drink and was very stubborn about driving under the influence! One Friday I decided to stay home with my kids and received a call from him to go and get him at the police station! He had been driving back from the club under the influence and was stopped on the freeway, I tried to get him out but they kept him overnight. The next day when he came home he refused to speak to me because he thought I left him there on purpose!

Another drinking problem with him was that the flirting with other women got more aggressive! When confronted he would deny it and would tell me that it was all my imagination...

This sometimes would get out of hand and people would notice it and bring it to my attention! One occasion was at a wedding we attended for one of Victor's family members, on our frequent trips to Thornton, we always stopped by Crows Crossing and visited with Victor's cousins, I really liked his cousin Thomas and his sister Cecilia! He was an intellectual that wrote poems and worked in an Aviary in town, we visited with them and many times they joined us at the Thornton Festival.

We were also invited to the wedding of one of their family members and parked our RV outside their home for that weekend...at times like this I would ask our friend and neighbor to keep an eye on my mother and kids since they lived next door. Maria Cecilia absolutely loved me and at this wedding she noticed that Victor was flirting with his cousin! The flirting continued even when we got together at Thomas house the next day! She made a loud comment in front of everyone of how wonderful I was and how lucky Victor was to have me as his wife! I was embarrassed but a bit later she drew me aside and told me that this comment was to shame him for all the flirting he had been doing in front of the family. Of course, I blamed it on his drinking but she would not accept that as an excuse.... When I confronted him with it, he denied it as usual!

I really felt sorry for her brother Thomas! He wasn't feeling well physically and he blamed it on working for the Aviary, he claimed that all of his health problems had started after working there! He read some of his poems to us and I could tell that he was a very intelligent man that was very loved and respected by his family…

Thru Victor's job we also made some friends that we got together with, Jimmy that worked with him and his wife Cindi that was a hairstylist, we became quite close with this couple! Went out to dinner often at a Mexican restaurant nearby and were invited to Jimmy's birthday party as well. The party was held at their home and it was filled with their family and friends, a black African woman approached me and told me "I bet your husband is really good in bed!" I looked straight at her and said, "Actually we are really good in bed together." She kept an eye on him the rest of the night and so did I because I knew how Victor liked to be watched by other women! I certainly didn't want a scene in front of Cindi…

Victor knew how to be the life of the party anywhere we went and even how to be a good sport…. On Halloween one year we were invited to a party at the Portuguese Family and went to look for costumes, I couldn't get him to buy anything serious to match my outfit… he decided to go dressed as a Mumu Cow with bells and everything! When we got to the party, just about everybody was dressed up and he got the reaction he was expecting from his friends! They gathered around him and teased him to death!

One year he dressed up as a woman with big breasts… this on Victor was hilarious because he was 6 foot 2 inches and did not make a pretty woman! His friends all decided to make a move on him that night and we ended up having a great time…. until of course his drinking got out of hand and that was usually when the fun would stop, unfortunately Victor did not know when to stop drinking!

When we got together with family like with my brother Carlos Henrique and Rosa… he was lower key, we loved to get together for barbecues and to play cards. Usually at their barbecues we were introduced to many of their friends including a very young woman (16) that loved Danny and was going thru depression, my own grandfather had committed suicide due to depression and I took her comments very seriously when she started to make comments like "I'm tired of living", I knocked on her parent's door and told them about what I heard her say and all they said was "She is just depressed because we are not allowing her to go out with a boy she meet at school."

I told them about my grandfather and how serious depression was but they saw her reaction as a sign of rebellion….

That same week, their daughter took a gun to the nearby park and shot her herself by placing the gun inside of her mouth! She left a note that nobody really cared about her… the whole community was shaken by this tragedy and her parents were devastated…There are people like my grandfather that do not give anyone a warning…but she had given quite a few people signs that she was depressed, many people if they don't have anyone to share their feelings with they just decide to end it all...

CHAPTER 30

An unexpected tragedy!

*I*t seemed that all around us there was always tragedies and I was hoping that with my family the tragedies would be over with for many years to come…

Since my grandmother had lived to the ripe old age of 91, I thought I was going to be blessed with having my mother with me at least until that age, I shared that with my mother… but she pointed out to me that she had many health problems (health problems my grandma didn't have) and doubted she would be able to live that long! She knew diabetes and heart problems were serious problems and so did I!

I had managed to get a position at a doctor's office and as soon as I come in my father-in-law that was visiting us complained about Danny! He was playing outside with his friends and he told me "You know, you have to watch your son Danny! He plays outside and then comes in, brings one or two of his buddies… opens the refrigerator and invites them to eat or drink! This costs you guys' money!" I told him "Danny is just a very giving child, I will talk to him but I'm sure he is just sharing a drink or a snack to be polite." He shrugged his shoulders and left it at that… this was one man that I didn't like to argue with… I had been thru so much that I could care less if someone was being blessed by my son!

I had been worried about my mother getting sick again because of what she had told me but my brother Carlos Henrique was the one that surprised us all!

He was looking very pale and had lost even the ability to play soccer with my husband! I used to join them on soccer practices and watched my brother stop running and stop to catch his breath! I knew something was wrong! I discussed my worries with Victor and he also felt the same…

When I received the call from my sister-in-law that he had gone to see his doctor and been diagnosed with lung cancer I got very angry! He had not listened to me when I had almost begged him to quit smoking …our internal joke with each other used to be "You give up the smoking and I will lose the weight." We all cope with stress in different ways, mine up until the time I had joined the gym had been food for comfort. His… like my father was cigarettes! Sometimes it's also the product of unhappiness….

His doctor had only given him a couple of months to live because his cancer was very aggressive! He tried everything from shark pills to seeing a healer and even picked up a Bible for the first time! Victor and my brother were good friends and he actually told my husband "I was never able to quit smoking before and isn't funny that after I started reading the Bible now I don't want to smoke any longer?"

His doctor told him to prepare himself and his family for what was to come, there were many trips to the ER when he couldn't breathe! My sister-in-law called me one night and asked me to go with her and my brother to Kaiser. He was placed in a room while we waited for the doctor to examine him, I looked at my brother sitting on the table and a strong feeling came over me that I needed to embrace him with all my heart! I placed my arms around him and had to back out because my brother actually cringed! When I looked at him questionably, he told me that he couldn't handle an embrace because it hurt him too much physically!

If anyone ever says that cancer doesn't hurt, they are lying! My brother was proof of it!

I kept working at the doctor's office and carried all my stress on my back! I would come home with my back full of spasms and Victor would give me massages so that I would be able to go to work the next day...

What hurts the most about seeing someone that you love going thru cancer is how helpless you feel! They were also going thru a bad financial situation because he was no longer working, every chance I got I would take groceries to their home and helped as much as I could without interfering...

I believe it's a mother's worst nightmare to see a son or a daughter die before they do, my brother's illness took a tool on my mother! She ended up at Brookside with pneumonia and almost died! While in the waiting room I prayed and prayed to God to please help her because I could not handle losing my brother and my mother at the same time! She managed to get better and was able to come home! My brother on the other hand was not getting better and considering Chemotherapy, something he had been advised not to do because his cancer was way too advanced…but he was so desperate to live… after all he was only 46 years old!!

The same week Carlos Henrique decided to have the chemotherapy treatment my husband convinced me for us to take my mother and the kids for a short camping trip to Morro Bay, mostly to take my mother and me away from the stress we were all going thru…. I didn't want to leave my brother but Victor refused to give up on the trip! So, I called my brother's doctor and he assured me that most cancer patients don't die from one day to the next, sometimes it takes weeks, even months! I went to see my brother before we were to leave and what I saw broke my heart! I would carry that memory forever engraved in my mind of my brother sitting in a chair with his feet soaking in warm water! I asked Rosa about it and she told me that he was having a hard time feeling his legs! I did not want to leave and told him so and he replied, "Take mom away for a few days, she needs it… I will be ok."

On the way to Morro Bay my heart was aching so bad I could hardly speak to anyone! My mother kept on asking me if I was ok… all I could do was hide what I was feeling and was very angry with my husband for taking us away…even the weather in Morro Bay was gloomy and grey!

That same night while sitting in our motor home I had the weirdest feeling that my brother was standing by me! I received an urgent call from my sister-in-law that my brother had passed away that same night! I looked at my mother sleeping and didn't have the heart to wake her up and tell her the news! We were about 3 to 4 hours away from home and not close enough to a hospital if she needed it, I got up and went to a bathroom near our parking space… alone I cried and cried until I was calm enough to return to our motor home and speak to Victor about it…

Early the next morning we told my mother that we had decided to go home due to bad weather…I didn't want to tell her until we got home in case something happened and she had to be admitted to a hospital.

When we finally got home, I approached my mother and before I had a chance to say anything, she said "It was not the bad weather right?" I hugged her and told her "No Mama, it's Carlos Henrique! He passed away last night! His doctors said that it was the Chemotherapy that killed him, otherwise he would have survived another month or longer." We cried together…both of us feeling awful that we had not been with him when he passed away!

This had proved to be another bad year for us, unfortunately this was something that only him could have prevented from happening…

This was the second son my mother had lost and for me the second brother! Something my sister-in-law friends forgot all about when we arrived at their home! I was attacked verbally by everyone in the leaving room "How could you leave him when you knew he was dying?"

Everybody forgot that I was also watching over my mother and that I had asked his doctor before I left about his condition, I did explain to anyone who was willing to listen but most of them had already made up their minds that I was guilty before proven innocent…

I tried to contact his daughter Carla but we had lost touch, she had moved from Quebec, she had tried to call me one night while I was sleeping and I had written her number down incorrectly, unfortunately was not able to locate her after that...

We prepared for his funeral… I was dreading going to the rosary and to the funeral not only because of seeing my favorite brother in a coffin but also having to face all the stares!

My head was full of memories of him as I walked to the Wilson and Kratzer mortuary in San Pablo! I remembered his contagious laugh, the complements he used to give me when he saw me all dressed up, his affectionate hugs, his love for soccer and barbecues! As I entered the mortuary my heart was beating extremely fast and I had huge lump in my throat! I looked at the coffin and saw him there, walked over and whispered to him "Carlos Henrique you could have been alive if you had listened to me." The tears were starting to come out and a very close friend of my sister-in-law approached me and said in a very sympathetic voice "I feel so sorry for you because you have been thru so much already… and I know how close you were to him." I couldn't even speak! I just nodded in gratitude because he was the only one in that room that spoke to me from his heart!

The worst part was knowing that if something happened to our mother, I would have to face it alone...

I was glad that before he died I had called my brother Jose Carlos to ask him to call Carlos Henrique since he didn't have long to live, instead, he called Rosa! I was never told what they discussed but I did call him again to tell him that our brother had died, I could tell that he was very emotional! I also made sure that he spoke to my mother and informed him that her health was also declining….

I had pictures of my 3 brothers together (just a year apart), my mother used to call them "A escadinha" The the staircase in English! They had done so many things together and they had a strong bond that was very hard to break…Now there was only one left…

CHAPTER 31

Learning to live without a favorite brother and my mother gets ill!

*A*fter his funeral we went thru the motions of living, preparing for the Holidays that year was extremely painful because my heart wasn't in it! I paid extra attention to my mother but nothing helped! She was heartbroken and not feeling well! It didn't help that Victor made a comment to me that she unfortunately overheard about becoming a burden to us! I saw her standing there at the door of her room that she had shared with my father and when I looked at her, she smiled but I knew she had heard him ...it would take a long time before I was able to forgive him for that stupid remark!

My routine now had changed… after I dropped off the kids at school, I prepared a lunch for my mother and I while waiting to pick up the kids at school, I watched soap operas like General Hospital, got hooked on the Oprah show and spent as much time as I could with my mother…

Many times, I would wake her up with a cup of coffee (like my father used to do) and one particular morning when I went to see her, she complained that that one side of her mouth was numb! We both looked at each other because this was not good news (we both knew about strokes) and I immediately made an appointment with her regular doctor for the next day.

Her doctor made very angry! When told of her symptoms he blamed them on her diabetes, I requested a brain scan… he told me that there was no need and that those types of tests were very expensive!

We left …on our way home I looked at my mother and all I could see was disappointment! I turned to her and said, "Don't you dare give up, this is not like my mother, we are going to see another doctor and get a second opinion." She smiled at me and agreed, that same day I found another doctor and made an appointment for her… he ordered a brain scan and we found out that she had a small stroke and was placed on medication. She was extremely upset with her old doctor… he had been our family doctor for years and she didn't expect his reaction! Little did she know that I called his medical office and told his assistant to make sure to tell him that my mother had a small stroke and we would not be returning to his office…

Unfortunately, it seemed that everyday something showed up! My mother grew weaker and she lost her appetite! She was having trouble chewing so I mashed everything and worse of all was her loss of equilibrium! She used a walker to get about and looking at her that way broke my heart! Depression set in and I couldn't see her that way! I called her doctor and told him to take a look at the medicines she was taking to see if they could also be the blame… he did switch her medications… but nothing helped…

She kept on having small strokes and would not allow anyone to bathe her or take care of her and I struggled to take care of the kids and her at the same time! I placed a small bell on her nightstand for her to use when she had to go to the bathroom or needed me for anything (our house was quite long). I hated to leave her by herself and go and pick up the kids from school! I always made sure she went to the bathroom before I left and came back one day to see her laying on the side of the bed trying to get up by herself!

My mother would sacrifice anything for anyone but didn't like sacrificing anyone for her needs. We had tried before she got worse to take her camping and took her to her favorite place (Pismo Beach) and that turned out an ordeal! My husband loved to take walks around the park at night but my mother was afraid to be left alone and was too weak to go walking with us…this created an argument with him but I refused to leave her… I knew she was afraid to die alone…something he could not understand….

I had tried time and time again to convince my mother that with the right treatment and with her fighting spirit she would get better, but she kept on having small strokes and her blood pressure kept on going up sometimes way too high! Many times, I would have to take her to the hospital to stabilize her blood pressure…all these medical problems only reenforced her idea that she would not survive this …

My mother probably didn't realize how much she meant to me! She was not only my mother but my best friend! One of the worse days for me was when she asked me to look thru her closet to help choose her clothes for her burial!

I didn't want to accept this, so I kept on calling her doctor to switch her medications… but nothing helped …it got to the point I was afraid to leave her alone! I had a hard time sleeping at night afraid she would try to get out of bed by herself … fall or finding her dead one day!

She fought me about everything! She lost her appetite, didn't want me to bathe her and didn't want anybody else do it either! She really scared me when she started not wanting to get out of bed in the mornings …this for me brought out the fear of pneumonia!

I was desperate for help but unfortunately, we only had a nurse came by once or twice a week to check on her blood pressure and diabetes, I ended up one day in the hospital with her due to her blood pressure and bad headaches! They admitted her, ran a CT scan and found out that the medicines she was taking were not stopping the strokes! Her doctor came in and asked me how she was doing at home and I had to tell him the truth, he suggested a clinic near where we lived, where they would be able to watch her 24 hours a day and give her physical therapy. I didn't want to leave her in anyone else's hands but he told me it would be a short stay until she got strong enough to come home…

I agreed because I was exhausted but I felt so bad in placing her in a place that I had sworn never again to use for a family member and a place I knew she was not going to like!

She was taken from the Hospital to the clinic that same week in an ambulance and that day proved to be a nerve-racking day! I had to drop the kids at school and was trying to be there to meet her at the hospital because I knew she had a fear of ambulances! Unfortunately, did not make it on time and had to meet her at the clinic! After she got admitted I told her "Mama this is not forever, please help me with this! Promise me that you are going to do everything they ask of you and as soon as you are stronger, I'm taking you home." Her answer to me was "I can't go back home because Victor does not want me there." I fought with myself not to cry and told her "It's not what he wants, it's what I want."

All my life I had been raised to treat older people with respect and kindness and I refused to let my mother be treated badly…. I had decided to fight for her to live and not be pushed into giving up!

CHAPTER 32

Exhausted and in need of help!

I told my mother that I would be at the clinic every day right after I dropped the kids at school, I left as they were getting her comfortable in her room, stopped by the lounge and burst into tears! A nurse met me there and assured me that she would be in good hands but I knew that not everyone did this kind of work because they loved taking care of the elderly mostly because of the money. I made sure I was there every morning right after I dropped off the kids at school, checked her food, made sure her needs were met and encouraged her to get well so that I could take her home…

Many times, after I dropped my kids off to school, I would go directly to the physical rehabilitation center and meet her there… they were working on movement and speech and there was always a smile of welcome from my mother when she saw me! God only knows how much it hurt me inside to see her in this place! She would tell me in Portuguese" Aqui vem o meu sol." There comes my sunshine!

I stayed with her most of the day… had lunch with her, went to pick up the kids, took them home, fixed dinner for my family and went back to check on her before bedtime! One night I happened to check on the glass backdoor and it wouldn't lock! This door led to an alley to other buildings… I realized that this posed a real danger not only to my mother but to her roommate! I stopped by the front desk and asked them to have a repair man fix the door immediately since I knew of cases of women that been raped while in these facilities and they agreed. I also knew that requests like these were sometimes ignored, so that night when I got home, I spoke to Victor and asked him before we went to bed for him to go by the clinic and check on the door or I would not be able to sleep! He agreed even though he was not happy about it! When he came back he told me that they had fixed it and that she was asleep when he left, that did not stop me from checking it the next morning…

I reminded him that night that we too will be old someday and that in this life "We reap what we sow."

At night I stayed until she was placed in bed for the night but one night there was no one around! I tried to move her from her wheelchair to her bed but her body was so stiff that she could not help me to help her! We both had tears of frustration in our eyes and when I asked her to help me a little bit, she just looked at me with her beautiful blue eyes and said "Nao posso." That meant "I can't."

We waited and after ringing the bell for a nurse for quite a while finally one showed up and between both of us, we were able to move her into her bed! In a way I was glad she was there because my mother had made a comment to me that morning that had me worried! She had told me that she was hungry and that when they gave her food, she felt that the food was not going to her stomach! The night nurse told me that they would check on that the next morning…

With places like these unfortunately you have to keep an eye on things …otherwise the nurses in the morning forget to check on what happened the night before…

That night when I got home, I was exhausted… physically and mentally and couldn't handle this alone anymore! I decided to call my aunt Mathilde (my mother's sister) and spoke to her about my mother's condition… I told her how I was feeling and asked her if she had any suggestions… she paused and told me that she was getting on the first plane to California! I knew what a sacrifice this would be for her because she was afraid to fly!

I couldn't wait to tell my mother about her sister coming over but her only comment was that she loved us and didn't want to leave us, when I checked with the nursing staff about my mother not feeling that her food was going in her stomach, they told me that they had to check with her doctor and that she might have to be placed on a feeding tube!

I hated the feeling of helplessness that I felt when I looked at her! I hoped that when she finally saw her sister that her depression would improve but unfortunately that didn't happen! I got a call from the nursing home late that night that my mother was being transferred to Brookside Hospital!

When I got to the clinic my mother's roommate informed me that she had been trying to ring for the nurse quite a few times because she had seen my mother throw up and choke on her own vomit!

Neglect is one of the major reasons we sometimes loose our elderly!

The ambulance came and took my mother to Brookside, they placed her in one of their rooms.... right in front of me I saw my mother have a grand mal seizure and her whole body shook from head to foot! I had never seen a seizure of this magnitude and my whole body went into shock! I ran to the nearest bathroom and got sick! By the time I was able to pull myself together and was allowed back in the room my mother was in a coma...

My mother never got to see her sister! We picked up my aunt at the airport and updated her on my mother's situation, we spent our days traveling to the Hospital back and forth wondering how long she was going to last that way! Her temperature would rise every day and I never saw her beautiful blue eyes look back at me again... Victor also decided to go and see her... probably out of guilt! When he came back out he told me that he had promised her that he would take care of me for the rest of our lives...

One night as I was preparing for bed, I went to say goodnight to my aunt in our living room, she was already fast asleep and when I looked at her… she looked very pale! I got this weird feeling that she was not well and that something was going to happen to her!

I walked off the room not wanting another death in our family! I loved my aunt like she was my second mother but nonetheless I was prepared to ask her to get a physical and probably have her scream at me…

Of course, the next day when I did just that she told me that she was fine but was having a hard time recuperating from her husband's death (both were heavy smokers), she did admit to me that she was having a hard time eating and was experiencing loss of taste and her tongue was full of patches! I made an appointment for her at a clinic in Berkeley, they found out that she had thrush and gave her medicine for it and the doctor advised her to brush her tongue on a daily basis… that helped somewhat but I had the suspicion that there was something else going on with her physically that was causing the thrush...

My mother before she had been transferred to the Hospital had told me about a dream she had of my grandmother… in this dream she kept insisting that my mother tell me to take care of myself! How could I take care of myself when I was worried about everybody else?

One Sunday night as we were getting ready to leave the hospital, I cornered one of the Doctor's on duty and asked him what chance did my mother had of coming out of the coma… He looked straight at me and told us in front of my mother, something I didn't like (I do believe that coma patients can sometimes hear what is being said) that the reason my mother was still with us was because she wanted to and when she wanted to go, she would! He also told me that even if she came out of it, she would be living the rest of her life like a vegetable…something that she did not deserve or want!

My sister-in-law Rosa and I held my mother's hands and told her not to worry about either one of us because we would take care of each other. I felt like I was saying goodbye to my mother and for some reason I felt like a huge weight had been taken off my shoulders! Before I left her room for the night I looked back at and whispered, "I love you, Mama." I think she needed the reassurance that we would be ok without her because when I got home later that night, I received a call from a very uncaring nurse to let me know in her own words "Your mother is dead, she was taken to the morgue and if you want to see her you will have to wait until tomorrow." I was very shaken and once I hung up, my aunt and I hugged and cried together!

All I could think about was that I had lost not only my mother but also my best friend and that now I was truly alone in this world!

My mother passed away before Thanksgiving… that would make it a Holiday to remember and not in a good way!

CHAPTER 33

Life after losing a beloved mother and my favorite aunt…

*M*y kids also had lost the opportunity to get to know their grandmother…

Thank God I had my aunt Mathilde with me to help me make the arrangements for the funeral! I asked the funeral home that when they did my mother's hair to fix it the way that I used to and took a picture with me, when my aunt and I entered the funeral parlor for the first time and saw her laying in the coffin it all felt so unreal to me!

I was informed that when people die they lose the natural curl in their hair, so she looked different but I knew she was no longer in pain! I placed a rosary in my mother's hands and cried until I couldn't cry anymore!

After the funeral it was really tough for me! I blamed Victor for my mother giving up and contemplated leaving with my aunt and my kids! My aunt as wise as she was told me to make an appointment to see someone and to get a second opinion on what I was thinking about… I made an appointment with a Pastor at our church and took my aunt with me, he was very understanding, took my hands in his and said "When we are grieving for someone it's not the time to make important decisions, give yourself some time to heal first."

I couldn't look at my home anymore! I didn't even like my place anymore, it just felt empty without my family! There was nothing but empty space!

The next thing I had to face was seeing my aunt leave! She had stayed with us thru Thanksgiving but she wanted to join her kids for Christmas, we took her to the airport and when we got home I cried and cried! My husband asked me "Why are you crying so much? She will come back someday." I looked at him and told him "I have the feeling that this will be the last time I will see her alive and told him about the premonition I had in our living room." I didn't even know if my husband believed in premonitions but I did...

One day after I dropped off the kids at school, I drove to the Nursing Home my mother had been.... parked the car outside and just let the tears go! There was such an ache in my heart that I couldn't even breathe right! I tried the following week to start cleaning her room and couldn't stay there long! It felt so empty without her! I found a top of hers (that was her favorite) and her favorite ring and wore both in the house to feel close to her...

Christmas that year was awful! My kids missed her as well, especially Carlos! My mother had spent quite a lot of time talking to him about God, our family history and our beliefs...

After the Holidays were over, I started to get pressured by my husband to get back to work, the main reason of course was money because we were not being helped financially by my parents any longer. The second reason he gave me that I didn't buy for a minute was that it would be good for me after so many losses...

Depression hit me very hard! I tried to fill a void that cannot be filled by anything.... I changed the rooms in my house with a new look, rearranged the furniture and nothing helped! The worst room to clean and rearrange was my mother's! Carlos wanted to have that room and I couldn't find the strength to go thru her closet (it was like I could feel her presence there). It helped that he kept on insisting on having his privacy and I was finally able to get it ready for Carlos to move in...

I found a position nearby at an eye Doctor's office has a scheduler and receptionist and dealt with for the first time in my life with anxiety and panic attacks! It didn't help that the people that I worked with were very rude to me and to each other! I spoke to my husband about giving up this job but he made me feel very guilty and kept the pressure on me to work…

At that point I decided that if I had to work, I was going to work in a place I enjoyed! So, I started looking elsewhere and found a position in a nearby Bank and what a difference!

The people there were friendly and willing to train someone new! I had no trouble learning and even managed to make a few friends!

I also managed to lose some weight and Victor insisted on taking me dancing to a Portuguese Dance in El Cerrito, as much as I loved to speak my native language and be among Portuguese people, I also dreaded being around some of them…. they had the tendency of not thinking twice before giving you a smart remark!

The first person that greeted me was a Portuguese man that knew me and my family and the first words out of his mouth was "Well, look at you! You are still alive! I thought that you also had died with the rest of your family!" I looked straight at him and said, "I would have given my life for them! I don't wish this on anybody… do you realize how many family members I have lost?" He became very serious and shook my hand! I asked him "And how is your wife?" He said, "Sadly still very depressed!" His comments had been out of place since his only daughter had died at the age of 16 in a car accident in Portugal! The reason his wife was still depressed was because they had sent their daughter to Portugal to keep her away from a boyfriend that they didn't like… In the end because of their stubbornness, they had lost their only daughter!

I left him there… Victor and I went to sit to have dinner but unfortunately this incident pretty much spoiled the night for me and we went home early!

I made a point of keeping in touch with my aunt Mathilde, I knew she wasn't feeling well… she had been going to different doctors but they couldn't pinpoint what was wrong! There were two things she refused to give up… the antidepressants she had been taking for a long time and smoking! I had spoken to her about both and her response had been always the same "I refuse to get fat or depressed."

One late afternoon I got a call from one of my cousins to let me know that she been admitted to the Hospital waiting to be operated on her intestines! Her doctor had found a tumor that needed to be removed… My first thought was to get on a plane and go see her but fear kept me from getting on a plane! It wasn't so much fear of flying it was the fear of facing another death of someone I loved…

On January of 1997 I got a call from one of my cousins to let me know that the doctors had found pancreatic cancer and when they gave her chemo… just like my brother she had died right after that! I remembered that when I had taken her to a doctor that they had found that she had thrush, later I did some research and I found out that was a sign of candidiasis! This illness when left untreated can lead to other serious illnesses, I often wondered if that had been treated if her cancer could have been prevented?

I got a lot of understanding and love from my cousin when she called me to advise me of her passing but I didn't dare to share with her my suspicions because I knew it would be very hard to prove…

I felt that everyone I loved was being taken away from me one by one, she had always been my biggest supporter and loved life! My biggest regret was that I let fear keep me away from her to be there for her like she had been there for me!

Chapter 34

Dealing with grief
and getting back to work.

My job and my kids helped me thru grief for a while and I was just getting used to my job when the bank I worked for got bought out! I found myself without a job and friends! In a way it was a good thing! I had made a friend that was way too good looking and one that Victor liked to flirt with!

He even brought it out to my oldest son attention what a looker she was in front of me...

Fortunately, I found another position in Berkeley in a company called MCSI as an accounts receivable clerk, I started with this company in 1998 and made great personal friendships!

Going to work became something to look forward to not to dread! Victor and I meet with some of my co-workers for personal parties and even managed to have a small gathering at my house…

I bragged at work about our camping trips and one of our favorite places for camping was the KOA Campground in Petaluma, we got a small group together and met at the campground for the weekend, we also convinced my oldest son to come with his girlfriend and we all gathered by the pool area. Unfortunately, that day I got extremely embarrassed! One of my friends touched me on my shoulder and said "Mary, look at Carlos! He has his girlfriend all over him! In front of all these kids she is French kissing him full on the mouth!" I looked at Carlos, signaled him to look around, he knew what I was referring to and after a while they left the pool area, nobody liked this girl that Carlos was involved with… she was very possessive and I for some reason didn't trust her…

Carlos complained about her occasionally and once we were back at home I had a conversation with him, he said he had tried to break it off before but was unable to! He complained that she was very possessive and insecure, probably the reason she behaved that way at the campground!

One day while he was out and I was by myself I went to his room and searched thru his things… I knew this would not sit well with him but I had a suspicion about this girl…I actually found a letter from her to him saying that she could hardly wait to get pregnant and have a baby! I was very upset because she was only 16 years old! When he got home, I asked him to come and talk to me and showed him the letter, he was upset that I had gone thru his things but I explained to him "Carlos, this is a good thing that I found this letter! She is too young to have a baby and her parents will force you to get married… this is exactly what happened to your dad before I met him. He was forced into a marriage with someone he didn't love and that didn't last… Do you think I want that for my son?" He calmed down and agreed to have a talk with her about giving up this idea, I told him that he either had conversation with her or I would go to her parents and showed them the letter myself…

Their relationship didn't last long and it was a good thing because he found out that she was not a trustworthy person…sometimes we as parents have to take chances in order to open the eyes of our kids…

Christmas that year was much better! The company I worked for had Christmas Parties every year and we had lots of fun!

One of our biggest bosses at MCSi invited a great number of employees to attend a pre-Christmas party at his own house (a big home up on the hills), I bought Victor a new shirt and a new dress for me, when we got there, we were amazed how many cars and people were there! I asked Victor beforehand to please watch his drinking because after all we were going to be around "big shots!" he said he would but right after I introduced him to a few people he started to drink! Unfortunately, Victor liked being the life of the party!

We were approached by our boss and his wife and she made a comment to Victor "Wow! What a nice shirt! Where did you get it?" instead of saying "Thank you, my wife bought it for me." He said "Why? Do you want to buy it from me?" She looked embarrassed, smiled and walked away! Of course, I was extremely upset and told Victor "See what I mean about drinking too much? She is the wife of one our biggest bosses!"

He made a comment about not liking stuck up people, I had to remind him that I had just started this job and like everyone else I wanted to make a good impression. We left soon after that… The next Monday when I told the girls at work, they assured me that since everyone had been drinking, they would not hold it against me…

It helped being around people after my mother's death! I also found another way to help with the grief that I was carrying… I did it by working out and finding good emotional support, Kaiser had grieving groups and I joined one… It helped immensely to be with others that were going thru the same grief and be able to talk about it…

Thru the years I had lost track of personal friends and one of them was a good friend of mine that lived across from my parent's place… Sylvia was one of them that had moved and that we had lost touch! One day I passed by the duplex where my parents had lived and knocked on her door and nobody answered. A neighbor saw me, came out and confirmed that she had moved away, I didn't know why suddenly I was thinking about her, but it wasn't too long after that I had a dream about her! She was walking on the street towards me with a smile on her face and told me that she was going to visit my mother in heaven and then I woke up!

The day after my sister-in-law Rosa called me to tell me "You never guess who passed away yesterday? Your friend Sylvia." I was sad that I had lost touch with her but very touched that she had remembered me before she left this world! I told Rosa about my dream and she said "Boy! You are giving me the chills!"

CHAPTER 35

A big life change and a very scary experience!

The year I turned 41 on February of 1999 everything changed!! It all started with depression, food allergies, night sweats and hair loss!

I didn't know where all of these symptoms were coming from because I was happy with my job, had many friends and even the grief that I had been carrying had gotten better!

I scheduled an appointment with the OBGYN Dept at Kaiser with a medical doctor to get to the bottom of my symptoms, they ran tests and couldn't find anything…... so they told me to go see a psychiatrist!

I scheduled an appointment with a NP that specialized in depression and anxiety disorders…she told me that probably I was starting pre-menopause and was already handling it the right way by exercising and avoiding certain foods… unfortunately my mother had not prepared me for this stage in life and thank God I had found an understanding person!

Victor and I still took our camping trips even to spiritual places like Thornton, CA and I actually needed to go there to pray for me and my family…

This festival always scheduled in the middle of October was done in the honor of Lady of Fatima…. a lot of people got together to pray for miracles, attend masses, dancing, free food and bullfights….

This was a place where you could see a large Portuguese Community… they loved to attend this Festival and catch up with their friends on what was going on in their lives. Some people would do barbecues in front of their trailers, drink and chat with old friends, Saturday night was a special night for a lot of people even from out of town, that was the night when the procession took place… They arrived mostly in cars and buses...

A mass of people would get together holding candles…they would follow the local priest that was in front of the procession in a car that carried the statue of Lady of Fatima, the rosary was prayed by all that followed, we would also pray for our needs and of our families...

Victor and I went to the bullfight that Saturday and as much as I loved to see these great acts of bravery… I ended up leaving early! This was a spectacular event where you got to see the "forcados and cava-leiros" "men on foot and on horseback" they challenged the bull and put on a show for the audience!

I started to feel unwell and by the time I got to my motor home I had a sore throat, chills and fever and my joints were hurting! I took Tylenol and after a while fell asleep….

That Saturday night along with a huge crowd of people I held my candle up and prayed that I would end up finding a cure for whatever was going on with me and prayed for my family…

After the procession we usually ended up watching Fados and Cantoria (Portuguese traditional singing) before going to bed, the younger people on the other hand would attend local dances and mingle...

The next day Sunday (the day we usually left) a lot of people would attend Mass and go watch the parade, the Queens chosen for that event would be upfront and marching bands along with various Portuguese organizations from California in the back. After the parade the "Bodo de Leite" (people handing out small Portuguese sweet breads with a small carton of milk) took place and some people would stay for the following Monday to see yet more bullfights...

Every time I left this festival…. I marveled of the amount of people we would see there from all nationalities! I always left sad when the festival was over with but ready to go back the next year!

Once back home I started to read books about pre-menopause and started to identify my symptoms including the change in my periods, I decided to be persistent, went from doctor to doctor and was even insulted! My family was a bit scared of all the changes they saw in me… and I was scared of my depression… I even contemplated suicide one day while driving!!

Who came to my rescue was my youngest son, Danny! He kept calling me at work to ask me if I was ok and to tell me that he loved me…

What didn't help was the visit that I got from my sister-in-law Rosa to tell me about a weird dream she had about my mother sitting in a wheelchair crying! I took it as a sign that I was really sick and that she was worried about me.! After I was told about this dream I wasn't able to sleep correctly… even my relationships changed because they noticed that Mary wasn't the outgoing person she used to be! Most of the times I could be found sitting alone somewhere and that was not definitely me…

As if what I was going thru wasn't enough my oldest son (17) was being traumatized in High School and wanted to quit before graduating! We had many arguments about this… we finally gave in and let him finish high school at night so that he could graduate, I was very upset because I wanted him to have a graduation ceremony… but we had to work with him… the important thing was that he would be able to graduate!

I suspected Carlos was also going thru hormonal changes like I was and that made me a little more understanding than others… it also showed that all my reading helped me and him…

I don't know how I managed to work some days! Even a kind word from someone was enough to make me cry and many times I would get in my car after work and let the tears go…

My sister-in-law once again came to see me to tell me about yet another dream, this one affected me even worse! She told me about a dream she had with my mother and grandmother and that they had moved in a house near me… I took this as a sign that they were waiting for me to die! From that day on I gave up on making plans for the future! These dreams made things worse between my sister-in-law and me… they made me resent her because she had not listened when I had asked her not to tell me about any other dreams…they were affecting me in a very negative way! So, I stayed away from her instead….

As if this wasn't enough… I also had a dream about my mother! I was in a room with her… hitting her with a blue nightgown she used to have and screaming at her that I did not want to die! I kept on telling her that I wanted to see my children grow up, have grandchildren some day and then the dream changed! I found myself in a room with a man that was kneeling next to me and has he came closer he brought his mouth close to mine and I felt him take my breath away! I kept repeating to him what I had been telling my mother!

Just before I woke up, I got a glimpse of his face and it was a frightening face! I found myself sweating and weak as a kitten with my heart beating 100 miles an hour! I turned to Victor and found him looking at me! The first words out of his mouth were "What was that awful smell?" The funny thing was that I didn't smell anything! I was just scared! I tried to disregard this nightmare as just a bad dream but a week after I remembered a conversation I had with a friend of mine about dreams, she told me that a week prior to her niece's death that she had smelled a very particular smell in her car and that at the time she had thought that death was near…. her niece passed away soon after!

When I shared this conversation with my husband, he told me that's exactly how he would have described the smell the night of my nightmare!

Imagine how I felt!

I walked around thinking that my days were counted and afraid to go to sleep in fear that I would not wake up! Wondering how long I had with my family...

My family didn't know how to help me… Danny who was about 9 years old and very close to me did not leave my side…he called me every day at work to check on me…

My depression was very evident to all of those that were close to me, I had tests after tests, hoping to beat death and nothing was conclusive! I had one Doctor that refused to see me again because she didn't know how to help me!

Just like my mother would have done I reached out to God! I sat on my bed, crying and praying at the same time pleading with Him to give me another chance in life! I asked Him to help me find a way for me to live long enough to see my children grow up and to have a grandchild… In turn I promised Him to pray the rosary every day and to help people along the way that needed my help…. I didn't wait to see the miracle happen I started to pray the rosary that same night…

I didn't know what was so special about me to have been given signs but since I was a baby… I had been told by my mother that I was a special child…

From the day I reached out to God desperately wanting to live things started to change in a big way!

I had found a sympathetic Doctor at Kaiser that saw how traumatized I was and referred me to a nurse practitioner that specialized in mind and body healing! She suggested that I researched my symptoms by reading books and to find the reason for my symptoms, I went to a public library and found that some of my symptoms could be related to endometriosis, this information was the beginning of a lot more research that I would have to do down the line…

I was obsessed in finding an answer and refused to give up…

Meanwhile Danny's communion was coming up in May and I had no time to do any further research… while preparing for this event I was feeling physically awful! My husband trying to cheer me up the night before the communion asked me to go to our friend's house and play cards to help both of us relax and sleep better…

Chapter 36

A sign from God?

When we arrived our friends were already sitting at the table, I waited until they were all playing… went to the front door… looked up at the sky and spoke to God "God I need your help! Please remember my prayer! Forgive me if I have done anything wrong! I will keep my promise to you to help people for the rest of my life." I left… trying not to cry and went to join my friends at the table…

My sister-in-law Rosa was by the table and asked me if I wanted something to drink and I asked her for a 7-up, she gave me the glass… I sat there not wanting to play and not wanting to speak to anyone in case they wanted to ask me how I was! Suddenly I felt a teardrop on my forehead! I looked up to check if there was a whole in the ceiling and there was not! It was a sunny day outside…how could this be explained!

Was this a sign from Heaven?

I placed my life in God's hands from that day forward! Gave up control and let Him guide me from that moment on…so this meant prayer before making decisions! I also decided that I was not going to share this experience with anyone in fear of being made fun of…

Even though I wasn't feeling well Danny's communion went really well the next day, our church was filled with families and we ended up at our house where I had all kinds of food prepared, we truly enjoyed ourselves after all the work we had done and I prepared myself for my doctor's appointment the next day…

The next morning, I went to my OBGYN doctor and told her about the research I had done… she placed me on a low birth control pill to help with the endometriosis, in case my symptoms were from that… When I went back after 3 weeks, she could tell the difference! Both the depression and the physical symptoms had gotten better!

At Kaiser they had given me tests for ovarian cancer among other tests and they were all fine, the NP that had been referred to me also referred me to a depression group, I loved this group and met wonderful people from all walks of life… engineers, nurses, teachers and even found another woman that also suffered from endometriosis!

I continued to attend the depression group and continued with the birth control pills for a while…

I truly believe that people sometimes are placed in your life for a reason and others are there to try to deter you from your destiny, some are also used to help you! One of my closest friends after my mother passed away, Sra Fatima called me one day very shaken about a dream she had about my mother! She told me that in this dream my mother had spoken to her and asked her to get close to me because I needed a friend! Something she took very seriously! She called me very often to come over and see her or go out shopping with her, she became my confidante and friend! God knows how I needed someone to confide in and trust!

Along the way I also met people like doctors and nurses that in the beginning were all smiles when they first meet you but if they can't help you and if you keep on being persistent then the story changes… I heard it all…

"You are just wasting doctors time and insurance money."

"You just have to accept the fact that you are getting older."

"You know it wouldn't hurt you to lose a few pounds."

"What you need honey is to try Prozac and see a psychiatrist."

These comments were mostly from women! It made me wonder if they ever experienced health problems, instead of being sympathetic they forgot to be human...

Another doctor I found was a specialist in Berkeley... I was having trouble digesting foods! I had really bad acid reflux and suspected I had a hiatal hernia. Victor and I went to the consultation and the doctor actually said to me "What makes you think, you have one?" I told him "I have done research and I know how I feel!" He didn't look like he wanted to even hear me out but I insisted on a test, he finally agreed to schedule an Endoscopy, Victor sided with the doctor that this probably was not necessary... but I was determined to have the test anyway...

On the day of the test, I was nervous of course but they gave me something to relax, the doctor inserted a long tube down my throat all the way down to the esophagus and took samples... after the test was done, I waited in a room for the doctor and made sure Victor was with me, the doctor came in and told me that in fact I did have a small hiatal hernia... that I would have to be placed on antibiotics and gave me a prescription. Before I left, I told him in front of my husband "Sometimes a patient knows her body best, we are not all paranoid!" I believe Victor was probably impressed that I was not afraid to express my feelings to a doctor...

The next day I got the prescription for the antibiotics and was amazed of the amount he wanted me to take! After a couple of days, I couldn't function with all the medicine I was taking so I called the doctor's office, told him how I felt and he agreed with me that I would have to be placed on smaller dosages... I did try the smaller dosages but not even that agreed with me!

On my own I started to do research and found out that eating smaller meals actually helped, losing weight, distressing and placing my head on a higher pillow. Taking these measures took longer but after a while I did start to see remarkable results! This was one doctor that never saw me again!

My belief in medications even off the counter were minimal to say the least! I would see adds on TV about medications and pay attention to the side effects, just knowing the side effects made me stay away from medicines prescribed by doctors… in a lot of cases you ended up with something else you didn't ask for! My own mother had been placed on a medicine for arthritis and ended up with an ulcer in her stomach!

I did find exceptions with certain doctors that I met that did restore some of my faith in mankind! I felt very alone with all of this… what helped me was that I got into the habit of talking to God…

Because I loved my family my prayers were not for me only, I included them as well... People sometimes can be selfish while praying…

Our conversations were one sided but somehow… I knew He had heard me because something strange happened! I started to see crows that squawked at me when I went somewhere and that had never happened before! They didn't scare me they just annoyed me…

This made me pursue God with a vengeance! If somebody else had heard my prayer… then He had as well! Even in my car I would speak to Him "If you really exist and you heard me, please give me a sign that you have because I need you desperately!"

Something else bothered me… I now had resentment towards two people because of the dreams… my sister-in-law and my mother, even though she was no longer alive! Because of the strong bond between my mother and myself I had asked her before she died not to contact me after she was gone. Plain and simple I had been very afraid of the supernatural...my sister-in-law on the other hand had explained to me that she had told me about the dreams because she had been worried about me! She also told me that she had actually prayed for me in Fatima…

When I confided in my husband about how I felt, he told me that my mother loved me way too much to hurt me! None-the-less I felt betrayed and angry because of all these dreams that almost had made me give up! My only hope now was that God had come to my rescue…

I couldn't make myself believe that my mother's motives could have been to let me know that I was very sick and that she was there for me (maybe because I had always been there for her as well).

I was a mess emotionally and any negative comment or conversation about death or illnesses I immediately took it personally...it didn't help to have my own husband try to look at my ears to see if they were pale, an old fashioned believe about people who are close to dying!!

I kept seeing different doctors in the hope that maybe I was missing something! One thing in common with all these doctors was that they all agreed that I should avoid surgery since surgery for people with severe endometriosis meant removing the uterus, the ovaries and if the intestines were affected that meant another separate surgery...

If like me, you happened to have a baby by caesarian… you could have endo around the scars…. doctors preferred that instead of taking risks with surgery…you should keep on trying to keep it under control by taking medicines instead until you reach menopause…

CHAPTER 37

A bit of hope from two cousins!

What helped me immensely was a visit from my oldest cousin from Bethel wanting me to meet her in San Francisco! I was thrilled to see her and arranged to meet her at the hotel she was staying for dinner.

As I sat there in front of her, she reminded me so much of my aunt Mathilde and of my own mother! The same friendly attitude, the same charm and the same ability to make me feel that everything would be fine!

She looked at me and asked me "So, Sao, how are you really doing?" I asked my cousin to meet me in the bathroom, with tears rolling down my face I shared with her everything that had happened to me and waited for her to call me crazy! But instead, she embraced me and said "My God, sweetie, you have been carrying all this pain inside of you with no one to share it with? Why didn't you tell me about this sooner?" I told her that I was afraid of being thought as a lunatic or paranoid woman and that she was the first person that I ever had shared this with…

My cousin insisted that I contact a friend of hers in Florida, she truly believed that this woman would be the first step towards healing me emotionally and give me back the hope that I had lost…

I agreed because I knew my cousin was a very smart business-woman and I needed to get hope from somewhere!

She believed in this woman because she had contacted her to check if she was doing everything well regarding her business and everything this woman had told her was right on the money…

She also had given her suggestions about people to contact to get more help with her cause and told her what to expect for the future ..I was skeptical about psychics because I had been raised to believe in God first and foremost…but I also been accosted by a gypsy in Portugal that had read my hand when I was just 15…that day she told me that I was going to travel to the US and get married really young and that had happened..

Before I left, we hugged and promised each other to keep in touch, I finally got to call this woman well prepared to hear the worst and instead she told me a lot of stuff about my family that was extremely right! While on the phone she taped a cassette for me to listen to that included what to expect for the future…This would show me if she was right…

I listened to that tape every time that I was down and waited for the stuff that she had predicted to come to pass and a lot of it did…

There were a lot of setbacks with my health! The birth control pills I had been taking raised my blood pressure and my doctor switched me to another medicine without estrogen that would allow me to feel better…

Victor would irritate me by telling me that my physical problems were not that bad and to let it go…. one day I sat with him and said "Victor do you realize that if I don't get these health problems under control, I will have a hard time even keeping a job? How you feel physically affects your job performance, even constipation can affect your ability to think clearly, your mood and even your concentration!" He shrugged it off but I also told him "I know you understand where I'm coming from… the next time your hemorrhoids act up and you can't go to the bathroom let me know how you feel that day!" He was silent after that and I think I had made my point…

Carlos was also giving us a lot of problems and making mistakes left and right! He hurt my feelings badly… no longer the child that confided in his mother or asked for advice…

It helped that I continued to attend support meetings, people shared their experiences with each other including what they were going thru with their children… so I didn't feel all alone raising two boys that I loved with all my heart!

I knew I had to make many changes in my life in order to heal! I had learned that healing was both physical and spiritual from Anne Marie (the psychic that I contacted), she told me that I had always been there for everyone, said yes way too often even when I couldn't handle it and forgot myself in the process...

All those years of taking care of my family and neglecting myself had brought about illness and depression! You can't afford to let go of your needs while you are taking care of others...

I couldn't go back and undo the damage that had happened... but I had learned a valuable lesson!

I looked at myself in the mirror and couldn't believe that this over-weight woman with sad eyes was me!

I managed to go places with my family even though I wanted to hide from everyone! I didn't look like myself and of all things to happen… my family and I were invited to a company picnic at Six Flags in Vallejo. My friends had promised to meet with us along with other colleagues at the park, they had reserved a table for lunch and the husband of a friend of mine took a picture of me that day, I asked my friend to send me that picture because I needed motivation to change my life…. when I finally received the copy of the picture… I couldn't believe my eyes!

The woman on the picture didn't even look like me!

I was so bloated and pale and a shadow of the woman I had been!

One of the things that also hurt quite a lot was that I heard from someone that I was considered lazy in the way I was keeping my home!

Little did they know what I was going thru physically! It's like the old saying "Don't judge people until you have been in their shoes!" There were days that I just wanted to give up but somehow… I knew that God was working behind the scenes…

It was in one of those days that I received a letter from my cousin Saozinha in Portugal reminding me that the women of our family did not give up! She herself had her been thru so much! Losing her first husband in a car accident, the illness that had affected her youngest son of her second marriage…etc…

Her letter had a message I couldn't ignore, don't you dare give up! She had managed with her letter to give me the push that I needed it…

Physically there were many setbacks! In order to stop the heavy bleeding that I was experiencing monthly I had been placed on Depo Provera shots that unfortunately had helped me to gain the weight that I was now carrying! I also noticed something that frightened me quite a bit and that was that my uterus had dropped down and I could feel it with my fingers! Unfortunately, I had become quite addicted to this medicine because it stopped the bleeding but on the other hand it was giving me serious side effects!

After waking up one night seeing the whole room spinning around me, I had decided to give it up completely but before I could the doctor had me scheduled for a pelvic ultrasound, that turned out to be a horrendous experience! The tech asked me to laydown flat with my head lowered and when I did the room started to spin again! It was all I could do to stay still for this test and actually needed help to get up! All the test showed was that my uterus was quite low as I suspected but now it was up to me do something about it…

CHAPTER 38

Taking a natural approach to healing physically and emotionally!

I found a natural doctor that took me off the Depo and placed me on a different medicine, she wanted to place me on pills for diabetes because my blood sugar was high but I knew that once on medicine for diabetes I would have to stick to it… in most cases if pills stop being effective then insulin! Like my mother…No way was I going to follow that path!

Don't know how but I convinced the Doctor to give me 3 months off the medicine and work on getting the weight off (I was told that because of the Depo Provera it could take me a year), at this point I was at least 50 pounds overweight and experiencing night sweats like someone on full menopause, headaches, dizziness and also losing hair everywhere!

I managed to surprise her… by the time I went back after 3 months, I had lost 15 pounds, the night sweats had stopped and so had the dizziness! I was glad that someone had taken a picture of me at that time so that I could prove to myself that things can be undone if you really have the will to do it…

For some reason I had a strong urge to write about my life! For me it was like writing a journal of what had taken place… Many times, I would be writing and crying at the same time! I didn't know that I was being observed by someone while doing this! Carlos had seen me writing and surprised me one day by coming home with a book in how to publish a book! He made me smile that day!

We had an argument that same week because I found out that he had started smoking and I told him "Carlos, can you blame me for not wanting you to smoke? Don't you think that I have suffered enough by losing my father and brother to lung cancer?" He left me crying that day… but he also needed to be reminded that he had lost a grandfather that he loved because of smoking.

It was while writing in my living room with the TV on that I saw a program on TV about a doctor called Dr.Liebgold, also known by the name of Dr.Fear! He was being interviewed and bragging that there was no fear he could not conquer! I was very intrigued and said to myself "Really? Let's see what you can do with mine!"

I wrote his name down and started searching for him… found out that he was conducting anxiety and phobias classes in Vallejo at a Kaiser Facility.

I enrolled in the next class… found a gym nearby so that I could work on my body both physically and mentally…

My first steps on the treadmill were baby steps and when I tried to use weights my arms trembled! I fought constantly with my mind that was trying to convince me that I was not strong enough to go to a gym! That did not work... I was determined to change my life… my image and ignore fear...

As my workouts got better and stronger… I was able to eat better and started to see the pounds coming off… even my mental state got better!

My first class with Dr. Liebgold was surprising to say the least! I certainly did not expect to see over 60 people in one room that just like me were suffering from panic disorders! I was amazed when I registered that the person that was helping me was none other than his wife Carol! She also worked in the same branch at Mechanics Bank that I did on the top level and we actually knew each other!

I immediately took a liking to this small doctor with a wonderful sense of humor! I loved his statement to all of us that he had learned thru a Chinese saying that when "The student is ready the teacher will appear"!

Who better to teach you about fear than a doctor that had conquered fear himself?

He was using what he had learned to help other people and he had suffered a tragic loss himself! His son had committed suicide because of an anxiety disorder… this had prompt him to make the decision to help others…

I had the feeling that this class was God's doing and maybe a way for me one day to help others!

We were asked to introduce ourselves and reveal in front of everyone what had brought us there… this by all means was not easy to do but it helped to be in front of people that were going thru similar situations…

I was the last to speak but after I had heard all their statements… I realized that I was not alone and not like some of them I had already started working on improving my life!

We were asked to do homework… including a victory card for every fear we faced and to share it with others! The first time I read my victory card I was amazed what I had accomplished despite the fear!

On Mother's Day I asked my husband and Danny to go to the Marina nearby and let me walk alone for a while (I had become afraid of being alone because of having to deal with fearful thoughts), the path at the Marina was a long one but I managed to walk it and met with them at the other end of the park, Victor totally surprised me by his comment when I was done! He said to me "Such is your will to live! I would have given up a long time ago!" I looked at him and said very seriously "Victor, how could you expect me to give up? I have two sons that still need their mother!" He got silent after that and I went home and wrote on my victory card for that day what my victory had been…

My fears were so bad that I was afraid of sleeping without a light on in my room! I bought myself a night light… it would take me a long time to sleep without that nightlight!

I learned so much from this wonderful doctor even small things that helped a lot…. including learning to recognize that due to my complexes I had worried what people thought about me and had a hard time with confrontations!

Confrontations sometimes are also best avoided when dealing with family!

For one class we were asked to dress down, different shoes, no makeup, etc... For me this was a big one because no matter what I always left the house with makeup and everything matching! That day I surprised myself by wearing sweats, hardly any makeup and different shoes! I was very surprised that Danny and Victor didn't even notice it until I brought it up!

In one of the Phobease classes I learned the most valuable lesson of all! If you let yourself believe what your brain tells you either positive or negative it can make a huge difference whether you live or die!

Our teacher taught us to visualize what we wanted to overcome and when the negative thought came to visualize a red stop sign (I practiced this daily). Somedays I felt like I had a demon inside of me that wanted me dead and used my thoughts to prevent me from going forward...

CHAPTER 39

One step forward, two steps back!

*I*t seemed that for every step forward I took two back!

I'm a true believer that everything in life happens for a reason and what happened to me was either going to kill me or make me stronger!

The physical symptoms had gotten better because the Depo had been taken away... but I knew the mental would take longer...

I felt so bad for what my family had gone thru... not only because of all the deaths in our family but also because of what happened to me! At one point I had thought about leaving them and start over by myself somewhere... but I loved them too much to leave them... when I mentioned this to Victor, he became upset! So, my only solution was to find a way to heal! He surprised me one day when he was getting ready to go to work, I happened to be awake, he looked at me and said, "How would I ever manage to live without you!" That showed me that he needed me in his life and made me even more determined to heal...

I completed the first set of classes with Dr.Liebgold and on the day of the graduation on the way home in the car with Danny and my husband I burst into tears! I knew that I was not over this yet and still had a way to go! They both reminded me how far I had come... but I was so overwhelmed by emotion that I couldn't even speak...

Each class that I had attended I had hoped to meet someone that had gone thru a similar situation like mine... but I was always disappointed! Instead, I had been given tools to use to combat the fears I lived with...

The tools however worked and I had seen quite a bit of improvement!

My routine was the same every day, I prayed, I worked out, read self-help books to help me grow and hid the truth how I felt inside even at work...

I had lost at total of 45 pounds! My friends at work had seen me do it and they were very proud of me! I also made a special friend at work that was like a sister to me and the only one I confided in...I was told many times what an inspiration I was to everyone but inside I felt like I had ways to go...

One thing I knew for sure was that I was not going back to the way I was 2 years ago! I was thankful for each day that I was alive and for making a difference in people's lives...

I also learned that Dr.Liebgold had other people trained by him conducting fear classes for young children from the ages of 6 thru 14, I knew that I had to enroll Danny... he had developed fear and anxiety... most of it because he was afraid of losing me, whenever we went somewhere Danny was always near me and suffered from anxiety when I was far from him! I had tried to help him with what I had learned on those classes... but it didn't help! I believed that just like me Danny needed to be around children his own age that were going thru the same thing... After what I had been thru I didn't want him to suffer with fears for the rest of his life...

Those children were taught to identify their fear, Dr.Liebgold had found a name for people and children to identify the fear as the "Boo" (the negative voice in your head) and how to defeat it..

Danny did really good in those classes... I had tried to convince Victor to attend some classes with me but of course he refused (Portuguese pride), I knew he needed them as much as me... but he denied he had a problem and called it stress...

I worked on my fears together with Danny and many times we were both surprised how much happier we were now compared to before...

We took a vacation to Pismo as a family… I decided to take my car, managed to find a temporary pass and worked out at a local gym! I had taken with me my friend Sra Fatima that had become like a mother to me after my mother's death, I had clung to her and she became my anchor...

While Victor stayed behind and took off in my car and went exploring nearby towns, Santa Barbara (Danny absolutely loved this town), Saint Luis Obispo and Solvang...

We also took off shopping to Santa Maria and found a shopping mall nearby!

I had forgotten due to my fears how good it felt to be independent and managed to surprise myself by joining a group of people in a restaurant and sang Karaoke! I sang my heart out to a song by Cheer and felt her words all the way to my heart … "I will survive" became my favorite song!

I knew that I still had a lot of work to do and continued the phobias classes on my own… by the time Christmas came up I had lost a total of 55 pounds and the gym I attended asked me to place my picture on their wall to help inspire people to lose weight. No matter what I wanted to keep my promise to God and help others when given the opportunity…

After the Holidays I knew I had to make some important decisions regarding my health, I could tell the medicine I was taking was not effective any longer and my uterus was way too low...

On the way home from work feeling a bit depressed and knowing I had to make major decisions very soon I looked at the bumper sticker of car in front of me and it read "Expect miracles."

The following week another appeared in front of me that read... "Dreams do come true."

Could all of this be a coincidence or was God sending me messages?

Victor went with me to my next doctor's appointment… when they took my blood pressure it was up and my doctor informed me that she had to take me off of the medication, I kept insisting that I could feel my uterus with my fingers and was even afraid to workout afraid that it would drop! She finally agreed to give me a laparoscopy to check both on my uterus and on my ovaries. One of the problems regarding this appointment was having to be put to sleep and facing the fear of not being able to wake up! I kept silent but Victor immediately jumped up and said, "Of course she will do it, she can't keep on living like this!" When I saw his reaction, I knew I had to confront this fear and needed to find out what was wrong with my uterus...

The weekend before my procedure for the following Monday I spoke to my husband about the fear that I was facing regarding this appointment, he was working on his Avery that he had built in the back of our house... this hobby of his had turned out to be a side job (he made quite a bit of money on it), he stopped to talk to me and reassured me that I had accomplished quite a lot to go backwards! He also had been affected by what I had gone thru and didn't want to go thru it again... at that point I knew when he told me this that no matter what the doctor said I had to do I would have to do it for my sake and for the sake of my family...

I had to rely on what I had learned at Dr.Liebgold class and on my faith in God...

CHAPTER 40

Starting to face major fears and life changes!

$\mathcal{M}$y doctor had given me 2 weeks to prepare for a Hysteroscopy and I fought with myself not to allow any negative thoughts to invade my mind… including the fear I had about cancer after what I had seen my family go thru!

She also had given me a low dose of valium to take and I took it the morning of the procedure and Victor and I took off to Kaiser.

Before we left, I had to reassure Danny before he left for school that this was a one-day procedure and that I would be home that same afternoon...

When I went inside the surgery room prepared to be put to sleep, I realized how far I had come! If this had happened 2 years prior… I would have not done it! What a leap of faith this was for me!

They put me to sleep and to my surprise I was awake and alive to talk about it in a very short time!!

My doctor came in and informed me that there was no evidence of cancer! I had a couple of small fibroids and of course she was able to admit what I had known all along that my uterus was too low! She also informed me that I might need surgery soon to remove it…at this point I was just happy that I had wakened up from the procedure and that no cancer had been found!

When I got home… I had flowers waiting for me and calls from my friends to find out how I was and happy that everything had gone fine!

On the other hand, my husband had to face a major change in his life after 33 years of working for Myers… he was forced into an early retirement! His company closed down and on the last week on his job he tore a muscle in his arm and was scheduled for surgery!

I went back to my Phoboease class and bragged to all with a shaky voice of my biggest victory yet! They all clapped and cheered! I told them that if I had listened to the negative voice inside of me… I would still be living with the fear of having cancer instead of taking the risk to find out! I felt incredibly brave at that moment!!

Many times, I questioned myself what in the world had happened to me! How had I gone from the outgoing and brave girl that had come to the US by herself to the woman I was now!!

Dr. Liebgold because of the difference he had seen in me had asked me if I wanted to become a co-facilitator in his class and I accepted! This was my opportunity to give back to others what I learned…

I started helping another co-facilitator at the class by putting together a group of people that had fears of traveling and flying… we arranged a trip to the Napa Airport and meet with the pilot that happened to be a woman that also had conquered fears of her own and worked with Dr.Liebgold.

She had arranged a small seminar about flying and safety that we all had to attend prior to flying, also for a small flight of 4 people at a time to go around the airport, we had 16 people together and even managed to have lunch with Sue…our pilot, I had not flown in over 10 years! It had been a bad experience for me but I also needed to face this fear in case I had the chance to go see my oldest brother Jose Carlos in Portugal. I kept on thinking about him and had the feeling that he was not well, I had tried to call him but I was never able to reach him…

I arranged for 16 people to fly with another pilot on short trips around the strip and for me and 2 other people to fly with Sue after the seminar. I remembered what Dr.Liebgold had said "People that never had fears probably would never know the real joy of living because they have not experienced fear at a high level, for fearful people the joy of living again is duplicated once the fear is conquered…it's like starting over!" Victor and Danny were with me that day and waiting outside for me…The pilot had informed us that we would not actually fly but could just take the plane for a ride around the strip and then take off and go for a flight…if we choose to… I was delighted but as we got close to the end of the strip the pilot looked at us and said, "You could always change your mind and go up anyway" I looked at the women next to me and they both said, "Let's do it!" I could have killed them both! I knew this would be for our benefit and I wanted my family to be proud of me as well…but I was so scared! So, we went up and all I could hear was the beating of my heart! Before the anxiety was able to take over, the woman next to me grabbed my hands and I relaxed long enough to start admiring the view! I could not believe that I was up in a four-seater airplane with 3 other people flying around the clouds! As we came down, I could see the remaining group waiting for us, we climbed out and heard cheers and applause from everyone! We took pictures to remember this day by!

Victor and Danny could not believe that I had done this… and neither could I! We had to wait for another trip for another 3 people, included on that group was a woman that had to take a flight to Italy with her husband, she had shared with me she had never been able to fly without being heavily sedated!

Before she climbed on board, she looked right at me and said, "I'm going to defeat fear today" We were all cheering for her and for the others on the small plane! To our surprise we saw the plane land and then take off one more time! When they landed…they told me that they had requested a second time because of the lady that would be flying to Italy very soon…

I went back home proud of myself and of all the others including my new friend that now would not be afraid to fly to see her family in

Italy! Fear in a way was like being terrorized…it made us afraid of living and of taking risks!

Before I had my procedure at Kaiser my mother had came to me in a dream! I was facing her… yelling and saying over and over that I was not going to give up and that I was going to live! As I kept saying these words, I could see the illness living my body! The next thing I saw was my mother and I sitting on a couch together, I asked her if what I had was Cancer, she looked straight at me and shook her head "No." Her eyes were sad however! She had gone to the top of a hill and pointed to a bus filled with people that I knew without a doubt were destined for Heaven…. I woke up in a cold sweat and with the full understanding of what the dream was about …she was trying to tell me not to give up because if I did I would end up losing my life…For 3 long years I had felt resentment and anger towards my mother who had come back into my life to warn me…not waiting to take me to Heaven but to warn me that in order to live I would have to fight to get better!

I now was able to visit the cemetery where my family was… pray for them and miss them without resentment!

Danny who was now 11 years old surprised me one day by telling me that sometimes people that have passed away come back to this world either because their work here is not finished or to warn someone they love! This out of a mouth of a child!!

I was now able to look at my mother's pictures and remember her with love!

Physically I was also better but unfortunately after my procedure I had been placed on Depo-Provera once again because of the over bleeding…I had told my doctor that I could not go on feeling good physically 1 week out of the whole month! I explained to her that I had to work on my own since Victor was now retired and I was the one carrying the insurance for all of us...

CHAPTER 41

Victor faces surgery…

*L*ife continued regardless… and this time I had to help Victor that was scheduled to have surgery on his shoulder at the same Hospital my mother had stayed…

Danny had a great since of humor! He made me laugh one day by telling me that our lives seemed to be taken out of a soap opera and I couldn't agree more!!

How could he feel otherwise!! He probably compared our lives with the lives of his friends and saw that their lives were a lot happier than ours!

As I entered the hospital… immediately I saw two of the doctors that had treated my mother! They didn't recognize me, so I just went to check on Victor…

I sat in the waiting room fool of memories and worry for him for 3 and half hours! I had been in and out of hospitals with my family so much that I had become traumatized by the experience! I hated the smell of the hospitals and heart monitors and had to fight the compulsion to flee! I was finally informed that the surgery had gone well and that I could go and see him, as I came close to him… I said a silent thanks to God for keeping him alive and well…

Suddenly… he looked straight at me, struggled to get out of bed and exclaimed that he could not breathe!

He complained that his lower back was hurting him… making it harder for him to move or breathe!

He was panicking and he would not listen when I told him to wait for the doctors! Instead, he managed to stand up with me helping him (not easy, he was 6-2 and over 220lbs), when I looked at the heart monitor he was plugged into his blood pressure was way up and so was his heartbeat!

A couple of nurses surrounded him, managed to give him a shot for the pain and laid a hot towel behind his back…between both of them they finally managed to get him to lay down…

After what seemed like hours… he finally got some relief and his blood pressure went down! His doctor came in to check him and told us that most likely what happened to him was that he had been laying down in the same position for the surgery and ended up with a huge muscle spasm in his back…I was told to keep an eye on him in case this happened again and he was advised that unless his blood pressure went back to normal, he would not be able to be released…

When we finally got in the car to go home, I strapped him to the car seat and advised him not to move so that the stiches would not break open… but the car motion once again made his back hurt, so he yelled at me that he had to get out of the car! When I was able to look at him after stopping the car he was already bleeding from his shoulder! I helped him get out of the car so that he could breathe normally again… a nice guy with a tow truck got out and asked us if we needed help, I told him about Victor's surgery and asked him if he could help me place Victor back in the car. He did just that and when we finally got home I helped him to lay down, managed to give him something to drink…. and ran to the pharmacy to get pain killers and antibiotics before I had to pick up Danny from school…

Of course, when things go wrong, they tend to go wrong! The pharmacy could not find his pills because they had used his first name as the last! At this point I was extremely upset and when they finally found his medicine, I drove back home to find Victor sleeping peacefully!

I was finally able to let go of all the anguish and frustration I had been feeling all day! I let the tears go that I had been holding back all day long! I had to be strong for my husband and for Danny that was full of questions when he saw his father… by then I had managed to get my emotions under control…

I knew without a doubt that if this had happened 3 years prior… I would have not been able to handle this situation! The classes that I had taken with Dr, Liebgold had given me the tools I needed to fight the ever-present fear of losing another family member! On the other hand, the faith that my parents had installed in me as a child had given me the faith that I now needed to reach to God when I was afraid!

Victor managed to get better with time and with physical therapy… I also found out for myself that not all men are good patients!

Meanwhile we got a treadmill for our small living room where I would walk and run while watching TV, I was doing just that when Victor and Carlos got into a big argument right in front of me! I watched Carlos get verbally abusive towards his father and finally got enough… stopped my walking, looked at Carlos and said "Carlos, if you spoke to my father the way you just spoke to your dad…he would have broken all your teeth! This is not respectful."

They both looked at me and the argument stopped right there! They left me in peace to finish my workout and I thought of how many times in a family there has to be a mediator!

Chapter 42

From a student to a teacher and facing major surgery!

I got prepared to once again go back to Dr. Liebgold's classes… this time not as a student but as a Co-Facilitator! A role I would absolutely learn to enjoy!

Me! The woman that at one point had no hope for herself was now giving hope to others!

I couldn't believe that we had over 100 people join our classes! I recognized myself in a lot of situations that they were going thru! It just seemed so natural to help others, it was like I had been born to fulfill this role all my life!

I felt for each one of them! The woman across from me that was losing her husband and didn't know how she was going to survive without him, another one that loved her children so much that she worried constantly that something awful could happen to them…etc.! These were all "What If's" "What if this happens?" These types of worries would and could keep people from enjoying their lives and keep them living in fear…

This class became an instruction and a half! We were instructed in how to recognize hoarding in someone and help them thru it and even OCD (Over compulsive Disorder), OCD I believe is a little bit in on all of us (the need to re-check on things) that also can get out of order if you let it!

The one that touched my heart the most was a young man by the name of Daniel! He confided in me that there was not one day that he didn't suffer from anxiety and panic attacks! Just like me they had told him that there was nothing wrong with him, again…an antidepressant was prescribed, was not effective and the reason for him being in our classes…

I shared my story with him and saw hope in his eyes! After all I was now a Co-Facilitator for this class! Just like him I had come to this class thinking that nobody would be able to help me and there I was sharing my story with someone else and bringing him hope!

By helping others, I was helping myself and it also made my life worthwhile!

As far as my physical problems… they were not over! The shots of Depo-Provera I was taking were causing the bleeding to come back (now stronger than before) and the pounds that I had managed to lose were coming back! I could feel my uterus with my fingers and was even afraid to work out and have it drop off on me...

My doctor wanted to keep me on the Depo because of the over bleeding but I wanted a second opinion, at work I shared what I was going thru physically with a Sales Rep that just had a hysterectomy and swore that she felt a lot better! She also gave me the name of the doctor she was seeing at Alta Bates Hospital and told me not to delay in making an appointment…

I scheduled the appointment with him already knowing that he was going to recommend surgery! At this point I was willing to do anything after another episode of dizziness that happened in my bedroom, I woke up one night to see the whole room spinning around me! I reached out to Victor and asked him to go to the kitchen… grab me a banana and a glass of water, I was very lucky that after eating ½ of a banana and drinking the water the spinning stopped! This was the second time that happened to me while taking Depo…

I took my husband with me to meet this new doctor and we liked him right away! After he examined me he told me "You have a very sick uterus there and it needs to be removed! I think after two kid's you guys should be fine without anymore…. correct?"

I knew that he was right! I had enough of Depo and of not being able to have a life… Once again… I had to face surgery and the fear of being put to sleep! In our Phoboease classes we had learned to write down our worst-case scenario on any situation that was causing us fear…when I got home, I wrote down what I was fearing regarding this surgery (this list was to be reviewed after the situation was faced) and hoped for the best…

The day of the surgery I kissed and hugged Victor and Danny and they both reassured me that I was going to do fine… they waited for me in the waiting room and I was escorted to the Pre-Op room. The room was filled with people that were scheduled to be operated on that morning, I was by myself and kept seeing one by one of the patients there escorted to the surgery room…I was supposed to be operated early that morning! I finally asked a nurse after an hour passed and she was amazed that I was still in the Pre-Op room! She went to find out why and came back to tell me that another woman had to be taken to the surgery room as an emergency… for her it had been a life-or-death situation! For me it meant that I had to wait for the surgery room to be available…They allowed my husband and son to be by my side until the room was available, for me this waiting was a torture! I was already nervous and questioning myself if this somehow was a sign for me not to do the surgery…

It got to the point that I asked for my clothes so that I could leave but my husband would not let me… between him and the nurses they convinced me to stay! It was after 12PM when they finally came to grab me to take me to the surgery room….my doctor was waiting for me and of course apologizing …All I asked of him was to consider that I loved my family and if it came to a decision of keeping the sick uterus or dying that I preferred to live with pain rather than losing my life, he looked surprised of what I said to him, he told me as he put me to sleep that I would be ok and that he had done many surgeries just like mine…

I drifted off to sleep with my doctor's hand holding mine and to my surprise woke up in the recovery room with a nurse asking me if I was in pain!

I was just so grateful to be alive!!

I was given morphine for the pain and that was not making feel very good… Once I was transferred to my room, I asked the nurse to stop the morphine and give me extra-strength Tylenol, I also told her that I wanted to make a speedy recovery and she advised me that as soon as possible to start walking...

Victor and Danny were waiting for me in my room, they had a beautiful blue necklace for me …. relief was written all over their faces!

The next morning…. I was already walking slowly down the hallway with no bleeding whatsoever! The lady next to me had the same surgery done by another doctor and was full of pain and bleeding! I considered myself very lucky indeed!!

When my doctor came in he was very pleased that I was walking already! He asked me to lay down because he had something to remove from my uterus!

Plain speaking I was scared! What in God's name did he have to remove?...

To my surprise once he had me laying down… he asked me to relax, open my legs and started to pull out a long cord very slowly that had been placed there to stop any bleeding! He also made very happy by telling me that he had not removed my ovaries because they were still healthy and he didn't want me to go into early menopause…

The day after I was allowed to go home and made another appointment to see my doctor for a few weeks after…. even I was amazed that I was back at work after 3 weeks! I made a point of getting my worse scenario list out… crossed out each written doubt with an exclamation point on each one and got it ready to take it to my next Phoboease class!

I went to my follow up appointment and was not surprised by what the doctor had to say! Thru the biopsy they had done of my uterus they had found that I had Adenomyosis (I actually looked it up on the Internet and found out that it was the beginning of Endometriosis) and I was also informed that when he took out my uterus it felt spongy to the touch and it was enlarged! I was very glad that I had made the right decision of removing a very sick organ from my body! This also meant no more periods!!

Of course, I was still worried that I had the beginning of Endometriosis or that I might still have it somewhere else in my body! My doctor placed me on a very low birth control pill because he felt that I was pre-menopausal, I was not happy with this decision and told him that I had been placed on birth control before and it always raised my blood pressure… but he told me to try them anyway for a while…

Also… a warning about pre-menopausal women! When your hormones start to change it's almost like the transition from being a teenager to womanhood! Once back at work I was not prepared to experience a physical attraction towards a younger man, but it did happen! He worked for the same company that I did and I would see him at work just about every day… Our eyes would meet and I knew he felt the attraction as well… but I fought it… Besides being married and not wanting to be unfaithful to my husband was also the fact that he was quite a bit younger than I was! Believe me this was extremely difficult! Even my girlfriends knew about it! They teased me constantly it and I had to them "I have read enough about these kinds of affairs… besides that they don't work I also don't want to give this kind of example to my kids." After a while he got the message and so did my friends…

CHAPTER 43

Dealing with depression…

*A*gain… birth control pills of course brought more problems! One of them was moodiness! I had ups and downs and didn't like the depression that I was experiencing! Sometimes I would go to the kitchen at work by myself and just sit there! One of our supervisors actually stopped by my table one day and said to me "Mary, what's up with you lately, you never used to be this way? You used to always have a happy smile for everyone, now it's like you are about to cry all the time!" I really liked this guy, we had known each other since I started working there, he was always nice to everyone so I had to come up with a quick excuse "Fred, I'm going thru some health problems that I will have to deal with sooner or later but thank you for asking!" He nodded and said "I want to see you smile again, all right?" I said "Yes" but I knew it would take some time before I felt like myself again…

I knew this Mary he was seeing was a very different woman from the woman that along with two of her best friends had sung to him "Santa Baby" on a Christmas week to cheer him up…

It wasn't long before my blood pressure once again went up and I had to be placed on Depo again to control other physical symptoms that had not been diagnosed…I knew without a shadow of a doubt that my body couldn't handle birth control pills of any kind!

This meant also the weight gain… something I hated because I had learned to eat correctly and exercise but the medicine at the same time would help me feel better physically now that the uterus was not there…

The worst part was also knowing that I was married to a man that did not admire heavy women and constantly looked at anyone that happened to be good looking and slim! That unfortunately had not changed! I had the feeling that it would never change…

I felt less attractive to him and our sexual life had changed! Desperate for a solution I attended an Endometriosis Seminar with him …I didn't like the fact that they informed the women there that this was a life-long illness!

That day I told my husband that I didn't want him to be stuck with a woman that might have an illness to cope with for the rest of her life…I gave him the option to get out of the marriage… he refused saying that he was there for the long run….

I even felt selfish for not having the guts to get out of the marriage at that point and give him the opportunity to be with someone more attractive and with less health problems!

What a journey this life of mine had turned out to be!!

On the other hand, everyone from the Phoboease class were very proud of me! When I went back to share my last victory… they couldn't believe that I was already back to work and back at the classes 3 weeks after my surgery! However, I knew my road to recovery (physically and mentally) was going to take a while! It was a good thing that I was too stubborn to give up…

I kept on helping in the classes because for some reason these people really listened when I gave them advice! It also helped to take my mind off my problems…

When you are helping others, you forget about yourself in the process and after all…. this had been my promise to God! Some people when fulfilling promises do so after the miracle is done… in my book you start fulfilling the promise as soon as you make it (that is how you see God work in your life).

My husband and I also had to make a difficult decision regarding our home that we had been living in for over 25 years, this house that I had lived in since the age of 16 was now a house that had nothing but bad memories because of all the family members that I had lost!

Because of how I felt about this home and because Danny would have to start High School at Richmond High the next year…we had to make a decision to move or stay, I hated the thought of Danny being exposed to gangs and drug abuse at that High School! I had brought up the subject of moving somewhere else to Victor before but because our home was paid for he had refused to discuss it! Now we were given an opportunity to change things for Danny and for me…

My father-in-law's house in San Leandro had become vacant (he had moved back east and had it rented) and he called us to ask if we would like to rent it since he wanted someone there that he could trust…

For us it meant a better education for Danny and a change of scenery for us! We discussed it as a family and agreed to rent our home… Danny was extremely happy not to have to go to the High School he was afraid of...

CHAPTER 44

Moving back to San Leandro and leaving memories behind...

I went to St. Joseph's Cemetery and visited my family… with tears running down my face I explained to my mother and father that had I loved my home but now I had to make this move and my reasons for it! This also meant less trips to the Cemetery for me but in the long run it would be worth it for all of us to get another chance to restart somewhere else…

We started the moving process and moved in the week before Christmas with rain nonstop!

It was one of the worse storms we had ever seen in the Bay Area! It was like Mother Nature was revolting that we were moving but I was determined to have us moved by Christmas Eve! We managed to get moved and had our Christmas tree up and our presents under the tree!

There were big adjustments to be made! Register Danny in his new High School, finding good tenants for our home… adjusting to traffic, etc.

For Victor it was better… he was closer to his friends in San Leandro including of course Familia Portuguesa the local Portuguese Club that knew us so well and that we both loved…

He immediately managed to make a couple of new friends that lived nearby…

I also had to make changes with my career! My job as data manager had become very boring and unfulfilling and I knew I had to make some hard decisions, unfortunately, I was married to a man that was afraid of making changes… if I had to make changes in our lives it would have to be me making them…

For months because of my health issues, I hadn't written a word! Once I was settled in our new place I started to write about my experience with my surgery and the move we had to make… Writing for me was like cleansing of my soul and it helped me to heal...

I had to keep on confronting fears it seemed if I wanted to or not! The next one would be to act as chaperone for a field trip that would take place in Alcatraz! For me that meant having to take the Bart for the first time in years and also the ferry to Alcatraz…no big deal for anyone else! For me it was a different story! Fears if not confronted they tend to escalate...

We went as a group of people that included students and families, the Bart was a little scarry because we would travel thru a tunnel on the way to San Francisco… the Ferry was even worse because the water was quite choppy that day! Once inside the Ferry I looked back at the bay and could not believe that I was inside of a boat with my son and approaching Alcatraz!

Once we docked… we had to climb all the way up the hill! I had to wait and breathe deeply because I found myself out of breath many times! Danny (the reason behind my pushing) stayed by my side, worried that I was not feeling well …but we finally made it all the way to the top…

I was not prepared to see what I saw!

The conditions that these prisoners were living in was deplorable! Even if they had been guilty of many crimes in my point of view, they were still human beings! It was bad enough being locked up… sometimes for the rest of their lives and had to suffer many things that were uncalled for!

Throughout the tour we listened to a video cassette describing the cells and the conditions that these prisoners went thru… at one point we heard the voice of a man asking us to imagine living in a cage watching the world go by!

Funny…that's exactly how I felt about living with fear and anxiety! Living in a cage with no bars watching the world go by! Only when you start taking risks are you able to break free from the ropes that hold you captive…

If the only way to break free was to take risks…then I was willing to do it!

Because of how I felt physically that day and being afraid of not being able to breathe correctly I made an appointment with a natural doctor that specialized in Endometriosis. I had at this point gained quite a bit of weight and after a series of tests she shared with me that I needed to be off the Depo that I was on for good! She informed me that my sodium was very low… that I was at the border line for diabetes once again and wanted me to start on pills, this for me was a turning point! I immediately told her that I would get off it… but I also wanted to lose weight and then be re-tested… no way would I accept being placed on a treatment for diabetes, I knew from my mother's experience that from pills eventually you would have to be placed on Insulin shots…

She told me that it would take a long time to lose the weight because of being on the Depo… I told her to give me 3 months and then we would do the lab work one more time… for the first time I had a doctor look at me with a lot of respect and tell me "Mary you have the ability to heal."

My next step was to go to the local library and research all the foods that I would have to eat in order to lose the weight.

I joined Curves for a workout routine and started working on myself…by the time I went to see her (3 months) I had managed to lose 15 pounds and managed to surprise her in the process! I could of course have looked for more trouble at the library, researched all the symptoms I was having and found other reasons to worry but this could also backfire on you and get you in a state of fear!

Every opportunity I got I researched the subject of fears and enrolled in a seminar in Oakland, CA given by Dr. Albert Ellis PHD and 2 other speakers. The subject would be Rational Emotive Behavior Therapy, Doctor Ellis proved to be a very intelligent older man with a great sense of humor!

His theory regarding fear was all related to the thought process… merely changing your negative thought to a positive one and challenging the negative one would you be able to stop the fear and change your life…

I took notes for me and for others and kept my gaze glued to these speakers afraid of missing a word!

This concept was pretty much the same that Dr.Liebgold taught us in his classes but he had encouraged us to attend the seminar so that we as students learned as much as we could because after all… knowledge is power!

CHAPTER 45

Refusing to listening to negative thoughts…

I used all the knowledge I had learned to my benefit… if I had listened to all the negative thoughts that had entered my mind… I could have lost my life…

If you don't confront the fear it can lead to paranoia or even suicide!

Clear example of this concept was a young woman I met at the classes by the name of Sara, she was extremely thin and suffered from anorexia! We became close friends, I shared with her all I had learned, encouraged her to eat and face her fears… one of them was for her to register and try to get chosen for the American Idol since she loved to sing! She made it as far as Los Angeles and kept us informed, I told her it didn't matter if she won or not! The important thing was that she had denied the voice in her head that told her she was not good enough and did it anyway! I also encouraged her to do something we had been taught at Dr.Liebgold class and that was to visualize what you want to accomplish even if doesn't come to pass as long as it's a positive image…

She was not chosen but came back to our applause because for her this was a victory worth talking about! We kept close contact but Sara still listened to the negative voice in her head and kept on missing classes and at one point didn't show up anymore…I often wondered if she had ever been able to get over anorexia or if she ended up dying from it…

There was another voice that I had learned to listen to if it was positive and that was the quiet voice of the Holy Spirit! I had an experience I would never forget! We had been notified that my brother-in-law wife's mother had passed away, there was so much fighting back and forth between the family regarding who got what that was incredible!

This lady had been nothing but kindness to me while she was alive! We left for the rosary…. I could tell that there was tension in the room because of all the fighting that had been going on… Victor, Danny and I sat behind my sister-in-law's brother, I saw this young man that suffered from a severe blood disorder and had converted to Christianity get up on his own and sing a Christian song to his mother right from his seat! He managed to show all of them how much love and respect he had for his mother! It took courage for him to do this in a Catholic Chapel!

After everyone had a chance to share a story or a memory about her, I had this incredible push to go and speak and shared this with Victor, he turned around and said to me "You are a wonderful speaker, go up there and speak from the heart." The best advice I had ever been given at Dr. Liebgold's class was to imagine the worst-case scenario in any situation and expect it to turn around in your favor! I did just that before I got my nerve to speak!

I got up… was nervous but I knew what I had to say was extremely important! I walked to the Podium… spoke from my heart… shared with a room full of people that this lady had been nothing but kindness to me when she was alive! I told them that I believed with all my heart that her last wishes at this time were that she would be remembered with love and respect and not to have her family fight over what was left!

When we left the Chapel, I was shocked that some of the family members shook my hand to thank me for what I had said and that what I had done had taken courage but needed to be said! Victor hugged me and told me that he was proud of me! To my surprise when I got to my kitchen by myself… I danced with happiness! That my friends is…. the work of the Holy Spirit!

Living life meant taking risks and another I would have to take was to look for another position! I had been working for MCSi in Berkeley for 5 years and loved the people I worked with… they had become like family to me and unfortunately, they had been bought out by another company that laid off quite a few people! Our company had made investments that had not been very wise, this had left many people afraid that they would be losing their jobs very soon! Some people started to look for other companies to work for… one of them was our Accounting Manager that found another position in a company in San Carlos.

Some of our accounting crew…including myself were offered other positions but in another branch, I knew I needed the change, so I accepted! I would be working for the Service Dept for the same company in Fremont, this time the challenge would be not only to learn a different field but to have to answer to two male supervisors that had a superiority complex! One of them stole my ideas in how to improve Servicing and the other one the Service Manager had such a bad attitude that I had to tell him one day "Juan in order for me and you to work together you are going to have to tell me how to talk to you! I don't like to feel like I have to approach you with caution."

He knew by looking at me that I was very serious and from that day forward he started to treat me with more respect...

Victor on the other hand found ways to amuse himself when I couldn't go with him… he loved bullfights and "Cantorias" (Portuguese old fashion singing) and as soon as he knew about a Portuguese festival around, he immediately made plans, either with his friends or with his brother and made frequent trips to Manteca and Gustine for their festivals… I did attend a few with him, this was not only a way to keep our culture alive but a way for us to see friends that we hadn't seen for quite a while…

I continued to lose weight and found that I needed something stronger then Curves as far as exercising, took my husband to check out 24 hours Fitness in San Leandro and we both became members, he had watched me not only loose quite a bit of weight but also watched as

I went from walking to running! I believe at this point he was starting to feel intimidated how I was changing and fought with me about joining the gym, I did anyway because my body was craving the stronger exercise and sweating made me feel absolutely wonderful...

CHAPTER 46

Unexpected visitors and premonitions…

*V*ictor and I also had a couple of visitors from back east, one was his younger sister that we took to the Portuguese club Victor went to and had dinner together… I was polite but very cautious… She asked me how I was, I told her that I had managed to survive all of the losses in my family but it would take some time to heal, she actually squeezed my hand and apologized for how they had treated me when Victor and I first got married! I accepted her apology but what I didn't tell her that day was that what they did to me had left scars that I would probably carry with me for the rest of my life!

We went by the Saddle Rack to show her the place and the next day she would be spending it with her other brother, her oldest sister also made us a visit later that year and just like her youngest sister apologized! We were visiting Sausalito and I remember how uncomfortable I was that day! It took them years to finally admit that they had been wrong about me!

They didn't know that I had become afraid of speaking to them… afraid that whatever I said could become misinterpreted….

I had changed quite a bit and one thing for sure I would have loved that they had done this and had been there for me when I needed the family support… My appearance changed as well and we once again started to attend a few Portuguese dances… for the first time in my life

I had a married man with 3 daughters flirt out right with me in front of my husband!

I was amazed because he was also a friend of Victor's and they saw each other frequently (they both raised birds), he would come by our house and I would catch him looking at me! At one point I told Victor about his flirting and asked him to keep him away from me… I didn't respect a man with growing daughters flirting with me in front of my husband!

I also was experiencing something that bother me quite a bit and that was that every time I went to a Portuguese function, I was looked at sometimes with admiration and other times with pity! Maybe because people knew what I had gone thru with my family and felt sorry for me?

I would find out the real reason for it much later…

At a dinner and dance that Victor and I attended I had someone make a comment to me that made me think! A friend of ours grabbed my hand and whispered in my ear "You know Sao…I don't know if anyone has ever told you this…but you have brought out the best in Victor!" I looked at her questionably and she explained "Some women can either bring out the best in a man or the worst and he has changed since being with you!"

That was the first time someone besides my mother had told me this!

I shared with her that maybe the reason he had changed was also because I prayed for him…she just raised an eyebrow at me!

That week we had a bit of a scare with Carlos… I was out shopping when I received a call from Victor to let me know that Carlos had been admitted to the Hospital (immediately you think the worst), when I finally reached the facility, he already been admitted… they operated on him and took his appendix out! I was so happy that he was ok!!

As I waited in the waiting room to see him, I got a glimpse of a guy that could have been my oldest brother twin! I got this strangest premonition that my brother was ill! I shared this with Victor and we tried to call him but we were never able to reach him! I prayed that I was wrong!

Carlos stayed in hospital until he was well enough to be released but the worry about my brother never left and unfortunately, I didn't know anyone in the area we lived in to ask if they had been to Acores lately and had seen my brother...

At one of the many functions Victor and I attended I came across a man that had just arrived from Acores... knew my older brother Jose Carlos and had seen him! I had kept trying to contact him with no success, he didn't answer his phone and his family refused to contact us! I had been really worried about him! I knew he did not take care of himself and I had the feeling that something was wrong! It seemed that everywhere I went I saw someone that looked like him!

I shared my worries with a man that had just seen him and he said that he was quite heavy, had a red complexion and was drinking quite heavily!

I was not surprised! I told my brother's friend about a conversation I had with my brother when he had come to visit us in San Pablo years prior about not taking care of himself, at that time he had been quite heavy and I could tell that he was drinking and smoking!

It was not easy to talk to my brother about anything! He was very set in his ways! I reminded him of our family history and of what my mother and I had gone thru for years taking care of our dad...

His response to me was "When it's over, it's over."

I told him that was not necessarily always true! How you take care of yourself can also affect others around you in a big way! He just shrugged it off and I could tell he was not willing to listen...

CHAPTER 47

And the last brother dies!

Two weeks after our conversation with my brother's friend, my husband and I received a call from a distant cousin in Canada to give us his condolences! When I asked whom he was referring to I was told that my brother had died a few days ago from a major heart attack while washing his car! I didn't even know the precise day or time that he had died but had felt it in my heart that something awful had happened!

Nobody had called me from his immediate family! I could not believe it!

Family issues aside, death is something that cannot be used as weapon against someone!

I was devastated and angry to the point I could not even cry! I took the next day off... that did not help so I went back to work the next day. My friends were very sympathetic, it helped that they felt my pain for not being there to attend his funeral... but it did not relieve the pain and regret that I felt inside! I tried to remember the words that his friend had said to me "I told him that his sister was very worried about him and I'm sure if he wanted to, he would have found a way to reach you."

It finally hit me on the third day! On the way to pick up some food for our family I found my myself not being able to hold back the tears! After I picked up our dinner... I parked my car in the parking lot and let go of the tears of grief I had inside of me! I screamed and cried until I couldn't cry anymore…

I spoke to him like he was there "You fool! If you had told me that you had any kind of heart problem, I would have paid for your trip here for you to see a specialist, why didn't you call me when you knew that I was worried about you.?" Once calm I was finally able to drive home….

By the time I got home with our food, my family knew by my face that it had finally hit me in a big way! As we sat at our dinner table to eat, I tried to get my emotions together since I had a Phoboease class to go to that evening… However, it didn't help that my husband made a very stupid comment that evening at the dinner table…

He looked at me across the table and said, "There is nothing you can do, he is dead and life goes on."

I looked at him and said, "Easy enough for you to say, you haven't lost any family members and I have lost way too many."

That night at the class I shared my feelings with all the co-facilitators and also with the new students, they wanted to give me all their support and I wanted them to understand that fear sometimes can stop you from doing something important! Like visiting a brother for the last time and having to live for the rest of your life with regret!

They understood my point! I also shared with them how important it is to listen to someone when they are trying to help you because after all they could very well save your life!

Jose Carlos was only 54 years old when he died but it seemed to me that my brother had always lived all his life as an older individual! Due to all the tragedies that happened in our family he didn't have time to enjoy being a teenager, he had given up studying to help us financially and he was forced to grow up way too fast!

He was probably no more than 18 years old when he took on the role of a caregiver when my father and my two brothers went to jail… my mother and I had depended on him because what my mother made had not been enough to help us financially…

Out of my 3 brothers he had been the only one that at the age of 10 had asked my mother to be my godfather! Victor asked Jose, my brother's friend to call me because I was carrying a lot of guilt and was always sad… One night I got a call from him to tell me that in the 6 months he had been in the islands he had seen him many times… had spoken about me to him and he had told him "Tell her that she will always be my sister and my goddaughter and if I'm staying away is to keep the peace in my family."

Now I knew why he had stopped contacting me! His words had made it a bit easier for me… but I was very different from my brothers, I would have not stopped communicating with my own family to avoid conflict with a spouse! Family is blood after all…

Avoiding conflict was his reason to keep away but had also kept him from the one person that would have done anything to help him live a longer life… Even have him see a Specialist here in the US!

I arranged for a special mass for my brother the following week and invited his friend Jose and his wife to attend… I was finally able to hug this man that had in a way given me a gift of much needed peace…

That day on the way to the church I had seen nothing but rain and clouds but as we left the church together… I looked up and saw the most vivid beautiful rainbow that went from one end of the church to the other! This was like a gift from Heaven!

I would no longer see my three older brothers leave home together (a escadinha- the staircase) going out to explore the town or to see a movie together…they were all gone from my life and they left me with a heart full of memories….

I had lost since 1990 a total of 7 family members that I knew I would see in Heaven someday! Unfortunately, something that my husband did not believe in, for him when you died your life was over… no coming back! The loss of all my family members had also led me to my next decision…

I knew that in life there were no guarantees and from that day forward I started to put money aside in a Savings Account for a vacation somewhere, it would be wonderful to see where I was born, where my brother was buried, even to go back to "Caxias" where I had spent my teen years…

All I had left was my aunt Carmen… 3 cousins in Portugal, my other cousins in Ohio and of course my husband and two boys! Much had been taken from me… but I also had found some amazing friends along the way and a strength I did not know I possessed!

I had been so traumatized by all the very personal losses in my life that at one point every time I saw my husband leave with the kids somewhere I would be anxious all day! Afraid something would happen to them away from me! To the point that one day when they had gone fishing, I asked a good friend of mine to drive me to Stinson Beach to check if they had arrived safely! I knew that road very well, full of curves and uphill! I was only able to rest once we parked the car and I saw them below fishing! I used another tool here, confront the fear and see for yourself so that the fear is not allowed to escalate…

My health was not improving either… I coped with hormonal imbalances, night sweats, food allergies, hot flashes, constipation, bloating and nothing seemed to really work, so once again I had to confront other fears…

I joined the Endometriosis Foundation and read their newsletters just in case these symptoms could be related to Endo and not just Pre-Menopause as I had been told, some doctors I saw actually told me to hang in there… that the chance was that when I actually went thru full Menopause, I would probably feel a lot better! This was told to me in my early forties! How do you face years of feeling this way until you do hit Menopause living with 3 guys and not a woman in the house?

CHAPTER 48

A wall is created and an extraordinary meeting happens in Pismo!

*A*s if that was not enough my husband and I were now separated by an invisible wall that I had not created! He was depressed most of the time and it was extremely hard to make him spend time with me! He was only happy when he was out with his friends… especially on Friday nights that now had extended to the other weekdays as well…

I tried to convince him for us to seek Marriage Counseling but he refused and that made me angry that he was not even willing to try to save our marriage!

Our sex life also was not the same and that made him resentful and much harder to talk to…

On one of my many attempts to talk to him he blamed my depression and illness for the drift between us! I could not believe that this man that had seen all that had happened in our lives was now blaming me for everything!

The day after our conversation I started taking Saint John's Wart daily (a natural antidepressant), I had tried Prozac… advised by a doctor and had a huge anxiety attack while taking a shower! That had prompt me to do research and seek a more natural approach…

I found myself spending most of my free time with Danny, especially Friday nights…we would go out grocery shopping… grab a game for Danny, fix something for both of us for dinner and ended up falling asleep in my living room waiting for my husband to come home…. most of the time after 2AM…

Friends are not always sympathetic when you keep on sharing sad stories, after a while you realize that you have one person that is always willing to listen and always on your side and that is God…

My faith and what I had learned on my Phoboease classes kept me going! I become an expert in hiding what I was going thru at work and with my husband's side of the family…at home I tried my best to hide it from my son's …especially from Danny because I knew he worried a lot about me and even from Victor since I didn't want a bad atmosphere in our home…

I was surprised when I received a call from a support person from the Endometriosis Foundation, she had suffered for years from Endo and had a huge number of surgeries! She believed that for her this illness had become a lifetime sentence! We were actually seeing the same doctor…

I had scheduled a follow-up appointment with my doctor and after a pelvic examination and lab work, she found that I was depleted of estrogen (that's why sexual intercourse had become so painful), she found small hernias and also that the vaginal wall had dropped down! Of course, she recommended surgery to correct all these issues and told me she would use a laser to destroy any endo that she found…

I listened carefully but was very skeptical about surgeries! She placed me on a gentler medication to replace my estrogen… went thru extensive testing and scheduled the surgery for 3 months after! I found out that my body did not like Depo at all!

I also had to find a way to get a down payment of $4000 dollars for this surgery since she was not part of my medical insurance, besides medical expenses I had to deal with other expenses, like braces for

Danny! Every single time I saw my doctor I had to pay up front and that became a big burden on us...

I decided to postpone the surgery and used all the info I had gathered thru years of research to start on a health program that included eating healthy and exercising as much as I could. This change was something that actually helped my husband as well since he had found out that his cholesterol was high, his blood pressure and his blood sugar! Victor just like me did not want to depend on medications...

We started a walking program together and in the space of a month he had lost 23 pounds and was feeling much better! As for me being off the Depo itself had helped quite a bit with the bloating, sweats, dizziness, etc... and the Saint John's Wort helped immensely with the depression....

Our kitty (Foxy) that we had brought with us cared a lot for me! If I stayed in bed and didn't want to get up to eat breakfast, she would jump on top of my chest and would lick my nose! She would not give up until I got up to eat...

It didn't help having other problems to deal with while I was working by myself and coping with my health issues! Danny was having problems in High School... Carlos had lost a good job and was having problems finding another and that left him depressed...

Victor on the other hand was experiencing daily headaches from stress! I was feeling overwhelmed after finding out that my company was filling for bankruptcy! If I didn't find another job soon... we would have to do without my income and medical insurance for me and for our family...

My doctor had advised me to get my health back on track before considering surgery and I totally agreed! My family and I had decided that summer to take a much-needed vacation to Pismo Beach (our favorite spot) and get some rest and relaxation.

One of the things my doctor had advised me to do was to keep a daily journal of how I felt and when I had a chance to read it, I could not believe that I was managing to live each day feeling so poorly! This list of symptoms was quite extensive…from night sweats, hot flashes, headaches, hair loss, feeling spacy, nosebleeds, nausea, out of breath and pains coming from my right hip down my leg!

Even shopping was not a pleasure for me anymore because of the way that I felt… I stayed behind in our motor home resting while my husband and Danny took a walk in Saint Luis Obispo, they actually met a young man that made quite an impression on them! He had been talking to a woman that was very depressed, they overheard the conversation and they were very impressed! They convinced me to go find him and speak to him…

We went back and found him near a Barnes & Noble's store sitting in a wheelchair! My first impression of him was that he had a smile that lit up his whole face and beautiful blue eyes! He looked at me and asked me if he could help me in anyway and somehow… I knew I could trust him!

We sat alone in front of the store and I shared my story with him… the tragedies, the triumphs and what I was going thru physically… even that I had almost committed suicide…

He listened carefully and then proceeded to tell me his story, he had made some real bad decisions regarding investments, found out he had multiple sclerosis and tried to kill himself with a knife 3 times! He ended up in a clinic that helped him to heal physically as well as mentally. That clinic proved to be a blessing because he was at the point of becoming homeless and provided him with a roof over his head!

Joshua instead of finding his illness an obstacle to overcome had found it an inconvenience in his life! Just like me… he had promised God to help others along the way… he now had a place to live in Saint Luis Obispo and managed to feel happy despite his illness! He radiated peace and love and that's what drew people to him...

I told him what I saw in him and he thanked me when it was I that had to thank him for being such an inspiration to me and to others!

Before I left he gave me really good advice and even some suggestions on books that I should read that would help me in my healing process...

I shared with Joshua about the book that I was writing and he gave me his permission to write about him so that I could share his story with others. He didn't seek people to help, he waited until they came to him for advice… then he helped them and gave them hope!

I left him without wanting to leave him! The first thing I did when we got back to our motor home was to tell my family his story and wrote it down on my journal…

On one of my good days, I managed to enjoy something I loved and that was sightseeing with my family, I convinced my husband and Danny on a Sunday morning to see some beautiful houses up on the hills. Once we arrived I started to have a nosebleed! My family asked me if I wanted to go back to the motor home, I told them why I wanted to stay "I want to keep my dreams alive… the nosebleed will stop eventually." It did and we ended up enjoying the experience of make believe we could afford a new home…

That same evening after dinner we went out on the pier… Danny went up to the Video Room where the kids played and stayed there for a bit with Victor. I went for a walk near the pier and had the worst experience ever! I walked into the public restroom and coming out of the stall to wash my hands I started to hallucinate and thought that I had seen my aunt Mathilde!

I knew that it was time to go back home the next day… see my doctor and go thru the list of all my symptoms while on vacation, I knew I had to make some hard decisions regarding my next treatment...

When I met with her, she had found thru a test that I had taken previously that I had a serious yeast growth on my bowel! She recommended I start taking Nystatin for the yeast overgrowth and enzymes to help me digest food better.

We agreed on holding off any future surgeries and take these medicines to see how they worked, it was amazing how just combining these two medicines how my health started to improve!

For one thing… the sweats and the bloating were gone, the nosebleeds and I started to sleep better!

My family and friends even noticed the difference in me! I knew something they didn't know! There was more going on besides poor health! There were years of neglect not only with my body but my soul as well!

The doctor that I had learned to respect and care for had also decided to retire and pursue a writing career! When I received her letter, I cried because that left me once again without someone to rely on! On our last appointment she told me in her office once again "Mary you have the ability to heal yourself." She probably saw that I unlike other patients had the willingness to change and heal on my own! Sometimes even by doing research and helping yourself you still need a helping hand along the way…

I called my friend Peg that day and we both shared the same disappointment regarding our doctor! She had another Doctor that she recommended and we both made future appointments.

I kept my appointment with the next doctor, he recommended that I keep the same treatment… above all told me to keep a close watch on the food I consumed and exercised moderately every day, I took his advice to heart...

At this point I also needed to trust my instinct…

CHAPTER 49

Spiritual growth...

I was really searching for a way to heal spiritually as well and one day while switching channels I heard Dr. Charles Stanley speak (a Christian Minister) and I couldn't take my eyes off of the screen!

Intouch Ministries became part of my life that day! He was an older gentleman with a gentle smile and lot of wisdom and I was willing to listen!

I bought some of his books and learned that not only God existed but Satan as well and that we as God's children need the knowledge to learn how to defeat him…something that was not taught to me by my parents…

I had been raised Catholic all my life but in our Church they didn't instruct anyone the way this minister did! Catholic religion was all about rituals and singing but not much Bible reading! Something that Dr. Stanley emphasized…

To follow along when he was preaching, I bought a New Revelations Bible, learned how God created this world and read beautiful stories that drew me like a magnet…

Sunday nights were dedicated to hear him speak… he had my full attention when he spoke about reaching your full potential in life…

I also bought his tapes and listened every day in my car on the way to work, thru his teachings I became a much calmer and self-assured woman! I felt compelled to explain my life change to my family and friends but it was hard for them to understand unless like me they had been thru hell and back!

This wonderful speaker became my mentor and was guiding me how to live a much happier and fulfilled life...

I still attended Catholic Mass every chance I got (even Portuguese Masses) because I knew God was everywhere... but thru Dr. Stanley I learned to really identify the Holy Spirit! I recognized what he was talking about when I attended a Mass one Sunday and saw this black African woman singing in the Choir! She left the Choir still singing and strolled thru the aisles as if possessed by something utterly beautiful!

I looked at her and I remembered thinking "Whatever she has I want it."

She had the most beautiful smile on her face and happiness radiated from her!

Later in one of Dr.Stanley's tapes I learned how the Holy Spirit can take possession of someone specially if they are glorifying God and use them to display to others what they need to see or crave!

I was on the road to finally heal physically and mentally with God's help!

It didn't surprise me one bit when I received a call from my friend in Napa (the pilot that was connected with Dr.Liebgold's class) with an invitation to join her at a Launch in Emeryville for Melaleuca products... She had tried to convince me to buy these products before but I had been too sick to even consider it... since I felt better now I decided to take her up on her offer and met her there...

I was captivated by this company right from the start! They sold everything from soaps to supplements to household products but what got my attention was that most of their products were made from tree tea oil, antifungal and did not give you adverse reactions...

That day not only did I became a customer for life but also a Representative for the Company and found a partner to work with...

While in Emeryville that afternoon I drove to Berkeley and stopped at a bookstore… when going thru some books I found a book that would be instrumental in my physical well-being! "The Yeast Connection, a medical Breakthrough."

This book written by Dr.William G Crook MD caught my eye! The message on the cover read "If you feel sick all the time, this book could change your life" and it did!

When I finally had the chance to read it, I realized that what I had was related to a yeast imbalance (candida) not only endometriosis…

I learned that candida is present in everybody's body but it could get out of control if you are living a very stressful life, not eating properly, taking birth control pills and other factors such as sexual intercourse… but it is treatable!

CHAPTER 50

Finally finding the answer thru research!

$\mathcal{I}$n my small living room that night by myself I cried because I had finally thru my own research found the answer to most of my health problems!

Thru this book I learned that I needed to switch to organic foods, cut out the carbs, the sweets and along with the medication I was taking also exercise moderately… It could take a while…. but it would work…

I also learned about the allergies that came along with the yeast overgrowth and switched all the household products in my house to natural ones (Melaleuca), soaps, cleansers, shampoos, etc.…

When I went to my doctor's appointment that week, I took the book to show him what I had found… hopefully have him read it and help someone else… He respected what I believed in and what I had accomplished so far… whether he actually believed it that was another story!

That year I learned about patience! Due to the Depo Provera shots sometimes it would take me 3 weeks to lose 1 or 3 pounds but by the end of that year I had lost a total of 60lbs! I had my blood work done again and the results even amazed the doctor! No need for medication for diabetes or blood pressure and I looked a lot healthier!

There were still bad days especially if I didn't eat correctly or ate something that was not fresh… the symptoms would flare up again and

I still had pain in my joints especially on my right side that refused to leave unless I moved around...

Those were the days that I would get discouraged and would confide in my family or very close friends… and of course prayer was always there as a resource when friends were too busy to listen…

From romance novels I switched to instruction books that taught me how to help my body to heal and showed me examples of how other people had healed themselves thru research and reading…

I learned that for you to really heal you also have to heal your mind as well as your body… the body works with the spirit…

I learned to let go of past resentments, anger and sorrow! After forgiving my mother the next person I had to forgive and make peace with was my sister-in-law, Rosa. I took Victor with me to visit her at her home (she was laying down in her bed) and explained to her why I had stayed away for so long, she couldn't believe I had taken her dreams the wrong way! I had to explain to her that at the time I was very sick and unfortunately took those dreams has warnings that my life was about to end instead of concerns from a family that loved me dearly….

I hugged her and told her that we would start our friendship over again… she also shared with me that at one point she had been so concerned about me that when she went to Fatima (Portugal) she had prayed for me! I left feeling much better and thankful that Dr. Charles Stanley also reenforced his belief that we cannot live a life full of resentments, he had given me the courage to do what I had just done…

I saw this man of God has my own personal mentor and had to find a way to thank him personally! While watching one of his programs on TV I saw an advertisement for a Cruise to join Dr, Stanley in Alaska, I immediately took action and decided to use my own personal savings to book the trip…

It had taken me over 2 years to save this money that I had planned to use for a trip to Portugal but it would be worth it to finally meet a man I truly admired!

My next move was to find someone to go with me! I thought of my friend Sue (the flight instructor and my partner as a Melaleuca Representative) and called her to ask her if she wanted to go with me since Victor had no interest in a cruise. She was not enthusiastic about it because she liked cruises with dancing, gambling and drinking… but I explained to her my need to meet Dr.Stanley and told her that I would need her support since this meant flying and taking a Cruise Ship! She finally said "Ok, I will go but we will have to get a room with a veranda, I insist on that." I agreed…

If this opportunity had been there even 3 or 5 years prior, I would have not considered it… all the work I had done on myself had paid off and I was now willing to take a higher risk…

I rehearsed in my mind over and over how I would approach Dr. Stanley to thank him personally for what I had learned from him and for the hope that he had brought to my life!

I knew I had changed (for the better) and that I would never be the same! This unfortunately brought conflict from those that knew you… some friends that knew how much I had suffered accepted and were happy for me and others were jealous of my new self-confidence…

I still had to deal with physical symptoms that I knew needed further healing but by this time I knew that there had to be other treatments out there… and that somehow with God's help I would find the answer…

Chapter 51

A very important workshop is found thru research...

While doing research for other treatments I found out about a workshop regarding Candida scheduled at the Nikko Hotel in San Francisco for May of 2004, this workshop was designed for doctors and people in the medical field only... but I was determined to get some answers from the experts! I found a way to register for the event as a medical assistant and prepared for this very important workshop...

The Sunday before I went to mass with Danny and prayed for guidance, courage and protection for the next week as never before...

On the day of the workshop the room was filled with doctors and other people involved in the medical field, I was sitting among them pretending to be one of them and hoping that I would not be discovered! Among these doctors on the panel was Dr. Has, I had done some research on him before hand and wanted to hear him speak...

I paid special attention to the questions and answers being thrown across the room back and forth and took notes...

Others went to the microphone and placed questions before the panel, I heard one of the speakers announce that only 10 minutes remained of the workshop and if someone had a question to ask the panel... they had to do it at this time!

I knew this was my only chance to speak up! I gathered all my courage and stood up! I had a huge knot on my stomach! I asked them to forgive me for being there not as medical assistant or a nurse but as a patient! I shared with them that had gone thru hell for the last 5 years and needed some answers how to further heal from candida. I also told them what I had done already and that what I had heard so far overwhelmed me! But that no matter what I would still do anything to heal!!

I was amazed that I was not thrown out of there! Instead, I was told that I would need to keep on switching treatments to eliminate the candida, take Vitamin C and find a dentist to take all the mercury feelings out of my teeth! Mercury feelings I learned destroy the healthy bacteria and allowed the overgrowth of candida… this also prevents your gut from healing…

I sat in my chair and wrote everything that I had learned and was approached by two other doctors that gave me yet more advise! I think they were very impressed with my courage, Dr. Has come by and shook my hand! I already had made an appointment with him for the following week and he told me that he was looking forward to our visit! I left that workshop with tears of gratitude realizing that not all doctors were created equal and that I had been very blessed that day in finding human kindness!

The decision that I had made a long time ago of instead of feeling sorry for myself of finding a solution had paid off!

My husband was waiting downstairs in the lobby of the hotel for me and as we walked towards the parking lot to find our car, I was approached by a woman that had been at the workshop by the name of Anne Marie! She had heard me speak, grabbed my hand and said, "Also in order for you to heal you will have to let go of the anger that has been inside of you since you were 5 years old and forgive." I asked her how she knew and she simply said "Because of who I am."

She told us that she had to catch a plane back to Washington and could not take too long…I grabbed her arm and told her "Anne Marie

209

when I started on this road of healing myself, I did a lot of research… found out that I needed to let go of resentment and anger and I did."

She looked straight into my eyes and said to me "But you have not forgiven yourself."

I was stunned but had to admit that I had never thought of that!

I remember that once I started getting information in how to heal I asked God in my kitchen "Why me? Why didn't the family that I lost receive the same guidance? And why do I feel guilty that I'm still alive and they are not?"

I asked her what I needed to do and she told me to write on a piece of paper the words "I forgive you" and use aroma therapy (lavender) to repeat these words over and over until my heart and mind believed it…

Somehow, I knew that she might be able to help me further and I was very intrigued because nobody had approached me this way, so before she left, we exchanged cards and I thanked her for her advice…

When we got to the car, I looked at her card and it read "Anne Marie Healing Artist from a Healing Center in Bellevue, WA."

Since Victor had not been able to attend the workshop, I shared everything with him and he was very impressed of what I had learned! I also told him that I was amazed and very grateful of what had been given to me that day!

In one of Dr, Stanley's cassettes I had listened to what he had stated, that when you pray… sometimes you can see God working in your life! That doesn't mean that you don't do your part as well… It's almost like teamwork!

I kept my appointment with Dr.Has, he discussed with me the importance of detoxification and how it played an important role with constipation. As an example, he shared a story with me of a man that suffered from unexplained pains everywhere, once trained how to detoxify he went back to see him later and …surprisingly the pains had gone away!

He had actually written a few books about the subject and I did buy one of them, as far as treatment he wanted me to switch the Nystatin I was taking to the power form and after a while switch to Nizoral.

I took Nizoral for a couple of weeks and started to develop a sore throat... one morning after clearing my throat I spit up blood and that scarred me enough to stop the medication immediately and went back to Nystatin...

He also added on a detoxification protocol that unfortunately back-fired on me! Instead of helping, after 2 days even my knees hurt! Once again, I had to give up on another treatment that did not work!

My habit had become... if something didn't work immediately pray about it and let it go!

CHAPTER 52

The right doctor is finally found at someone's house!

I had an Endometriosis meeting that afternoon at Peg's house, the room was full of women that were dealing with endo by either switching medicines or doing surgeries after surgeries and looked way too happy about discussing their symptoms with others instead of looking for a solution!

I shared with them what I learned at the workshop in San Francisco and told them that I believed that it had to be a better way! Suddenly, a woman stood up and shared with all of us that she had found a holistic doctor in San Francisco that claimed that you could not detoxify until you healed the gut first and that made sense to me!

That's why the detoxification did not work with me the first time!

This same woman also informed all of us that this doctor also knew how to heal the leaky gut! Something I believed I had from a book that I had read from Dr. Jordan Ruben, I took immediate action and asked her for the name and phone number of the doctor in San Francisco and she gave it to me gladly...

I took the time to share with this group of women my own personal road to recovery... from changing my foods to organic, to switching medications, moderate exercise, including all of the research I had done and continued to do... and I heard Peg say to all of the women there that Endo was an incurable and a chronic condition that we all would have to deal with for the rest of our lives and that made me angry! I stood up and said to all of them "Why are all of you accepting this label of having a chronic and uncurable illness instead of pursuing a way to heal and prove this label wrong?"

They got very silent and probably thought that I was a bit "naïve" but I also shared with them how my health had changed just by making health changes that made sense instead of relying in surgeries that left you weak and not healed anyway...I vowed that day that not only would I show them all wrong but also that this would be the last meeting I would attend with them!

They preferred to brag about how many surgeries they had and how awful they felt! I stood up to leave and the husband of one of those women shook my hand on the way out and thanked me for my speech and my passion for what I believed in!

Just maybe I had stirred some doubts in these women or husbands to search for another way...

Like the Bible says, "Plant a seed and then go on."

That same week I did some research on Dr, Gabrielle Francis the holistic doctor that I was referred to on the internet and liked what I saw! I e-mailed her office to ask for an appointment, followed up with a phone call and made the appointment for the following week...

Victor and I found her on Dolores Street in San Francisco, I liked her immediatcly! She was beautiful and had a very calming personality... her office surprised me! Totally different from any doctor's office I had been in! Full of color, cushions and Indian décor and her office had a very serene atmosphere....

The place was spotless, the scent of incense was in the air and soothing music in the background...not your regular doctor's office for sure!

Once I sat down with Victor on the couch, I got my paperwork out and my medical records (all of this had been requested by her office) and I felt totally calm, something that didn't happened with any other doctor!

I had gotten totally afraid of side effects from regular medications and who could blame me that I trusted a Holistic Doctor a lot more?

She sat in front of me… introduced herself to us, asked how I was feeling and asked me to give her a list of my symptoms, she then proceeded to review all the paperwork including medical records …I was very much taken back from what she told me! She looked straight at me and asked me "I see that they found a parasite in your stool last year…. has anyone treated you for it?"

I was amazed, I hadn't even been told about it!

She told me… no problem with this one! I can treat you for it in 3 months with an alternation of treatments and then proceeded to ask me questions with an absolute assurance that left me quite impressed!

She also looked at all the medicines I was taking and actually cringed! She told me that I was taking way too many medicines and that she was going to take me off a few at the time. One in particular that amazed me was Advil!

Because of the pains I had been experiencing I had been taking this over the counter medicine for a while and according to Dr.Francis this medicine taken in excess could cause Leaky Gut! Since she suspected that I suffered from it she wanted me off it immediately and had me switch to Tylenol if I really needed it…She actually drew right in front of me a drawing of what leaky gut looked like and warned me that I would probably have to drink a healing smoothie for a long time but she wanted me to have a stool test first...

She probably felt at one point that I was interviewing her the way she was interviewing me… but I had learned to do this when discussing my health with doctors, I had also learned to write my questions on a piece of paper before going into a doctor's office… most of us because of being nervous around doctors forget what we need to ask and remember after we get home!

Before I left, she gave me the medicine for the parasite… a form to submit for a stool test, a short guide regarding foods allowed and I knew that all of this was going to make a difference in my life!

We discussed the Alaskan cruise coming up and she agreed that to treat the gut and the candida it would be after I came back, she then would have a healing protocol for me that would include a smoothie every morning and foods to also avoid…

I felt so comfortable with her that I actually shared with her that I suspected that my husband and Danny also suffered from the yeast syndrome since I also had noticed similar symptoms on them… she agreed that we might have to consider have them tested for candida in the near future…

As I prepared to leave, we joked about sharing the same birthday, she hugged me and promised me that I would be able to eat a lot better once I started to follow her protocol. I could hardly wait to come back from the cruise to start on her healing protocol she had designed just for me!

CHAPTER 53

Preparing for the Alaskan cruise and choosing the right doctor.

*T*he next weekend Sue and I got together to discuss our plans for our cruise and to design a plan to make our partnership with Melaleuca more successful. That Saturday morning while at her place I received a call from Dr. Has asking me how I was feeling... he had taken my chart home to review it! I shared with him my symptoms (in a way I was interviewing him) and not once did he mention my parasite! When I told him that I thought that I had leaky gut he told me that he could have me tested, I asked him how he planned to treat it and he said with plenty of antibiotics... Red Flag!

For me that was a No! I had done enough research on antibiotics to know that along with killing the bad bacteria they also killed the good bacteria and when you are treating the gut it doesn't make any sense...

I told him that I was going on a cruise and didn't want to make any decisions at that time but his call at that moment helped me to make the decision to follow Dr. Francis plan instead of his....

That same weekend at Sue's house we watched together a video from Dr.Andrew Weil about your own's body ability to heal and went shopping for clothes for our cruise...

After dinner we watched a girlie movie in our comfortable clothes… this for me was totally new…doing something with a girlfriend and not with my family!

I had traveled by myself all the way to Napa… went back on Sunday by myself and found a vase of flowers on my doorstep! I asked my family and friends if they had placed them there… nobody claimed that the beautiful gift was their idea! All I could think of was that maybe it was from someone that I had helped before and were expressing their gratitude…

One afternoon while Victor was watching TV, he came across a documentary regarding Dr. Lorraine Day and how she had healed the holistic way! He called me to watch the program with him, I was so taken by her that I ordered a book that she had written and tapes as well…

When days later I got her book, I couldn't put it down! She had years back been diagnosed with invasive breast cancer… had rejected standard treatments because of their harmful side effects and instead had chosen to heal herself by changing to a holistic lifestyle!

She explained something in the book that is very important for people to understand about miracles from God! I thought that just by God pointing His finger at you that you would be healed or by sending you a Healer. Most of the healing that comes from God includes you doing your part and Him working behind the scenes, sending you the people to help you... In turn you turn around and help others from what you have learned...

Step by step I took steps to help me to heal… another was to find a dentist that would be able to take the mercury fillings out of my mouth, the same day that I had found Dr.Has I also had found Dr. Gallaher D.D.S in Sunnyvale that used mostly natural products. He proved to be very knowledgeable about Candida and agreed that I would have to remove all my mercury feelings, I had not told him about my gut problems…. he surprised me by telling me that the small cyst I had on top of my gum above my front tooth was a sign of problems in the small intestine and showed me a picture he had in his office!

He also advised me to start using flaxseed and cod liver oils on my diet… We started to remove little by little the mercury from my feelings… it was scarry at first because it was like being attached to a vacuum that sucked the mercury out of your mouth! They placed googles on my eyes to protected them…

In my quest to heal I also had friends giving me comments like "Wow! you go all over the place to find doctors" Unlike other people I prayed and asked for God's guidance…. I had enough wisdom in me to be able to tell who would be good for me and who would not!

The days grew closer to finally go on this much anticipated cruise and I even got a call from Dr, Francis asking me how I felt! She informed me that she would be sending me thru the mail my healing protocol and wished me a good time in Alaska. She asked me if I would be going thru the inside passage… I told her that I would and she made a wonderful comment!

"Mary, the inside passage will be like a transition for you from illness to healing!"

The day of departure finally arrived and Victor took me to the Oakland airport to meet with Sue…she was already waiting for me! As we stepped on the plane on route to Seattle, Washington, Sue grabbed my hand and asked me if I was ok! I smiled and drew my cassette from Dr.Charles Stanley about facing your fears and listened to it as we started to climb up..

We spoke along the way, when we finally arrived at the Washington's airport, I was grinning from ear to ear… she told me that I looked like a schoolgirl! I had conquered a great fear that day!

I had the biggest rush that could not be compared to anything I had ever felt and told her so! Flying was a big one for me!

We proceeded to the Hotel we would be staying that night and immediately I called Anne Marie so that she would meet with us somewhere.

CHAPTER 54

Meeting with God's messenger and the glimpse of a beautiful ship!

We met her at her apartment and even though Sue was skeptical about this meeting I convinced her to have an open heart about it! She knew things about her that truly surprised her and then Anne Marie told me something that amazed me!

She told me that evil had entered my life but that I also had God's protection and that I had a phenomenal potential as a healer! That totally surprised me!

Sue was advised that she was not doing with her life what she was supposed to be doing and her answer was "How can I just follow my heart and drop everything?"

Anne Marie asked her "How would you like to have my job?"

She said, "I'm guided by God and most of the times I have to go to strangers, like Mary for example and give them a message whether I'm believed or not! How easy do you think that is?"

We left an hour later tired and overwhelmed by what we had heard and feeling like we had just met with a messenger from God!

The next morning, we stopped by the Hotel's buffet for breakfast... as I looked at all the selections with all my digestive problems, I knew my selection was going to be very limited! I placed a small amount of scrambled eggs and a slice of melon on my plate... Sue exclaimed in front of the couple that was also going to join us on the cruise "Is that all you are going to eat?"

I knew I would have to explain later to her that since it was very unlikely that we would see organic foods on the ship and since I was experiencing allergic reactions to just about everything I ate that chances were that she would see me eat very little on this trip...

I was embarrassed to say the least and just told her that I wasn't very hungry that morning and afraid to get sick on the ship (I actually had bought bands to wear on my wrists for seasickness) and would try eating better later...

Once we were done with breakfast, we meet outside with a group of people that were waiting for a bus to take us to the ship, once we arrived... I couldn't believe the size of the ship and how beautiful it was!

When we got inside the ship, we grabbed a brochure that had the date of the cruise -07/11 thru 07/18/2004 and took pictures together!

I forgot how I felt physically and could hardly wait to meet this wonderful man that had become like a father figure to me!

Buffets were everywhere and I wondered if I ever would be able to eat normally again! We ate a small lunch and waited to be told to go to our cabin. Once there we were like two schoolgirls admiring every-thing... just like I promised Sue a room with a beautiful verandah! It made our room look bigger and I knew the views on the way to Alaska would be magnificent!

We gathered our purses and set out to the Queen's lounge where Dr. Charles Stanley would be giving a welcome on-board speech, I saw him stroll across the stage with that familiar soft smile of his, it was all I could do to hold my tears! This felt so unreal to be near someone that I had admired so and that had changed my life so much!

Sue and I went back to our cabin to get ready for dinner and I shared with her my eating problems so that I would not get smart remarks in front of people. Once in line for dinner we met with two other ladies that just like us were traveling together and we decided to sit at the same table.

Gigi and Joan proved to be delightful dinner companions and a friendship developed right away between all four of us, we took pictures everywhere to keep all these memories alive!

Joan connected with Sue because she was also a former pilot and Gigi connected with me because our personalities were very similar and she actually came from a Portuguese background!

Since this was a table for 6 people another two people joined us, Helen a former catholic that had converted to the Christian faith and her son Jeff that was there as her companion since her husband had passed away a year before.

Our dinners together became something that we looked forward to! We used that time to share our experiences on the trip and laugh together!

Getting my sea legs was another thing! On my second day I still felt odd even though I was using my wrist bands and I missed Victor dreadfully! I wished with all my heart he was there...

I think he was feeling the same way because when I checked my cell phone, he had left 3 messages that I could not reply to because I was too far offshore to call him back! This was our first time away from each other for so long and I could hardly wait to share with him all what I had experienced so far!

The first 2 days I relied heavily on Sue because of how I felt and because this experience was too new for me... but on the 3rd day I started to venture out and decided to check out the gym on the ship, the stores and even managed to read a bit in a lounge with a great view... even though the fear was still there!

That night after dinner our new friends suggested we all go out for a stroll on deck... I was not very thrilled because the ocean was pretty rough but I was there to confront fears and off we went! The walk turned out to be a power walk and it felt wonderful to feel the sea breeze across my face! We walked until we were tired... sat in the lounge talking about our lives and the families left behind until we couldn't keep our eyes open any longer and then decided to go back to our cabins...

The next morning, we would be arriving at our first port Juneau, for some reason I woke up at 5.30am that morning completely rested and as much as I tried… I couldn't go back to sleep! I felt like something or someone was pushing me to go to the verandah! I tiptoed across the room not to wake up Sue… opened the curtains and I was met with the most magnificent sunrise I had ever seen! The ocean was like glass, reflecting back millions of stars from the rays of the sun…and I was taken back from such beauty!

Tears fell from my eyes from the beauty I was witnessing and I couldn't keep it to myself! I woke up Sue that was upset of being waken up so early and then forgot to be upset and instead took pictures of the great sunrise we had in front of our eyes!!

Maybe someone was reminding me to also enjoy the journey along the way…

CHAPTER 55

Making stops here and there and a meeting much waited for…

Once we docked in Juneau, Sue and I went to see a Glazier that was breathtaking and a salmon cannery, in the observatory I was finally able to call Victor and I could tell that he missed me as much as I missed him!

He made me feel wonderful by giving me his love and support to finish this trip and told me that he understood my motives for taking the trip with Sue.

Our next stop that afternoon we were scheduled to go on an excursion to Sitka, so we had time to sit and read in our verandah while watching seaplanes go by… we both marveled how at peace we felt that afternoon!

Later while in Sitka we got to see a marvelous performance by Russian dancers that was amazing! We saw a place where eagles were kept after being injured…. even managed to do some shopping for souvenirs!

Next day it would be Ketchikan! This little town was full of little shops everywhere… we strolled around town and took pictures whiling enjoying the beautiful weather!

There were times that I felt like pinching myself to believe that this was really me in Alaska!

Physically I wasn't feeling well… one day when I got out of the shower, I looked down at my stomach and it was yellow! I knew it was from taking too much Nystatin! I knew once I went back home I would have to hurry up and start on the healing protocol Dr.Francis had designed for me and I could hardly wait!

I finally meet Dr, Stanley and even managed to shake his hand while he was signing his newest book! He was surrounded by his staff but I managed to thank him for making such a difference in my life, when he shook my hand, he held on to it and asked me if the bands were actually helping me! I told him yes… I could tell he was having problems with his eyes and I had the strangest impulse to place my hands over his eyes as if I could heal him!

I could tell that Sue was impressed with him as well and I managed to thank someone that needed to know that his program was helping people just like me!

While working out a bit on the gym I got to meet another man that I admired and that had also made a difference in my life, Dr. Jordan looked healthy and wonderful after 10 years of being cured! I shook his hand to thank him for the knowledge I had acquired thru his book, he was gracious, kind and hoped that just like him I would find my way with God's help to finally heal!

Our last stop would be British Columbia and I loved this city on site!

The marina where we docked was beautiful and we had a double decker bus waiting for us to take us to the Bouchard Gardens.

Our bus driver had a wonderful accent and a wicked sense of humor! I joked with Sue that he actually looked like Robert Redford!

From our windows we could see flowerpots hanging from every establishment and the light posts were different and beautiful! I imagined what they would be like at nighttime!

Getting to the Bouchard Gardens proved to be extremely difficult because of the heavy traffic and our bus driver decided to take the back streets, Sue and I had decided to go up to the highest level of the bus, we were hanging tight while our bus driver was driving thru curves (it almost seemed like a Disney movie) …while driving he kept us entertained and explained that we needed to get there on time to be able to see the gardens and to experience a magnificent fireworks display!

When we finally arrived almost at nighttime all we had time to do was to see a few layouts of the most beautiful flowers I had ever seen and get ready for the fireworks display...

For me the fireworks display was like the icing on the cake!

We all sat on the grass while the display of the most beautiful fireworks I had ever seen took place right in front of my eyes! There were dancing cups and saucers, people, animals and also the ones that shoot out all the way to the sky!

This was a beautiful ending to what turned out to be a very inspirational and wonderful journey!

Sue and I didn't want to end this trip but unfortunately, we both had to go back to work the following week! The next day we would be arriving in Seattle and from there we would be flying back to Oakland.

Traveling to Alaska had left both of us with a desire to travel more and to experience the peace and happiness we both had experienced! When I spoke to Sue on the phone one day about how much we both missed Alaska we both agreed that our consolation was that in 3 weeks' time we would be taking off again to Salt Lake City, Utah to attend a Melaleuca Convention!

Chapter 56

Another fear is conquered and another trip is scheduled!

his time we would be taking a smaller plane of only 50 people! I did experience that oh so familiar feeling of fear on a smaller scale! I reminded myself of where I had been and did not want fear to be a roadblock in my life!

I started the protocol that Dr. Francis had designed for me, starting with the treatment of the parasite and I was starting to feel better… little by little.

Once we got to the Hotel, they could not find our reservation! They found out that our reservation had been done beforehand and misplaced so they had no choice but to place us on the 18th floor, the Executive Suite of all places!

The view was spectacular and our beds were wonderful!

I was very different from my family because everywhere I went I always found a way to take care of myself, I knew that how I felt physically affected me in every way and I had much to learn on this trip…

At the hotel that night I had the chance to experience the dry sauna, I had pains everywhere and decided to ask Sue if she wanted to join me and her answer to me was "You got to be kidding! I will not go to a place where I cannot breathe… you better be careful!"

I went downstairs without her and enjoyed the dry sauna for a while… took a shower and was amazed that the pains were gone and I was able to get a good night sleep!

We attended workshops together the 4 days we were there and even managed to take walks, find good places to eat and enjoyed meeting new people…

I liked Salt Lake City quite a lot! A very spiritual city! Sue and I passed by a Mormon Temple… I wondered what kind of services they held!

We did manage to see a lot of Melaleuca products and had a wonderful catered dinner at the end… I didn't know if I could ever become as successful as some of them had managed to become but I also had agreed to take this trip to please Sue since she had agreed to come with me to Alaska. I loved their products but I was so very skeptical about making Melaleuca my first priority in my life since my healing would have to come first…

The highlight of this trip was to hear Scott Hamilton speak at the convention and his speech moved me to tears!

He not only shared his ups and downs in the Ice-Skating business but also his battle with testicular cancer! He felt that his life had been a series of curses and blessings! He even spoke about his mother's battle with cancer! I felt for him but I also knew that in my family a lot of what had happened could have been prevented if they took better care of themselves...

Sue asked me before we were set to leave Salt Lake City to go with her to visit a Mormon couple she knew in Spanish Fork and of course I agreed…

I was glad I had a chance to meet them, Steve and Kim were trying to raise two kids while dealing with her illness, she had been diagnosed with Epstein Barr and their little girl suffered from Gerd!

Steve and I connected spiritually in a big way, just like me he had always felt different from everyone else and alone in this world! It was like talking to a long-lost brother and I knew I had to help them in any way I could! We started by discussing their food choices and I realized that their food choices were not helping them or their little girl...

Inside our rented car I had the book that I had bought on the ship from Dr,Jordan, he signed it but I didn't have the time to read it so I gave it to Kim. I shared with her my own digestive problems that had improved quite a bit just by switching to organic foods, the Maker's Diet from Dr. Jordan had all kinds of excellent information that would benefit both mother and daughter.

Kim also suffered from severe digestive problems was still breast-feeding her little girl and I had the feeling that whatever Kim was eating was not agreeing with her little girl and was perpetuating her problems with Gerd. I gave her good advice "Kim, you have nothing to lose, this change could benefit you both!" Kim and Steve agreed to read the book and to make the necessary food changes for both mother and daughter...

When we left, I felt that somehow God had meant for me to be there and Sue was a witness how you can be used as a vessel or a messenger for God... just like Anne Marie!

It felt wonderful to be able to help someone without expecting "Nothing"in return!

Chapter 57

Receiving instruction that finally made a difference!

Once again back at home I had a call from Dr. Francis office, she wanted to discuss my treatments…she was appalled at the amount of Nystatin I was taking to survive! She wanted me to get me off it little by little because in the long run it was making the leaky gut worse, I was also on a low blood pressure medication that she wanted me to give up as soon as my health improved…

Unfortunately, when constipation exists the blood pressure as the tendency to go up… I knew because I checked my blood pressure when I was constipated versus when I had great bowel movements and there was a big difference…

Everything is connected to the gut… if the intestines don't function correctly, it can affect every part of your body, it can produce toxicity in your body and make you look older and tired!

I got off the Nystatin and followed her instructions to the letter! Little by little I started to see the changes, no more nose bleeds, my eyelashes and nails were growing back up and the fat around my waist that I had been carrying even after losing 70 pounds started to diminish along with water retention!

Even more amazing was that the pains that I had been suffering down my right leg were going away with the treatment for the parasite!

Thru Dr, Francis I was given a great education regarding what foods to eat and what to avoid and where to look for groceries at a reasonable price, the first time Victor and I shopped at Wholefoods… I looked around and saw the amount of organic foods that I would be able to eat without side effects and started to cry! Victor turned around and asked me "Why are you crying?" I looked at him and said, "Now I know that I don't have to go hungry again and that I will be able to eat a variety of foods." He smiled… for him this was not important but for me was a turning point for the better!

One of the things I noticed after I switched to just about everything organic was that I was looking younger and so did other people around me!

I also had Victor tested for yeast by Dr, Has office before I had given up on this doctor and it came back positive! That meant that he also should be treated but after seeing what regular medicines had done to my body he wanted to try to heal the holistic way, I worried about him! He was not committed like I was… had a lot of friends that were not a good influence and loved Portuguese food…

Physically he was a mess!

He had found out thru his regular doctor that he had bulging disks in his neck, carpal tunnel in both wrists, problems with his back and suffered pain in his right knee! I had read so much at this point that I also knew that a lot of his problems could well be related to the yeast imbalance because he also suffered from bloating and digestive problems. Unfortunately, he blamed everything on arthritis and he was very stubborn! I prayed for him to listen to me so that he could also have a better life…

It did not help that our financial problems were getting worse every month because of all the medical expenses! Most of the doctors that I had to see I had to pay out of pocket… also pay for the herbs and the smoothie that I was now taking… but when it comes to your life money should be the last thing you should worry about…

I had to explain to Victor many times when he asked me how long it would take me to heal that when treating yourself the holistic way it could take a lot longer but in the long run the cure was worth it… it was not like regular medicine that most of the time just gave you side effects instead of allowing you to heal…I had experienced that myself!

For the first time in our lives, we had to take a loan against our house in San Pablo and it was one of the most difficult decisions we had to make! We could not live tight the way we had before and Victor also wanted to be treated by Dr, Francis.

Not all men are created equal! Victor was the type of guy that loved discussing issues before going to sleep at night or start an argument, this was something I hadn't seen my parents do and could keep you from sleeping! I flat out refused to discuss anything that was negative at bedtime and after a while he learned to respect my wishes…

It was a different story while eating out…he loved to discuss everything that he had on his mind! Something changed when I first started to get sick, we would be waiting for our food to arrive, and he would blab away without giving me a chance to speak and many times, I found myself so exasperated that I would give up on speaking…that's when I found out that as a woman, I was losing my voice in this relationship!

CHAPTER 58

Finding a good church that felt like a home....

*J*decided to look for a Christian church and find out for myself
if I belonged there or not... Danny and I started to seek a few
Christian churches and a couple we found did not meet our expecta-
tions, so we simply left and kept on searching...

Besides Dr. Stanley I had found another minister by the name of
Joel Osteen that help me in my spiritual growth... this young man had
the power to make anyone believe in himself and on my worse days he
was the one that had the power to bring me up!

It seemed that just about anyone that I had a connection with was
Christian! One of them was Peg from the Endometriosis group that
happen to call me one day to ask how I was doing! Of course, I was
honest with her... she had taken a different path to heal but understood
my motives, when I shared with her that I was looking for a Christian
church she invited me and Danny to join them the following Sunday
and I accepted...

Danny and I entered the church that was full of people and immediately we were greeted very graciously, the pastor at this church had
the same demeanor that Dr, Charles Stanley had... and I felt at home
for the first time in a long time!

When I finally shook his hand and introduced myself to him, I asked him how to read the Bible so that I could understand it and enjoy it, he gave me the name of an easy Bible to understand… I ended up buying a New Living Translation Bible with large print that made reading a pleasure for me!

I felt sorry for Victor because he was seeing a new me that he did not like! He wanted the old Mary back… but the old Mary could not go back! He also wanted me to perform in bed the same way I had before but now I could not! I actually asked God one day out loud in my room what was permissible in the bedroom!

Now I was not trying to please my husband only but God himself because I knew I owed Him my life…something that only I believed in….

The type of sex Victor wanted from me…now made me feel dirty!

He also did not like my new independence and confidence and he was not the only one! Even some friends of mine had a hard time accepting the new me but the true friends stayed to see me heal…

I kept praying to God to also help Victor heal physically as well as spiritually because I did not want to lose my husband, my marriage was important to me and to my children! I spoke to God as if I was speaking to a good loving father and would remind Him that Victor had been there for me thru the bad times, had not deserted me or his children and that he did have a good heart…

I constantly had to reassure him on everything, even with my writing! I was keeping track on my computer of all the data and research I had done… the events and experiences in case one day I decided to write a book about it…he happened to see me writing and said "I wish I could be as smart as you!" I turned around grabbed his hands in mine and told him "Victor! God gives each one of us different gifts, look how you learned how to remodel our home and even learned how to build an Avery and raise birds! This is something I could not do!" I actually made him smile that day!

I also found out that Peg held weekly Bible meetings and started to attend them on a regular basis…. I wanted to learn with other people how to understand the Bible and found good loving people that welcomed anyone!

At work it was a different matter!

I had always been like a chameleon! I was able to adjust to different environments, different attitudes and different situations very easily... but also knew how to avoid discussing certain issues like religion and healthy habits with people that could take it the wrong way…

If I succumbed to temptation by eating the wrong foods to appease them, I ended up paying for it physically and mentally! I did worry that they would think that I was obsessed with losing weight and found a way to explain my healthy eating by telling people that I had food allergies… it didn't help that I now had a good figure, so some believed me… some did not!

What they didn't know was that I would love to eat what they ate! Sometimes I would sit at these functions, smell the aromas from the food, see the beautiful desserts and avoid them! I brought my own salad along and from the food selection in front of me I choose foods that I would not react to!

I got my courage and determination from reading books that would inspire me and prayed that people would not judge me but instead accepted the new person that I was becoming! In a way my heart was the same as before I just had to change to heal and not everyone was able to accept that! Only someone that had been in your shoes could understand your motives for changing…

As for my family they had no other alternative but to watch me in the process!

I now had been in a treatment for the leaky gut and candida for 3 and half months, had the mercury taken from my feelings (so had Victor) and knew that I had not gotten rid of all of it…. I did feel a lot better and looked a lot healthier but every time that my husband and I had intercourse my symptoms returned! For the first time in our married life, I asked my husband to use a condom at least until I healed!

He did not like using condoms (probably never did thru out his lifetime) but he agreed and then the stupid thing would either come off or break and I would run to the bathroom in tears to wash myself in fear of getting the symptoms back!

He also refused to buy the condoms, so I was the one buying them!

Little did he know that I did not like the condoms either! I had every intention later on after both of us healed of giving them up…

This was a constant struggle with us because my husband was the type of guy that only felt like a man if he performed well in bed… but I refused to go backwards and jeopardize my health!

Dr. Francis had advised me to join a local gym to use a steam room to detoxify and I also kept my membership at Curves for a while which turned out to be a good thing! We were notified that they had an upcoming video from Dr. K Steven Whiting about woman's health coming up the following Tuesday, the title of the video was "Women Cheating Death." The discussion would be about heart disease, diabetes and candida and that caught my attention!

My husband had tried to have me cancel the membership at Curves but something kept me from doing it (intuition maybe) and ended up receiving extremely important information that would be essential for our healing!

The following Tuesday night I was there with my eyes glued to the screen!

CHAPTER 59

A video that would reveal much needed information!

To anybody else the information that I received that night would have scared anyone but for me it became my glimmer of hope! Dr. Whiting explained on the video that candida takes root in many parts of the body that simple meds cannot reach and that by using a combination of Aloe Vera, Noni Juice and liquid oxygen can you eliminate the candida! He went on to explain that this combination localizes candidiasis and kills it even if the disease has become systemic and has spread to other parts of the body, like stomach, lungs, brain, etc... With systemic conditions the treatment would have to be repeated...

All along I had tried to tell doctors that I had felt that this illness had spread to other parts of my body and had been ignored!

I could hardly wait to tell Victor about what I had learned that night and went home with a bottle of the Oxy Aloe under my arm to start the next morning on an empty stomach...

I also read the booklet that I received from Dr, Whiting regarding systemic candidiasis "Eliminating Yeast Infections & Systemic Candidiasis" and found out that chances are that if you have it so could your husband and family as well! …imagine that!

My suspicion was that both my boys had it as well and that meant that both would have to be tested!

My youngest had problems concentrating in school, food cravings, mood swings, heartburn and unexplained rashes on his back and chest… these symptoms would become aggravated after he splurged on foods that were not good for him…

Carlos at a younger age also had allergies even with certain detergents that I used to wash their clothes with…I had to keep on switching products until I was able to find one that would not bring out rashes in his body….

It was hard enough to explain this knowledge to my children but even harder to convince them to take the stool test! They refused to do it so I had to convince them to have the bowel movement and then I would the test and ship it out…. it takes love to be able to do a stool test for someone and I had plenty of it!

The owner of Curves also shared with me that she had suffered from constipation for years and that the only thing that had helped her was drinking Herbal Aloe, I happened to come across that product at my girlfriend's beauty shop one day and bought it…

I used the combination of both Aloe's (3 doses of each) and both the candida and the constipation improved dramatically!

As soon as I saw that this was working, I contacted Herbal Answers the company that dispensed the Herbal Aloe and started an account of my own…

I liked that this potent tonic worked not only for candida but for diabetes, cancer, asthma, blood pressure and other illnesses…

At that time, I saw everything that came my way in a form of healing as a gift from God and I thanked Him immediately!

It was hard to convince my family that these holistic treatments would work and even less to have them believe what the tests revealed!

They had seen firsthand the research I had done and my total commitment to a cure but my husband first and foremost concern was the cost of everything and how long before you see a cure. This made it very hard for me because I didn't doubt that I was being guided to a cure and prayed that they too would be healed…

Victor believed that his health problems were too serious to be healed the holistic way… but I was determined to prove him wrong!

Every time that doubt was there because of my husband's negativity I would pray… God would always find a way to bring someone along that would restore my faith and keep me going…

When I prayed, I prayed on my knees… almost like in a trance and felt like God was telling me now that you know me very well it's time for you to get closer to my Son! What I knew about Jesus Christ was what I had learned from my mother but now I was introduced to Him at Church weekly… they used clips of movies to have us see how He had changed the world and I was captivated!

It was not easy from my attention to switch from God to His Son because I was very attached to God… but I learned to study his life and I was intrigued enough to pursue this relationship… I would get on my knees by a cross I had above my bed and would pray for me and for my family…

Chapter 60

A transformation
that was hard to accept…

ible study also became a habit with me and I loved going to church… this was hard to accept by Victor that was now seeing a very different spiritual Mary! He actually at one point thought that I must have a crush on someone at church! Little did he know that I just wanted him to change with me so that all of us could heal and introduce him to very decent people!

It didn't help that I was now 80 pounds lighter, had a small waist and glowed of good health! This was intimidating enough not speaking of all the complements I got from our friends made in front of him!

The difference in me was so big from the picture they had taken of me at Six Flags in Vallejo that at the gym, the manager of the 24hr Fitness Club asked me for a recent picture of me and a short story how I had lost the weight to be placed on one of their boards as members went by! At first, I didn't want to but then I thought that this would be a great way to inspire people! I managed to place a picture of a before and after picture of me with a story attached and gave it to the manager, I was very surprised how many people came to me to congratulate me or ask for advice!

Who was not taking my advice was my own husband, he tried to follow the diet and protocol that had been given to us to please me not because he believed in it… He cheated on his diet frequently and because of his problems with his back he couldn't exercise the way I did but even so his health had improved! He still had lapses of memory that only I could tell! He would get frustrated when he tried to perform sexually with a condom for our protection and then could not perform… It didn't matter to him that I also had lost my sexual drive, not only because of some of the treatments I had been given but also because I had become scared of having intercourse with him. However, I was determined to find a way to heal us both so that our sex life would improve, I made sacrifices that not everyone would have done… I got up at 5AM each morning to prepare my lunch for work and also to follow the protocol that had been given to me by Dr.Francis… there were days that I would feel overwhelmed and would have to remind myself how far I had come!

Unfortunately, most men are very impatient when dealing with illnesses! They expect quick results after years of mistreating their bodies, it takes time to undo all the damage…

We as spouses or family are also responsible for turning a blind eye when we see someone not taking care of themselves or in a bad situation and keep silent! After we bring it up it's then up to them if they do something about it!

Example of this was the unfortunate suicide of a young man that was the son of a Portuguese couple my parents were friends of…. they raised him being afraid of commitment with a woman…. even stopped him from getting a car (too expensive) … in the long run after they passed away, he became a loner, got addicted to drugs and killed himself in their own home!

We as parents are very responsible for what is said or unsaid to our kids…a life of isolation can very well lead to suicide or even violence against others!

I found on my own that on helping someone you also must watch out for yourself and turn a blind eye if your safety is at risk…I encountered a situation in Berkeley one day while shopping that left me debating if I should interfere or not!

As I was getting out of my car, I saw a couple arguing furiously… at one point, the man seemed about to strike her and I stood there for a minute debating whether or not to interfere…. but I was also afraid for my safety since the guy was pretty big! I was very relieved when another man approached the couple and told him that if he didn't stop the verbal abuse… he was going to call the police….

Thank God! The guy stopped the abuse and actually left!

At home my advice was always there for my family as my mother had done with all of us…

On his best days, Victor would thank me for being strong and persistent and on his worse days, everything would get on his nerves… me, the kids, the house and he would blame us for all his stress! His solution for stress was to take off to spend the day with his friends and would end up in a Portuguese club somewhere eating what he desired and playing cards!

Danny and I ended up spending a lot of time alone together… most of the times when I tried to contact my husband by phone, he was not available and my worry was that he was jeopardizing his treatment …

When we met his nights out with his friends that he had insisted on was one night a week… now they had turned into 3 nights a week! I found myself resentful that I was handling my illness, working, taking care of all our needs on my own and found myself sometimes exhausted physically and mentally! There were times I longed to have someone place their loving arms around me and take care of me instead of me having to take care of everyone!

I found myself asking "Why do I need a husband! If I end up doing everything by myself and I'm always alone?" Then I would remind myself that the kids loved their father and that we had many years invested in this relationship to give it up ….

One day at lunch time at work I went to look around at the shops at the San Carlos marketplace and found a shop that intrigued me that sold inspirational books, plaques, pictures and calendars. I found a particular calendar that drew my attention with Jesus Christ picture on in… it said, "Peace, I leave you, peace I give you." When I looked directly at His eyes it was like He was giving me the peace that I so much needed in my life! I bought the calendar and brought it home…it became my most precious possession…

I knew that if I didn't place pressure on my family to eat correctly, to drink the smoothies I made for them and drink the Aloe they would have given up a long time ago!

By the time Victor and Danny started on the second treatment I had the results for my oldest son and he tested for candida as well! His test came back positive with a picture of a parasite! I was extremely upset because I knew I would have a hard time convincing him that he needed to be treated and I was right! He started the treatment… but it was short lived (even after I showed him the pictures), he would not commit to the treatment because unfortunately Carlos loved junk food and was probably too young to understand how serious this illness could become…

It's like the old saying goes, "You can lead a horse to water but you cannot make him drink it!"

I would get extremely frustrated with Victor and the kids as they questioned me about everything! They would forget to take the Aloe on an empty stomach like we had been advised, they would jeopardize their diet and then question me why it was taking so long to heal!

I prayed for God to help me with my family so that they healed as well not just me! I knew that God worked behind the scenes, so I kept on fighting and praying for all our sakes!

I remembered one of my mother's sayings "O ultimo a rir e que se ri melhor ." The last one to laugh laughs the hardest! I truly believed that one day I would be able to show them all who had been right all along!

CHAPTER 61

Trying to save a marriage.

*V*ictor on the other hand had become sexually frustrated because he didn't want to use condoms even for a short little while until we got better, he became a very resentful and angry man and would stay by himself in his little living room downstairs. He would take care of his birds (canaries), speak to his friends on the phone and pretty much ignored his family! I sat in the living room upstairs by myself… many times would go and ask him to join me so that he could see a show with me on TV and he would always give me a lame excuse not to join me….

We were sharing the same bed but pretty much living like strangers!

He would come home at 1 or 2 AM in the morning and when I would question him about it… he would refuse to talk to me and go to sleep. I became very scared for our marriage and when I shared that with him, he acted like I was the one responsible for what was happening to our marriage! I would try to convince him to go out with me and he would refuse! He would get all dressed up and leave to go out with his friends, making the comment that he could not handle the stress in our house!

On the other hand, I refused to give up on my marriage and arranged for a weekend trip to Lake Tahoe for both of us that turned into a complete fiasco!

I had made plans for us to go to a Resort to get pampered and unfortunately by the time we got there because of the traffic we lost our appointment! I immediately turned around and told him "This is not totally lost Victor, we both love Lake Tahoe, let's stay at our motel, go gambling, eat out, go sightseeing, etc... What do you think?"

His response was "I'm not in the mood, let's go back home." I drove us back home and in the 3 hours that it took us to get home I got nothing but insults from him! He finally shared with me all that he was resentful for... even the years we had been spending together and blamed all the stress he had on our family! By the time I got home I went straight into my room and burst into tears and spoke to my mother's picture. "You were wrong Mom in saying that my husband loved me immensely! All I could see in his eyes today was resentment...not love!"

Victor had also applied for disability because of damage to his shoulder (from work) and was waiting for a good sum of money... One Friday after he left for San Jose to spend time with his buddies, I checked the mail and found a check for him, I knew he had been waiting for this check and I was extremely happy for him! So, I called him and told him that I wanted to take him out to dinner at Sousa's restaurant, he didn't want to go but I insisted and told him "I will drive to the club myself so that we can have dinner together and drive back home. I have something important to show you." He finally agreed! I told the kids I was meeting their dad for dinner and left... When I got to the Portuguese club, I entered the building and asked up front for him...

The guy that met with me at the door was one of his friends and when we reached him by the bar he said to Victor "So, this is your wife! Wow! She is a beautiful woman! You are a very lucky man!" He said thank you, grabbed my hand and we proceeded to his car to go have dinner, when we got to the restaurant, I took a minute to enjoy it... this Portuguese restaurant always had the best foods, we knew the chef and the ambiance was awesome! I listened for a minute to the fado (Portuguese traditional song) and when he asked me what was so important that it couldn't wait until he got home, I took the check out and gave it to him and said, "I wanted to give you something that would make you happy." He looked at it and said "Wow, it finally got here!" He placed it in his pocket, we had our meal together and not even a "Thank you!" not even a smile my way! We finished our meal in silence and drove back to the club… I got in my car and drove back home completely disappointed!

Our anniversary was coming up and refusing on giving up on a man that I still loved I planned a trip for both of us to Hawaii, I had a friend mine loan us a place in Maui and even rented us a car! I paid for everything on my own and told him to get prepared and to buy luggage because I was taking him on a surprise trip. He out right told me that he didn't want to leave the country because his knee was bothering him! I finally had to tell him that this was our anniversary trip to Hawaii and to finally have the honeymoon we never had together… but he refused to budge! In the end I had to cancel everything and lost all the money I had paid for this trip! I was devastated that he wouldn't even try!

I gave up temporarily and concentrated on working together with a team of people that were working on a Christmas party for our company, because we were doing so well they had booked it at a Hotel in San Carlos! I had volunteered to help put it together with my friend Beth and we all set out to look for the perfect outfit. I found mine and asked Victor to come with me to the Men's Warehouse to look for a suit for him… this turned out to be a nightmare! He argued with me over how much it would cost us, that he didn't want to wear a tie, etc… I almost had to plead with him to do this for me, told him that all my friends would be there and that this was something that I had helped put together… we finally got out of there with a suit and a tie!

The night of the party we had Danny take our picture together and drove to San Carlos, the place was beautifully decorated and we booked a room with a discount for the night. We greeted our friends and danced a bit… but I could tell that Victor's mind was elsewhere! He kept on complaining about his back and checking his cell phone… I had hoped to bring us back together but instead he called it a night much too soon and said that he was going up to our room to rest his back.

I stayed behind to say good night to my friends and saw only pity in their eyes! Once I got to our room, he had just gotten off the phone with someone but would not tell me who it was.... I looked at him laying next to me without making a move in my direction and I knew something was very wrong! He was definitely hiding something from me!

We went back home the next morning and all I got was the silent treatment...

I had experienced this distance from him before when we had attended Portuguese functions and had noticed the same look of pity that come my way from our friends at these places… Sometimes I wondered if they knew something I didn't!

CHAPTER 62

Dealing with suspicion and Betrayal!

*H*e had developed a friendship with a Mexican guy that also raised birds and of all things to bring home he brought a parrot that my kids and I didn't care for… he would squawk continually… besides being loud he made me very nervous! Many times, I asked Victor to get rid of him, instead he kept on pressuring me to hold him…of course I refused!

He also received a suspicious call one morning when we went out for a walk while driving back… I looked at him and he was biting his lower lip and told whoever was on the phone that he would call him back! I could tell he was nervous and when I asked him who that was… he just told me "Just a friend of mine, I will call him back later."

My friends at work kept noticing my depression and sadness and opened my eyes! They told me to pay attention to what he was doing… He had bought new clothes, was wearing cologne and even wearing an earring! Also, when I tried to contact him on the phone… he was never available…

In short… they suspected he had a girlfriend on the side! I was not prepared for this because I finally had learned to trust him!

My boss and friend convinced me to hire a private detective to have him followed and I agreed, I also paid for him to keep track of his phone calls and learned from the detective how to keep track of the calls myself! He followed him to a night club that he and a friend of his attended (pretending to be at a Portuguese club), unfortunately he was not able to get the pictures that I wanted because they changed their minds! I desperately wanted evidence that he was cheating… otherwise I refused to leave him.

When I finally got a call from his Mexican friend to inform me that Victor had been cheating on me for over a year… I was not surprised but was extremely angry that he had been blaming me for his unhappiness while all along he had been having an affair!

This guy also had something else in mind on calling me! He wanted to take me out and I almost laughed at him! What a time to ask this of a woman!

I hung up the phone…headed for the bathroom and got sick! I asked Danny to go to the gym with me because I needed to get my emotions under control before I saw my husband again! Danny sensed that something was wrong because he heard the phone ring…. I refused to tell him anything about his father until I knew for certain that what I had just heard was correct so instead I made up a story about a friend of mine being in trouble. I worked out like crazy and by the time I used the steam and went to take a shower the tears finally came out! When I left to go home, I was much calmer and able to handle anything that came my way!

He was not home when we got there and I was not able to sleep that night! I kept thinking about what she looked like and the word betrayal kept on ringing in my ears!

The next morning, Victor sensed something was wrong and kept on asking me what was wrong! I was not ready to discuss his betrayal yet … that afternoon I had a consultation with Dr, Francis in San Francisco and didn't want to drive there upset… He wanted to drive me but I refused! I needed the time alone….

When I got to Dr. Francis's office, she could tell by my face that I was upset about something… She gave me an Acupuncture treatment with Aroma Therapy discussed my treatments and we finally discussed my marriage, this time as woman to woman! This discussion turned out to be very important! She convinced me to confront him otherwise I would have no peace. I had learned to respect and trust this wonderful woman that had become more than just my doctor...

When I got home, I was surprised he was there... like he sensed something was wrong! I asked him to take me out to dinner so that we could talk and he agreed. He sat across from me and as I looked at his hands across the table I thought "Those hands that you used to caress my body have now been caressing another woman's body and those lips that used to kiss mine have been kissing another woman's lips and I cannot bare it!"

I had been with this man since I was 15 years old! He had become more than just my husband, he had been my confidant, my friend and my lover and now a total stranger to me!

When I finally looked straight at his eyes and told him that I knew about the affair he tried to deny it but once I told him that his friend had called me to tell me he got silent! I told him that I had actually hired a private detective before his friend's call and then he had no choice but to admit it…...He didn't act like he was sorry and resentment towards me was all over his face!

It was all I could do to keep my meal down and when we finally left the restaurant there was nothing but silence between us! Now I knew why every time his friend had called him before he had always acted nervous!

When we got home, I stopped by the kitchen to get me some tea, he stopped by to give me a brief apology without looking like he was remorseful for what he had done and left me with the difficult task of having to share this information with my sons! I now understood why he didn't want to go on trips with me….

I asked my sons to meet me in the living room and was amazed that they were not surprised! They both suspected all along that their father had another woman on the side, especially Danny! Now I knew why weeks prior he had come to my room to asked me "Mom, supposed you found out that dad was cheating on you, would you forgive him?" At the time I told him that was a very difficult question to answer because I loved him... but I also knew that this was not something a woman should accept especially because this was a bad example for children to witness…

My sons loved us both and whatever decision we came up with they would accept it, of my two sons Danny was the angriest because he had witnessed how much I had tried to work on my marriage and how lonely I was...

Victor did not come to me and tell me the affair was over and that left me thinking that he had feelings for the other woman… after dedicating over 30 years of my life to one single man that made me angry and sad!

I went to work the next Monday morning full of pain and sorrow and prayed for peace in my heart because I couldn't even concentrate on my work! While working that afternoon I got this feeling that I should leave and go home! My boss and friend (the one that had convinced me to hire the private detective) agreed that I should trust my intuition and go...

Driving thru the San Mateo bridge on the way home I prayed that if Victor was planning to leave that I was not too late to stop him...

When I got home, he was still there! I asked him to come and talk to me in the car so that we could have privacy and he agreed, I asked him what he had been planning to do and he told me that he was preparing to leave before I got home! I asked him why he didn't even want to wait until we could talk before he made that decision and found out that the same friend that called me to tell me of his affair was also feeding him all kinds of lies about me… adding fuel to the fire! Probably thinking that once our marriage was over he could come after me! I also shared with my husband the conversation I had with his friend on the day that I had found out about his affair and he was amazed!

This time Victor was honest with me! He confessed about the double life he was living! The other woman, the night clubs, the friends that were not good for him and when I looked at him, he actually had tears in his eyes!

CHAPTER 63

Giving someone you love a second chance.

That night we kissed and made love like before without protection, I was still worried about us contaminating each other with candida back and forth. I also knew that I was taking a risk of infecting myself with something else he might have gotten from another woman… but I loved him enough to give us another chance, I also needed to prove to him that I had never stopped loving him and just wanted desperately for both of us to heal….

The next morning the symptoms were back along with vaginal burning! I was afraid to ask him to be patient and give me time to heal before we were intimate this way when there was another woman out there willing to do whatever he asked…. He knew me well enough to know when I was worried about something and he insisted on finding out! I told him what was on my mind and he agreed to be patient…. I was doubtful but after all he had placed his hands on the Bible for me to show me that he was serious!

I asked him to prove to me that he was serious about his decision to make our marriage work, to take me to meet this woman he had the affair with and to let me talk to her. I was adamant about this, so he agreed. He took me to the Blue Pheasant the night club he had met her… I was very surprised that she was a brunette and she was just as surprised that I was there!

I asked her to sit with me on a nearby table and shared with her the fact that Victor and I had been married for over 30 years… something she said she didn't know about! When I asked her if she wanted to see the pictures of our kids, she flat out refused to see them! I told her that Victor and I were planning to make our marriage work and she told me that she had been thru a situation like this before and that second chances never worked…

I had another motive for meeting her (something Victor didn't know) and that was to do something he should have taken responsibility for… to inform her that he had candida and that she might end up one day with the symptoms as well. I told her about my own struggle with this illness, that he didn't believe in using protection and left in her hand a booklet from Dr, Whiting for her to review… I then left to join Victor on the dance floor...

After a short break he left to go to the bathroom and when I looked up, he had gone to the bar instead! Has he passed by her he caressed her leg and smiled at her! At that precise moment I knew this affair was not over!

We danced for a while but I didn't tell him about what I had seen! However, it made me suspicious that our relationship would never be the same...

I went back to work the following Monday and when my friends questioned me about our marriage, I told them that I was willing to give him another chance... but they told me that I was a fool and to watch him closely...

Something kept nagging at me and that was the fact that I could not get a hold of him on the phone and when I spoke to him directly… he could not meet my eyes! I had learned that truthful people are always able to meet you eye to eye when carrying conversations…

Something really strange also happened at work! I tried to call him and when he answered the phone, he was carrying a conversation with her on the other end and called her "Babe" … for some reason he didn't know that I was on the line as well! I hung up before he could tell that I had heard him…

The next day I cornered him in our bedroom and made him sit down in our bed, I looked at him in the eyes and said "Victor, have you looked at yourself in the mirror lately? You don't look the same, it's like you have this evil look in your eyes… when I try to talk to you about anything you can't even look at me in the eyes!" He looked at me sarcastically, smiled and started instead to defend himself by pointing the finger at me!

I suspected that when I had decided to trust God in taking care of me, He also had opened my spiritual eyes! I was now able to see and understand many things that I had not before, something that could not be explained to everyone! To any other person the only way you could explain it is by calling it "intuition."

He actually blamed me for the affair …for not being the same Mary as before and the attitude was back again! I decided to let go for now…

When I shared this with my friends we came up with a plan! One of them was to contact the detective one more time and find out how to get to his phone log…. Once I found out how to look for different phone numbers by going thru our phone bill… finding her number was easy and I found out that he was calling her on a daily basis…I also found out where she lived and convinced Danny to go with me, I parked in front of her apartment complex waiting to see my husband go up and then catch them together… I explained to Danny that this was the only way for me to convince myself that he was still having the affair and he agreed to wait with me…After a couple of hours we found a way to get in the lobby… found a buzzer with her name on it, she answered but pretended to be her sister! She claimed that her sister was not in at the time… but I knew better….

We had no other choice but to leave… I was surprised by getting a phone call from my husband asking me what I had been doing at her apartment! I asked him in turn how did he know! He told me that she had called him freaked out that I had been there and afraid to talk to me…. I told him that I had not been there to do her harm just to confirm that the affair was still going on….

CHAPTER 64

Disappointment and yet another chance is given!

The next day he finally admitted that they were still seeing each other and I told him that it was over! After all he had even moved some of his clothes to Carlos old room just to give us space… so I had been told and to give us a chance to heal as well… but now I knew that he was not willing to work on our marriage…

Danny himself had opened my eyes "Mom, every time I turn around dad takes more and more clothes out of your closet and takes it downstairs… are you sure that he wants to work with you on your marriage? He also seems way too happy about it!" He was right and I promised him to keep an eye on his father…

That same night I had a birthday party to go to for my best friend and decided to go my myself, I dressed up and when I got there enjoying myself was impossible! I was too hurt and decided to go home early….

I kept on praying that God would change his mind and would remind him of the family that he had… it was never on my mind to get even by cheating myself… even though Victor had asked me that himself one day by saying to me "So, now is payback time, right?"

I told him "Two wrongs don't make a right and I don't want any more bad examples for our sons."

In two weeks, I would be celebrating my 47th birthday and I had also chosen that day to be baptized in the church that I was attending…. instead of being happy about these two very special events my heart was full of sorrow…I truly believed that God was working on Victor as well because one day I caught him looking thru our family pictures and smiling but without saying a word! I smiled as well knowing that God was working behind the scenes….

I knew from experience that even if you pray for people, it's really up to them if they listen… that's why God gave us free will…. because of this I also started to look for an apartment for me and Danny to move to just in case we could not make this work. Many times, I would pass by Victor's room downstairs and heard him talk to the other woman on the phone and I would leave with my heart broken one more time….

Two days before my birthday I was out with my friends having lunch when I got a call from him asking me what I wanted for my birthday! I told him that what I wanted I would not be able to get and that was a faithful, loving supportive husband. He surprised me by telling me that he could grant me that wish and asked me to go out to dinner with him that night and I agreed.

We had many issues to discuss… we discussed them reasonably and without anger, once again, he promised me that he wanted to work on our marriage and this for me was a true miracle! Just a week ago he had been so confused that he had told me that he could not promise me that he could ever be faithful!

I also asked him as a favor to me and to his kids to get rid of the parrot. He agreed to look for someone to give to and we found a Portuguese friend of ours that liked birds and asked her if she would like to buy it, she agreed to come over and look at the bird and she immediately liked the parrot! We had to advise her that he was extremely loud but she didn't care and took it anyway.

Victor was no longer married to a timid and naïve 15-year-old but a much more self-confident assured woman and instead of being proud of what I had achieved he had become jealous and insecure…. one of my husband's biggest problems was also that he was easily influenced by the advice of friends that did not have his best interest at heart….

The difference with me was that I listened to what my friends had to say and then prayed about it and refused to decide in the spur of the moment…

On the day of my baptism and my birthday he was at my church with Danny and some of my closest friends and it turned out to be a wonderful experience! Even my friends from Bible study were extremely surprised to see him there and asked me to give a testimonial at church the next Sunday and I agreed. I also had asked some of my personal friends to meet me at my church and then proceed to celebrate at our home…unfortunately because of my marriage problems I also had lost a few friends …in situations like this is when you find out who your true friends are…

When we got home, I had flowers waiting for me on our table, a cake, gifts and a wonderful meal that we all shared together….

I believe my biggest birthday gift was how I was doing physically! I was not only looking younger… but I was now able to run, to sleep better and even my hair was growing back! Better yet! I was even able to eat out with my friends without having too many bad side effects….

Unfortunately, my marriage problems were not over as I suspected! He constantly blamed me and my newfound religion (Christianity) for his unfaithfulness and I had to remind him "Excuse me Victor! God did not place the other woman in your bed! It was your decision so take responsibility for what you have done."

He had become my biggest critic! He would look at me and give me remarks like "You have no breasts, your butt is way too small, can you ever manage to be on time for anything?"

It was like he was constantly comparing me to someone else and I was falling short!

He tried to come home sooner not to upset me but most times he failed and was stressed out to the limit!

He was not healing like I was, he kept on promising me that he was trying but I knew he cheated on his diet, I also caught him smelling like liquor when he came home at night and I knew he could not drink while on treatment. I confronted him about it but of course he denied it and I also suspected the affair was still going on…. When confronted about what he was doing and that we were wasting money, he laughed about it and would tell me that he would try to do better the next day!

CHAPTER 65

Facing the truth is not easy!

*H*is birthday was a week after mine and his friends were throwing him a birthday party at the Portuguese Club and for the first time in a long time, he asked me to come with him…so I got all dressed up and we took off…

When we got to the club they had a table with food and a birthday cake set up! It was like I didn't exist once we were close to his friends! He left me alone at the table and when I looked back… reality set in! He was surrounded by his friends, raising their glasses and laughing out loud! At that precise moment I knew without a doubt that I would have a fight in my hands to get him away from this environment and that he would never change! We ate dinner, had some cake, socialized for a bit and went back home in silence. He asked me if something was wrong and I said "Nothing!" because I didn't want to spoil his birthday….

I knew that this would be a never-ending cycle with our illness if we both didn't heal…. I had read enough books and done enough research to know what I was talking about and was becoming very annoyed with all his excuses!

My mother had once told me "Burro velho nao aprende linguas" this meant "You can't teach an old dog new tricks." She had been absolutely right!

I read a book that was instrumental for my education from Donna Gates "The Body Ecology Diet" explained that candida affects a woman or a man in a different way… that if both of you are not being treated at the same time and willing to commit to a cure that the illness will always be there!

That's why whenever we had intercourse the day after I always felt worse! I knew that out of the two of us I was the only one that was very committed to diet, exercise and following a treatment…

I was so desperate one time that I got on my knees and prayed to God that the lies and deceit would stop! I asked Him to give me the strength to confront him… I loved him but I didn't want him to jeopardize my health! I also had lost trust in my husband not only by committing himself to a cure but even trying to being faithful!

One day stuck in traffic coming home from work I let go of the tears that I did not want anyone to see and when I looked up in front of me, I saw a bumper sticker on a car that said, "Trust is everything."

It was like God was telling me that he had heard my prayers! Sometimes He amazed me how He managed to send me a message at the precise moment I needed to hear it!

This message gave me the courage to confront him! That same night I asked him to talk to me in private and asked him outright how he was doing with his treatment and his diet. He flat out told me that he didn't want to do the treatment any longer and that he didn't believe in this candida bull shit!

I had been right all along! He had agreed to do the treatment to keep me near him and to appease me… I had read out loud to him quite a bit of the research I had done and he had gone with me to see Dr. Francis many times! He had heard our conversations regarding this illness… how could he be so blind?

Not speaking that I was living proof that if you dedicated yourself to a cure, you could actually heal from this illness! He had seen firsthand how much healthier I had become and had even made a comment aloud to me "Look at you, there is nothing wrong with you!" Amazing… how people forget!

I gave up at this point and Danny and I resumed our looking for another place to live without telling him about it… I had promised Danny that the place we would go would be a safe place, the first couple of tries were not successful but we refused to give up….

Part of me still hoped for a miracle but he didn't show any signs of changing! He had become way too comfortable with his new lifestyle! The girl on the side, the friends, playing cards all afternoon without a care in the world, eat and drink to his heart desire…in another word… Living in denial!

I suspected from what I had read in Dr, Whiting's booklet that I had contracted this illness from him…from all the years that he had not practiced safe sex but had not told him of my suspicions for fear of adding fuel to the fire!

I had open communication with doctors… one of them was Dr.Jeri from Herbal Answers, I called her one day to find out about the dosage for the Herbal Aloe that I was taking and she happened to mention that you could really see results if you doubled the dosage! I decided to convince Victor to try and double the dosage of the Aloe just one more time and he agreed probably just to shut me up….

After a few days I got a call from him at work totally amazed that he had gotten up that morning without any pain anywhere and I thought if this doesn't convince him nothing would!

I doubted that he would stick to it because after all this would be expensive and Victor was all about money! It also meant that he might heal enough that he would not have to apply for Disability… something that he was working on so that he would not have to go back to work…

We actually discussed this and he admitted to it!

For some people it's easier to suffer and get paid for it than try to heal and have a long and healthy life ahead of you….

Knowing all of this did not make me love him any less I just had less respect for him! I knew I was facing a very difficult decision in my life and I wondered how in the world was I going to leave him… it wasn't that I was afraid of facing life alone or if the finances got bad it was just the thought of losing him!

He didn't stick to the treatment just as I suspected! He told me to my face that to take the amount of the Aloe he took it would take a lot of money and we couldn't afford it! I told him "Victor this will not be forever, it's just for a few months then you can go down on the dosage." He didn't believe me of course or was looking for an excuse to live the life that he wanted to live….

One day after work and stuck in traffic my emotional state was so bad that I could hardly wait to go exercise! It was the only way that some days I could cope with all the stress I was under…

I got home one night too late to go to Curves or to go to the gym due to a traffic accident on the freeway… so I told Danny that I was going to the park nearby and run… He got worried that I was going out there alone at night but I had a huge knot on my throat and told him that I needed to release all the stress that I was under and headed out the door….

When I got to the park I started on a walk and then run and let the tears go…I screamed at my husband for being so weak, for the friends that placed all kinds of wrong ideas in his head, for his family influence, for his lack of love for me and cried out to God for justice!

I had lost so many family members but for me this was worse! I had a tremendous ache in my heart and ran back home still crying…. I must have looked like someone that had just lost someone to anyone that saw me on the street! When I knocked on my door a very relieved Danny was there to greet me but he could tell that I felt better!

CHAPTER 66

Deciding to move out….

*I*f Victor felt anything he didn't show it to me or to his kids but I did receive a call from his older sister trying to make things better between us! Once I told her my side of the story, she asked me what would take for Danny and me to stay, I told her that it would take a total commitment on his part of staying on our present treatment for at least 3 months without jeopardizing it! She asked me not to make a move, that she would talk to him and would call me back and I agreed…

She did call me back later to let me know that he was not willing to listen and I told her that I would talk to him one more time that night…

When he got home, I waited until he got to his room, knocked on the door and asked him if had a chance to speak to his sister, he replied that yes and his response was….

"Not 3 months, not 3 weeks not even 3 days, I'm finished with all of this!" I left him there and I knew it was time to pack….

We also had to get rid of something that we both loved and that was our small motor home, so we put it up for sale! The day we sold it and the guy came by to get it my own husband in front of Danny said "Are you happy now bitch?"

He had never spoken to me that way and Danny turned around and said "Dad, what's wrong with you, you never spoke to mom this way!"

He fell silent and didn't say anything… I reminded him how much I loved that little motor home and that it was me that had convinced him to buy it…

When I looked out the window and saw someone else drive our motor home out of our parking lot my heart was broken! I went to my room and cried… The next step would be even worse for me but it needed to be done….

Danny and I went looking once again for a place for ourselves, the first one we found Danny didn't like the location, he felt that it was not a safe place for us, the second was like a private residence. It was built almost like a basement! Way too dark and when we went outside and I looked around the corner I saw that they had placed a building next door for a fortune teller! That did it for me…I didn't want Danny to be tempted to go there when I was not around, so we kept on looking….

My supervisor at work knew I was looking for a place and suggested an apartment that she seen on the way home… the apartment complex was near Danny's High School and I placed my application there. However, I was having a hard time getting approved because according to them my income was not enough! Even after telling them that I would be getting child support from my husband was not enough to convince them! My answer of course was to pray! I remembered a Bible verse that said, "For with God nothing is impossible- Luke-1:37."

In my kitchen I said it out loud quite a few times… believe it or not I got a call from the apartment manager letting me know that we could move in if Victor co-signed for the apartment! I spoke to him and he actually agreed!

Danny was ecstatic about moving out from this home that had become scary and uncomfortable for both of us! Our rooms had become cold and full of mildew, when I had asked Victor to please help me clean and paint the rooms because this was no good for our breathing, he always said he didn't have the time… also because of his Avery outback that he didn't clean enough we were bombarded with small bugs everywhere that even got inside the cupboards….

One afternoon while attending Bible study I got a call from Danny asking me to come home early and I knew from the tone on his voice that something had happened! I left right after and when I got home Danny told me that while he was taking a shower, he had heard a hard knock on the door thinking it was me… he wrapped a towel around himself, opened the door and no one was there! He got totally freaked out!

We both knew that Danny was by himself that afternoon and no wonder he was spooked!!

It didn't help one bit that our cats walked around frightened most of the time and even I felt uneasy in that house! Everything had changed for us in that house! Our family was not the same and even Carlos had become quite aggressive while he lived there especially towards me!

My father-in-law while he had lived in that house also had cheated on my mother-in-law and had treated her quite badly (they did stay together) … it seemed that everyone that had lived in that house had experienced family issues, either bad Karma or something evil existed there!

While we got prepared to move, Victor made daily calls to his girl-friend and for some reason all 3 of us got ill! Danny kept putting pressure on me to hurry up and get us packed but many times I would have to stop to throw up and then start again! I even managed to make chicken soup for all of us!

As we prepared to leave the house with our stuff, I had the strangest compulsion to look back … instead I did what the Bible instructs us to do "Go forward and don't look back!" Exactly what I did!

CHAPTER 67

Moved from darkness into the light!

*T*hat day I even got Victor and Carlos to help us move out! Victor stopped by the office to co-sign for us and even managed to give me a comment on the way up to my apartment "Woman you have no butt! Look at you, you better start eating!"

I didn't respond…. I was just happy to be out of that house!

When I entered our apartment, it was like going from darkness into light!

Our place was right in front of the pool area where laughter and water splashing could be heard thru out the day and our place was surrounded by trees and flowers everywhere! We took our kitty Foxy with us and the she devil called Precious that Foxy didn't like… my husband didn't want to keep her, they were both Persian cats that had been with us for quite a while and that we refused to give up. Foxy many times would sit on Danny's back when he was watching TV or playing video games and he absolutely loved this cat….

I spent most of my free time decorating our place and loved that time! I went to a furniture store and bought my first Thomas Kinkade picture, it wasn't a real one… but I loved the way this artist painted! That week I did some research and found something amazing about this painter! He was a Christian that used lighting to bring out the best in his paintings, he loved his wife so much that hid her first initials on some of his paintings! In order to have more of his paintings in my apartment I bought imitations from Avon! Once I got the pictures, I bought frames and hung them in my apartment!

The nights for me proved to be awful! That's when I would miss my husband the most… something I didn't share with Danny so that he didn't worry about me...

I waited for about 3 months before going for a divorce to give him time to come to his senses and to realize that he missed his family, instead all I heard from various friends was that he was attending different functions, even Portuguese dances with different women so I finally got the picture! From that day on I worked on my thoughts and stopped crying for him….

One of the most important prayers I did was to ask God that he hardened my heart against this man…. I had loved him way too long! I needed to get strong enough to be able to see him somewhere and not let it affect me in the least ...

Unfortunately, I also had decided to let go of Carlos for a while…. He had hurt me quite a lot, so I was very surprised to get a call from him at work one day asking me "Mom, please don't give up on me! I know I have hurt you quite a lot and I don't know how to say this but I think there was something evil in that home, that's why I moved out, can we please work on our relationship?" I was so moved by my oldest son's words that I started to cry! I totally agreed with him, nothing had been the same after we had moved to that house! I did promise him that no way was I going to give up on him and that same day on my break time I looked up the history of that house….

Unfortunately, sometimes if you don't have the right tools somethings are hard to find… all I could do was to go by my own experience and my mother's-in-laws! She had shared with me when I arrived from Portugal that she had found out that a very mean alcoholic man had died at that house…

My sons became my priority! Every time they asked for something from me, I did my best to comply! Danny really liked octopus made the Portuguese way and since his birthday was coming up, I went to the Portuguese store bought it and brought it home to surprise him! That night while Danny was out with his brother, I opened up the box and found that the octopus was not cut in pieces! I looked at it and was scared to even touch it! I got a small kitchen hammer and a knife and set out to cut it… it was sliding all over the place and I was scared the stupid thing would come alive! I managed to cut it in small pieces, season it and cooked it, I also made Danny's favorite lasagna and garlic bread. The next day Carlos and his girlfriend showed up, we had a terrific dinner and they all laughed about my fight with the octopus!

Victor on the other hand always took them out for their birthdays and catered to their needs… of course my kids always made sure they come home with some kind of news, they would only tell me what would make me laugh! They knew I had been hurt enough….

He was out there flashing women in front of our friends and I decided to finally file for divorce. That same week I started searching for a good lawyer and was blessed that I received that information from a good friend of mine at church!

I was referred to a petite Jewish lawyer that was not intimidated by anyone and she liked me right from the first moment she met me! She became my greatest ally! I flat out told her that I didn't want spousal support from him but she convinced me to request child support for Danny since he was only 16 and in High School… he would be able to use this income for school.

Believe me it took guts to do what I did! I was the one that served him the papers! I knocked on his door, gave him the envelope and he asked me "What is this!" I told him "These are the divorce papers, please sign them and return them to my lawyer as soon as possible." He was fuming! He asked me "Why you?" I knew what he meant and responded "Me, because my lawyer and I were afraid that you would refuse to accept the papers if they were delivered by a stranger." He tried to intimidate me but I refused to bite the bait! I told him instead to call my lawyer if he had any questions and left! I called her and he did try to argue regarding the child support because I was requesting half of his pension! She wasn't the type of a person that you could try to intimidate so he passed by my place the next afternoon, caught me walking home after work and started to tell me off in the parking lot!

I looked straight at him and told him "Victor, I'm only asking for what is fair! I have worked right along your side since I was 18 and Danny deserves a bit of help from his father, you are very lucky I didn't ask for spousal support!"

He tried to fight with me but I walked away with my head held straight, the last remark I heard from him was "The money for Danny better be for him only and not used for nothing else." I didn't even answer back because he didn't deserve it and walked away!

This lawyer had definitely helped me to became stronger and had given me confidence… it helps to have a woman on your side!

Chapter 68

Giving up toxic relationships and God's vengeance!

My friends worried about me arranged for a dinner get together and couldn't believe the changes in me! Some changes had been easy.... others more difficult... like giving up a man that had become toxic!

I also had to give up other things that were hurting me physically and that was a full body girdle that was placing a lot of pressure on my chest area and was causing me acid reflux.... I found out that these types of girdles could cause lack of blood flow to your organs! This was a habit due to lack of self-esteem that was very hard to break.... the next one was the false eyelashes that were preventing my real eye-lashes from growing!

Experts say that it takes 3 weeks to give up a bad habit and 3 weeks to develop a new one... I truly believed in this concept! I also believed in rewarding myself occasionally... one of the rewards I gave myself every other week was the gift of flowers! I made sure to stop at Trader Joe's bought myself a small bunch of flowers and placed them on my table, this would become a good habit for me for years to come!

Friends told me that I looked younger and happier even after all I had gone thru... little did they know how much these changes had cost me emotionally and financially!

I was so determined to heal that I did research on everything and did I make any mistakes? You bet! Sometimes out of desperation you can also try things that are no good for you…. for example, a friend of mine talked me into trying a mattress that was filled with magnets… the point was that by laying on top of it would increase your energy and help you to heal you faster! The first time I tried it… it seemed to work, the second time I was depleted of energy and felt really weak…from there the mattress went into the garbage and that was that!

On the other hand, it seemed that God was taking justice in His hands because the people that were involved in our breakup also were getting taken care of and I didn't have to lift a finger! Victor's friend that had lured him to the nightclub where he had met his girlfriend also had lost his wife…. just like me his wife found out thru someone else about his affair and threw him out! He didn't stay with the other woman either and lost both…

My husband's best friend that had called me to tell me about Victor's affair had contracted throat cancer…coincidence?

After all the Bible says "An eye for an eye …a tooth for a tooth…"

I wanted to study ministry and asked my Pastor at church how could I achieve this dream and he told me that I would have to study for it! When I asked him if he had any suggestions, he suggested Patten University in Oakland. Without knowing how I was going to pay for this education I called their office and met with a counselor, I was amazed that I was able to get government funding and got prepared to enroll in classes!

For me this would mean quite a bit of sacrificing! I would have to work, go to classes at nighttime 3 or 4 days a week and keep up with my diet and exercise! I knew that this education would help not only to further my education but also keep me too busy to think…

Thru Dr, Francis I also learned how to detoxify at home when I didn't have time to go to the gym, I used the treadmill in the little gym downstairs that belonged to the apartment complex… finished by using an Epsom Salt bath followed by a cooler shower, it was incredible how good that made me feel!

As soon as I was done with the bath, I drank 1 or 3 ounces of the Herbal Aloe on an empty stomach…straight to my room and used the Herbal Aloe Gel on my stomach and on any part of my body that was hurting, I could feel the soothing and healing power of this juice as soon as I took it! I made sure to split the dosages thru out the day, always half an hour before a meal and included it with my smoothie in the morning. This juice had so many benefits! It was antibacterial, antiviral, known as a cancer treatment and a treatment for diabetes, arthritis, asthma, ulcers… even digestive disorders and had an extreme calming effect!

This healing protocol even helped me when I was bombarded with homework and gave me a wonderful night sleep!

I was still hurting inside and prayed that God would send someone into my life someday that shared my beliefs, would respect me and love me for who I was and especially someone that would not be a womanizer. One of the things that I had learned by reading the Bible was that a healthier relationship was better when both partners shared the same beliefs and respected each other! Between me and Victor these elements were not there….

Chapter 69

Not all that glitters is gold!

Sometimes we have to give God time and like the saying goes "Not all that glitters is gold" that proved to be right! One day at church this good-looking guy showed up and started taking an interest in me! After all I had been thru, I was extremely flattered! I prayed that he would be the right one...

I shared everything with Danny including this bit of news with him, I believe since he communicated back and forth with his father that he probably told him about the new guy... I started to get calls from Victor asking about this new person in my life!

This is where the typical proverb applies "I want my cake and eat it to." That was not going to work with me! I had told Victor once "If I'm not good enough to be your wife I'm also not good enough to be your mistress."

Victor and Danny had planned a trip to Pismo and he suggested that I join them as a chaperone but I knew better! I would be setting myself up to get hurt once again and even though I was tired and needed a vacation I decided to let them go and stayed behind which proved to be a good decision....

I had discussed with my boss and good friend the need to get off earlier in order to make it to classes on time, even suggested taking half hour for lunch but she became very stubborn with me and refused to allow me to change my working schedule… so I knew I had to look for work closer to home!

I found a company about 10 minutes away from my apartment and a boss that would allow me to get off early to attend my classes at Patten and I was thrilled to make this change!

This position was also closer to home and to Patten University…

I gave my 2 weeks' notice at my old job and my boss was not happy with my decision! She told me that she would give me my full pay and have a week for myself…. I truly needed to rest, to get prepared to start college and have my car fixed.

Meanwhile I got a call from Victor to alert me on being careful with guys because after all most men were liars including him! I was amazed that he actually admitted that for the last 4 years he also had one night stands not just the affair! When I asked him why this information now… he said that it was a warning to help me to be careful with guys out there!

I was glad I had not gone to Pismo with them! I was devastated by this piece of news and found myself very lucky that I had not contracted something really serious from him!

He hated to use protection in any form! In his own words "I don't feel a thing."

I was out shopping when I got his call… dropped everything and went home so that I could let the tears flow… I decided to call my friend Sue and share this bit of information with her and was told "Do you realize what time this is? Too late for so much drama!" I looked at my watch… it was after 10PM and realized that sometimes friends are not always there when you need them, so I hung up… got my emotions under control and went to sleep…

I was getting disappointed with the guy at church as well… I caught him staring at another woman and I decided to investigate him a bit… I found out he was a martial arts instructor and decided to join the institute he belonged to and learn self-defense …knowing very well my body was not going to take it for very long…but it also gave me time to observe him…

Right from the start something wasn't right, when I entered the Institute, I saw him kneel and bow down before a picture (Buddhism) and it didn't set well with me since as a Christian you are not supposed to "bow down before other gods" that's in the Bible and after all he was attending a Christian church regularly and got baptized at our church the same day I did!

This was a man that had asked me to take him to Patten because he wanted me to introduce him to my teacher for Bible Studies, of course I had done that, he had been quite impressed with Patten and with the teacher…this made me wonder about his religious background and how truthful he was!

After 2 weeks of getting banged up I found myself placing ice on my shoulder and the last time I saw him giving us a demonstration of certain moves to another instructor I witnessed something that appalled me!

He was practicing a move on a female instructor on the floor, when he touched her breast! She scolded him for it and he apologized but the class grew silent… I knew then and there that this guy who professed to want to know God was also a player!

He kept showing up at church and flirting with me and with another woman that was afraid of him…. when I asked her about him, she told me that he was stalking her and that she had told him that she was not interested! When he showed up at church one Sunday, I had a meeting with him outside, told him flat out to stop coming to our church or I was going to tell the pastor the information I had learned from the other woman and called him a faker!

I actually quoted something from the Bible to him "Don't do unto others what you don't want done unto you." He looked at me and left…

They say that our eyes are the windows to our soul, unfortunately… we are not always able to look into someone's eyes and tell what their souls are like! It would be wonderful if we could! When it comes to men it would be wonderful to have the ability to even read their minds!

He stopped coming around and I decided to dedicate my life to my sons, to work, to school and leave men alone! I had become very distrusting of men and was more interested in healing physically and spiritually…

A friend of mine had once told me "Success is your best revenge" and I truly believed it!

I was out to prove everybody wrong, even those that believed that because I had been very young when I married Victor and had not been on my own that I was not going to make it…. even my father-in-law had called me to insult me and to tell me that I would not amount to nothing after hearing of my decision to file for divorce! I paid no attention to him because I knew I had done nothing wrong and refused to be blamed for something that his son had done. I was not like my mother and my mother-in-law that had forgiven infidelity, had lost trust in their husbands and lived miserable lives…for me it was bigger than that! My life had been at stake! Something he would never understand because he had not gone thru what I had gone thru! I also had been told by a friend "Once a player…always a player!"

That weekend when I went to get my haircut by Cindi, she asked me how I was doing, I told her that I was getting ready to change my life, to start college and to take care of myself and she told me how proud she was of me! Just like me she believed that Victor would never change! She and her husband had seen him at Costco with his girlfriend and when he saw them… he came towards them to introduce her. She actually told me, "Without an ounce of guilt or shame." When he tried to bring up my name and started bad mouthing me, she told him "Victor, stop right there! You forget that we have known both of you for years and she is not here to defend herself!" That's what a good friend is supposed to do! I thanked her for coming to my defense…sometimes we have to place ourselves in someone's shoes…

When I left, I knew that I would have a friend for life always there when I needed to reach out!

Thru another friend of ours were started the process of selling our home (another heartbreaker) and because of Victor's refusal of getting permits for the work that had been done in our home we had no choice but to sell it as it is and lost money in the process...

CHAPTER 70

Starting College and facing doubts!

*O*n the other hand, was my own self-doubt regarding starting college at my age! On my way to Patten to take a test that afternoon I was filled with anxiety and had my eyes fixed ...not really seeing nothing ahead when the traffic forced me to look up and on the bumper sticker of the car in front of me, I read "Failure is not an option!"

I looked at it twice to double check that I was reading it correctly and for the first time that day I laughed out loud!

I get it God! No turning back! Full speed ahead!

I'm glad I didn't listen to my fear that day and worked hard on everything I did, at Patten because of my dedication and hard work I was getting A's and B's… at work I was given more responsibility and my confidence grew!

When I moved to my apartment, I placed a couple of pictures of Jesus Christ, one by my computer for inspiration and one in my bedroom… the funny thing was that nobody that visited my apartment ever gave me a nasty comment about His picture! If they had asked me why His picture, I would have told them "After all I have been thru, I felt that I needed all the peace that only Him could give me…and protection."

I was treated with respect and kindness at Patten by my instructors and fellow students something I had been lacking in my personal life and grew to love this University with all my heart!

At my church I was also treated with kindness and formed lasting relationships that helped me not to feel isolated and appreciated...

I was asked if I wanted to be part of their Care & Prayer Ministry and I accepted, I helped anyone by praying with them or for them and used my own testimony to help people have faith in God...

Everyone marveled at my energy but little they know how many times I would fall asleep in front of my computer! Between working 40 hours a week, attending classes at Patten at night, having to workout at the gym, being involved in ministry at Church, fixing dinner after classes for me and Danny and doing homework! All of this before going to bed! No wonder I found myself exhausted most of the time... but it also helped to get rid of the grief I was carrying of having lost a husband!

I did push myself to the limit... but I was also determined to show those who were making bets how long I would last that I had a will of iron and that I refused to go back home with my tail between my legs...

In January of 2006 my divorce became final and thank goodness I had listened to one of my oldest cousins advise, not only asked for child support for Danny but also for something she totally convince me to do and that was to also apply for half of his pension. She had to remind me that I had been married to him for over 30 years and that I had been working along his side since I was very young...

She had been right in telling me not to let my pride get in the way, that someday I could end up needing this income and she turned out to be very right! Thank God I had a woman on my side!

I didn't know how to feel after the divorce! I still loved him dearly but I also didn't want to be his punching bag or jeopardize my health in the process not speaking that I had lost trust in him!

I certainly didn't want to risk forgiving him and not knowing if while he had been out there going from woman to woman if he had gotten infected with another sexual transmitted disease or even worse AIDS...

I prayed for him and for Carlos that had moved back with his father and hoped that they both found a bit of happiness in their lives...

With the money we received from the sale of our home we paid our bills, my car and Victor bought himself a 5th wheel that he used often to go camping with his girlfriend. I found it funny that while Danny and I had lived at the house nothing had been fixed by him and found out from my son Carlos that he had fixed the house, gotten rid of the bugs and painted the place once his girlfriend moved in!

Some of our old friends couldn't believe the changes in him and now spoke about him without respect where once they had been envious of our relationship and our love for one another! We looked incredible when we danced together but that did not make a healthy relationship...

CHAPTER 71

Once a player always a player!

*E*ven by myself I managed to go to the Thornton Festival that year! I knew he probably would be there and I was right but he had gone by himself! I had planned to go back home right after the procession, I saw him along with some of his personal friends by the food stands playing the flirt… this time with me! Probably placing bets with his friends how fast he could get me back! I said hello and headed for the bullfights and on the way there I saw his cousin Thomas, even with everything that had happened between me and Victor he come towards me and shook my hand! All I could see on his gaze was respect!

I went up the stairs and saw Victor sitting on a bench with his youngest brother and I sat somewhere else. After the bullfight was over I went down to eat, bought Portuguese goodies to take to work and sat down to listen to music until it was time for the procession. He approached me and asked me to dance, I politely declined…. and told him that I would be leaving right after the procession, he just looked at me! He probably thought that I was there because of him! As usual I got my candle and prayed for my kids, as soon as the procession was over… I headed home, I was so relieved to be back at my place! If I stayed longer… he would have made himself a nuisance and we would have probably become the talk of the town!

Carlos's birthday also came around and we decided to meet at Chevy's, I dressed up for the occasion and brought Carlos's birthday gift with me. I knew where my son was living so I bought him a chain with a cross, when I reached the table where he was sitting I placed it around his neck. Probably something that he wouldn't have bought for himself but my sons loved me enough to not make fun of something as sacred as a cross!

My ex-husband had a stupid smirk on his face but I didn't care! We ate lunch together, spoke to our sons about what was new in their lives and when it was time to leave Victor walked me to my car. He leaned against the car… playing Don Juan and said, "You are looking really good, how about going out with me for dinner once in a while, we can still remain friends, right?"

I knew what remaining friends meant in his book so I looked straight into his eyes and said, "I know what being friends with you means and I don't think your girlfriend would appreciate it… see you later Victor, I have a lot to do today." He also looked for excuses to call me even thought his girlfriend was living with him… probably had placed a bet with someone that he could get me back anytime he chose....

I wanted to make sure that just like my mother I installed in my children good principals… very often I would share with Danny my experiences at Patten and took him with me to church on Sunday's. I prayed the Rosary at night just as I had promised God that had I would… I was not ashamed to pray, it was something that I had been doing since I was little girl…

I kept studying and applying myself to my studies at Patten and was doing research for a class at the San Leandro J.A Freitas Library when I was approached by a reporter doing research on Portuguese ancestry. He asked me what I was researching and I told him that I was actually looking for a Portuguese book to help me with an essay. He surprised me by asking me if he could take my picture for the San Leandro Daily Review and of course I agreed! The article was printed on March 11,

2006, I bought the paper, showed it to my sons and friends and even showed it to my friends at Patten…

That same year, my nephew Sammy got married to Wendy on July 23, 2006 and my family was invited. I wasn't looking forward to being there because a lot of my old acquaintances and Victor would be there and I wasn't looking forward to being interrogated… The ceremony and reception were going to take place in San Pablo…when I finally got to the reception I was surprised to see and old girlfriend of mine and of course my ex-husband.

I was approached by an old guy that had been drinking way too much and wanted to dance the afternoon away with me…Out of the corner of my eye I could see Victor looking at both of us with a smirk on his face and I could read in his expression "I can do better than that!" He didn't ask me to dance however, probably like the fact that I was very uncomfortable!

As soon as I managed to get away from the annoying guy, I went to the veranda to get some air and I was approached by my girlfriend that flat out asked me to look down below, when I looked down Victor was downstairs talking to someone… I turned around and said, "You have something on your mind?" she replied, "I miss you guys together, do you still love him?" "I said "Lia, I will always love that man but I will never be able to trust him again, he has hurt me quite badly." She hugged me and said that she understood but I wondered how much understanding Portuguese people had towards women that refused to be married to men that cheated on them… Later she also would be divorced from her husband for totally different reasons! It's like the old saying goes "Who are we to judge anyone?"

I went home happy that I had not succumbed to temptation and had left with my pride intact…. a lot of people didn't know the whole truth and they judged me regardless….

My health was always my first priority and something came up that discouraged me! I had been taken the Oxy Aloe from Dr. Whiting and the Herbal Aloe from Herbal Answers together and done a remarkable recovery but for some reason the old symptoms were coming back, I thought "Now what?"

Since my symptoms first started I had noticed floaters in front of my eyes back when I was working for Mechanics Bank…. fungus had also started to grow on my toenails and neither had improved!

If one thing I had learned thru reading books from Dr. Stanley and Joel Osteen was to always have a backup plan for anything in life, mine always included getting in touch with God first before making a decision and many times He would show me the next step to take!

CHAPTER 72

Healing sometimes comes from unexpected sources!

I was at work one day feeling pretty awful and decided to go to the bathroom to pray, I pleaded with God to find another way for me to heal and was surprised to hear from my oldest cousin! I had confided in her about my struggles with Candida and she sent me an e-mail with a website to look up…. this proved to be instrumental in my healing!

Thru her research she had found a company called Whole Approach that had a different protocol to be followed every 3 months! I was excited about it but decided to have Dr. Francis check out the website and give me her stamp of approval before I started ordering any product. She perused the website, gave me her approval but advised me to take extra Vitamin C.

Thru this website I found out why my former treatment had stopped working! Candida can take on many forms…. if you kill one form others can resurface and can only be eliminated by taking different treatments every 3 months to stop the cycle…

I contacted Linda at Whole Approach, she was there every time I had a question regarding any treatment! She actually gave me hope by sharing with me that she also had suffered from candida! She also shared with me that she had been free of this illness for 15 years and finished by giving me hope that one day I would also be free of it…

My hope was that I in turn one day would be able to help someone that had this illness… so for me it became extremely important to document every defeat and every victory… took pictures of the foods that I was preparing to show people that even though you had to be extremely careful of what you ate you could also become very inventive with your meals. I'm a true believer that food must appeal to the eye before it appeals to your mouth!

I also switched my diet around every day…. my lunches consisted of a chicken meal so that I could get enough protein in me for the day (always with vegetables and a salad) dinner consisted of either salmon, baked or grilled (omega 3) or eggs. Always served with different vegetables… a carb and a salad, I also incorporated a small little bowl of fruit on the side to add more vitamin C and banana for potassium to my diet. I found that switching foods also worked to bring candida out and made your diet more interesting!

It made a total difference to really season your foods in order to enjoy them! Most people believed that healthy meals meant boring food with no flavor! On the contrary you can make healthy foods extraordinary by using herbs, butters and pre-season them before cooking! I had friends of mine ask me for recipes because they loved my food! Little did they know that sometimes I wished with all my heart that I was able to eat anything without repercussions! It was not easy seeing someone eat foods that you miss and have to look away!

Before I got ready to leave for the grocery store, I made sure to look at my refrigerator and cupboards to see what I needed and made a small list, this prevented me from over buying and overspending…

I looked at all the vegetables and salads I bought and made sure they were free of bacteria…. even the chicken and the salmon I bought were always looked at twice by me. I actually shopped at one market in Alameda where I refused to buy either the chicken or the salmon because you could smell them!

Many times, I would ask a grocery clerk to let me smell the poultry or fish before I bought them…. after all you are paying for your groceries and I could care less if I got a dirty look!

Eating healthy takes practice but you also have to make sure that you have enough fat in your diet…mainly doing research and finding out what fats are actually good for you…

I kept taking pictures of the fungus in my nails and even of the bowel movements, especially if they had particles of candida to keep me motivated.

What I tried I had Danny try but for him it was extremely hard to follow a protocol and a diet, he was exposed to all kinds of temptations at school and was forever eating the wrong foods…. He liked carbs and sugars and many times I caught him throwing the smoothie I made for him down the toilet!

This would make me extremely angry or sad! How could this child of mine ever heal from this illness!

I followed him one night to the nearest liquor store and caught him buying candy and ice cream. At first, I was really scared that he was buying liquor or cigarettes…. I didn't know if I should be happy that it was junk food instead of liquor that he carried with him but I still gave him a great speech about letting me waste my money on treatments when he was not willing to let go of the wrong foods and threw his bag in the garbage…

But I felt very sorry for him to have to follow a treatment being a teenager at school! I actually cried one day when he shared with me that when he drank the smoothie and went to school he would fall asleep in class! I suspected that he probably snacked on top of the smoothie and this of course was a lot of food to digest while seating down. I had been told by Dr, Francis that this smoothie that she had designed for us was a meal in itself and we should not consume any other foods between half of hour to 1 hour after...

It's hard seeing someone you love battle with symptoms that you know where they come from and not be able to convince them that you have the answer if they just be willing to listen! I watched Danny get extremely tired to the point that he would fall asleep for hours and had to shake him to wake him up to go to school! He developed rashes on his chest and back that refused to go away, he suffered from stomach problems, mood swings and frequent colds. I wished with all my heart that I had a camera so that I could film him when he fell asleep to convince him of what I was seeing with my own eyes!

His way of keeping awake to do his homework was to drink energy drinks and one day he got scared because his heart was racing and he was anxious. He knocked on my bedroom door to ask me to help him and I asked him how many of the energy drinks he had drank and he said, "a couple" I told him to flush all the caffeine out by drinking plenty of water and after a while he was finally able to go to sleep for a few hours…he learned a valuable lesson that day…not to exceed on caffeine!

Sometimes I wished that I could lock him up in a cellar and try to heal him without the influence of anyone so that I could give him a better future… but I was also afraid to create a gap between us and risk losing my son as well!

When in doubt…Pray!

CHAPTER 73

Reconnecting with my son...

*T*hat was exactly what I did and the next day I received an e-mail from a former friend of mine with a great idea in how to spend time with your kids. She had taken a trip with her family to the Pinnacles in Gilroy and swore up and down that Danny would enjoy it and that this trip would benefit both of us! I was skeptical because after all this involved mountain climbing and I thought "How in the world do I convince a teenager to go on a trip like this with his mother?"

That Friday night I took a chance and told Danny that on Saturday we would be getting up early and leave for Gilroy and told him he would enjoy it. At first, he griped that he didn't want to go anywhere so I had to come up with a solution and told him "Danny it's been a while since we enjoyed a day together by ourselves and I will buy you a new pair of shoes on the way back, what do you say?" When nothing works.... a little bribe works miracles!

He finally agreed and the next morning I packed a couple of back packs with a light lunch and we set out to Gilroy, Danny sat by me in the car and kept on asking me where we were going like a little kid... I refused to tell him because I didn't want him to argue with me. He joked with a friend of his on the phone that his mother was kidnapping him... I was just happy to have this time alone with my son....

When we finally got there we went by the main office… not being experienced with mountain climbing we asked the lady at the service desk where we should start, she suggested that we take the easiest trail and direct us to the "Moses Trail."

We set out to find the trail and we were both a little intimidated but I told Danny "If other people can do it, we can also."

The path we took was easy at first and then it got progressively worse… there were stones, curves, bushes and sights of huge mountains all around us! Danny particularly enjoyed the caves and we stopped to take pictures, went up a steep narrow trail…. only large enough for one person at a time that led us to a beautiful resting place…. this lagoon was surrounded by flat rocks, squirrels playing around the water's edge and we liked it so much that we decided to sit on a rock and had our lunch there! We watched the squirrels for a while and went up the trail one more time…. it led us to the top of a mountain with a beautiful view all around us and we took pictures.

After all this was God's creation and we took time to enjoy the view! We stood there for a bit mesmerized for what was in front of us!

Needless to say, the trail down was much easier! I was a bit sad that this climbing trip was over with but just as I promised my son we set out to the Gilroy outlets, I bought him a new pair of shoes and took him to one of his favorite places to eat "Chevy's" of course….

I was surprised that Danny did not want to go home yet and suggested we go out to see a movie! We did just that and it was well after 11PM when we got home…. exhausted but happy and Danny actually bragged to his friend the next day about our adventure!

I kept hoping for a better life for Danny but my son was also going thru puberty and being influenced by friends at high school that were not living their lives like us…. at this age every teenager wants to fit in with the crowd and be popular… they could care less about their future…

One sport Danny loved was basketball! He was tall enough and played often with his friends and I decided to invest $1,000 for a personal trainer at my gym so that he could have someone give him the training he needed to be a success at this sport. Unfortunately, he wasn't very consistent and became obsessed with video games and making money…. he got himself a part-time job at a local grocery store and I watched his grades slip down….

I was becoming seriously in debt because unfortunately all the candida treatments I had bought for me and Danny were not paid for by insurance, neither were the smoothies or the organic foods! The money I got from my ex-husband was barely enough to help with the rent and I also had bills to pay including Danny's ortho treatments…

There was no other choice but to charge credit cards to the max and for me it became "Rob Peter to pay Paul."

I didn't tell anyone for fear that someone would tell me "If you stop all these treatments and eat normally you will be able to do a lot better." For me that was impossible…. this was my only solution to be able to heal! In my heart, I knew that my life was not going to be like this forever… that someday I would be healed enough to be on a cheaper protocol…

Not everyone did what I did and that was to research when in doubt and I also researched what could happen if you left candida untreated. I found something that convinced me if necessary, I would have to stay on a candida treatment for the rest of my life and that was "that candida left untreated can lead to cancer." Imagine how I felt having the family history that I had!

Meanwhile Danny gave up on his dreams of basketball and dedicated himself to play video games and making money … I also found out from one of his bank statements that he was using his ATM card to buy food at McDonalds, Taco Bell and even at work! That day I became extremely angry and decided to take him off of everything including the smoothie! I told him that from that day forth the smoothies and treatments were being stopped and told him why. It didn't face him one bit…. he was probably happy that he didn't have to hide food from me anymore…

I was brokenhearted but too angry to admit it!

The next day while I was using the steam room at the gym my ex-husband walked in and asked me what was going on with Danny and me! I asked him why and he said that Danny had told him that I had taken him off everything and I told him why.... he looked straight at me and said, "You know, you told me once that if I didn't heal from candida then you wouldn't either, doesn't that apply to you and Danny as well?" He also had bad news, his cousin Thomas had passed away! I wondered if anyone had the idea of having an autopsy done to find out if he had been right about his illness being caused by working for the Aviary... such a waste! He was an incredible man!

I had lost touch with his sister Maria Cecilia that had moved a couple of times...I knew that with her I would always have her support.... but I didn't want to ask Victor for her whereabouts...

Of course, Victor was trying to help but I did point out to him that Danny and I were not intimate with each other but for Danny's sake the next day much to his displeasure I started him again on the treatments and on the smoothie knowing fully well that he was not dedicated but I also saw that he felt better on the treatments than without...

Once in a while if I found a funny or moving story in the Bible, I would read it to Danny and I come across the book of Daniel.... this young man and his 3 companions had refused to eat the food that the king and the royal family ate because they believed that by eating healthy, they would be stronger than them... they had a contest for 10 days and they won therefore they were allowed to stay in court safe from harm! I wanted to show Danny proof that eating healthier could actually make you stronger not weaker! He enjoyed the story... but refused to change his eating habits...

CHAPTER 74

Physical Improvement worth bragging about!

$\mathcal{A}$s for me I had managed to lose another 20 pounds and something wonderful happened that nobody knew about! Over the years because of this illness, I had lost the feeling that comes when you are about to have a bowel movement and suddenly... I started to get that feeling back and was actually a bit worried at first until I realized that this was an incredible improvement!

Along with the progress also came the die-off from the treatments! The only thing that helped me was extra vitamin C, working out and the steam room. I also found out that if I had headaches from die-off, I could get rid of them by eating extra chicken at a meal along with a cup of coffee! Headaches would probably make any normal person use an off the counter pill but I wanted to keep myself on a natural path as much as possible. I remembered my mother that had been placed on medicine for arthritis and ended up with an ulcer!

At the gym I also joined a speed biking class that had a wonderful instructor! The routines were done at the sound of music and I also joined a Zumba class so that I would not get bored with the same exercise routine each day. I got compliments from everyone about the way I looked and how much energy I had but it seemed that when it came to

292

my own family they were too blind to see or refused to see it! Probably because they didn't want to make the changes themselves...

A guy at the gym stopped me to ask me what was my routine (unusual) and what kept me so young? I looked at him and said, "You actually look pretty good yourself, what have you been doing?" He shared with me that he had been doing Botox treatments and was not too happy with them.... I was very sincere with him and spoke to him like I would speak to a girlfriend "You know it's a combination of eating as organic as possible, exercising and using the steam room every other day. Also, it helps to use good products on your face, for me it's been Melaleuca Products." He smiled and thanked me! Many times, I would see women in the steam using a mask at the same time as they detox-ified.... even using hair masks! Something I didn't agree with... After all the rest of us were inhaling the toxics from whatever products they were using!

A person that saw my improvement and always cheered me on was Dr.Francis! Because she had been so instrumental in my earlier healing, I invited her to come and have lunch with me at my apartment and was elated when she accepted! We enjoyed a homecooked meal that she loved! My doctor and friend that had given me good advice when I needed a friend was there also to applaud the changes in me and in my life!

I really tried to invest in my time wisely and I don't know how I managed to get A's and B's on my tests! Maybe it was my determination to succeed!

It was not always easy attending classes at Patten... I also had to deal with jealousy from other students, one in particular that wanted to become a minister! He saw me read to myself an essay that I was getting ready to submit and asked me if he could read it briefly.... just to get an idea how to write an essay, I felt sorry for him and let him read it for a bit... Unfortunately, he ended up copying the text from my paper and got into trouble with the teacher!

One class that I was attending I also came across discrimination due to favoritism! A group of students brought up at the registrar's office and the teacher was spoken to and disciplined, this was one thing that I really liked about this college…. they really listened to what the students had to say!

Other classes were wonderful to attend including Environmental Studies! This class did not only have a wonderful teacher but the students themselves were not only young but fun to be with! It was at this class that I got to know Al Gore and how much he cared for our environment! We all watched a documentary that he did regarding our planet and the steps he was taking to improve it!

I also made a point to attend church on Sunday and study the Bible… that was also a requirement at Patten…I listened to cassettes in my car of ministers like Dr, Charles Stanley and Joel Osteen with whom I learned to face anything with confidence and faith…

I used what I had been thru to help others and at my church they were starting new groups for the coming year that would benefit people who were struggling with difficult situations. I volunteered to start a group for people that were going thru grief or divorce…. When helping someone in these situations they will believe you a lot faster if you have been thru it yourself….

Thanksgiving at my apartment with Danny was always celebrated with me cooking the traditional turkey, stuffing, corn souffle, etc. While the turkey slowly cooked in the oven I would get in my car and attended a special service at Patten…. this was a wonderful way to give thanks, sing and see teachers and fellow students in a different light! After the service was done, I would drive back home…. take my turkey out of the oven and my kids would join me for a late lunch….

On Christmas Eve I was offered at church the role of leader for the Care and Prayer Ministry Group that was led by a church member that due to personal reasons had to give it up and I accepted it without reservations….

I gave Danny that Christmas a basketball gift of season tickets for 4 games plus another 2 in order to bring back to his heart his dreams but unfortunately that did not actually change his mind about using sports as a career…Christmas Day Carlos and his girlfriend come over and we shared a good meal together…. these were the only times I would let myself eat Portuguese Foods and one year I even bought a Portuguese Bolo Rei… this traditional King Cake was delicious, in my country they had a tradition, they placed a little gift inside the cake (small piece of jewelry) and a fava bean… Whoever got the fava bean (broad bean) had to pay for the Bolo Rei the next year! These were family gatherings that I treasured…

While I succeeded in college Danny struggled to finish High School…

CHAPTER 75

Making a difference in people's lives….

*I*n January of 2007 my new support group was started on the 1st Sunday of each month and 3 women joined…. each one there for different reasons, one because of the death of a brother, another because of a separation between her and a fiancé and the last a pending divorce. Between what I had gone thru myself and the Counseling classes I was taking at Patten I was able to give them sound advice and I was very pleased with the results! It was like I had been born for this!

One woman in particular absorbed every word that I said, the one that was going thru the divorce! It was awesome to see her grow more and more confident! I had become her role model and she loved her new independence!

I did not know that I could have that kind of impact on someone's life! For me it was not that this gave me any kind of power but that I was now able to turn around, fulfill my promise to God and help others along the way….

On Sunday's before I went to the Care and Prayer Ministry room to pray with someone, I prayed that God would send me someone that really needed my encouragement or guidance that day and it was amazing how many people needed someone to pray with!!

It was awesome how prayer worked! I was given an opportunity to help someone feel less alone…. Dorothy was an elderly woman that loved to attend our church services and lived alone in an apartment complex with her small dog. We started talking one day after the service and when we started talking about favorite foods, she shared with me that she went hungry sometimes because she didn't know how to cook for herself!

I asked her to give me her address and surprised her one Saturday by showing up with a container (enough for a week) of homemade Portuguese soup, she loved the food and most of all the company! I felt so sorry for her! I decided to make a weekly trip to her apartment, spend time with her and helped her come up with a food plan. Trader Joes was within walking distance, I wrote down for her meals that were already prepared that she could buy at the store and store them in her refrigerator. Our friendship lasted for quite a while, I had the feeling that she also suffered from loneliness...

Many times, friends at our church when they saw me enter the building, they approached me to ask me how I was doing and smiling I would tell them "Up to no good as usual!" They always laughed at this comment.... especially an older gentleman that was our greeter! He became very dear to me! He had a problem with his balance and every time I saw him... I had to reminded him to get his cane, he would smile and then go and get it!

As long as I remember I had a great fondness for the elderly and for children! In a lot of families, they can be the most neglected human beings on this planet! Most of the time they are also the most silent ones in their suffering...

I was approaching my graduation at Patten and was asked by the editor of the school paper, professor Dr. Gunkel to give a testimony along with my picture of how my relationship with God had started and what had led me to Patten University on May of 2007. After 2 years of hard work and dedication I graduated from Patten University with a Certificate of Ministry and celebrated with my sons and friends.... it was a day of triumph for me and a day I would never forget!!

One thing for sure I didn't want my experience with Patten to be over with and prayed that God somehow would give me direction and He did!

I spoke with someone at the Registrar's office at Patten that told me that I could continue my education with an Associate Degree this time…. It would mean another 2 ½ years of sacrifice but I also loved Patten too much to leave it at this point…

Everyone at Patten had read my personal testimony in the school paper and stopped me often to congratulate me in how I changed my life! Little did they know how many sacrifices I had to make but like I told someone…. sometimes sacrificing can also bring you rewards!

One thing I found out thru a class at Patten was that I had to improve my public speaking and after some research I found Toastmasters, a non-profit organization that trains people in public speaking and leadership skills, I loved it right from the beginning! I had always been shy when speaking in class, this experience would also benefit me there and when speaking to people at church.

♦

CHAPTER 76

Danny's High School graduation and trying to be a good parent…

$\mathcal{I}$kept my grades up but Danny was struggling to graduate from High School! In order for him to graduate I had to intervene and make sure all his class requirements were done, I called his teachers and made sure that he attended every class…. he agreed because he really wanted to graduate. Danny called me at work on the day before his graduation almost in tears that he was 5 credits short! All I could do was to calm him down and told him to ask around how could this be resolved and prayed…

It wasn't too long before I got a call that same day from Danny's counselor to let me know not to worry because his business teacher had forgotten to add in the computer the credits owed to him for working at the grocery store. That thank God meant that Danny would be able to graduate the next day, June11th!

I loved the experience! I didn't get to see Carlos's graduate because he graduated thru night school so there was no graduation ceremony, I even made the time to design the graduation cards for Danny to send to family and friends. On the day of the graduation my ex-husband was there, some our friends and we took lots of pictures…a day to remember!

We had the reception at our apartment and I found out that Danny was planning to take a year off to work instead of enrolling in college! I knew if Danny took a year off, he would never make it to college… so one day by myself at home I enrolled him thru the internet in a college that had a basketball court and so that he would stay also convinced his best friend to enroll! Danny promised to give it a try and I just hoped that he would give it a chance...

Some friends of mine had advised me to give up and let him make his own choices and mistakes but I was not made that way! I believed in giving my kids advice and direction and then let them do their own decisions… this way my conscience was clear that I done my job as a parent…At the time that Carlos had been a teenager I had been too sick to be the parent I wanted to be but that didn't stop me now by encouraging him every opportunity I got. He had always dreamed of being a film director and I told him to look at my life, how it had changed and that there was always a second opportunity!

His father had not been great of giving him praise for whatever he did correctly, many times I had caught him calling Carlos an idiot and that he would never amount to nothing! Words like this can be deadly for a child that in turn will stop believing in themselves… I had always stopped him when I caught him doing this…. but this was also a cycle learned from previous relationships and Victor had learned this from his own father, I refused for this to be repeated in my family…

Being a parent isn't always easy especially when dealing with teenagers! Sometimes we say one thing, their friends say another and they usually go by what their friends say, after all… we are considered "Too old! Or too old fashioned!" Perfect example of this was what happened near where we lived. I was on my way to the supermarket one day when I noticed a memorial full of flowers by the train tracks with the picture of a young woman, when I got home that afternoon, I asked Danny about it… the young woman actually had attended Danny's High School, he told me that on her way home...she had been wearing her headphones, didn't hear the train coming and was hit and killed instantly!!

On the news they had advised teenagers to be extremely careful using headphones while walking because they would not be able to listen to outside noises! Probably if the parent of this young woman had advised her not to use headphones while walking…she probably would have told them that there was no harm on using them and that they were old fashioned!

It's unfortunate that sometimes it takes a tragedy for other children to listen!

Since my finances were not doing well, I tried becoming a Melaleuca rep and found out that people would buy the products, loved them but to be able to get the preferred prices they would have to spend about $60 dollars each month (35 points) … for most people this was hard to afford so they would cancel their memberships and I would not be able to get a decent commission! So, I gave up on being a rep and learned to love the products for myself… one of them that became my favorite was the Gold Bar, an antifungal soap made with tea tree oil… among others…

CHAPTER 77

A unforgettable trip to Chicago!

*F*unny that same week I received an e-mail from my cousin inviting me to join her in a company that she believed in that had natural products! I told her that I would like to try them first before trying to sell them and she sent me samples. I tried the beauty products, liked them and decided to become a sales rep on the side, I got permission to demonstrate the products at Curves and 24hr fitness… women would buy small orders and then unfortunately would not re-buy and I wondered if this was going to work! Before I had a chance to give up on this company, I got an invitation from my cousin to join her in Chicago for a week of training and to meet the founder of the company, I decided to accept the offer and got ready to fly there… I was looking forward to being with my cousin and to explore a new city.

I did like Chicago but found the weather a bit colder than California, the city was beautiful, I loved my cousin's place and being with her! I set out to learn all I could about this company that my cousin was so excited about… I didn't want to disappoint her, so I used the products daily while I was there. I was also told that they wanted me eventually to take the place of the founder of the company …I wasn't sure I wanted to make my living this way! I was still attending college and the pull that I felt was to go into ministry… this part-time job for me was only to help me pay bills...

There was also something that I didn't like about the products, I knew just like me a lot of women didn't like using too many products on their faces to achieve results and this also added up costs... because I didn't want to hurt my cousin's feelings... I decided to keep this to myself...

I managed while I was there to walk to the local gym, used the steam and shopped at the Wholefoods market... my new lifestyle went everywhere with me... I would say the best days for me in Chicago were the Friday and Saturday before I was to leave! That Friday night I had reserved my time to attend a speech given at the Convention Center by Dr. Creflo Dollar, he focused on the suffering that Brazilian people were going thru... I was touched by his call to everyone to help the families in Brazil that were living in poverty! That night I was one of many that contributed to this cause...

Unfortunately, I was left without a ride back home because my cousin and her husband had gone out to dinner... I didn't get scared instead I looked around and found a limo outside with a driver. I asked him how to get a taxi and told him I was new in town... he said that he had be waiting for people that had found another ride and told me "Hop in, I will take home with no charge." I got in a little nervous but I looked inside and realized that this was actually a brand-new limo... a new experience for me! I decided to enjoy it and got home safe! Even my cousin was surprised how I had managed to get back to her home safe and sound!

That Saturday morning my cousin and I enjoyed breakfast together, went to a Farmers Market and passed by Lake Michigan and had a ball seeing the Chicago Air and Water Show! We finished with a ride thru Oak Street on a convertible, took pictures and watched the Blue Angeles flying above us! It was an awesome experience that I would never forget!

I went back home knowing that the goal my cousin had in mind would take me away from college and from my sons and I was not about to give up on neither... I didn't want to hurt her feelings because I knew she and her husband really wanted this for me, so I continued to sell the products as much as I could. No matter how much I tried I couldn't get anyone to place a second order, they kept on complaining about the prices and that to achieve results they had to use an accumulation of products that they didn't like...

After a while I had to give up because even with demonstrations made at Curves, gyms and even supermarkets I couldn't make enough money to make it worth my time! I was becoming exhausted by juggling work, college, ministry, sales and trying to take care of me and Danny! My cousin of course got angry and I received an e-mail from her that really hurt my feelings! I tried to explain to her how I felt but she wouldn't listen and stopped talking to me...

I believed in finishing what I started and I couldn't stop college and give up on my family just to make someone else happy... so I gave up on explaining how I felt and went back to I had been doing previously...

CHAPTER 78

Making a difference in someone's life...

*M*eanwhile at church I came across someone that I had met at Bible Study! Helena had seen me at my worst while going thru betrayal and coping with an illness, she couldn't believe how I had changed both physically and personally! I looked strong and walked with a new confidence... Helena on the other hand looked tired and sad and I felt this incredible need to help her! Our friendship started with phone calls and talking in church. I found out that she was suffering from severe joint pain, stomach problems and that her husband was dying from lung cancer...the sadness that I saw in her eyes was not only depression caused by being mistreated by her husband but also because of not feeling well...

When I finally by her invitation visited her at her home, I saw with my own eyes the reason for her depression! Anger and resentment were abundant in this house and Helena was struggling to survive in an environment that was suffocating her...no wonder all she could focus on was on her health and the need to give up!

Our friendship grew and I often would take Helena to my apartment to get her away from that environment, we would sit and read the Bible together and I fixed her home cooked meals. It was amazing how much her mood would improve by positive reinforcement and proper nutrition!

305

I brought it up to her attention and she informed me that at home they didn't trust her in the kitchen and many times she gave up on cooking for herself! Her son cooked for all three of them but she wasn't eating enough and she had lost quite a bit of weight! I started taking Helena grocery shopping with me and introduced her to organic foods, to books that I been reading regarding nutrition and helped her by being there to really listen when she wanted to talk...

I took her on a Saturday to the Lady of Fatima Festival in Thornton and showed her what faith was all about...she loved the festival, especially the procession and we came back home in a great mood!

We also attended a Women of Faith conference together and heard testimonies from a group of women of how God had transformed their lives! Helena loved to hear their stories and it actually renewed her faith...

Little by little she changed right before my eyes, when she called me, she was not only focusing on her health issues but she now was also showing concern for her husband! She would ask me to read the Bible to her, we would pray together and even attended Bible Study... She gained some of the weight she had lost and started to take interest in the way she dressed and best of all she had a new will to live!

I cannot tell you what an impact seeing these changes in a person has on another person if you are partly responsible for these changes! The first time I saw Helena really smile and laugh out loud I was ecstatic!

She also called me one day and surprised me by asking me if I could find a picture of Jesus anywhere (she loved mine), she wanted to place His picture in her bedroom. At first, I looked everywhere (even the store I had bought mine) and since I couldn't find one... I printed a beautiful picture of Him from the internet, bought a frame and delivered it to her one day... she was very touched and immediately took it to her room...

By helping Helena unfortunately, I also had to confront her husband and son! They were afraid of her spending time with me because after all I was a divorced, independent woman from a different culture!

Once they saw that I was very serious about keeping my relationship with her they stopped interfering, I knew if I gave up on her she could very well go back to depression and sooner or later she would have to face her husband's death. Since I had dealt with cancer before I knew she was going to need me…

My plan was to help her become strong enough to be able to deal with her husband's death when it came and to stand on her own two feet…

CHAPTER 79

Two very important incidents that could have been tragic!

*A*nd then something strange happened to me at work! I started to get sleepy and would struggle to stay awake after my lunch hour! This had happened to me while driving as well! I almost had a very serious accident on the way home from visiting Carlos and his girlfriend… we had a great time with them playing Mini Golf and I asked Danny to keep on talking to me while I was driving back because I felt very tired… unfortunately Danny decided to talk to someone on the phone and I must of closed my eyes for a second because I found myself within an inch of the car in front of me hearing Danny scream out my name!!

All I had time to do was to steer the car to the right and by doing so I lost control of the car! Went over the embarkment… came down again and all I could do was to pray out loud for God to help us! Suddenly, I felt like someone was telling me to let go of the wheel and did so… believe it or not the car came to a stop at the side of the road with a rear flat tire, a hole on the other back tire and a damaged motor mount! Danny and I were amazed that we had managed to survive this accident without anyone being hurt!

I managed very slowly to drive the car back to our apartment complex and parked it for the night, I knew the next morning I would have to take it to be fixed and meanwhile I heard Danny call his brother and exclaim that without God's help we would have not made it!

It was a wonderful thing to know that both my sons believed in God!

This incident also made me realize that I was pushing myself way too hard! I read in the Bible that even the Apostles had been forced by Jesus Christ to take time off… I was so driven that I had an extremely hard time to slow down! This could happen to anyone and unfortunately could cause health problems down the road…. We both called this a Heavenly intervention and we were so happy to be home!

You never know where help may come from someday! I had proof of that because I also ended up needing Helena's help one day! I had just picked up Helena to bring her up to my apartment when on the way up we were stopped by a man that took a hold of my purse! Knowing very well that inside I had my driver's license, money and credit cards I refused to let go of it…. he lifted his fist and was getting ready to strike me down when I heard Helena scream "Let it go." I did just that and because of Helena's scream some of our neighbors heard the commotion and called the police…

Once we got to my apartment, I was frozen and in shock for a minute and went to my room… prayed and calmed myself down. I looked up at the picture of Jesus Christ I had up on my wall, asked Him for help and suddenly I knew what to do! I called my bank froze my ATM card and called my credit card holders. I was also informed that I would not be able to access my funds until I was given a new ATM card and checks to use…. that left me with no income and I knew I was going to need money for groceries and gas for the next day! I felt violated that night! This man had taken more than just money and credit cards, he also had taken family pictures and my address book…

In a way something good came out of this! I learned to look into my checking account each day to check on recent transitions so that I knew right away if someone had found a way to use my debit card!

Helena in my living room had called her family and within a few minutes they were over my apartment with cash in their hands enough to buy groceries and gas for my car the next day!

My church also come to my rescue by donating $500 for any expenses with my car and other unforeseen expenses!

It was hard replacing everything but even harder having to deal with the feeling of uneasiness I now had every time I came home alone! I even hid my purse in a bag! It took a while to feel comfortable around my apartment, many times Danny would meet me downstairs and we walked up to our apartment together...

At work keeping awake after my lunch hour had become a constant struggle and I started to put two and two together and realized that I was taking a small blood pressure pill at lunch that could be causing me side effects and that would have to be adjusted. My supervisor had noticed that I was struggling to keep awake and told me to do something about it, he refused to believe that this could be the blood pressure medicine and blamed it on me being tired and pushing myself too hard!

At this point because there had been layoffs in our company, I knew that I was also at risk of losing my job and decided to schedule an appointment with my personal doctor and had blood work done. My doctor had me decrease the amount of the blood pressure medicine gradually that I was taking since I had lost quite a bit of weight.... he told me that he would not be surprised if I managed to completely get out of it! I also asked my doctor to write a note that I could give my supervisor so that he wouldn't use this incident to fire me and he did...

Back at work that week I showed my supervisor the bottle of the medicine I was taking.... showed him the side effects, the letter from my doctor and I was surprised when he asked me to speak to my doctor! I gave him his number since I had nothing to hide.... Things went from bad to worse in this company.... branches were closing, people were let go without references and I was getting worried that the same thing would happen to me since they also had a good reason in their point of view...

I had been working for this company for over 2 years, had done great work even while attending college so I wasn't about to give up this job this easy!

I scheduled a meeting with the vice-president of the company and explained the situation, I showed her the letter from my doctor…. she suggested that my supervisor and I have a meeting and come to an agreement to our mutual benefit. The meeting was scheduled but I knew that what they were trying to do was to let go of me instead of laying me off…

I prayed before entering his office but he also had a meeting with the vice-president prior to our meeting, she wasn't happy that he had not given me my two month review due to what was going on with my health so when I entered his office he was a lot more mellow! He gave me a reference letter for future employment and informed me that I would be able to use the internet at work half of hour at the time, in the morning and in the afternoon… also use the fax machine and receive calls regarding employment.

My last day would be November 16th. In order to get this reference letter and extra time to stay, I was asked to sign a letter that I was living of my own accord… I could hardly wait…. the place was now deserted and the atmosphere was very tense…

God knows I could use the money and the time off to look for work! Being able to look for another position at work saved me time since at home I had to dedicate any extra time I had to study and finish my semester at college. While at work I watched my supervisor interview candidates for my position and went from being glad to being extremely angry!

Looking for work let me tell you it takes work! I had to try to find a job near my apartment and college that also paid enough to pay the rent and that would definitely take time...

I performed my job to the best of my ability to the last day and got out of there with grace and dignity…. said goodbye to friends left behind and left justice up to God…after all my supervisor had seen me get better and I now knew that he had been looking for an excuse to let me go!

CHAPTER 80

Losing a job and got a better one…

*F*rom that point on I lived near my computer, looked for work, finished assignments for college, went for interviews and prayed for a good job asap!

Helena also lost her husband to cancer but was strong enough to survive it! Unfortunately, she also would have to stay strong enough to deal with her son that was very set in his ways and had old fashioned values…

Thanksgiving for me and Danny was different that year… Both my sons would be going to their uncle's house to have dinner and my ex-husband had agreed to be there as well…. as for me I decided to do something different and volunteered to serve the homeless for the Salvation Army in Oakland. I had never done this before but it turned to be a very rewarding experience! I helped to serve a Thanksgiving meal to many people and I was startled by a man that entered the building…... he was handsome, tall, had a beard and looked (you guessed it!) like Jesus Christ! I couldn't take my eyes off him!

Unfortunately, I was not in charge of serving his table! I watched him eat and socialize with other guys… I and other servers proceeded to help clean tables and when I looked up, he was gone! For the rest of my life, I wondered if he was just a homeless guy wanting a warm meal or if Jesus Christ had showed up out of the blue to mingle with the poor…. like we read about in the Bible!

That Christmas I refused to wallow in misery, sang Christmas songs at home and attended church services. My sons upset about what had happened to me at work wanted me to take the company to court because I had been intimidated into signing a form that I was leaving of my own accord. I told them that I refused to do that because I wanted God (who sees all) to be my justice and explained to them that this kind of action would not benefit me while looking for another job…

I was told that the vice-president's mother had passed away just before Christmas and decided without telling anyone to attend the services to offer my sympathies. I reached out to her and told her that I also had lost my mother before Thanksgiving one year… I knew how these memories unfortunately stay with you forever…I left feeling that God's blessing was upon me and that I had showed her that I was woman with integrity and honor….

Within a few days I received a call from a company in San Ramon for an interview and a couple of days after I was offered a position as a Credit Rep with better pay, better benefits and willing to work with me on finishing my degree at college! I accepted this new challenge knowing that this meant that I would have to learn a new industry but willing to do it!

I was there just a couple of months when everyone was called into a general meeting held by our vice president, everyone was scared not knowing what to expect…. we were informed that due to inflation they would be forced to lay off people and boy was I scared!

My heart skipped a beat and I thought "What am I going to do now if this also affects me?"

They were a few people laid off that day but fortunately for me my department did not get touched and that was a blessing!

At work I had to deal with women that were too stubborn to listen! I had done enough research on my own to know that when going thru pre-menopause, if you exercised and changed your eating habits the

313

symptoms would improve dramatically! Unfortunately, when I shared this with my co-workers that used fans on their desks due to hot flashes, they ignored me! Sometimes when we don't want to change our life-style it just easier to suffer… the problem here is that people around you also end up suffering! Working or living with someone that suffers from mood swings can be awful!

I had dealt with women going thru menopause before at MCSi… sometimes afraid to go inside someone's office for fear of being yelled at for no reason!

I finally came to the conclusion that I was better off just leaving women alone when there were too stubborn to change their ways!

Meanwhile at college I also had to deal with a new class in Communications that instead of building my self-esteem made me doubt myself… even with the experience I was getting at Toastmasters! The teacher every time I had to speak in front of the class would find a reason to criticize me and my grades went down because of him! I actually asked him what he suggested I do to improve my grades! I told him about the training that I was receiving at Toastmasters and shared with him that I had won contests and received ribbons for my speeches. He was not impressed! I happened not to like this teacher and told him that is attitude towards me was not helping me to do better… instead brought my self-esteem down. He did get a little bit better after our conversation…. probably because I had the guts to stand up to him…

My health on the hand was another issue! Candida was not com-pletely gone from my body, I was forced to do another round of treat-ments from Whole Approach and that left me discouraged! I called Linda and shared with her how I was feeling, she encouraged me by telling me that for some people it could take up to 2 years or more to get rid of the candida depending how long they had it and not to give up! I was happy that I had received this information from someone that had the illness and survived it! I sent her a picture of Danny and me with a sincere thank you!

I looked back to realize how far I had come as well…. from an unhealthy size 20 to a much healthier and younger size 8/10…. that was quite an accomplishment that nobody could deny!

I was very glad that I had that conversation with Linda because I still had to put up with stupid comments from friends and family, like "How come you are not healed yet?" "How long have you been on those treatments now?"

I also knew something they didn't know is what candida looks like in the intestines! As this stuff was coming out of me, I took pictures and then went on the internet to look for pictures to compare them with… and found out that these treatments were bringing this stuff out! Even the fungus on my toenails was actually disappearing little by little...

CHAPTER 81

Some people refuse to change!

I always managed to sidetrack negative comments but there was one in particular that left me foaming at the mouth!

I had taken the day off to stay home due to car problems, my ex-husband called me to let me know that he would be picking up Danny to take him to the DMV and to let him know that he was on the way. I woke up Danny and asked him to please don't tell his father that I was home that day… I was not in the mood to see him and went in my room and closed the door…

It wasn't too long after, that Victor entered my kitchen, looked at my kitchen table and made a remark out loud "I see that your mother is still on this Candida shit!" Next, he looked at the picture of Jesus that I had by my computer and remarked "I don't believe on any of this crap!" Victor had been the only person that ever had dared to make that kind of comment about that picture!

In my room I bit my tongue and held my breath because what I wanted to do was to burst into the kitchen and let him have it!

This man was now so full of conceit it was incredible! It was thanks to him that I developed this illness to begin with! I felt so sorry for Danny because I knew that he was trying his best to have his father leave the apartment. When his father asked him if he wanted to stay and study the DMV book…he told him that he preferred to leave and study the book on the way to the DMV office…

Once they were both gone… I regained my composure enough to sit in front of my computer and finish my assignments for that week for college…

I also used my weekends when I had free time to visit St. Joseph's cemetery in San Pablo to see my family, bring them flowers and visit old friends, it never failed that I would hear of Victor's latest comments about me! They ranged from all the money that I was using in organic foods and treatments to my newfound religion! On one of those trips, I took Danny with me so that we could visit Ken, an old friend of our family…he absolutely loved me and the kids and was very saddened by what had happened to our marriage. Victor and I used to take the kids to their home, Ken would play cards with Carlos that always made him laugh by accusing him of cheating! After our visit we went by our old home…. thinking that it was there, instead we saw a duplex!

Both of us were brokenhearted! Danny called his brother and told him "Guess what bro? our home in San Pablo is now a duplex!" Carlos asked him how I was and Danny told him "She is upset of course but there is nothing we can do about it!" We left and I made a promise to myself that day that one day if I could find a way to help my sons have a home of their own I would! Hopefully a bigger and better one!

Because of all the stupid comments I was hearing from people that knew me very well I really wanted the chance to tell him off and that chance came one Saturday morning! He called me with an excuse and asked me what was wrong! I finally told him that I had overheard his conversation with Danny in our living room and that I had just visited some friends of ours in San Pablo and was informed of his latest comments regarding my lifestyle…I challenged him that day to start being real to me instead of being one person in front of me and another in the back of me! Of course, he twisted the truth and finished by letting me know that he still thought of me constantly!

My answer to him was that he had made his choice in how he wanted to live is life and to let me live mine!

Frankly I had lost my trust in him, all I wanted was for him to be happy with his girlfriend and leave me alone... I told him that day that I did not go around talking badly about him to his children or friends and expected the same respect back...

CHAPTER 82

Overcoming challenging situations…

*I*t seemed that I was always dealing with situations that challenged me but I always managed to fight back including an incident with my car! While at lunch break doing an errand… I was hit sideways on the passenger side! The car that hit me was an old pickup truck and was hardly damaged but my car was hit pretty badly and had to be towed!

I was overwhelmed and thought of how I was going to cope with no car, a deductible of $500 I needed to pay and higher insurance rates.

The guy that hit me came around and we exchanged information…. he actually gave me a lift to my job and that same afternoon I got a rent a car so that I could keep working. Within a few days my insurance company called me to tell me that they didn't want to fix the car… instead they were going to pay off the remaining amount owed on the car and give me $400 back to use towards another car!

Where in the world can you find a car for $400?

My insurance company had given me until May 16th to keep the rental car but after that I was on my own!

I kept it for another week…. unwilling to give up my legs and the day I finally had to return the rental car in San Ramon I walked to work and yes…praised God that I still had two legs to walk to work and thanked Him for the next car He would provide me with!

When I got to work, I shared what I was going thru with my supervisor, she informed me that there was a bus that stopped right by my job that went straight to the Bart station and stopped at the San Leandro Bart station. Once I arrived there I would have to walk to my apartment or to the 24-hour fitness club nearby, before I tried this route, I was offered to be picked up by a co-worker that lived near me… I accepted that option first but it didn't work out! She made us constantly late each morning and I ended up being called to my manager's office where I was informed that this could not continue! I could end up losing my job!

So…this left me with no alternative but to use the bus and Bart option! I fixed my meals and studied and most nights ended up going to bed at 11PM! I found myself sometimes falling asleep in front of the computer…but refused to give up!

Many people would have resorted to eating TV dinners for lunch and dinner to get more sleep! I refused! I had seen for myself what eating healthy could do for your concentration at work! Eating healthy just like anything else can become a habit…. you actually start to enjoy preparing your own meals and being creative!

Maybe because of being this kind of person God always managed to bring to me people that helped me even with grocery shopping! Not only to take me back and forth but to help me bring the groceries up to my apartment!

Even at Patten I was offered help when I most needed it! I found out that in order to finish my degree I would have to pass an algebra class and I panicked!

I had never been great at math in high school and I knew algebra was going to be a challenge! When I got to the class I met this wonderful young instructor from Brazil… once I shared my worries with him he immediately volunteered to tutor me on the side for free!

That meant that I would have to meet with him on campus before my classes begun or after they were over with… he really took his time with me and it paid off because I started getting A's and B's!

My best subject by far was the Counseling Class! This class was like the continuation of what I had learned thru Dr.Howard Liebgold! I got re-trained in Phobias, OCD, Hoarding, Depression, etc and also learned a valuable lesson thru this class! We had a young man join us that was in charge of producing the videos for our class… when I looked at him, I thought "If anyone looked at this young man anywhere, they would actually be afraid of him!" He was full of tattoos, had a beard and long hair! I sat right behind him and had a chance to see him working on the videos! He totally surprised me when I heard him speak about Jesus Christ with admiration! That goes to show that you cannot judge a book by its cover!

I strictly forbade my sons of sharing with my ex-husband what I was going thru at college or with my finances because I did not want his fake sympathy or admiration in any way! I scraped and found a way to go to cheaper supermarkets like Trader Joes to be able to eat the organic foods that I needed to heal and if I had problems on anything I would go to anyone but him…

It was enough having friends ask me when I was going to get a new car! They thought I made enough to pay for a high rent and afford a car payment. I was too proud to admit that the income that I received was just enough to get by and was not about to make a mistake to make anyone happy…

I also used my knowledge to help those that helped me or to give them encouragement if they needed it…. even on the bus that I took to work I managed to minister to a bus driver that was seeking a deeper relationship with God! I shared my own transition from Catholicism to Christianity with him, my family history and we developed a great friendship!

As far as my health goes it was a constant struggle! I saw improvements but I also dropped from a size 8/10 to a size 5/6! It didn't help having friends and family making comments how I looked! I always found an excuse…. that I ate really good and that I was just too busy and couldn't keep the weight on… My clothes were getting baggy on me and I could not afford to buy new clothes, a friend of mine at work looked at me one day and asked me what size I was... I shared with her that I could not afford to buy new clothes and she surprised me one day by bringing to work a bunch of clothes from her closet that fit me perfectly!

I had shared my dilemma with clothing at my church as well and was given clothing from church members that wanted to help me.... pretty soon I found myself with a closet full of extremely nice clothes...

On the days that I felt discouraged I listened to Joel Osteen and filled myself with positive thoughts and faith! I even managed to read inspirational books like the "Battlefield of the Mind" by Joyce Myers that helped recognize the thought process and used positive affirmations to keep a positive mind...

I knew that if my hands were tied at the moment God's were not and that He worked behind the scenes, so many times I had to remind myself of this fact and pressed on...

At home my relationship with Danny grew worse... he refused the candida treatments, he started smoking (something that broke my heart) and now had a steady girlfriend that he was having sex with...

He had given up college and had been promoted as a head clerk at the grocery store he worked for.... he was so intelligent and stubborn at the same time!

Many nights I picked up Danny at the grocery store late at night because he wasn't driving yet.... I didn't mind, we had become partners when we had moved out of the house we had lived in... sacrifices can be made if you really love someone...

However, I had a reality check one night when I was standing up and praying instead of kneeling to keep awake and found myself waking up with my face on the mattress and realized that I had fallen asleep while standing up!

That happened quite a few times and I knew I was spreading myself too thin! Unfortunately... I had no one that I could rely on...

Chapter 83

Betrayal in a big way!

*V*ictor actually tried to talk to Danny about giving up at least the smoking because of our family history but he was too stubborn to listen! He was getting ready to leave for Portugal and had even promised Danny that he would take him to Pismo and give him $200 when he came back if he quit smoking, that unfortunately did not help!

My ex-husband called me prior to talking to Danny to let me know that he was leaving on vacation to Portugal and without me asking him he told me that he would not be taking his girlfriend with him… when I asked him why he stated that he no longer trusted her! He had caught her going out with other guys… my answer to him was "Now you know how I felt!"

Once in Portugal he soon found a new love interest… believe it or not one of my first cousins!

I didn't learn this information from him… I was told by my oldest son one day when we got together with Danny to go and eat out. My response to my son was that with his father there was no boundaries but this one did surprise me! Maybe a bit of retaliation on his part because of our breakup! He constantly bragged about his conquests to his sons… little did he know that they were actually ashamed of his behavior and wondered what had happened to their father!

He had also gone to the island of Azores and was running with the bulls, a traditional event that almost got him stabbed by a bull! He was trying to relieve his childhood and probably thought that if all this information got back to me that I would react…but I could care less! He had hurt me too much for me to care…

It wasn't too long after that I got a call from my cousin Saozinha in Portugal (we were more like sisters than cousins) asking me how I was… it didn't surprise me because we had always kept in close contact… I shared with her that I knew that my ex-husband was dating her oldest sister and that this would not affect our relationship at all! Because both were my cousins, I also had to tell her about candida and how thru sex it could contaminate the other partner just in case her sister had health problems later on…. She felt sorry for what I had been thru but also told me that from what she had witnessed about Victor he had a way with women and could charm anyone!

I knew that! I had seen it myself but that didn't give him the right to go around infecting other women when he had been educated thru me and doctors as well about candida….

It was funny how one piece of information can lead to another! My sister-in-law, Rosa called me one day to tell me that my godmother's husband was pretty sick! I had lost touch with her after her first husband had passed away, she had moved to the islands of Azores and now was taking care of her second husband. I asked my sister-in-law to give me her phone number and called her that same day, this was one woman that always been on my side and she was delighted to hear from me!

She told me that I was correct, Ernesto was bedridden and she was taking care of him but she also shared something with me that I could not believe! In her own words "You know that Victor came by to see Ernesto and brought your sister-in-law with him! Rumors are going around that they are dating!"

It took a while to digest this one! If this was true, even this would be beneath him! She had been married to my brother Jose Carlos and Victor had not only been his brother-in-law but his best friend!

I hung up and promised to keep in touch with her, it seemed to me that my ex-husband's motives for dating women that I knew or were related to me was to try to hurt me and make me jealous…. little did he know that he made me sick with his actions….

As for me I concentrated on my work and in developing friendships with strong women!

At the company I worked for they ended up needing another person that was familiar with collections and I actually referred a former supervisor of mine that had worked with me on another company. She was hired, we developed a close friendship and shared our lunches together…. it was awesome to have someone that I trusted near me!

She knew that I took public transportation like she did and often teased me about the bus driver that I had met and developed a friendship with… Stan was a tall fairly good-looking man older than I was and also divorced. I told her many times that I was burned out about men but she kept on insisting that I should give him a chance, I laughed it off but he actually surprised me one day by asking me out for lunch and I accepted.

CHAPTER 84

Starting new relationships…

We developed a close relationship and even managed to go grocery shopping together! We went for walks in the marina and I even cooked for him in my apartment, this was a strictly a platonic relationship, he often held my hand and kissed me lightly but that was it! I found out that he had many food allergies and introduced him to Dr. Francis. He liked her immediately, she ran a few tests on him and we found out that he also suffered from candida!

And you guess it! He also had been married to someone that had not been faithful!

He actually told her "I want to be just like Mary!" and she told him "Follow her example and advice because she has come a long way!"

He liked my food so much that he even asked me to teach him how to cook, he especially loved my green beans and salmon. One day he asked me why my food tasted so good and I told him "Any food that you cook with love comes out good." He complained that when he tried making my dishes at his place, they never came out the same! His weight was up a bit and so was his blood pressure and it would be for his benefit to lose some weight!

I knew for a fact that unless a person really enjoyed their food they would never stick to a program! I also convinced him to join the 24-hr fitness club, join me for a few workouts and he was placed on Linda's protocol for candida. Little by little he started to lose weight and was taken off blood pressure medication gradually.... Some of things he was into totally amazed me! Like the day he admitted to me of taking baths and using dishwashing liquid as soap! I got him off of that in a hurry and introduced him to the Gold Bar from Melaleuca instead... he absolutely loved the experience and even switched laundry products that he was using! He looked a lot better and became involved in my church! He attended services often with me and became an usher.... something he really enjoyed...

There was something that bother me about our relationship! I had been with a very sexual man that all I had to do was to touch him and he was ready to hit the sack! I was now involved with a man that could lay down with me on the couch... hug me and never once had I seen him aroused!

He hinted that he wanted to marry me and I had to discuss my concerns with him...... he finally admitted that he had problems performing in bed and blamed it on being traumatized by his ex-wife! I told him that we would discuss this with Dr. Francis and find a natural way to heal instead of medicines that could harm your health instead and he agreed....

We also attended a Joel Osteen event together at the Oakland Coliseum that he enjoyed but he admitted that women ministers were still his favorites.

Stan also loved to see me write.... many times, he would sit by me on the couch and asked me to read to him what I had written, he even believed that I could become a wonderful minister one day!

He bragged about his weight loss and how happy he was with his life change to me and to some of his friends at work...One thing he absolutely hated was to go shopping in Berkeley, the people there like he said, "Freak me out", for me this was funny from a man that drove a bus for a living!

However, he loved Santa Cruz! We took take many trips out there and used his yellow convertible Toyota with reverse gears! We took turns driving his car because he wanted me to have that experience and I loved it!

One trip that we really enjoyed together was at the Santa Cruz Monarch Butterfly Grove! We saw the most beautiful butterflies! We managed to have the time to stop by a beach nearby, got our feet wet and stopped at the Whole Foods Market for lunch, drove to the Santa Cruz Boardwalk, walked around and then drove back home…...These were the trips that we loved the most and always went back home with fresh vegetables for us to cook….

On one of our shopping trips to Berkeley after we did our grocery shopping, we stopped for lunch at one of our favorite healthy restaurants. I had been in between treatments and was trying to get off one candida treatment to start another when something really scared me! I hadn't experienced it in a long time! We ordered our meal and suddenly my nose started to bleed! I got scared but at the same time I thought of taking 2 capsules of the candida treatment from Whole Approach that I had with me and within a few minutes of taking them the bleeding completely stopped! Right after that I was able to eat and enjoy my meal! Now I knew for sure where these nosebleeds came from!

Many times, Stan would help me bring the groceries up to my apartment and I would do his laundry with mine so that we can spend more time together. While doing our laundry we made a new friend by the name of Larisa…. she was from Indian culture, married to a man that was not treating her with the respect she deserved but a man that she loved non the less….

She would often stop by my apartment (she lived a couples of doors down from me) or I would stop by hers…. I always encouraged her to fight for her happiness since she had such a cheerful nature, especially when her husband wasn't around! Just like Stan… she also joined me at the gym for a short while and was able to lose quite a bit of weight and gain self-esteem!

I pretty much got used to using the Bart station and the bus as a method of transportation and was surprised to receive a call from my sister-in-law Rosa asking me if I was still in need of a car! I told her that of course I was! She surprised me even more by offering me her son's car since he was in the Army and had no use for it! All I had to do was go to San Pablo and pick it up!

She and my best friend picked me up at the Bart station and took me to her home. That day I was able to pick up an older silver Toyota RAV4 and drove it back home!

For me that also meant extra sleep something I really needed! I was so thankful that I finally had received a gift that I hadn't even asked for!

Now I didn't have to depend that much on Stan to take me grocery shopping and that was another blessing since he could become quite inpatient!

My girlfriend Helena was extremely happy that I had found someone to share my life with but I had my doubts since for some reason my sons didn't like him very much….

Chapter 85

Overcoming devastating news!

I had too much on my plate to worry about it! I had finals coming up and a lot of studying to do when I was hit with something else that I wasn't prepared for and that was Danny moving out! I was studying for a final exam when he came in and told me that we needed to have a talk and I told him "Danny, do we need to talk right now? I have an exam tonight to study for and I need to be able to concentrate on my work for this class." He replied, "Yes Mom we do, my girlfriend and I are moving in together, I just came in to grab my clothes…please don't get upset! I will come by to see you often…. this is not goodbye!"

I don't think Danny knew how devastating this was to me!

We had been together thru thick and thin and today of all days I had to see my son leave thru the front door with his luggage! We had our disagreements…but we loved each other dearly.! I had always been there to give him advice even when some of his friends got him into trouble or when he had doubts about anything…. I worried that this distance would affect our relationship….

When I saw him by the front door with his luggage ready to leave my heart was broken into two! I hugged him holding back the tears… after he left, alone in my apartment I let the tears go and kept on telling myself "It's time to let the apron strings go… this doesn't mean goodbye!"

That day I also made a promise to myself…that any discussions regarding candida with my sons or with my ex-husband were now over with…we as family or friends can help to a certain extent but it comes a time that you must let go, let each individual make their own decisions or choices regarding their own health and how to live their lives…

From my own experience I knew that to follow a holistic treatment of any kind it takes a lot of work and dedication…most people will choose to stay the way they are because they want to fit in today's society or it's cheaper…only those like me that have been near death will do anything to be able to heal!

I sat back down in front of my computer, prayed that God would keep this child of mine safe and also prayed for peace in my heart so that I would be able to pass this exam! It took me a while to get my emotions under control but I was still able to retain a lot of information that would help me with the exam! I asked Stan to go with me to Patten that night because I needed the emotional support…I don't know how I managed to finish my exam all I hoped for was that I would be able to pass….

I was very surprised that I was even able to get an A minus!

Danny's leaving left me with a difficult decision of keeping the 2-bedroom apartment or move to a smaller apartment to save on rent, so after waiting a little while to see if Danny would change his mind, I found a one-bedroom apartment a couple of doors down. I called a moving company to move my furniture and had to find another home for my cats since I found out that I couldn't keep them on the new apartment. I spoke to my kids and Danny immediately agreed to keep Foxy but nobody wanted Precious because she was way too wild! I ended up taking her to a shelter, since she was a very pretty cat she ended up getting adopted right away…

On the day of the move the guys from the moving company were late! Stan was there to help me but we couldn't move the furniture together because it was too heavy, so I had no other alternative but to call my sons and asked them to meet us at the apartment…. between all of us I moved to a smaller apartment that same day! I dedicated all my free time that wasn't much to begin with to decorate it a bit differently and kept it clean and neat.

It was a good thing that I had moved to a smaller apartment because one day when I got to work, I was informed that I along with other people were going to be laid-off due to a slow down! I was devastated! Once again unemployment and looking for work!

I also had to deal with Stan's difficult moods…. in this relationship that had lasted over a year he had not asked me once to see his townhouse in Concord and when I asked him why he always came up with an excuse! Either his place was not clean enough or he had more fun with me on mine, I finally concluded that he had something to hide but decided to drop the issue….

Stan's moods finally got the best of me….one day on our way home on a Saturday afternoon from grocery shopping Stan was behind a truck that stopped suddenly and forced him to bump unto it…. he got out looked at his truck… saw that there was no damage and started to yell at the poor driver that kept on apologizing! He explained that he was new to his job and pointed out that there was no damage to either car! Stan refused to listen but was forced to get in the truck because he was blocking the traffic…. once he got in, he looked at me and saw that I was upset and asked me "And why are you upset, don't you see that he is an incompetent driver?"

I had always tried to be honest with everybody and had to tell him how I felt! I told him that for one thing he was overreacting, there was no damage to either car, that all that he had accomplished was to embarrass the poor driver and create a scene! On the way to my apartment all he did was to tell me off…...that as his girlfriend I should always be on his side no matter what! I had to disagree with him and told him "You can't proclaim to be a Christian and have no compassion on you for other human beings, that scene was uncalled for!"

When we got upstairs with my groceries, he left them inside my door and said that he was going back home, when I asked him if he was staying for dinner he answered "No! After all I have done for you, do you think I deserve for you not to be on my side?"

That did it for me!

I looked him in the eyes and said "Stan, don't you think, you have that turned around?" He didn't answer because he knew I was right...

He had the ugliest look on his face I ever saw! When he left, I proceeded to put my groceries away... made my dinner and enjoyed it without any guilt!

After this incident he wouldn't answer his phone and did not show up at church services to help out! Worse of all did not answer their calls when they called him to check if he would be there to usher for the following Sunday!

At church they asked me about him and why he wasn't picking up their calls, they had relied on his help and now he was not showing up! I had to share with them that we had not spoken for a week but that I would find a way to get a hold of him. That Sunday when I got home from church I called him one more time and left him a message and half! I told him that there was one thing not to answer my calls and another to let the church down!

CHAPTER 86

Calling quits on a relationship and something to brag about!

$\mathcal{A}$nother week went by and I finally decided to take matters into my own hands!

I found his address and did something I hadn't done before and that was to drive to his place in Concord and check if he was home! I found out that he lived in a very nice town home, prayed before knocking on the door several times and waited.... he wasn't answering, so I decided to write a note and leave it by the door. He got out and exclaimed "So, now you are stalking me, isn't enough that you don't leave me alone with your phone calls?"

I told him that I was there not for me but for our Church and told him to read the note that I had written and also that this would be my last communication with him and left...when I got home that day, I sat in my living room and ripped apart all the pictures I had of him....

Surprise! I saw him at church the next Sunday! He ushered and acted like he didn't know me in front of my friends! I had no other choice but to share with them that we had split up, he didn't last long at church, after a while he stopped showing up... I was actually happy that this relationship was over! I had seen a picture of him I didn't like and was afraid of...

I concentrated on looking for work each day instead and managed to graduate from Patten with an Associate Degree after 4 and half years, one of my proudest moments was when I held my diploma in my hand! I had done it!!

Danny was there that day…. I dedicated that day to God that had been there since day one and wished with all my heart that my parents and brothers were there to see me!!

Outside after the ceremony we took lots of pictures with family and friends and had a luncheon at my apartment afterwards….

My work search now included church ministry because I knew I was good at it…. I looked everywhere even out of state including Stephen Ministries and unfortunately got no answer! I suspected that because I was a woman the doors were not opening for me as a minister, I shared with a friend of mine at Toastmasters what my deepest wish was, she had attended a Women of Faith Conference with me and she actually agreed that would be a role she saw me in!!

Meanwhile being unemployed and having to keep up with paying rent and housing expenses left me little money to live by! Unfortunately, I had no family to help me…. I was also too proud to share with my family what I was going thru financially, so I struggled for quite a while and started to get notices for back rent. My cousin had been so right in convincing me to get half of my pension from my ex-husband! This pension actually helped me with the rent each month but it was not enough! I was told that either I would come up with back rent or I would be evicted!

Victor on the other hand called me one day out of the blue to complain about his latest relationship with my cousin, in his own words "She is too high maintenance and too moody for me and nothing like you!" I stood silent for a minute and told him "Maybe things will get better for you if you stop getting into relationships with women that are my relatives just to hurt me! For your information it only makes me sick and even your kids don't think that this is the right thing to do!"

Of course, he denied it and then made the excuse that he was just checking on the kids…I told him that he could always go back to his first girlfriend and hung up!

I had my priorities right and I was considering renting a room from someone, if that happened, I needed to change my protocol regarding my meals and how I lived, I was used to preparing everything fresh…. from baked chicken to fish and other organic homemade dishes…. I did some research, shopped around and found natural chickens already made! All I had to do was to come up with a fresh sauce to place on top…. replaced fresh homemade salads by buying salad bags, added avocados, onions and beans to taste and even managed to cook salmon on a skillet instead of grilling it in the oven! The flavor was awesome! "When there is a will, there is a way!"

CHAPTER 87

Losing your favorite things and making changes…

*A*t church and Bible study I had shared what I was going thru regarding housing and a friend of mine introduce me to a church member that had a room for rent with use of her kitchen to prepare my meals! I had to accept this generous offer until I got on my feet….

I contacted a storage company, placed all my furniture and most of my belongings there for the time being…. took pictures of my furniture to try and sell what I could…. God knows I needed the money! Unfortunately had no luck there and the furniture stayed in storage….

When I finally moved into the room that I found in Castro Valley it would be an incredible experience that I would never forget!

The room was downstairs and it had another adjoining room that a guy was renting with 2 pit bulls! We had a bathroom door with 2 doors, I was scared to death of the dogs that were left all day in the room…. every time I had to leave to go upstairs to use the kitchen or to leave on an errand I would have to listen for the dogs afraid that they would attack me!

I could not afford to eat out, so I prepared my meals not only because of the protocol I had to follow to keep on healing but also to save money and found out soon enough that this got on the landlord's nerves! She didn't like sharing the kitchen (something that I should have been told right from the beginning) and soon after that she told me that the situation wasn't working out and asked me to find some other place to live!

Someone else from my church also heard about my situation and offered to rent me a room in her townhouse near our church in Alameda. I had learned from my last experience and told her right away that I had to cook my own meals…I explained that I also did a smoothie in the morning, prepared my meals and that meant that we would have to share the kitchen…. She immediately told me that would be fine with her that we could do our cooking at different times…. I agreed and moved in…...

At first it worked out and then she got tired of it and started to complain about everything! Sharing the kitchen, washing my water bottles, etc... I asked her to work with me and whatever was wrong we could fix it…. but to my surprise when I got home from looking for work at the local library, I found all my belongings including the picture of Jesus Christ out in front of her house! She did this without fear of repercussion! After all she was a Christian and had placed Jesus' picture outside with my belongings! Not only was I scared of where to go from there but deeply embarrassed!!

All I could think of doing was to call my girlfriend Larisa that still lived at my apartment complex and crying I told her what happened! She spoke with her husband and they agreed to let me stay for a while in their spare bedroom, she came by and helped me to put my belongings in my car and we proceeded to her apartment. They didn't have a regular bed all they had was an inflated bed but I didn't care all I needed was to find understanding and caring somewhere!

Larisa and I shared her small kitchen and the refrigerator something her husband who was a truck driver didn't like…. when he came home in between jobs he always complained and that created a big conflict between them!

I was also informed by the storage place that they would be having an auction for all my stuff that was on my space…. I had not been able to keep up with the storage payments that were too high to begin with!

When I got there…. I tried to bargain with people at the office and they would not budge! I got to my storage unit to see my things being removed and all I had time to do was to grab a couple of boxes with all my family pictures, my books and jewelry! It was heartbreaking to see all the stuff I had worked so hard for being taken away by someone else! When I got back to my car I cried for all that I had lost and once I was able to get my emotions under control I went back to Larisa's apartment…

It wasn't long before Larisa sat with me and told me that she was having arguments with her husband because of me staying there! She asked me to find another place as soon as possible and I asked her as my friend to give me a week or two to find another place and she agreed. I went back to the library to keep looking for work (at this point my income had run out from E.D.D) and did some research on shelters and found the House of Ruth nearby, a Christian organization that helped homeless people and I applied.

CHAPTER 88

Finding myself in a
Homeless Situation and Soliciting!

I was accepted and an interviewed by one of the managers and informed of their rules, one of them was being back at my room every night on time, attend Bible study and keep my room that I would be sharing with someone clean. One of the most difficult things I had to do every time I was given lodging somewhere was to explain that I had to have a smoothie every morning and make my own meals! Just like other people she didn't find a problem with that but every time I had to do a smoothie in the morning there was a problem… if somebody was in the kitchen, I would be asked to leave without making the smoothie and the same would happen with preparing my meals…

Unfortunately like many people that find themselves in difficult financial situations we have to come up with different solutions! I had tried borrowing money and it worked for a while but I didn't want to lose friends, so I had to stop doing that…. I kept a log of who I owed money to so that one day I would be able to pay back every cent and meant to do it!

People sometimes surprised me! Like a couple of friends of mine that called me from MCSi, one to give me clothes from her closet and another called me to meet her at a supermarket. I knew Diana very well (she wasn't the easiest person to get along with), when I met her at the supermarket my car was full of my belongings…. Imagine meeting with someone that worked with you and have her see that picture!!

I could tell she was touched by what she saw but I was very embarrassed to say the least!

She asked me to go inside the store with her, bought me groceries and once outside gave me a hug and placed a $100 bill on my hand!!

I prayed and prayed for a solution and one day after observing a homeless near a supermarket I decided to do something that would have appalled my parents and that was to start soliciting to make enough money to be able to survive! I researched the best places where you could make more money, where you would find the most sympathetic people and used my car to get to those places.

Most of the places were supermarkets, Lucky's, Safeway, the Hacienda Crossings Shopping Center especially by the Movie Theater…. Union City Shopping Center, the El Cerrito Shopping Center and stayed away from Alameda so that no one from Church would recognize me. I found my own way to tell my story… that this was a temporary situation for me, that I had no family to rely on…. a college degree and that I was looking for work faithfully but had not been able to find a position…. believe me I found sympathetic people but that did not make it any easier for me…

At first this was very hard for me! I had never done this before and felt degraded…. many times, I would ask God out loud "So this is what my college degree gave me?" "Why all the sacrificing?"

I didn't revolt against God however I prayed instead and sometimes I would see the hand of God even on those places where I went soliciting! Many times, I would come back home with $60 dollars or more in one afternoon! I gathered all the coins received, stopped by the nearest grocery store, used the coin changer and often bought my groceries that I needed for that day. I couldn't share this with anyone…. especially with my sons or family…afraid that they would judge me or that what I was doing would be told to Victor and his family!

Another unpleasant surprise was waiting for me one day coming back to the House of Ruth! The manager was waiting for me to let me know that they couldn't keep me because of my meal preparation that was always at inconvenient times…. according to her! She explained that they needed the kitchen free for their meetings…. Also mentioned that a couple of times I had come back home late (soliciting & traffic) and that was unacceptable….

So now there was no place to go! I asked Larisa if I could at least use her kitchen when her husband wasn't there to prepare my smoothie and my meals until I could find a place and decided to live in my car!

I parked my car in safe places, got up in the morning, went to gym where I worked out, got cleaned up and designed a routine. After lunch I always stopped by the library to apply for work, faxed resumes, etc. I used my evenings to do soliciting and Mary learned how to pee outside without anyone seeing her!

Do I sound angry?

Believe me I was…. extremely!

That day I wished with all my heart that people thought of others occasionally instead of themselves all the time! Sometimes even to just share what you are going thru! I found a lot of selfish listeners! They would require all your attention if the story was about them but once you started trying to share with them what you were going thru…. they stared into space and the attention span was gone! I had always prided myself into been a good listener, unfortunately I found that not many people had that skill!

On the first day that I started soliciting I looked around, saw the parked cars, the people walking around and thought of my father and mother and all I could think about was of what this intitled…I was now "Implorando por Ajuda" "Begging for Help." Nobody in my family had done this before and I knew if they had been alive, they would have not allowed me to do this! Unfortunately, I had no one to rely on except me….

I had done so much sacrificing to get my college degree and now I couldn't find work and couldn't find a decent person that would allow me to live with them, able to follow my protocol and give me enough time to look for work! I couldn't keep my car in the same location every night for safety reasons, so I had to find a safe location every night, one late night I stopped by Helena's house and asked her if I could park my car in front of her house just for one night. It was too late to look elsewhere; she spoke to her son and they both told me that they didn't want problems with the neighbors! Most likely they were afraid to be embarrassed… that's what I thought at the time…. So, I said goodnight! Very hurt by this experience (I would never have turned away anyone in this position) I went around the corner and found a dark spot to park my car… She didn't even have the decency to call me or look for me the next day!!

How can people forget so easily what someone has done for them?

I didn't allow this experience to make me a bitter person, there were many times that when I shared my story with someone, they would share theirs and I would end up counseling someone! I had the background for it and became an expert on hiding from the police….

One of my proudest moments was when someone listened to my advice! I had lost both my father and brother to lung cancer and became an advocate for the American Lung Association. I carried their cards and brochures to show what lung cancer looked like with me everywhere and if I saw someone smoke with intentions of quitting…. I would hand out the information I had and prayed that they got this information on time! I never did anything halfway!

Neither did the Holy Spirit! Many times, when I was really struggling for cash it seemed that God sent people my way when I had bills to pay! For example, Income Tax season was coming up and I didn't have the money to pay for the tax preparation, while I was out asking for help someone came up to me and placed a $100 dollar bill on my hand!!

CHAPTER 89

Losing a church
and a ministry that I loved!

I kept attending church without telling anyone what I was going thru when something happened that I was not prepared for! I walked into my favorite place to be on a Sunday morning and nothing was the same! My church was experiencing conflict in leadership and there were rumors going around regarding two favorite people of mine, the minister and his wife! Since I knew these two people very well, I refused to listen to gossip! Fortunately, they were exonerated by the outside consultant's report and by the group inside the church that examined all the evidence. Unfortunately gossip prevailed and these two people that had brought so many people to our church and made it a success decided to resign just before Christmas of 2009!

Our minister had taught us not only to pray but also taught us how to read the Bible, we were instructed to read it at home chapter by chapter and discuss it at church the following Sunday. They had a terrific Youth Ministry that loved our church and scheduled events that always brought us new members, there were times we had no seats available!!

I was also called to attend a meeting with two of the new board directors and informed that they no longer needed the Care & Prayer Ministry! When I asked why, they replied "We really have no need for this ministry, thank you for taking care of it for so long but the decision has been made."

Totally devastated by this decision I walked out of the meeting barely holding my tears, sat in my car and told myself that I would try to come back just a church member! I had lost not only two dear friends of mine but a ministry that I loved and believed in...

Attending church services on Sundays was never the same! There was a new sadness in our church.... not as many people attending and I didn't feel like I belonged there any longer! So, I finally decided to give up on church for a while...

I missed this connection with my church but I was not the only one that decided to leave due to what happened! Even personal friendships were affected! Nothing was the same!!

Even those that decided to stay were not the same, there was no happiness in our church any longer...

There were many times that I felt totally isolated from everyone, my life now consisted of trying to survive.... One night coming back from soliciting and exhausted while I was trying to find a place where to park my car for the night, drove too close to the curb.... my car flipped over twice and stopped! I was very lucky that I was alive!

My heart was racing so fast that I couldn't think clearly! I just prayed and prayed and finally calmed down... I called Larisa and told her what happened, she unfortunately couldn't come and get me because she was afraid to be by herself at nighttime... when I asked her what she suggested I do... she gave me the idea of calling her friends that lived a couple of doors down and so I did. Even though they knew me it took quite a bit of convincing to have Oscar came and get me because he happened to be living with a jealous girlfriend! I asked him to please ask his girlfriend, explain my situation and that this would be for a few nights only until I found a place to stay and he agreed....

He finally showed up and we both realized that there was no way my car could be fixed! We moved all my stuff to his car.... called the police and the car was towed away.... once again, I was without a car!!

Oscar and I took as much as we could that night to their apartment, I slept on their sofa but I knew that I would have to find a place to stay asap since this was a very uncomfortable position to be in!

Once in the library the next day I thought of how much I was making soliciting per day, decided to call motels around that had a microwave, a tiny refrigerator and would allow me to stay for a while. I found the Nimitz Motel in San Leandro that was been managed by a couple of Indian brothers.

Oscar helped me move in and once moved in I bought a portable stove that I could use to cook my vegetables and even found a laundry mat and a grocery store nearby…. even the library was within walking distance…

CHAPTER 90

Soliciting and living at a Motel…

I knew I had to work hard to keep up with the daily rate and knew that I had only me at this point to rely on…. I developed another routine….

Early morning, I would take the bus to the gym nearby, did my usual work out, 20 minutes treadmill, 10 to 15 minutes Stairmaster, weights and then the steam room. Took a shower, went back to the motel and had my smoothie. After eating a good lunch, I walked to the library to look for work. Once done proceed to get on the bus that would take me to whatever location I decided to take to do my soliciting for that night and that included taking the Bart. I prayed on the way there and came home only when I had enough money to pay for my room… if something happened that touched my heart… that night before I went to sleep… I wrote about it…

Even Larisa and her husband came by to see me, they didn't know how I was making the money and my excuse was that I was now a Melaleuca Representative. I used that same excuse at the motel when I didn't make enough money to pay for my room, they liked me so much they ran a tab for me to pay when I made extra…

Something amazing happened! I don't know if it was because of all the walking I was doing but I started for the first time in my life to have huge bowel movements! I was also still too thin but that I couldn't do nothing about!

My hope was that someone would show up while I was soliciting that would offer me a job or knew someone that would, so I shared my story with just about anyone that was willing to listen…. depending on the person I would either get a pat on the back and a generous amount of money or get insulted!

I approached a man once that actually told me that what I needed was a "Sugar Daddy." To this remark I replied, "I studied enough to get a job somewhere one day not to depend on a man to support me."

Many times, I stood back to observe people or places before soliciting, to keep myself safe or to choose to whom to go to for help. One afternoon I happened to be by the CVS Pharmacy in Union City and I overheard these two teenagers speaking about going inside the store to steal! I just couldn't stay silent! I approached both and said, "I happened to overhear your conversation just now, please don't do this, even if you don't get caught now you could get caught eventually and your lives could change forever! I speak from my heart, my two brothers were arrested as teenagers and placed on a Correctional Facility, they were both drafted to the Army and the oldest lost his life at 23." They looked at each other, looked at me, nodded and left! They probably didn't realize that I was soliciting! Unfortunately, a Security Guard showed up and I had to leave that location and walked away…

As the weather changed there were many times I had to do soliciting in the rain with an umbrella and had slow days and good days! Many times, coming back in the Bart I had to stop in the bathroom first before getting into the bus to go back to the motel, my hands would get so frozen from the cold that I couldn't unzip my pants!! Sometimes I would end up peeing my pants because I didn't unzip them on time!

Nobody knew how alone I felt living this life and not being able to talk about it with my family…but I'm sure God knew…

One night at the motel I got a call from Danny and I could tell he had been crying to let me know that our kitty "Foxy" had to be put to sleep! We both cried together…. this kitty had been such a big part of our lives!

It didn't surprise me that he had to put her to sleep, on my last visit to Danny's apartment Foxy came towards me and she broke my heart! She was so thin and I could tell she wasn't feeling well! Danny told me that he had taken her to the vet but the vet bills were becoming quite expensive, I was so proud of my son's heart! He had her cremated and kept her ashes as a memory of a cat that had loved us both dearly!

As far as soliciting I went as far as the El Cerrito Plaza…. while I was out there soliciting a Portuguese friend of mine that knew me and my family very well walked towards me, all I had time to do was to hide my bag! I had seen her son at Trader Joes in Emeryville once and told him that I was out shopping and made up the same excuse to her… she looked at me like she didn't believe me! I didn't care so I just told her that I was heading towards Ross and said goodbye, I knew this incident was going to backfire on me anyway and I was right!

Helena and I were out grocery shopping in Alameda at a natural food store one Saturday morning when I got a call from my oldest son Carlos with a straightforward question for me "Mom, Gilberta saw you at the El Cerrito Plaza and she swears that you are soliciting, her son also saw you at Trader Joes the other day as well, is this true?"

I hid from Helena to answer my son and told him "No Carlos, I'm working as a Melaleuca Rep and I was out shopping on both occasions, please don't worry about me!"

I don't know if he believed me but there was no way I could tell the truth to my sons! They were not doing well financially themselves and I knew by now that when people helped you it was short lived, not even Helena knew what I was doing behind the scenes….

One of my worst fears was to be recognized somewhere either by someone that knew me personally or by the police! I was out soliciting in the Fremont area that I usually went to and after passing by Sprouts and Starbucks when I saw that I was still short on money I walked further and stopped by Walgreens. I was approached by the local police and given my first citation! I was also advised that I would be taken to jail if they saw me there again…. this meant that this area would be off limits for a while. I walked to the Bart station, got on the next Bart, stopped on the next location and started all over again…. I had learned where all the good places were by now…

I didn't wish this life on anyone but I also helped the homeless when I could either financially or by giving them advice, I told a young man once "I have seen you at this location quite a few times, if you really need the money, change the location frequently and when telling your story…. do it from the heart, with sincerity and make sure you are looking at someone eye to eye, so that they believe you."

Sometimes while soliciting you have the chance to observe people and may even have the opportunity to help someone! I was given that opportunity to help someone in need at Jack London Square…... as I waited for people to get out of restaurants to ask for help, I looked to my left and a well-dressed gentleman was sitting on a park bench with his head down…. depression was written all over him! I couldn't help myself, took a chance and went and sat by him and said "I have been observing you and you have depression written all over you! I lost my grandfather due to depression, he committed suicide because he didn't have anyone to share what he is going thru at the time! Sometimes sharing your story with a total stranger can be easier than with family, believe it or not I went to Patten University and attended classes in Counseling there…... if I can help you let me know!"

He looked at me up and down, at the way I was dressed, at the bag that I was carrying and I got the message "So who are you to give me advice?" Sometimes you also have to be smart enough to walk away! I got up, looked straight into his eyes and said, "I will be around for quite a while if you change your mind." I walked to stand in front of the restaurant, collected as much as I could but he never came towards me, so I left after a while… When it got too dark to be there, I walked to the bus that would take me to the Bart station that would take me home…

CHAPTER 91

Almost getting arrested and a special wedding!

One of the places that helped me make quite a bit of money was the Hacienda Crossings Shopping Center and one the most dangerous places to do soliciting because police cars were seen there frequently! I managed to move from one store or restaurant to another and would hide for a while until they moved out of the area. I happened to be at Toys-R-Us and had found a few people willing to help when the Dublin police came by! The officer placed my hands behind my back, told me that I was being arrested for soliciting and read me my rights! I was extremely scared and all I could do was to pray!!

I looked straight at him and told him that this was my first time, that I was a graduate from Patten and even told him to look it up. I spoke from my heart and told him that I didn't have any family, that I was doing my best to find a job and to please give me a chance!

This was one of the times that I wished I could call God directly and ask Him for help!!

He went inside his car looked me up and found out that I didn't have a past record came back and told me "I'm going to let you go this time because you don't have a past record but I do not want to see you here ever again.... do you understand me?"

Relieved beyond measure, I promised him I would keep away from that area and headed towards the Bart station…. on the way there I spoke to God and told Him "So, when are you going to come to my rescue and get me out of this dangerous double life I'm living?"

I knew that I would have to come back because this was where I made the most money and stay away from the Toys-R-Us location. I was smart enough to know that I would have to wait a few days, the best days for soliciting there were always Fridays and Saturdays.

My bill at the Nimitz Motel was getting bigger and I was also told that I would have to move out for a week to another motel (office policy), register and come back again! I found someone that helped me to move my stuff to another motel in Hayward…. stayed there for a week and went back to the Nimitz. Those people must of really liked me or felt sorry for me because they accepted me back even with a past-due bill!

I also had to make a very hard decision and that was to take the very few gold rings I had and take them to a Pawn Shop, including my mother's ring! I needed the extra money to give it to the motel but that didn't make it any easier! When I got back to the Motel and counted the money I cried because like my father had done years ago, I had to sell my mother's ring to pay for lodging and I was glad she wasn't alive to see this! My aunt Carmen had a saying she was famous for "vao-se-os aneis ficam os dedos (let the rings go and keep your fingers instead) not much of a consolation when you happen to treasure anything that was handed over to you by your family!

I waited about a week to go back to the Hacienda on a Friday but to a different store, when I got on the bus that would take me to the Hacienda of all the people to see, Stan was driving the bus!

We looked at each other, I asked him how he was, he said fine and I told him that I was out shopping for the day at the Hacienda Shopping Center. He said no problem, I took my ticket and went to sit down thinking to myself how much this man had changed!

Even though I was scared I managed to the soliciting that afternoon by the movie theater, left a bit earlier in fear of being discovered and was able to make enough money to pay for my room that night!

Physically this lifestyle was taking a toll on me! I was way too thin and when before I was having great bowel movements now constipation was back full force! I was forced to look for constipation remedies off the counter, tried everything you can imagine (started with natural remedies first) and found one that worked. Unfortunately ended up just like my mother taking something off the counter (hers had been Correctol) for me the only one that worked was Ex-Lax Maximum strength. I knew that I could not afford to let constipation build up otherwise I could become very toxic...

Carlos surprised me one afternoon by inviting me to his wedding and I was thrilled because I knew this girl loved him dearly! I liked that she was outspoken and right from the beginning of their relationship she had told me "I'm going to marry your son, you raised a great man!"

Of course, I accepted and the date was set for May of 2011. I told my son that I would take the Bart there but someone would have to pick me up once I arrived. I set out to find me a dress and shoes for occasion and looked forward to being with my sons, I loved the ceremony! Both Carlos and Kristin had lost weight and looked beautiful together.... and to my surprise both my ex-husband, his brother and his family were there! I was embarrassed that day! I knew I was way too thin and that the people there that knew me were going to talk about me...

Carlos totally surprised me that day by placing a $100 bill on my hand! I refused to accept it! He insisted and said "Mom, please accept it, I know you need it." So, I did but I didn't want to take it! Afterall this was his wedding day! My son had a great heart and was worried about me! We went outside to take pictures and after that we sat down for the reception.

I stood up to toast the happy couple and shared something with them that had been given to me by their grandmother.... I told them "I was advised by my mother and she proved to be right to never go to bed at night angry with each other! Another I learned on my own was that communication is extremely important to keep a marriage strong." I raised my glass and wished them a very long and happy marriage together! Everyone clapped and when I looked up my ex-husband was looking in my direction and raised his glass!

I went outside to get some air later and both my ex-husband and my brother-in-law were leaning against the balcony talking to each other. I walked towards them gave them each a hug and a kiss on the cheek (the Portuguese way), I was surprised that my niece grabbed my waist and exclaimed out loud in a very nice way "My goodness look how tiny your waist is! You look wonderful!" Christine actually made my day!

I had the feeling that my ex-husband had in mind a reconciliation with me because he had not brought anyone with him and tried flirting with me, probably because one of our sons had told him that Stan and I were no longer together! I also suspected that they had told him that our Pastor had left our church and that I decided to stop attending services there, this man unfortunately never got it! Our marriage had broken up because of his unfaithfulness, lack of trust, lack of commitment on his part to get healed and it had nothing to do with religion! In my book God kept people together (marriage vows) not apart!!

When I left…. I felt more alone than ever but very proud that I acted like a lady in every sense of the word in front of my sons!

Because of my lifestyle and my divorce, I felt disconnected from everyone…not speaking of living in a motel instead of a home….

I reminded myself not to worry about what people thought about me but about what God thought about me! That's what was important!

Unfortunately, even though I used every resource within my power I could not find work! When I was out soliciting many times, people would give me hints of whom to contact regarding employment, I used the information and contacted whoever they suggested. I was also worried because I hadn't worked since the end of 2009 that my chances of finding work would be very slim (most employers would always ask what you were doing in between jobs). That did not stop me from trying!

I found myself going from one Bart Station to another, especially if the location that I was soliciting at didn't produce any money or police was present…. on the way home I would count the money that I had collected and the next morning I would pay for a one-night stay at the Motel…

My tab at the Nimitz was now pretty big! I had kept a log of how much I owed them and God bless them…. they were so patient!

CHAPTER 92

An encounter that changed my life!

*A*nd then…… probably because God works behind the scenes…. I was out once again on a Friday evening soliciting by the Hacienda movie theater when I was approached by a gentleman by the name of Jim that surprised me by being the 1st ever to ask me "Do you want to keep staying in this situation or do you want a job?" I couldn't believe it! How long had I waited for this! I finally had someone ask me the question that I had been waiting for and told him immediately "I would start working tomorrow if given the opportunity!"

I shared my story with him and asked him the question that sometimes I asked people that would get smart with me when I was out soliciting "Do you honestly think that a person with a college degree would keep herself soliciting if she could get a job instead?"

He looked straight at me gave me his card and said, "Meet me on Monday morning at this address, I'm the General Manager for a Waste Energy Saver Company and I'm going to give you the chance to get out of this lifestyle." I shook his hand, gave him my phone number and left for the day!

He had asked me what I was doing Saturday and I told him that besides doing grocery shopping I would have to do Soliciting that weekend because I had to pay the motel daily, to my surprise he called me Sunday and asked me where I was and I told him that I was getting ready to leave.... He asked me to meet him and his wife at the local Walmart...they were on their way to Church. When I arrived there, he introduced me to his wife and gave me enough money so that I would not have to go soliciting that day! I was so touched! I cried on my way to the motel! I paid my motel bill for the day, ate lunch, got my clothes and lunch ready for my first day at work the following day!

I also shared this bit of good news with the manager at the Motel so that they were aware that my situation had changed!

I also found out that this company wasn't far at all from the motel! I would be able to get a bus that stopped nearby and on Monday, February of 2013 I started working as a Telemarketer! I was ecstatic to say the least!

Jim introduced me to everyone at the office and I was amazed that nobody asked how I had gotten there! I'm sure there were a few curious ones!

I was trained how to make appointments, kept tally sheets, make daily phone calls, record info into spreadsheets, etc...

After a couple of days Jim called me into his office and asked me how I liked what I was doing.... besides thanking him from the bottom of my heart for this great opportunity I also shared with him that the next thing I needed to do was to find a room to rent because I was over my head at the Nimitz motel!

He actually gave me a great idea! He told me to place an ad on craigs list that I was looking for a room to rent!

He also asked me about the tab at the Nimitz and I told him that I would show it to him.... he amazed me even further by offering to pay the bill and then deduct a certain amount each week from my paycheck to pay him back! I was so grateful to this man! It was like an angel had arrived to help me!!

The next day I brought him the tab from the motel, he told me he was going to pay it off and he actually did! I also spoke to the manager at the motel about paying my bill weekly instead of daily until I found a place to live and he agreed! I walked to the local library and placed an ad on craigs list for a room.... specifically asked for a room with a bed and the use of a kitchen...

I was surprised to get a call from a man named Juan that had a room for rent! I met him and his wife the next day... they agreed to have me move in with use of a bathroom and the kitchen.... it was hard for me having to share living quarters again with other people because I was so used of having my independence but I couldn't keep on living in a motel forever!

I believed in not leaving things unfinished, so I decided to take a trip on a Saturday afternoon to visit the Walgreens in Fremont, the place where I had been given my first citation! I looked for the security guard that had called the police on me, at the time that I had shared my story with him, all he had said was not to come back again but I was there today with a mission. I found him, he looked at me and said, "You know, you should not be here." I told him "Before you call the police on me, I'm here to tell you that sometimes people go thru temporary situations in life where desperate measures must be made.... this doesn't mean that they are stuck! I'm also here to tell you that I finally found someone that believed in me enough to give me a job and I even found a place to live." I had dressed up for this occasion... I looked at him and said, "Do you mind if I enter your store to go shopping?" he smiled at me and nodded, I went inside bought a couple of things and left satisfied that I was able to show someone not to judge people too hard before you know their circumstances...

My friendship with Jim grew... I found out that he and his wife were also Christians, they attended church services together and he actually gave me a small Bible to read....

I had been living with Juan and his family for a while when he approached me one day to let me know that unfortunately his mother-in-law would be coming from Mexico and she needed my room to move in! I was disappointed to say the least but he gave me time to place another ad on craigs list to find another room and a letter of recommendation....

CHAPTER 93

Trying to find a place to fit in and moving on....

On April of 2013 I got a call from a Christian woman named Gill that had a room in her house for rent and asked me to meet her at her home. She came to pick me up and took me to her home...it was pretty close to where I worked and she showed me around. I really liked her home but because of what I had been thru already I asked her to sit with me and then told her that due to food allergies not only did I have to make a smoothie each morning but also prepare my own meals, she liked me on site and said, "I don't mind that at all, I wouldn't mind learning how to cook healthier meals with you!"

I liked that she was a neat person since I was that way also and got my things ready to move in......she actually helped me to move in and we set some house rules even in the kitchen. She very proudly showed me her room where she had a Bible sitting on her nightstand and I felt safe!

At work we started to experience a slow down after a while.... I had the feeling that I was going to be there just long enough to pay the bill at the Nimitz motel and then I would be let go as well!

Jim had shared with me that the Telemarking Dept was not producing much results and certain people would have to lose their jobs.... I told him that I didn't want to be left in the same position I was before and asked him to give me time to look for another job, he agreed and I found a glass company nearby that was looking for a temporary A/R Marketing Assistant! I left Jim knowing that I would be missing him immensely and started this other position on May of 2013…Working for someone else could turn out to be a very different experience than working for Jim but I had no choice…

Sometimes God brings someone to your life for a time or a reason and you have to be strong enough to know when to say goodbye….

My work once again consisted of answering phones, sending catalogs out, data entry and even updating spreadsheets, I liked this job and set out to make it permanent if I could...

I immediately made a very special friend, Chris was a lawyer that worked for the company and made friends very easily, he ended up coming to my rescue many times...

The experience at Gill's house on the other hand became a nightmare! At first everything was ok…. then she started finding things to pick at! First my bathing suit and towel in my bathroom (she had hers) was to be removed! I actually had to keep my wet clothes in my room to dry! She had given me a corner of her big kitchen to do my salad and cooking, after a while she started giving me side remarks like "This is not dinner, it's a Big Production". The heater on cold days could not be on unless she turned it on… most nights I slept with socks on! In the beginning she had given me a space in the refrigerator, now the amount of food I kept in the refrigerator irritated her!

I was constantly criticized for this or that and then there were days that she would ask me to sit with her and watch a movie and for peace's sake I would, even though I was always on edge! When the movie was over, she would close the TV and tell me "I'm going to my room and read the Bible" …it was a total up and down regarding her moods! I never knew when she got home from church what kind of mood she would be in!

One day after she came back from the grocery store, she told me to follow her outside and she showed me where the garbage pails were (something she should have done right from the beginning) one for gar-bage, one for plastic and another for boxes and told me "I'm not about to take out the garbage out for anybody." I just kept silent….

As soon as she complained about anything I made sure not to repeat the mistake and asked myself if this was a Christian woman where was the mercy and kindness? One day fed up with all the criticism I actually looked at her straight in the eyes and asked her "Gill, I don't seem to do anything right, please tell me what I have done to displease you so much?"

She looked at me and said, "I don't need a healer in my house!" and left me in the kitchen wondering where in God's name had that come from?

I had never professed to be a healer and had never given her the idea that I was one! Maybe because of the way I took care of myself?

In order to protect myself I kept note of all the incidents in writing for my own protection and prayed for her to change, I was so tired of moving around! Most of the time I was exhausted! Take the bus to work, bus to the gym, bus back home, make dinner, lunch for next day and back at the same routine the next day…

I used my weekends for cleaning my room, laundry (walked to the nearest laundry mat) and grocery shopping….and dealt with Gill's moods!

One particular weekend she was in a bad mood, opened the door of the refrigerator, threw all my food on the floor and told me to reorga-nize it! She actually trusted me one weekend to take care of her home when she went away somewhere to visit someone! I took the time to dust all the furniture and totally cleaned the kitchen but when she came back home it was like she didn't notice anything!

No matter what I did there was no pleasing her! I sacrificed and took insults but at the same time I noticed changes in my body that made it all worthwhile!

These treatments I was on were essential and what I saw occa-sionally made me keep up with all the sacrificing…. I had been on

Candactive from Wise Woman Herbals for a while when one morning after a really good bowel movement I looked down in the toilet and saw pieces of candida overgrowth! I googled it later and found the same images under "Images of Candida Intestinal Overgrowth" and when I wiped myself it smelled like semen! ...this had happened to me before! I knew what semen smelled like from my relationship with my ex-husband...I had been too scared to have sex with anyone and dedicated my life to healing myself instead, I was not sorry I had chosen to heal instead of letting myself develop another illness and die! I knew that Candida left untreated could lead to other very serious illnesses!

At the new company I worked for... the Marketing Dept was not making it even though we all worked hard! Seeing changes already I volunteered to help the accounting department and they told me they would keep that in mind. Because this company did not pay very well I found a way to make a little extra money on the side... when I shared my financial situation with Chris, he told me he had a catering job lined up for the next weekend coming up and he volunteered to take me and let me take his place! I certainly could use the extra money! So that Saturday I went with Chris and he trained me really quickly how to do catering and made over $100! By the time I came back home I was exhausted but the money helped!

On July of 2013, I was called to the President's office at the company I worked for and was informed that even though I had done a great job they didn't have a need for my position any longer! He reminded me that when I had accepted this position I knew it would be a temporary position! I was upset of course! This meant looking for work once again but he was nice enough to give me a good reference letter! I had left another friend behind that had a very caring heart and that was Chris!

CHAPTER 94

Another place & position and meeting a persistent man!

I kept looking for another position and found one the following month at the Hometown Buffet in San Leandro as a server and cashier, I really didn't care if this wasn't a clerical job! I needed to keep up with my expenses and I found some good people who were willing to train me! I learned how to prepare breads and desserts, serve as a backup as a cashier and maintained the dessert area clean… most nights after taking the bus home I would get home extremely tired but still glad that I was working!

It was funny that every time I had a question about anything I would be directed to a Spanish guy they called Chava! He was like an assistant supervisor that knew how to prepare any food on the menu, clean anything or answer any question…I started to notice that he was looking at me in a different way and I kept on being teased about it! I wasn't interested in a love affair! I had been thru a lot and preferred to be alone. He kept on smiling at me, coming by with any excuse to talk to me and when I sat down to eat dinner he would sit with me at the table, he made a point of becoming my friend…and I shared with him what I was going thru at Gill's house and he couldn't believe that I was still there! He actually rented a room at his sister's house and helped to take care of his elderly mother.

One day I came home from work to find an eviction notice on top of my dresser and I couldn't believe that she hadn't warned me about this coming!

When I knocked on her door and asked her why, her answer to me was "This is just not working." I asked her to give me some time, I knew this was not about money, this was about sharing your space with someone that was trying to live a healthier lifestyle! She agreed to give me until the end of September.

Once again, I used Craigs list and placed an ad for a room with the use of a kitchen… I saw a couple of places but I knew by now that sometimes if they said they were willing to share the kitchen that ended up not being the case!

I could not afford an apartment with the money I was making at Hometown Buffet, I even tried close friends to rent a room from… I had kept my friendship with Jim and Cindi, she had been doing my hair forever and I got in touch with her since I knew she had an extra room… unfortunately, she had agreed to rent it to Jim's nephew so that was out of the question…

It was better that I stayed away from family and friends anyway! There was nothing worse than living with someone to break up a friendship! People changed when you actually lived with them!

I finally had a guy call me with a room for rent and the use of a kitchen in a mobile home park… we agreed to meet by Walmart and I liked him on site! Jose was single and young and was buying a single wide mobile home, we agreed on the price of the room, sharing the bathroom and also the kitchen. He stated that he hardly cooked and that we could also share the refrigerator. This sounded too good to be true and since I had been thru this before I drew up a written contract that we both would sign to acknowledge and agree upon! That included that I would be making a smoothie each morning, using the refrigerator and cooking in the kitchen… also that if either one of us was not happy…a 30 days' notice would be given. He looked at me surprised that I had everything written down and I explained that I had been thru this road before.... people would agree on something verbally and then change their minds! He signed it, I signed it and I showed him a recommendation letter from Gill that I had with me so that he knew that he had a good person in his hands....

I was all set to move in the beginning of October of 2013. Chava had volunteered to help me move my stuff from Gill's house to the mobile home and I could hardly wait!

She also helped me that weekend to move the rest of my stuff and used her car... she liked the mobile home park! I told her that I would be going by her house occasionally to pickup my mail and she agreed....

I was glad that when I left I had taken with me all the notes she had written to me...I had learned the hard way how to protect myself! It seemed to me that from all of the experiences that I had gone thru in living with someone that there was always a black sheep in the household...

I actually told quite a few people that if I had the choice, I would eat like they did... it would save me time and money but unfortunately, I had an illness that required me to cook and eat as healthy as possible in order to heal!

Most of the time they nodded in agreement and then they would forget about it! I had made a point of not trying to change their eating habits or to help in anyway unless I was asked... I had learned that people sometimes can be very cruel if you try to change them (for example my own family).

On the other hand, Chava was becoming more persistent with me! He kept on asking me out and I told him that I would agree to go out to dinner or to a movie once in a while but not dating.... just as friends and he agreed...

Working at the Buffet wasn't bad... just a very physical job that left me pretty tired and did not pay enough to get by... so I kept on applying for other jobs and found a collection company in Hayward that dealt in collecting on consumer and commercial debts. I started in the beginning of January of 2014 as a Collector and kept Hometown Buffet as a weekend job so that I could put some money away for a rainy day…

Chava and I kept on seeing each other and I liked that he was a man that professed to love God! He prayed occasionally with me! I admired the fact that after almost killing himself drinking because of his mother's prayers he had given up drinking completely!

He, just like me had survived an unhappy marriage with an ex-wife that had cheated on him and had left him with 7 kids to raise by himself! They were all grown up and she ended up homeless! I liked him but I knew that he wanted more than a friendship… so I was very careful in not giving him the wrong impression and avoided meeting his mother and sister…

I had to stop by Gill's house one day to pick up my mail and knocked on her door, when I asked her for my mail… she was extremely abusive! She grabbed my arm after giving me my mail and told me to never come by her home unannounced and pushed me out the door! I looked back at her and said "And you call yourself a Christian! Was this necessary? Could you just have requested this without the need of becoming violent?" She slammed the door shut on me and until I had my mail forward to me, I made sure I called her beforehand…

CHAPTER 95

Helping a son and learning to accept changes!

*J*had never lost touch with my sons and found out that Danny was living near a church in Hayward…we had found the time once in a while to play mini golf or to go out to eat together but after a while I became a bit worried… Danny had not contacted me for a while so I decided on a surprise visit! I called him to meet me downstairs… when I saw him my heart broke in two and I now knew why he had kept away!

I had never seen Danny that heavy! I found out why! … He had broken up with his girlfriend and was extremely depressed! We talked… I told him that family is always there when going thru difficult situations and that I was his mother not his judge! I went home and alone in my room that night I cried and cried and prayed that God found someone to help him! I wrote a letter of encouragement to my son and went back with Chava to see him once again. Chava stayed downstairs… once alone with my son I spoke to him from the heart "Danny please read this letter when you are down, if you lost weight before you can do it again and this will give you the confidence that you need. You know my son…. you mean more to me than anyone else in this world."

We hugged and I departed with a heavy heart and was surprised to get a call from Danny one day that he was set to leave for Las Vegas! Carlos and Kristin had moved there to live with Kristin's mother that had health problems, of course, I was upset! This meant that both my boys would now be living far from me!

But I would have done anything to see Danny happy again!

On the weekend that Danny was set to move I met with Carlos at Danny's apartment, he had come down from Vegas to help his brother and I was surprised to see my ex-husband there as well! Carlos also did not like the way his brother looked or the depression he had been suffering… he knew something that I didn't know and that was that Danny was having a hard time financially! Carlos and his father convinced him to get a transfer from his company to another in Vegas and have him move in temporarily with his brother until he got on his feet. When I saw my two sons together with their father that day my heart was full of sorrow for what we had lost as a family due to a stubborn man that was too hardheaded to change!

That weekend I was heartbroken knowing that Danny now would not be close by and it was extremely hard to go back to work and concentrate on my job. My friends tried to console me by telling me that I would now have an excuse to go visit my kids in Vegas and take Chava with me…

My relationship with Chava helped somewhat, the friends I had at work and the gym but nothing can compare with having real family nearby.

I also found something amazing that I never knew before and that was what chemistry between a man and a woman was all about! Chava asked me out to dance with him at a nearby club and I accepted. Very close to where I lived was a Latin nightclub that Chava knew about and we decided to check it out! When he held me close to him to dance, I felt the chemistry between us and was very surprised!

By looking at Chava many people would have asked what I saw in him… he had lost all his hair before due to an illness but as he claimed "I do have big ears but also a big heart" I could testify to that! When it came to looks, he was completely different from Victor but he still attracted me because of his heart and the chemistry between us!

Chava was also a very interesting person! I found out that he was a former boxer, a very dedicated father but also a man that had quite a few weaknesses…I was amazed to find out that even though he had a strong personality he was very addicted to Nyquil at night… not because he was sick but because it helped him to go to sleep! I asked him to replace it with Chamomile tea because of being a former alcoholic, it was not a good idea to be taking Nyquil that had alcohol as an ingredient… He agreed and got very used to drinking the tea at night.

We kept on seeing each other and I also had to make another decision and that was to give up Hometown Buffet! I was exhausted by trying to hold on to two jobs at the same time! This decision became an easy one when after 3 months in the collection department I was offered another position in the same company making more money! They offered me a position in their Marketing Dept and for Section 8 (Housing), I met with the Vice-President and the EVP of Sales and Marketing and they liked me on site! I was told that I had plenty of time to learn both jobs…. Once offered this great opportunity I gave notice at Hometown Buffet… concentrated on learning everything about this new position and worked closely with both supervisors.

I made good friends even people that loved the fact that I was from a Portuguese background… Claudia for example that loved Portuguese food and as usual I kept my promise to help anyone, that included a young woman that suffered from Asthma. I shared with her what I knew about using a steam room and losing weight for better breathing… sometimes people are just too set on their ways to change their lives and sometimes it takes a person to be near death (like me) before they actually do something about it!

I had met a woman at the gym that while using the steam had shared with me that she suffered from asthma and had been able to let go of an inhaler just by exercising and using the steam room regularly…

Keeping my promise to God to always help those in need was essential to me but I also learned to recognize those that would listen and those that wouldn't. For example, at the gym that I still belonged to I had developed a friendship with a woman that loved to work out on the Stairmaster... many times while I worked out I watched her from behind, she held on to the machine while she pushed herself to the limit! By the end of the workout, she would be sweating profusely and on to the next machine! I once told her "Susan, I have the feeling that you are pushing yourself way too hard! All you need to have a terrific workout is to start on the treadmill to warm up, go to the next machine, do weight training and finish with the steam if what you are craving is the sweating? All in moderation!" She thanked me for the advice with a smile but continued doing it her way!

I had been working out for quite a while at the gym when I noticed that I hadn't seen her! One day coming out of the steam room I bumped into her! I hugged her and asked her why she hadn't been around, she shared with me that she had a heart attack and that the doctor had placed her on a light workout routine. I didn't want to tell her but she actually deserved a "I told you so!" Instead, I told her that I was glad that she was ok and left...

My quiet times at home were also essential for my wellbeing... in my room I read my Bible and prayed, unfortunately I never found a church like the one that I had belonged to! I did attend services at a nearby Christian church but did not develop a close relationship with anyone... the feeling wasn't the same so I would only attend services on Holidays...

CHAPTER 96

Making a difference in someone's life and a proposition!

*C*hava and I continued our relationship and he shared with me one day that he had an umbilical hernia that was extended. He used a black belt around his waist when he was working but still lifted heavy boxes when he knew he was not supposed to! I shared with him that my mother also had one but it wasn't near as big as his and that he should do something about it. He kept on delaying going to the doctor and one Saturday when I was cleaning my place he came by and asked me if he could lay down in my bed that he was not feeling well! He was pretty pale and when he laid down and took his waist belt off I saw that his hernia was extended and it looked inflamed! I immediately told him "Chava, we must get you to a hospital asap! You don't want the hernia to burst on you! This could be life threatening!"

For the first time he didn't fight me on this! He was also running a fever! I got him in the car and took him to the nearest Hospital... they admitted him and I called his sister for her to inform the rest of the family. He was taken to surgery and I waited by myself in the waiting room. His doctor came to see me late that evening and told me that he was very lucky that I had brought him in because the hernia not only needed to be removed but had become infected and could have become life-threatening! He stayed overnight… I left for the night and went back to see him the next day…

I found out that Chava was afraid of hospitals, I had an extremely hard time convincing him that he needed to stay a couple more days! He tried to get out of bed by himself and that made his blood pressure go up! I was finally able to calm him down and within a couple of days he was released and given some time off… he was also advised to take care when he went back to work… something he had a hard time doing because he liked to work hard…

After a few weeks off he went back to work, I advised him to listen to the doctor's advice and share with his supervisors what happened so that he would be placed on light duty for a while…unfortunately most of the jobs at Hometown Buffet involved having to do cleaning (even with mops) after the place closed down…

Life went back to normal…He went back to work and we started dating on a regular basis, he finally convinced me to meet his sister and mother that lived near my place… they were extremely grateful that I had been there when he needed someone to take charge on the day of his surgery…

Chava totally surprised me one day by coming by my place all dressed up! I looked at him and said, "Are we going to a place I'm not aware of?" He pulled out a little black box with a ring inside and asked me if I would consider marrying him! I was speechless for a moment and then I held his hands in mine and told him from the heart "Chava, I know you asked me before if I loved you and I will repeat this again… I will never be able to love you like I loved my ex-husband but we have an incredible chemistry between us, if you can accept that then I will accept your offer." He looked at me smiling and said, "Sure I will! I know you will grow to love me someday and I don't want to lose you."

Before we set a date, I told him that he had to agree to have a physical including being tested for candida… I was not about to get infected again and I knew that his ex-wife had not been faithful to him… he agreed and I made an appointment at the Marin Natural Medicine

Center. We met with the doctor there and besides blood work she ordered a stool test for Chava, we went back to get the results… she told us that everyone had a bit of Candida in their system and that we would be perfectly fine if we decided to get married. On the way home I placed a request on him that when we finally made love that he learned to withdrew instead of living his semen inside me… this was incredibly uncomfortable to ask but I didn't want to take a chance of becoming infected again! He agreed and understood because I had shared my story with him right from the beginning of our relationship….

We set the date for August of 2015, in North Highlands, since Chava knew Reverend William, we were asked to meet with him for a pre-wedding meeting… I was glad that they insisted on this meeting because I had a few doubts I needed to discuss with the Reverend…

Chava and I took a trip to Sacramento to have the meeting with the Reverend, after we had the meeting together, I asked Reverend William to speak to me alone and he agreed… Chava looked at me with a questioning look on his face but I told him that I would talk with him afterwards. I spoke to Reverend William from the heart and told him that one of things that I didn't like about Chava was that he had the tendency to lie! This was a problem because I had been married to a man previously that had hurt me quite a bit because of his lies! I certainly did not want to go thru that again!

He totally understood where I was coming from and told me "Every time you catch him doing that… confront him about it and tell him that if wants a lasting relationship with you he has to stop stretching the truth." He also shared with me that he had known Chava and his family for a long time… they were considered good people. I accepted his word and left feeling a bit better! Of course, Chava wanted to know what we had discussed…. I told him and he agreed to become more honest with me… he also had been lied to by his ex-wife and told me that he didn't want that kind of relationship with me…We stopped by his son's house to visit, had lunch out and drove back home.

At work my friends had found out that I was going to get married and arranged for a wedding shower for me! It turned out to be a great gathering and I went home with a few gifts. Chava on the other hand took me to his sister's house to share with her and his mother the good news and they were both thrilled!

His sister wanted to have the reception there at her house, I made the invitations and included my sons and some of my friends. I got surprised by a call from my ex-husband warning me not to trust this guy completely (Victor did not trust people from the Mexican culture) and I told him not to worry about me that I already had spoken to a few people that knew him and they assured me that he was a good guy.

The next step would be to speak to my sons and asked them if they could make it to the wedding, they both promised to make it and I asked Danny to walk me down the aisle. I told him to please make the sacrifice because I didn't have my father to do it for me, I knew he was skeptical but he agreed to do it. I also knew that in his heart Danny had hoped for a reconciliation between his father and me but that would never happen! Victor would never change and he was now living most of the time in Portugal.

I went shopping for myself and once again I would not be wearing the traditional white dress! I was a bit heavier and didn't feel comfortable wearing one, I bought a white top instead and once again no honeymoon scheduled! Between my first marriage and the second one neither one of the grooms thought about surprising me with a trip! So much for romanticism!

CHAPTER 97

Having doubts and getting married anyway!

Carlos called me and told me that he couldn't make it to the wedding because he had to work that weekend so the only family member that would be there would be Danny. I had met most of Chava's family and they all liked me but I was really disappointed with the amount of people at the church!

Because it was in Sacramento, his sister and his mother stayed behind and got the reception ready... Chava had stayed the night before at his son's house in Sacramento and was scheduled to meet me at the Church, I arrived with Danny and we sat in the church's lobby, I was still full of doubt and prayed for God to intervene! I didn't know why I felt like this but took it seriously because I had always been prone to premonitions...Nothing happened!!

I was too embarrassed to cancel the wedding at this time so I decided to give Chava a chance and when I heard the music... took Danny's arm and proceeded to walk down the aisle.... the Reverend was there waiting for us ready to perform the ceremony and I remember at that precise moment of thinking of what Danny must be feeling of seeing me marry someone else besides his father!

Once the ceremony was over with.... we signed our documents, took pictures with his family and proceeded down the aisle... Chava's kids were already waiting for us outside and halfway down the aisle he let go of my arm and went to join his kids!

I couldn't believe that he had left me walking in the middle of the church by myself and went to join his kids, they congratulated both of us… we got in the car together and drove to the reception. When I asked him what was that all about, he replied that he had been worried about his youngest son…. the night before they had taking him to the hospital with an overdose and since he was outside, he wanted to check if he was ok. I just shook my head and let it go! I didn't want to make a scene in front of my son that was sitting behind us. I suspected that Chava wanted to prove to everyone that he could get someone to marry him because when we were preparing for our wedding, he had always referred to the wedding as "I want this for my wedding." I would have to remind him that this was "Our wedding, not just yours!" That should have given me a hint that something was not right!

He rushed me to get ready for the reception, actually got annoyed with me because we were running a bit late and that same night he would be moving in with me as well… Jose had met him and he would be at the reception with his mother and father. Chava's family had hired a mariachi band and a taco truck among other foods… some of my friends from work showed up, we took plenty of pictures, my friend Larisa also showed up and was extremely happy that I had found a person to share my life with... I had a few personal friends that could not make it to the wedding… but Chava's boss showed up…We cut the cake, danced and ended up going home pretty tired!

Danny went back to Vegas with a promise that we would keep in touch with each other by phone, I knew that Danny didn't like where I was living but he understood that the prices for an apartment in our area were outrageous and we could not afford anything else at the time…

I convinced Chava to walk with me in the Marina after work, I drove directly from work and meet him there on the days that I didn't go to the gym. Since I didn't have a car, he would take me in his 49ers pickup truck to work so that I didn't have to use public transportation every day. I introduced him to some of the people at my job…as for entertainment we did some dancing at a local Mexican club and went to the movies occasionally. We also did some shopping once in a while, visited his mother and sister quite often and took frequent trips to Sacramento to visit his son and a personal friend of his…

After our wedding I found out something awesome about me! I had not had sexual intercourse with anyone since I had left my ex-husband, first because I didn't believe in going to bed with anyone unless I had feelings towards that person and second because I was afraid to get a sexual decease from someone… what I found out was that I still enjoyed sex quite a bit and could have an orgasm if I wanted too! Imagine that! This after 60! This proved that it pays to take care of yourself! On the other hand, Chava bragged that he certainly did not need Viagra!

Since my life had changed for the better what I was looking for was an opportunity to tell someone about it and show people that sometimes when we are helping someone it can change their lives forever, that opportunity came where I least expected!

CHAPTER 98

Thanking those that deserve it and losing another family member!

I had been working for CBA for a while when out shopping at the 99cent Store I came across Paul from the Nimitz Motel! We recognized each other and after shaking hands I told him "I'm so glad that we saw each other today because of you I was given another chance to start over! I know that the supervisor of the company I was working for came to you and paid the balance on my tab. I went to work for his company and was able to pay him back every cent! That was a temporary job, I now work for a Collections Company and just got married. Sometimes when we take a chance on people, they can certainly prove to us that they are in a temporary position and not taking advantage of anyone." He agreed with me, smiled and extended his hand! I could see a look of respect on his face! Mission Accomplished!!

There was another man I needed to thank and that was Jim, the gentleman that had offered me a way out of soliciting! I called him and he answered the phone! I told him "Jim, thank you for giving me the opportunity to start over in life, you were one of the few people that believed that I didn't want to stay in the position I was in! You believed in me and now I'm working for a Collections Company and just got married." He gave me his congratulations and I could tell that he was pleased that I was doing well. I hung up with a smile on my face because my motive of thanking these two men had been that they realized that taking a chance on someone can definitely be worth it!

Not everyone that is soliciting is doing it because it's a lifestyle for them but maybe because they have no other choice until given the opportunity to change their lifestyle…

Even Chava after hearing my story had asked me for help when we both worked for Hometown Buffet… we had worked with a guy that we suspected was homeless, he denied it and pretended that he was sleeping at his sister's house but Chava had seen him sleeping under an overpass! I told Chava to have him go by the Nimitz Motel that was nearby and start paying for a room weekly. While he worked at Hometown Buffet he had a roof over his head... Many times, I would see him at the local library, he was the type of guy that made everyone smile! From what he told me he was separated from his wife and a daughter that loved him dearly. I told him to change his life so that he could restart a relationship with his family, every so often I would see him out on the street but after a while we lost touch with him…

It's amazing how people can be different! I also became friends with a guy at the gym that split up from his wife and children and decided to live in his car because it was cheaper that paying rent on an apartment! He actually came to my rescue many times… even helped me out financially while I was at the Nimitz Motel… I told him to do what I did and stay there but he refused to leave his car…

At the gym there was only a handful of people that I shared with what I was going thru financially, one was a Portuguese couple that I befriended that also knew my ex-husband…. they helped me a little bit but one thing I knew I couldn't share with anyone was that I had been homeless! The gym was one place that Mary could be Mary…. give advice or encouragement if someone needed it and a place where I could be myself!

That part of my life I had been hidden from my cousins and from distant relatives because I did not want to be judged! I had managed to set a routine no matter the circumstances…. especially with work! I woke up early, had my smoothie, took the bus to the Bart station and then another Bus to my job…

While I was waiting for a Bus after work to take me back to the Bart station, I received a call from my cousin Saozinha in Portugal to tell me that her mother, my aunt Carmen had passed away! My last link with my mother… I really felt for my cousin… this was one person that just like me was extremely close to her family….

Little did she know what I had been thru all these years! I was not ashamed of what I done! I had to do what I had to do to survive but was afraid of sharing my story with her and have her share it with her sister… that in turn could share it with my ex-husband! We had kept in contact on the phone thru out the years, she knew that I had gotten married and that I was working but I kept secret what I knew could be divulged to someone else…

Chava also when thru a scare with his mother that while shopping in one of her favorite places, the 99 cents store, slipped on something on the floor and fractured her hip! She was taken to the hospital of course and from there to a nursing home… we didn't think she would actually recuperate quickly from the fall because of her age but she surprised us all by healing enough to go back home! I was glad I didn't wish a place like that for anyone! I had shared with Chava what my parents had gone thru, just like me he was glad that she would be back at his sister's house. I told him "Treasure each moment you have with her because you never know how long she will have here on earth." She liked me quite a lot and loved it when we would take the time to go and see her! Isolation with her was always there because she was very hard of hearing! Elderly people that suffer from hearing loss are often neglected because people don't like talking to people when they have to raise their voices to be heard. It's always a good thing to put yourself in someone else's shoes!

CHAPTER 99

Getting my independence back and dealing with disappointment!

One good thing that happened was that I finally had enough money put away to buy a used car! I was so tired of using public transportation and found one thru craigs list! At work they helped me to investigate the car's history and we made an appointment with the owner of the car for the following afternoon.

Chava and I met with the guy at a fast-food place, looked at the car and found it in good condition so I ended up with a 1997 Acura that had a few problems but definitely worth fixing! I loved being able to drive to work and have my independence back! My next step would be to find a place where to park it, we found one thru our landlord that knew an older couple that lived on the opposite side of the street… they had a parking available that they never used and were willing for a small monthly fee to let me park my car. They become close friends…. Roy was extremely tall and good hearted and introduced me to an older Portuguese man that shared my last name! Amazing!

I found out he had family but liked living by himself, loved linguica and loved to talk! Once he found out that I spoke Portuguese and English he immediately started to ask me to read some of his mail and translate it to him, I didn't mind at all! He made me laugh! Every time I did something for him he would give me and Sal a package of linguica…

Sal sometimes would disappoint me in judging people as soon as he met them instead of getting to know them first! Mr. Rose Lima was one of them!

If he found defects in people (like talking too much, drinking, smoking, etc) he immediately made comments and did not allow the friendship to develop!

Many times…I told myself that I should have listened to my inner voice and convinced Chava to keep our relationship the way it was for a while instead of letting him convince me to marry him. He really tried hard to be a good husband but he hid some really important information from me that was hard to accept!

I found out that he was not legal in the US…. had a least 3 DUI's that he had not paid for, other driving tickets and was driving each day with just a personal ID!

I was extremely upset with him for hiding this from me and part of me wondered if he had married me so that he could stay in the US legally but I decided to help him instead. I did some research at work to check how he could become legal, found out that he would have to pay his tickets and get a lawyer and I spoke to him about it. He knew that I was serious and made an appointment with a lawyer, he started doing community service and paying the tickets little by little…he was upset that it was expensive to get legal but he promised me that he would pursue the best way to achieve this… he also agreed that he was taking unnecessary risks every day while driving around...

Chapter 100

A miracle in Thornton, CA!!

I was at work one day when I got a strange premonition out of the blue! I had a strong feeling that I should go to Thornton in October and this feeling would not leave me alone! I spoke to Chava about it and told him that I would like for him to go as well, he agreed and we planned our trip together, we took turns driving there…when we arrived, I showed him around and hardly saw anyone I knew! He liked the Portuguese foods, the food stands they had on the streets and the saints on display, we shopped around a bit, listened to Portuguese music for a while and attended the evening mass. He was amazed at the amount of people there from all over the place and I also took him to my favorite place of prayer to the Lady of Sorrows Chapel. The inside of that Chapel was wonderful but my favorite statue outside was of Jesus' mother holding her Son in her arms after crucifixion! Outside the Chapel they had placed all the saints… I always stopped by one in particular because it had been my mother's favorite "Rainha Santa Isabel" she had a strong belief in this saint that had done so much good for so many people and performed so many miracles! I thanked her that day for helping my mother and apologized that she didn't have a chance to come thru with her promise that she had made to her when she left Coimbra behind…

People were getting ready for the evening procession that would take place right after the mass, we all got our candles ready, proceeded to follow the Priest that would be upfront in a small vehicle praying the rosary with the statue of Lady Mary on the back of the vehicle. All around us were people praying, holding candles and rosaries…. even people on their knees as a promise to Lady Mary….I explained to Chava that we could certainly pray in our own language… that this was the time to pray for miracles and to pray for our families. We both decided to pray for our son's, Chava had a son that concerned him quite a bit because of his addiction to drugs…

Suddenly everyone stopped praying and there were gasps everywhere! Chava and I looked up and on the left side of the night sky we saw two doves flying around and I thought "Doves at this hour?" and then I saw Her appear in white "Lady Mary." She was in her full glory up in the sky and I was trembling from head to foot!! All I could remember to do was to pray for my family with all my heart and for Chava and me… her image stayed there for a while and I don't know what made me say it…. maybe because the "Pastorinhos" had probably said the same thing when they saw Her, I looked up to her and said, "Lady Mary what can we do for you.?" Of course, there was no answer! I had heard that every time she appeared somewhere she had a request to make…

All around us there were people crying, kneeling and praying! It was a sight to behold! All I could think about was that someone should have taken pictures or a video of this awesome vision! After a while her image faded, Chava and I decided to leave to go back home since he worked the next day. We drove back to San Leandro totally amazed of what had happened and could hardly sleep that night!

I wondered and wondered if she had appeared there with a special request! In all the years that Victor and I had gone to this festival I had never witnessed this before…The following weekend Chava and I went to have dinner at the Hometown Buffet at the Southland Mall in Hayward… we sat down for dinner and shared what happened in Thornton with a few employees, we were amazed that they knew about it and they shared with us that this apparition of Lady Mary had been occurring every 4 years at that location!!

We finished our meal and went home that night in a thoughtful mood…

I also received a call while shopping from Victor asking how I was and I shared with him what had happened in Thornton and he surprised me by exclaiming "So, you saw your "Madrinha!" (Godmother)! What surprised me the most was that he wasn't making fun but actually believed me!

The following weekend I decided to take Chava to meet my good friend, Sra Fatima, we had never lost touch thru out the years… she had moved from her own home to a retirement home in Pinole. I didn't like seeing her there! She was living in a small apartment with a small dog and no longer driving! She had suffered for years from asthma, had been told a few years back to get rid of the carpet in her place and to get rid of too many ornaments (at one point she had collected over 1,000 Santa's) … this place where she was living had carpet wall to wall and because it was small, she didn't have a lot of space to put her things… so it was crowed as well!

She liked Chava on site and he liked her as well… this was a woman that loved God and really loved hearing about what happened at Thornton, my sons also liked her, she had gone with us camping and in a way she had become like a part of our family…

It was a good thing that she had a very outgoing personality and made friends easily otherwise this could have turned out to be a very lonely existence!

We went back home with the promise of keeping in touch…after all she had been there for me when I needed a friend!

CHAPTER 101

Having to deal with challenges and a special wedding!

$\mathcal{I}$ had promised myself not to neglect my health and noticed that no matter how much I tried I couldn't lose the extra pounds that I had on me! I was receiving a few wise cracks from Chava when we were in bed and even exercising harder did not help! I knew from experience that when this happened, I needed to change my candida treatment, so I did some research and decided to go back to Caproyl. I knew if I gave it time it would bring up the Candida out and the weight would drop off...

It was amazing that Caproyl also brought back my appetite! I could eat half of chicken and a big piece of fish with no problem!

One thing I learned by experience was to take stronger enzymes at night to help me improve my digestion...I paid extra for better-quality enzymes that even helped with constipation! Not letting go of my health also meant taking care of my teeth and I finally decided to do some research and found a natural dentist that used the most natural solutions. I was always afraid to react even with the anesthetics they used and had to make sure they didn't use mercury feelings because of the candida.

I found a dentist at Jack London Square in Oakland and even applied for Care Credit, I had quite a bit of work done on my mouth...I liked that they were very careful in using the most natural anesthetic available but was very disappointed that for some reason the feelings…. even the crowns they had done had dissolved really easy! I found myself later on in need to go back to the dentist again!

I was so upset of having spent money for nothing that I decided to leave the work on my mouth for later when I could afford it…

Not everything stays the same and Jose (my landlord) found a girl that captured his heart and started dating her… they were together for a while, they decided to get married and of course invited us…

We attended their wedding together, they were married in a catholic church and had a wonderful reception in a Hall nearby… we had a late lunch with them… took pictures, mingled with their family and friends that knew us very well and left happy that this wonderful couple had found each other! We knew that they were going to make it and they promised us that our living together was not going to change much….

Another adjustment that came our way was that Hometown Buffet also closed their doors in San Leandro and Chava was forced to look for work! He was a hard worker, so it didn't take him long to find a couple of jobs! One of them at a Taco Bell location that was further that I liked… He had been referred to that place by a former supervisor from Hometown that now was a supervisor for Taco Bell, I warned Chava to be careful driving by himself since I knew he was still driving with an ID card… but his answer was always the same!

He always claimed to be careful but he had not taken care of the DUI's either and one day I got a call from him to let me know that the police had stopped him on the way to work! He had been taken to jail so he called me to tell me that they had taken his truck and to ask me to call one of his sons to get the truck out and park it by his mother's house. The next day I drove to the Court House, met his kids there and saw Chava behind a screen with other guys dressed in orange. I was actually very upset at him for being there! He should have listened to me and paid a lawyer little by little to get him legal in the US instead of being placed in that position! I was amazed that they set him free!

However, he was told that he needed to take care of the DUI's asap and that he would have to have someone else drive him to work….

He came home and smiled at me like everything was ok! I looked at him and told him what my own father and brothers had been thru when I was just a child and told him that I refused to go thru this again! He promised me to get a ride to work and have me drive him around… the next day I got a hold of my good friend Chris that I had worked with that was a lawyer, he found the name of another lawyer that Chava could meet with to help him legalize his status in the US. Chava promised me to meet with this guy and I made the appointment for him… he attended that meeting but of course come back home saying that it was too expensive to get legal and I was fed up with his excuses!

So, he only drove around town and when we drove long distances I drove. Chava was not very happy that I did this but I contacted one of his supervisors that he got a ride from and asked her not to let him drive and to contact me if something happened to him at work…ICE had the habit of paying surprise visits to places that might have illegals working there, she agreed and I kept her number in case he was late coming home….

Chapter 102

News that affected me in a big way!

I did receive a call not from his supervisor but from my dearest friend Sra Fatima with bad news! She informed me that my sister-in-law Rosa had come back with my nephew from Portugal pretty sick and had a severe cold that refused to get better… her niece had taken her to the Hospital to run some tests and they had found uncurable cancer!!

I was devastated! Another family member with cancer! My relationship with Rosa went back years (since I was 14 years old) and I couldn't believe that I would end up losing her as well! My first thought was that I needed to see her and give her some hope, so I called her and arranged to go see her on a Saturday. I toke a bottle of Aloe Vera with me and hugged her with all my heart! She had started on radiation treatments and was also experimenting with another form of Aloe…the one that she was using did not match the quality of the Aloe that I had taken to her but she accepted anyway and said she would try it…

I spoke with her about switching her foods to organic as much as possible and told her about Dr.Lorraine Day…She also had been given a death sentence (cancer) and had turned it around by switching her foods and healing the natural way. Rosa was willing to listen to anyone because she didn't want to lose her life but she also shared with me that she had been sick for a long time and that she had waited too long, it would probably be too late for anything to work now! I didn't know that she had actually retired and now had a group of women to do the housecleaning for the companies that she had worked for...

Ana, her niece was taking her to all her appointments and fortunately she was surrounded by a lot of Portuguese friends that were willing to help her in anyway, they brought her food and visited her often… unfortunately I was not close by but we decided to keep in touch by phone as much as possible. Rosa had been there for me when I called her before deciding to get married, unsure of what I was doing, she had told me "Do it, you need a partner, children grow up and make their own lives and then you are left on your own."

She had not re-married after my brother had passed away but had decided to dedicate her life to her son Sammy and to enjoy her life as much as possible. I admired her quite a lot, she had come to this country hardly speaking English and had found a way to build her own little business and help Mexican women that she hired to work with her... All she asked of me was to pray for her and that I did! Besides me she had quite a few people praying including her best friend Paula that had moved to Portugal, she had converted to Christianity as well and when she came to visit Rosa she convinced her to attend a service at a Christian Church. She attended services often and when I visited her with Chava she would always try to put up a brave front but I knew she was suffering! She read the Bible often and that brought her peace...

Her cancer was aggressive but it was not like my brother's had been, my brother's had been a very rapid illness… in a few months he was gone! She had a long run-in front of her and my heart ached for my nephew that would be losing another parent to cancer!

Chava was also experiencing health problems! He felt lightheaded sometimes and even felt like throwing up! I made him have a physical, we found out that because of his drinking his liver had been affected and he would need to take Vitamin D on a regular basis. I decided to e-mail Dr, Jeri from Herbal Answers and ask her if taking Herbal Aloe would help him heal whatever damage had been done to his liver and she replied back that it would definitely help… I shared the e-mail with him and of course he told me that he couldn't afford it, because of my experience with my ex, I had requested from Chava right from the beginning of our marriage that our finances be kept separate and that we share the expenses but I knew him too well…. I told him that I would pay for the Herbal Aloe myself and set out to order it…

Within a few weeks Chava was noticing the difference! He felt much better but had to watch the amount of Aloe he took because if he took too much it would cause him to get constipated… then he would back off on the dosage a bit until he got regular. I also convinced him to start taking Estro-C daily to prevent him from getting sick…

Probably one my defects or virtues is that I have always been out-spoken! I have always preferred to say right out to a person what needs to be said instead of saying it behind their back (for me that is being a coward) and I warned Chava about this…. He said that I could always be honest with him, I absolutely hated when he spoke to one of his sons on the phone and would answer the phone by saying "What's up Niger?" I confronted him about it and he said that it was a joke but for me this was offensive! He also had the habit of judging people that drank too much, he would forget quite often what it had taken him to give up drinking and I would remind him gently "Chava, you have been there, alcohol is not easy to give up and in most cases when you give up a bad habit most of the time it's replaced by another!"

Whenever Chava spoke about people that were drinking too much, he would call them "drunks" I would have to remind him "Chava after hearing how you quit drinking after much prayer from your mother, I would have joined an AA meeting… shared my story and helped someone else to quit drinking."

He had told me once that it was a good idea but he never followed up on it! This had been a man that had been driving around with a bottle of whiskey between his legs! He had quit drinking by closing himself in a room for days, where after much suffering he was able to give it up completely... a great opportunity to help others, unfortunately he would judge instead of helping anyone!

At dinner time I made a point of us praying over our meals together and we also fought a bit too much! Chava was one person in front of his friends and family and another when alone with me! He had tried to impress me while dating but once married that had stopped! I didn't believe in this, my aunt Mathilde had once told me "Never let go of yourself, always use makeup every day and always look your best, the day that you go to the supermarket without makeup is the day you will see someone that knows you and will talk about you." Many times.... is the reason why men stray....

CHAPTER 103

Losing a good job
and gaining another….

At work I got really bad news on November of 2017! I got laid off from CBA! I loved this job, I had been there for over 3 years and made many friends! We had beautiful Christmas parties together even at restaurants! The day that I was let go (work reduction) I left in tears and had friends come and hug me goodbye… I called Chava and even him was upset about it but thank goodness that I was going to receive unemployment and had enough experience now to get another position elsewhere…

It took me a while to find another position but on April of 2018 I found another position at "Alcal" as a Credit Specialist and learned quite a few things, including lien releases… I didn't mind in the least and liked the people that I work with….

One of them was the first cancer survivor that I ever met, I was so impressed with this man! He was married with two kids but as a young man had been diagnosed with terminal cancer and had managed to survive it!

I told him about my family history and what my sister-in-law was going thru and we became friends… one of things I showed Dave was to use a vegie wash to wash his favorite foods, like tomatoes and strawberries…

I still struggled with what protocol to use to continue my healing… I had a stool test done by Doctors Data and it recommend I switch treatments around, unfortunately every time I switched treatments it made me become constipated (something I couldn't afford at work)! I would end up back with Caproyl and the psyllium mixture and afraid of running out of the product!

This made me try to contact Linda at Whole Approach and found out that the company had closed down, she had taken time off to take care of her ailing mother, I was so disappointed! This company had helped me and so many other people! Caproyl the way it was made by Whole Approach was not available by any other company so in order to extend it I started to use less of the product…

I also found out that using too much Caproyl could result in big time side effects…die off a lot of times included dizziness, accelerated heart rate, headaches and even sweats… at that point I had to decrease the dosage and then start slowly up again…

In life there are always unexpected surprises coming up and mine seemed to always be there!

Danny called me to let us know that he was coming to visit us and bring his girlfriend just for a weekend, he wanted to visit his cousin Sammy and my sister-in-law that was not doing very well. Before we set out to see her, we stopped to get her flowers… Danny tried driving my car around and we found that the A/C was leaking, this was something I had tried to fix before and learned to do without! We took off together to visit Sammy and his mother, she was extremely happy to see us but she looked so pale and sick! It was heartbreaking!!

She was a fighter, she prayed and prayed and when I asked her how she was feeling she told me "I would have preferred not to have all these treatments, chemotherapy has been worse than the illness itself, it has left me with no strength, no appetite and it didn't stop the spread of the cancer."

My heart ached for her and for my nephew! Unfortunately, all we could do was to give her as much love as we could and pray for her!

Danny, Sammy, his son (that been named after my brother Carlos) Lynn, Chava and I went out for lunch, took pictures and left that day with sadness in our hearts....

Danny and Lynn went back home... my son actually told me that he planned to come back if something happened to her because he knew that Sammy would definitely need the family support...

CHAPTER 104

Surprising News!

$\mathscr{I}$was surprised to receive a call from Danny instead asking us to come and visit him in Las Vegas since he was going to purpose to Lynn! This was an event I could not miss! I convinced Chava to take a few days off and we decided to drive to Vegas a few days before Christmas of 2019.

Driving with Chava proved to be a very stressful event! We didn't like the way we each other drove and he didn't like to stop to eat anywhere, this proved to be a challenge!

With my health problems I could not afford to skip any meals and choose my menu carefully because I knew if I ate a lot of carbs, it would affect me in every way. I had reservations at a La Quinta Inn in Las Vegas where we would stay and we processed in that direction, it was late in the evening when we finally reached the strip! I was amazed at the picture of the strip with all the lights! This sight never got old for me…I was always captivated!

I loved our Inn on sight! We registered and the next morning Danny and Lynn came to get us, I had paid for all the expenses…Chava unfortunately was not a generous man regarding money, he did something in front of my son that placed him in a bad light! As we were getting into the car, Chava looked down and right by the door on the floor there was a $100 dollar bill! He picked it up and smiling from ear to ear said

"Well, this made it worth my while to come here!" Danny knew that I was paying for this trip and asked me later "Mom, has he offered to at least help with gas or food with that money? Don't let him get away with this!" I told him "Let him deal with his conscience, sometimes it's better not to say anything."

That afternoon we had lunch together and proceeded to the Strip… Danny parked his car and we walked towards the Bellagio, took pictures by the water show and inside the Bellagio… Christmas time at the Bellagio was a site to behold!!

We didn't stop to gamble… we had a lot to see and would have to attend a Christmas Eve dinner at Lynn's family where Danny would propose, on the way there we saw beautiful Christmas lights everywhere! When we entered their home… they had a beautiful table filled with all kinds of food, the hospitality these people showed us was extremely kind! The Filipino culture is very warm, they love karaoke and card games! They greeted us like they knew us beforehand!

When I finally saw Danny on bended knee purposing to Lynn (that was very surprised) I knew this trip was worth it and wished that his father also had been there! Unfortunately, he couldn't make it but we took lots of pictures and sent some to him as well…in a way it was a good thing! Chava was very jealous of him and would have refused to come with me if he had been there.

We sang karaoke…. ate some wonderful food, talked and went back to La Quinta to get some rest…

Christmas Day, we went to Church for the Christmas mass and took pictures with Lynn's family outside the Church. Once the service was done, we processed to Carlos's house to eat a late lunch with his wife Kristin and his mother-in-law Deb. I was very proud of both of them, they had been taking care of two kids, a girl and a boy since they were babies, Kristin's sister had not been able to take care of them…. Instead of handing these beautiful children to social services they had decided to take care of them and of Kristin's mother that was dealing with a severe illness! We took lots of pictures, exchanged gifts and left late that afternoon since Chava had to work the following Monday. I knew my sons didn't want to see me leave and I certainly did not want to go either but I had a good job to go back to...

Before I left my sons, I left with them some very important information regarding smoking because I knew they were still struggling with this addiction. I had brought with me cards and brochures from the American Lung Association with actual pictures how lung cancer affects your lungs and I wanted to make sure they took this addiction very seriously! I knew they were using patches but I also knew that this was an addiction that was very easy to go back to… Pictures sometimes are worth a thousand words….

They were grateful for the information since they knew because of our health history that I didn't want to lose anyone else to this awful disease!

Chava was not in a good mood by the time we got ready to leave and it got worse when I asked him to stop for a late dinner! He didn't want to stop because he wanted to make it home early and I wanted him to stop to make sure we both had coffee to keep us awake. He had me so stressed out that by the time we stopped to eat at Denny's and Carlos called me to ask if we were close to arriving, I went outside to talk to him and burst into tears! He told me "I know you are not happy mom! Sooner or later, you are going to have to do something about it, don't let him control you, you have been thru enough!" I agreed! I told him not to worry about me and that we were almost in Sacramento and not far from home…meanwhile I got the silent treatment…

When we finally arrived home, we were both exhausted! The next Monday I was off and used that day to rest, to put away our stuff and prepared myself to go back to work on Tuesday, the next day I shared my pictures with Jose, his wife and my friends at work…

CHAPTER 105

The loss of yet another person dear to me!

$\mathcal{D}$anny had promised me that he was going to make the effort to come down to California if something happened to Rosa and unfortunately that happened way too soon!

I received a call from him on New Year's Eve of 2019 that my sister-in-law Rosa had passed away and her service was scheduled for the beginning of February. Danny once again would be traveling back to California to attend her funeral… he would be staying one night at a motel and leave the next day…

We set out to meet everyone at the Chapel where the services would be held at the same cemetery where my parents and my brother were buried, she had chosen to be cremated! Many people would be attending because she was well known by the Portuguese community…. as we entered the chapel quite a few people greeted me with surprised looks since they hadn't seen me for quite a while…

I walked into the foyer and saw a couple of stands with pictures of her family thru out the years and as my eyes moved back and forth… I did not see even one picture of me! To say the least my heart was broken!

We had known each other for so many years! She had been married to my brother and it was like I didn't exist!

We sat down behind Sra Fatima (my Portuguese friend) and heard a very heart felt speech from my nephew, personal friends and family. Many tears were shed that day and we all processed to the Columbarium on foot where her ashes would be stored. I entered the building followed by my son and his fiancée and was stopped by a Portuguese guy that my ex-husband and I knew from our dancing days. He of course exclaimed that I had really slimmed down and asked how I had been doing, I hugged him briefly and told him I was perfectly fine. Chava…a bit uncomfortable among all these Portuguese people stayed in the background...

Halfway down the building again I was stopped…believe it or not by the same man that years ago after I had lost my parents and my brothers had told me "Well, look at you! You are still alive! I thought you also had died!" He had the audacity of coming out with the same comments that he had thrown at me years prior at a dance! I looked at him and asked him "Still asking me the same old questions? It seems to me that you wish me dead! I just lost my sister-in-law that was married to my brother… do you think these questions are appropriate?"

He just looked at me, I looked at him straight in his eyes and said, "I wish you well, take care of yourself and say hello to your wife for me." I left him standing there and processed to attend the brief ceremony. Many people would miss her, she had changed for the better and I would miss her immensely! She was the last link between me and my brother!

When the ceremony was over, we left in our cars on the way to her home… They had a reception waiting with food and drinks, I met with Ana and her hubby and kids…. she had been extremely helpful with Rosa's illness and had always been close to me, we hugged and got caught up in our lives. I was extremely surprised when out of the blue my nephew came up the stairs to the kitchen with a picture of me and Rosa together!

It was like she had been there behind me at the chapel and knew how I felt about not having a picture of me with the other pictures! I felt that somehow, she had placed a request on him of finding a picture of both of us!

I'm a firm believer that when someone dies their soul stays behind to attend the funeral until it's time for them to leave... I just looked at my nephew, smiled and thanked him for the picture! We ate and reminisced about old times that we had shared with Rosa and the fact that her home would never be the same without her!

I left with a heavy heart also because my son would be living again the next day for Las Vegas and I would be left behind in California without my sons....

Chapter 106

Something to be proud of….

$\mathcal{T}$he beginning of the year was also when I liked to do my physicals especially before my birthday and what made me the happiest was that they showed no sign of diabetes or cholesterol! For me that was proof enough that I was eating the right foods and exercising the right way! I sacrificed by refusing to eat what many people were eating but my reward was the tests results!

I took an extra step for my future and sent an application to the San Francisco USCIS Dept of Immigration to become an American Citizen, I studied quite a bit and Chava and I drove to San Francisco to take the test… I passed with flying colors and all I had to do was to attend the Oath of Allegiance scheduled for February 26, 2020, the day before my birthday!

For me that was the biggest gift anyone could have given me! I wished with all my heart that my parents were alive to see me receive my Certificate of Naturalization!!

I had taken this step to protect my future but also to try to influence the man that I was married to…. I bought myself a red blazer and had Chava take the day off so that he would be there to witness it…On February 26th we drove to San Francisco… had to park the car quite far and walked to the building where the ceremonies would be held, the line was huge but I was finally able to get in! The families were separated from the people that would be doing the Oath… I walked downstairs and sat down among thousands of people from different countries and I was the only one from Portugal that day! I was extremely moved by the Ceremony and could hardly wait to call my sons and tell them about it!

Once the Ceremony was over… I walked outside with my certificate in my hand…. Chava found me and we had someone take pictures of both of us. Of course, he was already in a hurry to go back home but I had seen a booth to register to vote and refused to leave until I got registered! I had been waiting for years to have this opportunity!

I heard Chava say "What do you need this for? Let's get out of here, the traffic is going to be incredible!" I told him that it would only take a few minutes, proceeded to the booth and managed to get registered. On the way to the car all he did was gripe about the traffic and I told him "What happened to all the pride you had for me back there?" "Do you realize that I also did this to help you get determined about becoming legal in this country?"

Once in the car he calmed down and I finally had the time to call both my sons and send them the pictures we had taken…. they were both very proud of their mother…that afternoon we had dinner out to celebrate… the next day I would be working and celebrating my birthday with my friends.

I shared my experience and my pictures with them… they actually had a cake waiting for me and flowers! I placed the lay that I had bought outside the building prior to the ceremony and a little flag above my desk and took pictures. This was an unforgettable experience that I would recommend to anyone…. for me even more because it was done before my birthday!

CHAPTER 107

Changes, a separation and an unforgettable trip!

$\mathcal{M}$eanwhile Jose, my landlord found out that he was going to be a father and was extremely excited! They had a baby girl and that year they also decided to renovate the mobile home since Jose had finally paid it off! He told us that it would take some time because they had to apply for permits and had to wait for the rains to stop completely before they could demolish anything…

On the other hand, Chava and I unfortunately were not getting along! We fought constantly! I decided to get tough and ask him to stay at his sister's house for a while and try a short separation to see how we felt about each other, he agreed. He was not very happy about it but I didn't want to live the rest of my life with someone that refused to do anything to help himself...

Danny called me to ask me to come to Vegas for Christmas, he told me that this time his father would be joining us…. he was in California and would be driving to Vegas, he came up with the idea that maybe we could meet halfway (Pismo area) and drive the rest of the way together. I decided to rent a car and made a reservation at La Quinta Inn for that weekend. Victor also called me to ask me sarcastically if my husband would mind if we drove together to Vegas to see the kids…. I had to tell him that we were trying a short separation to see if were better off with or without each other….

He asked me where I would be staying, I told him about La Quinta and gave him all the information by phone so that he could also make his own reservation…

I drove up to a town near Pismo and we met at a Starbucks…. from there I followed him to a farm where he had his 5th wheel parked and he introduced me to a Portuguese couple that owned the farm…. They were keeping an eye on his 5th wheel when he stayed in Portugal. I liked them immediately and they also liked me…. Victor made a remark that made them smile about having good taste in women! Little did he know that I was giving him a last chance mostly because of my sons… especially Danny! He had never given up hope that we would reconcile one day, I didn't throw myself at him… stayed calm and decided to observe him on this trip…

From there we drove in my rental to Las Vegas and took turns driving because of his back…. we stopped often to put gas or to get coffee, it was late when we finally arrived at La Quinta due to traffic and registered in separate rooms. He made a comment about me joining him upstairs to stay in his room and I told him "No thanks Victor, I have my room downstairs, go get some rest… we have a full day tomorrow with the kids." I left for my room, unpacked a bit and got my clothes ready for the next day….

The next morning… he had already asked the front desk to change his room, his room was in an area too noisy for him to be able to sleep at night and they moved him one floor down.

We waited for Danny and Lynn to come and get us and drove up to Danny's apartment, we were met by Danny's cat "Bandit", when I first met this wonderful cat I had told Danny that he reminded me of "Hitler" because of his black mustache, he sat by us while we chatted for a while. We had lunch out together, went sightseeing and spent Christmas Eve together at Lynn's family, Victor joined the guy's outback for drinks and became the life of the party as usual! They had quite a spread of goodies laid out… I had brought with me some Portuguese goodies to share with them that night and they loved the sweet bread!

Once we were done with dinner and gifts…. Danny brought us back to La Quinta, the next morning Danny and Lynn would be back to get me so that we could attend services for Christmas Day at a Church nearby…. Victor stayed behind that morning to enjoy the indoor pool and breakfast, after the service we went back to pick him up and set out to Carlos's house. Victor absolutely loved the kids, we took pictures and had lunch together… He kept pressuring me to eat dessert and I had to remind him that I had to watch it because my mother had been diabetic and on insulin, I certainly didn't want to end up that way! He looked at me sarcastically and I told him "I must be doing something right because I just had a physical and because of the way I eat I have no diabetes or cholesterol!"

From what I had observed he was already taking medication for blood pressure and diabetes but had a hard time staying away from sweets…

My son's asked me how the trip had been on the way to Vegas…. I had to tell them the truth that because of his back he had not been a happy camper on his way to Vegas and I was not looking forward to driving back with him! Nonetheless this was a time we should enjoy being together as a family and they agreed. What made us both happy was that both of our boys had quit smoking and they were thriving in Las Vegas!

We stayed until late and spent one more night at La Quinta, the next morning, we checked out and drove back to Pismo… stopped by his friend's farm, stayed and chatted for a while…. I drove back home by myself and the next day I would have to go back to work and return the rental, Victor stayed on his 5th wheel that was parked by his friend's house. I wished that I had been able to talk to him like we used to…. but something had changed in a big way between us that we could not recapture! At one point while I was driving, he had reached out to touch my hand and then withdrew his hand… probably afraid to touch mine and to let himself feel anything!

CHAPTER 108

Two unexpected invitations and a disappointment…

Once back at work I shared with my friends the pictures that we had taken at Christmas time and was very surprised when I got a call from Victor asking me to join him at a New Year's Eve celebration in San Jose! I asked him what his reasoning was for this invitation …. he said that he wanted to make it up to me and in his own words "For being a pain in the ass on the trip to Vegas." Since Chava and I were still separated I decided to accept his invitation to see how he behaved around our friends in San Jose. I also knew that he was considering living permanently in Acores and that this could well be our last opportunity to dance together, I bought a beautiful top for New Year's Eve at Macy's and got ready for the dinner dance….

Chava called me to ask me what I had planned for New Year's Eve… I told him that I would be joining some friends in San Jose for dinner and left it at that! Our New Year's celebrations had always been the same… we would eat a special dinner, watch a special show on TV and wish each other Happy New Year! We would finish the night by calling our kids and then go to sleep!

When I arrived at the Portuguese Athletic Club in San Jose, Victor was waiting for me by the parking lot … we went up the stairs to join his friends and got ready for a great dinner of filet mignon and lobster!

They had a great conjunto (band) with great music…. that night they also had another New Year's Eve celebration downstairs. We had a full table including his friends from Pismo that we had just seen, we chatted and took pictures to send to our kids…. I wanted to make sure that Danny knew that I had tried.

Dinner was awesome! When it came to Portuguese cooking, Portuguese knew how to flavor food! We ate, had a few drinks to relax and after dinner the band started to play…. immediately Victor wanted to be the first (a habit he had from way back), we started to dance together and it was like time had stood still and we were better than ever!

It was funny that Victor's words to me while dancing were not "I miss dancing with you, we make a great team" instead he asked me twice "I'm not too bad after all, right?" I knew perfectly well of what he was referring to…. I just looked at him, shook my head and refused to answer him…

Some people that had known us finally realized who they were seeing dancing on the floor and came up to greet us, they told us how great we looked together and asked if we were back together once again! Victor immediately exclaimed "Oh, no… we are together just for tonight, still friends but I'm going back to Acores this week!" In between dances when we returned to our table a friend of ours pulled me to the side and whispered in my ear "You guys should get back together! When we see you dancing… we all can see how well you fit, it's marvelous to see!" I told her, "It's a bit too late! He is totally addicted with living in Portugal and loves his freedom!" She squeezed my hand and gave me a hug…

I also knew something that they didn't know! Something that he had shared with me and that was, that he was impotent! When he shared this with me, I told him "When a woman really loves a man that does not become a factor, my own mother went thru it with my father because of all the medications he was on and that did not stop her from loving him" but for Victor unless he could perform in bed…. he did not consider himself a real man…

We went back to dance a few more times and I knew we were being watched! He grabbed my hand and told me that we were going downstairs before midnight to check out the other dance…. the same thing happened! We were stopped by old friends…. glad to see us and asking if we were together again… We went back upstairs to be with our friends for the midnight dance and at midnight we all hugged each other…. Victor placed a light kiss on my lips and that was that! We had our "canja de galinha" (chicken soup) a traditional dish for New Year's Eve and champagne. Since I had to drive back to San Leandro by myself and didn't want to go back home too late…. I said goodbye to everyone and he stayed behind because he was staying at a friend's house nearby in San Jose…

My kids called me as usual to wish me a Happy New Year and I went to sleep pretty tired from all the dancing! I did not expect Victor to call me back since I knew that he would be leaving for Portugal that same week….

I was very surprised when he called me on New Year's Day to invite me out to lunch that same week without giving me a reason! I accepted mostly curious of what he had in mind and called Danny to tell him… he was excited and told me "Mom, this is good news! It could be that he still misses you and wants a second chance!" I didn't want to disappoint Danny because he really wanted his mother and father together again…. he had admitted that to me …but I had my doubts that our relationship would ever work again…

Two days after I was at work when I received another call from Victor to cancel the lunch because his friend where he had been staying had asked him to lunch that same day! He said that he couldn't very well refuse him because they were good friends…. I just wished him a good trip back to Portugal and advised him to take care of his diet while there because of his diabetes… his answer to me was "Well, I actually eat better there than here! Anyway! I had fun! It was great being with our kids but if I ever do this again, I will fly instead." We said goodbye over the phone and I had to call Danny and disappoint him, when I told

Danny about his father cancelling the lunch, he made me very proud by saying "You know Mom it's for the better! He will never change, let him be by himself in Portugal… that's what he loves!" I could tell that my son was disappointed! I felt more for him than for me!

CHAPTER 109

Giving someone another chance and finding temporary lodging…

*O*n the other hand, Chava showed up that same week with flowers, a bottle of expensive perfume and a handful of promises!!

To say the least I was very surprised! I knew that his mother loved me dearly and probably had placed quite a bit of pressure on him to work on our relationship. I had a straight talk with him and told him "Chava, if this is going to work, you will have to stop saying what I want to hear and see someone to get yourself legal asap…. show me that you mean what you say."

He promised me that he would… he also wanted to know what I had been doing during the Holidays…. he was surprised that I had taken a trip to Vegas by myself… had met with my ex-husband and had gone out for New Year's Eve! I looked at him and told him "I had a life before you showed up Chava and have always been independent! I'm a survivor and since you know that I was around my ex and nothing happened… now you can stop the jealousy and focus on fixing our relationship instead."

He moved back that weekend and I made another appointment for a legal consultation for him…This time he kept the appointment. When he came home… he discussed with me how much it was going to cost him but I told him that he could always work on a payment plan with this lawyer. He promised me that as soon as he had the money put together he would start the process… the problem was that every time he had extra money… he would spend it fixing his truck or buying tires! Every time I went outside and saw tires I would become extremely upset! He couldn't get it thru his head how important it was to become legal!

I actually asked him to start giving me out of his paycheck a certain amount of money to put aside so that he could afford to pay for his tickets and get legalized …the problem was that he kept on taking money out!

Frustrated to the limit… I gave up on trying to save money for him…

At our place our landlord decided that they were going to do renovations as soon as possible since the weather had improved but they still wanted to keep us! They started on their side of the mobile home and moved to his mother's house, that gave us time to look for temporary lodging. We looked at apartments but they were too expensive and we would have to come out with a down payment as well as the 1st month's payment...

I did some research and found Extended Stay America in Union City… it would allow us to stay there for a while with use of a kitchen and a refrigerator. Chava and I agreed to share the expenses, I became quite friendly with the manager there and showed him pictures of our place that was being renovated and was even able to get a discount! They did an awesome job at Extended Stay! While we were at work they cleaned our place, gave us fresh towels and they even had a laundry mat inside that we used to wash our clothes...

Chava liked Extended Stay America and he understood why we were there in the beginning! We took frequent trips to the Mobile Home Park to check how the repairs were going and to check on the mail. Unfortunately…. the repairs had been delayed because the permits were late and because of the weather! Soon we would have to decide whether to stay at the Extended Stay or look for lodging elsewhere…this was causing a lot of arguments between us because of the weekly expense….

Danny and Lynn also scheduled a weekend trip to California, they planned to see us and then stop on the way back at Pismo (my kids favorite place), they stopped by our place at Extended Stay and they actually like the place! I also took them to see the repairs they were doing at the Mobile Park, they agreed with me that since the landlord wanted us back it wouldn't make any sense to get an apartment...

We took a ride to the shopping center in Union City and stopped at Starbucks and as I sat there in front of my son… I remember thinking "Danny if you only knew how many trips I took out here years ago to do soliciting while hiding from police cars!" Danny's mind was on our situation and suggested Las Vegas to both of us one day but Chava had a job nearby, his mother, his kids and I also had my job… for the time being this option was out of the question….

They left the next morning and Chava and I had arguments after arguments because of the money we were paying weekly, he wanted a stable environment for both of us and I couldn't blame him! He had a friend that we both knew that wanted to rent us a trailer that he would be willing to move to a nearby Mobile Home Park. We would have to pay a partial payment to his friend and pay for the park separately… in the long run it would be cheaper than renting an apartment….

Before we agreed to this offer… we made another effort to look for an apartment, went to check out a couple that were way too expensive for our budget… one we both liked and made an appointment with the office manager. This place was convenient for both of us, it was close to my gym and both of our jobs! On the day of the appointment, we were walking outside with the office manager when we heard people come out of their apartments and ask him directly when was the pluming getting fixed?

That was a red flag and we got out of there real fast!

CHAPTER 110

Moving into a Trailer Park and dealing with distrust…

*B*efore we decided to move to the trailer that Chava's friend had available for us, we decided to stop by Juan mother's house and have a one-on-one discussion with them… we needed to see if it was worth it to move somewhere or not… They finally told us that they didn't know how long it was going to take for the Mobile Home to be fixed… not only because we had a lot of rain but because of the delay of the permits. We all agreed that it would be for our best interest to move somewhere else and save money until the whole project was done…

We started the whole process, filled out an application with the Trailer Park (relying on my credit) got approved and filled out an agreement with Chava's friend. He was also the mechanic that worked on our cars, we agreed to pay him half check, half money order each month and the trailer park separately.

I had made yet another appointment for Chava with a lawyer referred by a friend of mine to get him legalized here in the US, he kept the appointment but came home complaining that it was too expensive once again! I had heard the story before so the next day I called the lawyer myself and he told me that they could work with him on a payment plan but he also needed to pay his remaining traffic tickets! I was upset because I was not being told the whole truth but kept quiet for a while….

Chava's friend had taken pictures of the trailer and it was a nice one! I didn't mind at all moving there temporarily until we could either go back to Jose's place or put money away for a better place…. I went by his friend's place to give him our first payment and he surprised by telling me "If you don't mind, I would like to receive the monthly payments by your hand, I don't trust Chava very much and you shouldn't either." I looked at him surprised and he said, "Believe me, I know what I'm talking about! I have known him for many years." I told him that I would be paying him every month… thanked him and left….

That afternoon I had a talk with Chava and we ended up arguing! I told him "Chava, you promised me that you would stop the half-truths and would be straight-forth with me… why are you avoiding getting legal? Do you realize how dangerous it is to be driving every day with only an ID instead of a driver's license, not speaking of being caught by ICE?" He said (like always) that he would do it later when he was able to put the money away… the problem was that he could never manage to do it!

I was starting to suspect that Chava was relying on me (as a citizen) to keep him safe but I had done enough research to find out that he could also apply for citizenship after being married to me… I had requested an application for him but he needed everything in his past cleared up including DUI's…for him it was like he had all the time in the world…

Now there was also suspicion because of what I had been told by his personal friend and I asked him about it…his answer was that he didn't trust him either!

I didn't know at this point if I wanted to continue with our relationship or not and asked him to give me some time to think things over and find out if this relationship was worth it, he asked me what I had in mind and I told him " Since everything has been approved… go ahead and move your stuff into the trailer and give me a week or two by myself at Extended Stay so that I can have some time to think." He agreed to my surprise but kept in touch with me…. I had paid my rent at Extended Stay to the end of the month and didn't mind being there by myself…. but I was also a realist, I knew I could not stay there forever… I could not afford it! I was also trying to scare Chava into doing something about his life…It was my last attempt to help him realize that he needed to keep his promise to me of getting legal in this country…

One night while watching TV by myself I felt the whole room shake and realized that this was quite a strong earthquake! I called Danny and he said that they had felt it all the way in Vegas! This was something that I had always disliked about Portugal and California that they were both very prone to earthquakes! When Danny asked me if I was alone, I had to tell him the truth and he told me that he didn't like me being alone as often as I was….

I was very surprised when I received a nasty call from Chava asking me "So, have you decided if you are going to move into the trailer or not? Since I cannot afford to pay for the rent by myself, I asked my daughter and her friend to move in to help me pay for the rent. What do you think about that?" I was very upset and told him "Chava, you and I need to have a chat in person, I will find the time to come and talk to you." He agreed and hung up… what I didn't tell him was that I was headed to the trailer as soon as we finished talking! By the time I got there I was fuming! It didn't help that his daughter and her girlfriend were already living at the trailer!

I spoke to both directly and told his daughter my motives for asking her father for a couple of weeks by myself…. not leaving him but making him aware how serious it was not to be legal in the US!

I also told her that if it wasn't for my credit score her father would never been able to get the place. She started to apologize but this was mostly her father's fault for not being honest with his daughter, so I turned around… spoke directly to him and told him "Chava! What gave you the idea that I would be able to afford staying at Extended Stay America?" He got quiet and his daughter asked us if they could stay there until they were able to get a place of their own…. I turned to her and said, "I would not throw anyone out on the street (I had been there) but I also need you to grab your stuff from our bedroom and place it on the extra room in the back… it has a sofa bed that you can use." I looked at Chava and told him "I will help you find a place for both of them, just like this…. meanwhile please make room for our dishes in the kitchen since I see that the cupboards are pretty full." I will be moving in this weekend." He was silent…. he was seeing a sight of me he had never seen before but I didn't like being taken advantage of…

When I got back to my room at Extended Stay, I started to pack all my belongings and moved all my stuff by myself in my car …it took me two trips!

I said goodbye to the personnel at the front desk and thanked them for their wonderful service… when I got into my car, I looked back and felt pretty sad! I was leaving a place that I liked a lot and that I would definitely miss! To my surprise when I got to the trailer and exhausted there was no hot water and the electricity had not been turned on…. something I had to arrange for by myself. That week I got to know the manager of the park and she and I became good friends…

Meanwhile at work on my breaks I started to look for a place for Chava's daughter (knowing Chava he would not do anything about it) and made a couple of appointments…. because they did housecleaning and didn't have steady income they could not afford a Trailer Park or an apartment so they ended up back in Sacramento living with someone they knew…

CHAPTER 111

Trying to regain trust and dealing with a big epidemic!

*M*y relationship with Chava had suffered because of this…. I had lost trust in him but he wanted to make it work…. once they left it was better but I was left alone quite often because he switched schedules and worked weekends and even nightshifts! Many times, my sons would call me to ask me how I was, they didn't like what had happened with the moving to the trailer and that I was left alone quite often…... what helped me was that I spent the whole week at work… and even that changed!!

In January of 2020 California started to see cases of the Covid Epidemic and people were asked to stay at home if they were sick…. at the same time, we were hit with wildfires and had to use masks when going outside even while grocery shopping! When I went for walks in the Marina my heart would break when I looked across the bay and could see a red haze from all the fires! California was changing so much from when I had first gotten here from Bethel, Ohio…

Our world was changing and not for the better!

For the first time I witnessed something I had never seen in my life and that was Hoarding in a big way!

I saw people at grocery stores place loads of items on short supply in their baskets afraid that they would become unavailable in the future and uncaring of other people's needs!

Our environment at work had also changed! They gave us masks to use outside for protection and many people stayed home if their immune system was compromised in anyway…. As usual when something like this happens there are people that overreact! Our manager for example if we approached someone at another desk to ask a question if she was there, she would stop nearby and exclaim out loud "Stand back! At least 6 feet…. you know the rules." This was one angry individual! Anything would set her off and unfortunately, she also had favorites! I had made quite a few friendships including an Indian couple that worked there, the wife worked in our department and they both cleaned our offices after closing, he was extremely polite… reminded me of my father! Just like him he had broken his foot and was having a hard time recovering fast enough and I told him "My father was told that because he had broken his foot, every time the weather changed he would feel it." He agreed… that was happening already!

I also developed friendships with other young women there, one that joined us from Arizona that I liked very much and my immediate supervisor. I found myself many times giving advice to women because after all I had done extensive work in counseling at Patten…. some would listen and some would not…. that also went for weight loss since I had experience with that as well….

My promise to God was never forgotten no matter where I was….

No way was I prepared when I got called into an office with my manager and another person from HR! I was given a letter that due to the slowdown in our industry due to Covid, 15 positions were being eliminated… including mine! They gave me a copy of the letter and I was told to clear my desk immediately! My manager escorted me to my desk and refused to leave until I had all my stuff in a couple of bags, did not even give me time to say goodbye to anyone!

I felt like I had committed some kind of crime! I had made friends in this company and had given them two years of hard work and dedication! I was not able to speak to anyone… I didn't like the way this was done at all so once I was finished clearing my desk I stopped at HR and spoke to a young man "You know, I'm not some kind of criminal that I have to be watched over! I have never taken anything from anyone… I also need to place a special request and if I must speak to the head of HR so be it! I do not have a computer at home to apply for E.D.D… If I could get permission from someone to use one of your computers, I would appreciate it." He actually felt sorry for me and got permission for me to use a laptop while I was in his office and was able to apply for Unemployment and left….

I wondered on the way home if anyone was going to call me and tell me "Mary, we are sorry to see you go, wish you the best and you will be missed!" but no one did! As always when you leave most people feel relieved that they still there and have a job….

I had told my father before he got sick "Dad, take care of yourself first…. your health is more important! To any company most of the times you are no more than a number and once you leave… they will immediately replace you."

He heard but did he listen? Unfortunately… not!!

CHAPTER 112

Adjusting to being unemployed and living a different way...

Once I got home, I put away all my office stuff and once Chava got home, I told him about it…. he was supportive and told me "With all the experience you have you are going to find work sooner than you think." I sat out to develop a routine every day and one of my first priorities was to buy a laptop so that I could look for work every day! I was lucky that Jose (my former landlord) came by with his wife and baby to see the trailer and helped me install everything I needed on my laptop! I missed them quite a lot, this young couple had become like family to me…. there would always be a special place in my heart for them!

Chava and I also developed a routine every night, he would come home from work eat dinner with me while we watched "Enamorandonos", it became our favorite show! This show was like the Dating Game in Spanish! I developed a habit of watching Spanish novellas (short soap operas), this kept my Spanish alive, I needed Spanish even for work …. sometimes practiced Spanish with Chava, Portuguese I practiced with my friend Sra Fatima and with my cousin in Portugal.

Unfortunately, my kids because they knew their parents spoke English didn't want to try to speak Portuguese. Carlos had learned quite a bit with his grandmother and with me but then lost most of it when she passed away! It was funny how I would try to start a conversation in Portuguese with my kids and they would finish in English!

I was on the way home one night after working out at the gym when I received a call from Carlos, he actually surprised me with his request "Mom if you are still working out at the gym please stop for a while… covid cases have increased everywhere and I don't want to worry about you!" I was very touched by his call and told him that I was going to find another way to workout…. when we disconnected, I thought about what he said! Especially in my case it would be dangerous to keep on going to the gym since I always finished my routine by using the steam room …. The steam as wonderful as it can be can also be filled with bacteria in the air if not cleaned properly....

From that day forward I started walking in the Marina every day…. because I also needed the steam, I started using a warm shower in the morning and found to my surprise that it also helped me with constipation! If I woke up constipated and took a warm shower that would stimulate the bowel to move! What surprised me the most was that I found out that I was actually having better bowel movements! This stimulation could last for a couple of days but I also had to make sure I took a mild laxative the night before…. unfortunately, my bowel refused to produce a bowel movement unless I took it!

I found out something else that I had forgotten from a long time ago that warm showers can also help to calm your nerves and put you in a better frame of mind! I had noticed this before when dealing with Victor and Chava and always chose to discuss important issues with them after they took a shower!

Due to my concern with the use of laxatives I contacted Dr.Francis and discussed my concern…. I had tried other alternatives and for me nothing else worked, she ordered a stool test for me and advised me to switch treatments around (candida was still evident), she also advised me that because of the leaky gut and the laxative use to always incorporate the smoothie in the morning…

I also shared with her that a few years prior I had asked another doctor the same question about the laxative that I was taking... she told me that the Senna that was included in the product that I was taking was actually beneficial and not harmful in any way!

Whenever we had a chance to speak to each other, it was like old times! She always asked me "And how are you honey?" I always shared with her whatever had changed in my life...like my marriage to Chava... She surprised me by asking about the book that I had been writing and I told her that unfortunately because of everything that had happened in my life I had kept it in the back burner!

Before we disconnected, I told her that I would be sending her a picture of my wedding day and shared with her that day I had been so full of doubts that I wished with all my heart that I had her there to speak to.... she always managed to bring peace to my heart!

We both agreed that men are not everything and that women need to be independent! Because I was no longer going to the gym it became impossible to change protocol, I had tried changing treatments for the candida and found out that to have better bowel movements nothing worked better than Caproyl. Something amazing kept on happening! This treatment brought out candida like no other! I actually took pictures of it in the trailer and was amazed that this was happening without using the steam at the gym!

I kept these pictures to myself, it would be incredibly difficult to explain to anyone...even family! To see is to believe....

CHAPTER 113

Doing research
and witnessing sad events!

J had the habit of doing research about everything and many times found things that had helped people many years ago and used it in my diet…. for example…. the use of lemon juice every day. Scurvy was actually cured in sailors on a ship thousands of years ago by using the juice of lemons and oranges! Lack of vitamin C can be extremely harmful to a human being! Besides taking Vitamin C every day…. I sprinkled lemon juice on my chicken or fish every day…

As far as playing it as safe as I could I also made sure I had anti-bacterial soap everywhere for us to use when we got home, washed all our floors with Pine Sol and used plastic gloves when shopping. Chava asked me one day why the gloves and I told him "Why? Think about it! When people are shopping out there, they are touching everything with their hands, we forget and touch our face or eyes…if they are sick…. we are taking a risk of contamination!"

Unfortunately, sometimes men are harder to listen then women! Chava argued with me even about wearing masks and my ex-husband made fun of them on Facebook! I on the other hand did research on prior pandemics and found that the use of masks had been extremely successful, so I used them everywhere I went and saw that many people use them as well…

Going to supermarkets had now become a sad experience! We now had to stand outside in line and only a few people were allowed in to avoid exposure to many people in a store at the same time! I liked to observe people no matter where I went and especially how they handled difficult situations…. I saw people walking around with masks placed wrongly on their faces…. covering only the mouth area and not the nose! There were those that entered a store with no mask at all…. maybe fed up with all the protections required?

I also took another precaution, coming home from the supermarket I made sure to wash all my vegetables! That applied especially to avocados, vegetables and fruits, I still used a vegie wash for all my vegetables and fruits as I had before but washed them a lot better…

Many days I found myself walking in the rain at the Marina even with an umbrella! In order to keep up with my weight training I bought a couple of weights and did training while walking! This is when you have to not really care what people think of you and do it for your health! I didn't care if people look at me funny or not, I did for me!

Sometimes looking at other individuals around you can make you less self-conscious! When doing my daily walks, I had the chance to observe a father and son that also walked the Marina… the son was young and suffered from autism, when he walked it was like he was dancing and humming and picked little flowers along the way! I wondered about the mind of a young man that was stricken too early in life with this illness! His father had a hard time keeping up with him and would laugh and hug his son along the way! Seeing them always placed me in a good mood going home! God knows we needed to see people like them with everything that was going on all around us!

Everywhere I went people were walking around with masks, there were fires all around us and even looting! I would drive home from the Marina and see stores locked up in fear of being robbed and we were subjected to curfews just about every day!

After witnessing all of this it made you wonder if this was the beginning of the end of the world or if all of this would be over one day? I prayed every day that God would act and put a stop to all of this! I knew if I had to come back to this world the way it was now, I would much prefer to stay in Heaven!!

I shared with my kids what was going on around our area and they kept on insisting that we should move to Las Vegas. Danny came up with the idea that I should ask Chava to get a transfer from the Taco Bell he worked for to a Taco Bell in Vegas. He also believed that I probably would find work there much faster, I shared that idea with Chava but he was very stuck on his job and of being closer to his family…. of course, to pacify me he would agree to anything and then do nothing about it…

He was also experiencing pains in his groin, had tests done and it didn't surprise me that they found another hernia that needed to be removed! He made an appointment for the surgery and then backed out because he was afraid to be exposed to covid in a hospital setting. He also switched schedules around and now came home after 11 or 12 at night and worked late Saturday nights! Unfortunately, because of all the violence around us I became afraid of being alone in the trailer…. even when I shared with him how I felt he refused to change his schedule, I even suggested that he ask his supervisor for a change of schedule but he kept telling me that she needed him working those shifts…

CHAPTER 114

A call that I was not prepared for and two disappointments!

*A*nd then something happened that I was not prepared for! I was out shopping at Walmart when I received a call from Carlos to let me know that his father had been found at his place (in Acores) unconscious! They had taken him in an ambulance to a nearby hospital and found out he had a heart attack and a small stroke but was alive! I was in shock and my first thought was that I was glad that we had our last dance together!

He was at the hospital for a while until he was well enough to go back home! I was glad that he had someone living with him to watch over him, the kids promised me that they would keep me informed in case he got worse, this situation made realize one big thing! That I had forgiven him a long time ago because I felt sorry for him! I wished with all my heart that he would have remembered what I had told him a few years back when discussing health issues, he had told me what my oldest brother had told me before he passed away "When it's time to go, it's your time to go!" I had answered him "Not really Victor! We are also responsible for how we take care of ourselves, that can definitely extend our lives."

What happened to Victor also prompted me to get prepared in case something ever happened to me! I wrote a letter that I carried in my purse in case something happened to me with all the emergency numbers… for example my son's phone numbers, etc.… also that if I was in a car accident that I did not want to be placed on life support and my last wish was to be cremated. Whatever belonged to me went to both my son's and no one else, this is not easy to do! It's facing mortality! Something we all avoid doing...

When my parents passed away it had helped me immensely that they had an insurance policy with all the funeral costs provided for...I also paid monthly fees for this purpose, when someone close to you dies it's very hard to arrange for everything and worry about costs!

I found out thru Danny that Carlos had also gotten sick, he had been to the Hospital for shortness of breath and flu like symptoms and sent back home! I was really concerned! Being away from your kids when they are sick is extremely hard! I told Danny "If he gets sick again make sure you call me right away and I will be on the next plane!" He promised me that he would keep me updated but that he was home and already doing better....

Meanwhile my work search continued since I was hoping to a find a position nearby, went to a couple of interviews and nothing happened!

I took the time to clean up my closets and found Sue's phone number and called her right away, she was surprised to hear from me! My Melaleuca partner and friend had changed quite a bit! We met halfway as usual at a restaurant, hugged and laughed how time had changed both of us! I was taken back completely to find out that she had become a nudist and now loved to go camping using her RV instead of working for the Napa Airport!

We shared a lunch together, shared pictures of our kids and then she asked me how I was doing.... I told her that I was laid-off, she said "Wow! Sorry to hear about that!" she then smiled and proceeded to get money out of her wallet and flashed a wad of cash in front of my face just like saying "Well, look at this! I'm in no need of money!" I was so offended that I got my credit card out to pay for both of our lunches and she exclaimed "Don't you dare honey! I will pay for our lunches!" We said our goodbyes but I didn't make any future plans to see her again! I was so disappointed! When I got in my car I burst into tears and thought "What in the hell happened? Is anyone in this world able to be a true friend to someone?"

When I got home, I called Danny and shared this experience with him since he also knew Sue, he probably could hear the disappointment in my voice because he asked me "Mom, how are you doing with the job hunting?" I had to tell him the truth "Not so good! I had a couple of interviews but maybe because of Covid everything is a lot harder now." He reminded me that I could always come to visit him in Vegas and try looking for a position... then if I got chosen for a job then I could always stay in Vegas, he also reminded me to speak to Chava again and have him ask for a transfer... The Taco Bells in Vegas were always hiring.

Both of my sons were very concerned with all the fires and violence that was going on all around us and they wanted us nearby! I agreed to once again speak to Chava about it but I knew that he would make every excuse in the book... mostly because he didn't want to leave his mother and kids behind. I also had to remind him that I couldn't take too long to find another position because I was getting older... the Unemployment wasn't going to last forever! He agreed to give it some thought and discuss it with his family, they had planned a family get together and I decided not to go, I didn't want to place any pressure on him...what bother me the most was that instead of becoming more loving towards me he had become colder and had an attitude that didn't quit!

It became harder to talk to him so when he come back after the get together with his family, he told me that no way could he consider such a move and told me "What makes you think you can get a job in Las Vegas?" I was not surprised, I told him "Chava, what makes you think, I can't? Where is your faith in me? Why can't you try the transfer and then we can make an occasional trip back and forth to see your family?" He answered me "Well, then you go first and if you make it... then we can talk about it."

It was not like I was an idiot! I also reminded him that he had heard from Danny that the situation with Covid was better in Vegas....

For me marriage was a partnership and Chava was not willing to be a partner!

CHAPTER 115

Taking a chance in moving to Las Vegas and saying goodbyes…

$\mathcal{I}$continued communicating with Danny back and forth and he finally convinced me to go and visit and to bring quite a few things with me just in case I decided to stay… this meant of course that I would have to rent a very small U-Hall and drive to Vegas. Danny and Lynn booked a flight arriving in Oakland on May, 23rd of 2020 and I told Chava about it, he acted like he was happy to see them but not happy of the decision I had made of driving back with them to Vegas. I told him that I was going to go for a visit and would only stay if I ended up getting a job, I wasn't getting anywhere in California and things were getting worse instead of better!

Before I was set to move…. I said my goodbyes to some of my friends in case I didn't come back including the manager of the Trailer Park. I had to tell her the truth because my name was on the rental application but I promised her that I would call her immediately if I decided to stay in Vegas with my son's. Paulette (the trailer park manager) gave me her stamp of approval on what I was doing and shared with me something that actually made feel better about the decision to move out of California! She told me that I was getting out of the Bay Area just on time because we were once again going back to Phase I (shelter into place) and that also meant fewer jobs available!

I also went by Chava's friend place (the guy that had rented us the trailer) and explained what I was about to do…. he wasn't very happy about it because he didn't trust Chava with payments, I reminded him that he had a daughter that would probably move in and help him with the rent. I also called Jose (the owner of the Mobile Home) and told him that I needed to speak to him, he met me at the Mobile Home that was still being worked on and told him what I was about to do, he understood because he knew that I was having a hard time finding work. I had a few close friends that lived nearby that I said goodbye to and promised to keep updated…. some I just chose to contact by phone if the move proved to be a permanent one…

I finally picked up Danny and Lynn at the airport, they were wearing masks and I was very happy to see them! I had our sofa bed prepared ahead of time and even a Portuguese breakfast for the next morning…

They went with me to get a small U-Hall and we had someone connect my car to the back of the U-Hall, between the 3 of us we packed everything I wanted to take with me and set aside what I didn't need or want…

Chava showed up after work… was polite to them of course but kept to himself, he knew by now that I was not going back on my decision. Before dinner I did my daily walk around the park using my weights and prepared my son to what he would see every day once we got moved to Vegas, he didn't mind of course he just wanted me out of California!

The next morning, we had our breakfast, took some stuff from the refrigerator for a few days and cleaned as much as possible, Chava gave me a brief hug and told me to keep in touch… when we finally got in the truck and drove out of the Trailer Park, I didn't feel sad! I was so glad to be out of there and away from so much violence!

As far as Chava I was still hoping to change his mind and hoped that if I got a job that he would reconsider…

We drove out and Danny looked at me and said, "Don't worry Mom, you made the best decision… there are all kinds of opportunities in

Vegas and you also gave Chava plenty of time for him to consider a transfer…let's see if he does anything about it."

Again, I didn't look back! I had prayed for God's approval for this move because after all I was moving to a city that people called "the city of sin."

I felt that I had His approval and I had been quite a few times in Vegas to know that like any other city evil and sin exists in any place not just Las Vegas. Danny because of my religious beliefs had made sure that when in Vegas I had the chance to attend services at a couple of churches… went as far as pointing out to me because of the way I ate of the all the places where to buy my groceries…

We drove most of the day and stopped for a late lunch and gas… it was pretty late by the time we got to Danny's apartment. He lived on the 3rd floor and we moved most of what we could by ourselves, I really felt sorry for Danny because the day was extremely warm, any heavy boxes were taken upstairs by him and placed on the veranda! I was introduced to Lynn's best friend Jing, she had given me her room and was sleeping in the living room in a sleeper. The next day Danny and I went to return the U-Hall and got my car detached from the truck and was notified that my car was leaking oil! Unfortunately for me that meant taking the car to the nearest Acura Dealership and have it fixed, I called them and arranged for an appointment and that same week the car was again drivable!

Thank goodness Danny had given me a smart phone for Christmas! He convinced me by the statement he had given me "Mom, you have to get with the times and this smart phone will be able to get you anywhere without getting lost." It had taken me forever to give up my flip-phone but now I was extremely happy that I had! I certainly didn't want to rely on Danny to go to a supermarket or any other place.

CHAPTER 116

Adjusting to a new lifestyle in Vegas...

*T*hank God I was not easily frightened by new places or adjusting to a new lifestyle! Soon after I came up with a new walking program… with the Marina no longer available I walked around the apartment complex with my mask and my weights (found that people could careless how I looked) once done, stopped by my car to change my shoes, took my laxative and walked upstairs to my son's apartment and prepared my dinner.

One of the things I had to learn to do at my son's apartment was to take my shoes off at the door and use slippers, this was a Filipino custom that came from Danny's fiancé… it was also a good custom because of covid! I also took another precaution by cleaning doorknobs with a disinfecting wipe and cleaned kitchen surfaces daily…. We all took every precaution necessary to keep us safe in a time of crisis!

After a few days I started to look for work just to see if anyone would respond, I got on my laptop and applied for California and Nevada jobs. Back in California before I left, I had spoken to a paralegal about my situation with Sal, Marcel asked me if I wanted to start the paperwork to start the filing for the divorce, at the time I was upset with Sal and said yes but before I left I asked him to hold off on filling since I wanted to give Sal at least a month to reconsider.

That 4th of July was spent at my oldest son place with a terrific barbecue! I watched Carlos and the kids swim for a while on a very warm day! I marveled how mature he was and how wonderful he was with the kids! Jayden and Jordan were marvelous kids and very lucky that they had found a couple of very loving and responsible people to take care of all their needs!

I was also amazed how I had adjusted to the weather! The weather was not only warmer but also drier, hardly any rain …something I liked! Also found out that earthquakes in Nevada were very few… something I loved! The only thing I had a hard time adjusting to was the drivers in Vegas! They were very impatient and would honk at someone for the least thing!

Many times, I remembered the Portuguese saying "Passa por cima!" this was something I witnessed in Lisbon! Our traffic there would get quite hectic and while traveling with my cousin I saw many drivers yell out the window this saying that in English means "Jump over!"

One of things I found out about people in Vegas was that they used the word "Excuse me" a lot more than Californian's and got offended if you forgot to use that word! For me the most important word was "Thank you."

I was very surprised and pleased by the respect I saw for wildlife in this State! I was on my way out one morning stuck on the street like everyone else, thinking it was a traffic accident, looked out the window and saw a lineup of wild geese crossing the street! It looked like mother geese with her little ones following behind were on the way to the park and all the cars were stopped to let the family thru! I was so touched I called Danny to share this experience with him and we both laughed!

Both of my sons were thrilled to have me in Vegas but whether I stayed or went back to California depended if I was able to get a job or not!

To my surprise I got an interview with a Bond company on the Strip, they liked me quite a lot and told me they would be calling me for a second interview!

I also had applied at a mortgage company on Tivoli Village and was very surprised that a very nice guy called me for an interview! I accepted of course and found out that the place where they were located was very beautiful! Jeff met me downstairs and escorted me upstairs for the interview! Both of us used our masks and I found out that they were very shorthanded! One person had been left behind when the pandemic started to do all the work and they also needed someone that spoke Spanish, Jeff and I clicked! I liked him on the spot! He said he had a couple more interviews that week and would call me for sure that week to let me know... Danny told me "How much do you want to bet that you will get a job sooner rather than later?"

I was on my way out one Friday when I received two calls, one from the Bond company wanting a phone interview to check on my Spanish and the other from Jeff! The Bond company promised me to call me the following week to let me know if I got the job! Jeff on the other hand called me to let me know that he was very impressed with me and wanted me to start the following week!!

I was extremely happy and so were my son's because they didn't want me to go back to California....

While getting to know the area where we lived, I had the chance to see (like Danny had said) how many food places we had all around us and even bus stops, not for me but for Chava! I was extremely surprised that a man that professed to love me hadn't even called me to ask me if we had arrived safely!

That same afternoon I sent a message to E.D.D to let them know that I would be starting work the next Monday and stopped searching for work...

CHAPTER 117

A new opportunity arises in Vegas and getting divorced…

*T*he following Monday I was once again met by Jeff, he introduced me around and I immediately took a liking to everyone!

The job itself was not hard! They were overwhelmed with work and they needed a lot of help! It was a good thing that I was like a chameleon! I was already adapting to work, to new friends and to a new environment!!

I found that working for guys was much easier than working for women! Women tend to get jealous of other women…. much quicker to judge and even less patient! My manager proved to have the same background in banking that I did and was extremely patient when training someone! Our department was small but a very effective one!

It was a total surprise to me when I received a call from Chava one night asking me how I was doing! I told him "I'm surprised to hear from you! We arrived safely in case you care, I already managed to get a job at a mortgage company making almost as I was in California! I also found out that Danny was correct, there are a lot of food places out here and plenty of public transportation. How are you and your mom?" His response! "Congratulations! We are fine! I'm glad I stayed in California, my mother would have been extremely upset if I had left her behind!" So, from this short conversation I finally understood that he wouldn't be changing his mind, the next morning, I shared with Danny the conversation I had with Chava and he told me "I didn't think he was going to change his mind, Mom! I guess he didn't love you enough to make this move!"

The following Monday I contacted Marcel and told him to finalize the divorce papers…. I refused to be a long-distance wife and I had given him enough opportunities to change his mind… in the end I had proved him wrong!

I gave it my all at my job and even managed to give some good advice to those that would be willing to listen! To David that suffered from allergies to eat correctly because I knew it would help his digestive system! To both David and Jeff- vitamin C because of the covid pandemic and made them my own special coffee (a mixture of Starbucks French Roast with hazelnut cream and sugar-free hot chocolate mix) which they loved!

I liked the fact that this company really appreciated their employees and recognized them even on their birthdays! They would gather all the employees together, stopped by an employee's desk with a birthday cake and sang "Happy Birthday!" The girls at the front desk also decorated the desk of the person that would be celebrating their birthday the night before, when the birthday guy or girl arrived the next day… the desk was already decorated!

Of all things I was very surprised to find that our HR person came from a Portuguese background and loved our cod!

To my surprise not everyone really worried about covid! I took every precaution possible, I wore my mask everywhere, washed my hands faithfully and disinfected my desk before I left work. I found out that on the elevator that we had to use each day that not all people would use masks! I had a word with the cleaning lady that was not using her mask in the elevator. Lack of knowledge in your language can definitely hurt you! I spoke with her in Spanish and she understood how important it was to use a mask, after all we had visitors from other branches and other states that we could not possibly know if they had been exposed to covid!

By the end of July, I received the divorce papers and I knew that Chava had also received them! He never called to even admit he had the papers with him! I looked at the documents in my hand and couldn't even cry! I didn't like being divorced a second time! When I showed Danny the papers, he asked me if Chava had called me to protest and I told him "Not a word!" Danny said something that was very true "I guess Mom, he didn't love you enough to fight for you!"

To my surprise I did receive a call from him one night not to admit that he had received the papers but to share with me that he had gotten sick with covid thru his job and that they placed him on quarantine in a motel! I didn't mention the divorce papers just asked him how he was doing and he told me he was going back to work. I also decided not to tell him about my decision to help Danny buy a home…. he had lost much because he had decided not to believe in me!

It was a good thing that I believed in myself!!

Something else surprised me one day! I found out at lunch that I wasn't smelling food the way I usually did and was scared! I couldn't taste my food the way I usually did either! I didn't have a fever but a few body aches….

I had been trying to let go of caproyl to start a new treatment, so I had been without treatment for a few days and that's when I started to feel unwell! Instead of panicking I decided to once again start on caproyl and increased my vitamin C, it took a couple of weeks but I was once again able to start smelling and tasting my food! I did some research regarding the Caprylic Acid benefits and found out that it contains antibacterial, antiviral and anti-inflammatory properties! This information was extremely important because I needed to protect myself from covid and this seemed to work for some reason!

Also because of covid I switched my bath soap to Dial antibacterial… while in California I had heard a disc-jockey on the radio claim that one of the ways he kept covid at bay was by taking a warm shower every day and used an antibacterial soap! This was particularly important after being around a large group of people while shopping or at an event...

After my probation period Danny and I discussed checking into a home, I had told him many times that paying for an apartment was money out of your pocket and out the window and he agreed. I had been saving for a long time for a down payment to give Danny for a home (I knew he had not been able to do it) he also shared with me that his credit score was not high enough to qualify him for a loan. Danny and my supervisor both shared with me that the interest rates were really low!

This was the time to buy a home! My son was extremely happy when I told him how much I had been saving for the deposit and he set out to look for our new home, we scheduled a couple of appointments to view a few houses on a weekend and finally found one that we all loved!

CHAPTER 118

Buying a home together…
a reward in itself!

We got all the paperwork approved and Danny and I became co-owners of a home together, we both would be paying less each month than we would be paying on an apartment! The day we signed the papers for the house I looked at Danny and told him "This hopefully makes up for the loss of our home in San Pablo that I knew you really loved!" He smiled in agreement!

The next step would be to start packing all our stuff and our plan was to move in before Thanksgiving of 2020!

We all worked hard and managed to move in before Thanksgiving! We had much to give thanks for!!

Danny and Lynn also made sure the apartment we had been living in was cleaned up and we got prepared for Thanksgiving!

One day after parking my car outside I had a really good look at our home and tears of joy came into my eyes! I realized that I would no longer be under the mercy of anyone as a tenant! This was a big reward for me! I had been thru enough sorrow…. including the fact that I had lived in a car at one time!!

The first day I set foot on my new home I made a promise to myself, that nobody was ever going to play games or make me suffer again! Enough was enough already!!

I ordered cod from a Portuguese Store in California and some Portuguese products for the Holiday, I managed to make "pasteis de bacalhau" (cod fritters), seasoned the turkey, made Portuguese stuffing and rice-pudding. I wanted to make sure my kids had all the traditional foods that they loved cooked by me along with Filipino foods prepared by Lynn and Jing that I happened to like quite a lot! Carlos came over with his family and we took lots of pictures, Carlos and Kristin really liked our home! I really wished that what I had done for Danny I could also do for them one day!!

I took leftovers to my job and my co-workers loved them! The only time that I cooked Portuguese foods was on Holidays otherwise I ate as healthy as I could... Even when they had luncheons at work, I would always bring my own salad and added anything I found that was healthy to it...

My protocol remained the same.... I found that if I changed from caproyl to any other treatment it would make me constipated! I couldn't afford that at work... Constipation I found out many years ago affected my concentration big time and I needed my job!

I got many compliments at work how slim I was and some of my co-workers thought that I was trying on purpose to stay slim, little did they know that I actually wanted to gain weight and couldn't! Caproyl was one treatment that kept your weight down but helped immensely in getting hidden candida out!

My first Christmas in Las Vegas as a resident was extraordinary!

CHAPTER 119

Holidays spent with
my sons in Vegas!

Christmas Eve Carlos came over with his family and as usual I made my traditional Portuguese Dishes; I was very proud of my son's they actually asked me to pray over our meal before we shared all the wonderful foods we had prepared! We all contributed to our Holiday meal, Carlos and Kristin brought food to share and Lynn and Jing also shared their Filipino dishes with everyone as usual…

We took pictures together and after dinner we exchanged our gifts. Carlos shared with me that he also disinfected his place at work every chance he got…. he worked at a motorcycle shop and of course they had customer's come in frequently, so he made sure he used his mask and washed his hands frequently, I was very proud of him for doing this, especially because men are notorious for not washing their hands often!

My son and I had many interesting discussions about our family and when we spoke about the house in San Leandro that we had lived in, he believed just like me that something evil had lived in that house! This made me do some research on the house that Danny and I bought…. I found out that an older gentleman had lived in our home but couldn't find out too much more! Instead... You guessed it! I prayed every day for God to protect our home!

On Christmas Day we got together, went to an early service at a local church and went to the Bellagio to see a beautiful display of Christmas decorations! Took pictures as usual and ended up having dinner at Lynn's family.

We took some food ourselves, exchanged gifts, sang karaoke and took more pictures! Her family also had been at the church service and as usual they were the same courteous and kind people as before!

At work we also exchanged gifts and of course everyone took left-overs to work the following Monday! For me right after the Holiday meant right back to my routine of eating healthy, I couldn't afford to get candida back worse! I knew that for the rest of my life I would always have to watch my diet and exercise, this was something I had decided not to share with anyone unless they asked why I kept living and eating this way!

The pictures we had taken at Christmas had come out beautiful and I could hardly wait to send them to special friends and family, including Jim Amos, Dr. Francis, Sra Fatima my special friend …among others….

New Year's Eve was approaching and I was feeling pretty lonely! My New Year's Eve celebrations had always been so much fun (even with Victor)! With Chava they had not been that exciting…. he always worked that day! We would have a special dinner at home and then watch a Spanish show with a multitude of stars celebrating in different states…. my kids would call me at midnight and that was that!

I was expecting to spend New Year's Eve by myself but Danny called me to ask if I wanted to have a special dinner at home (just the 3 of us). They actually had plans to go over to Lynn's family but someone had gotten sick with covid, so they changed their plans…. we ended up having a good time! We had shrimp, rice pudding (Danny's favorite) among other goodies and took pictures as usual, a pleasant surprise was to be able to watch a fire work display right from our back door! Once the display was over, I went to my room and watched a special on TV… Not a bad night after all!

New Year's Day was pretty low key for us, it was just nice to be in our new home and praying that the following year would be a better one for all of us, hopefully there would be a way out of this pandemic we were all living with!

I decided since I now had medical benefits to start the new year by having a physical, scheduled it and had tests done. I could hardly wait to get the results back and I was extremely happy to find out that I had no sign of diabetes or cholesterol and everything else was fine!

Also had a pap-smear to check if everything was fine and was told that because of my hysterectomy this was a test I did not need to do every year unless problems arouse. It paid off that I had to eat correctly because of candida but even if I didn't have this illness, I would have kept eating correctly because of my family history.

Keeping healthy was essential and what helped was that I never got bored with my meals! I always found ways of being inventive! I found herbs that I learned to love that also helped with constipation, including Senna Power and Leaf from "Starwest Botanicals" and Adobo Seasoning. These herbs combined with White Onion powder, butter and olive oil made a sauce that once melted in the microwave become extremely delicious and could be added to either chicken, meat or fish…

One of the things I really appreciated about my son's was that they never made comments about my food or the way I exercised. Sometimes I enticed them to try my chicken or salmon…. they would try them and tell me that it was good but they were very set on their own diets and I learned that you can't change someone's diet unless they are willing to listen to you...

Carlos and Danny had a workout room in our garage (mainly with weights) that they used every so often…. Carlos came over after work and he stopped by the kitchen to say hello to me, one day he surprised me! I had my radio on and Roy Orbison's song was playing "Oh, Pretty Woman" my son come in the kitchen singing that song to me! I was glad that they liked having me in Vegas and I knew that their deepest wish was that their father was also here…. Unfortunately, he loved living in the Acores and now because of his health traveling here would be a lot more difficult.

Chapter 120

The biggest birthday gift I ever received!

The following month I would be celebrating my birthday and it would be my first one in Vegas! I knew my sons wanted to take me out for lunch and so I prepared for it…. my birthday was on a Saturday, we went out for lunch and they surprised me with gifts and a birthday cake! The following Monday when I got to work I was surprised to see my desk all decorated with gifts and cards! My co-workers also had bought me a birthday cake, sang to me and my supervisor asked me what I wanted for lunch! It turned out to be a wonderful day with pretty special people!

Right after my birthday I got the biggest birthday gift anyone could ever receive and that was the news that I was going to be a grandmother! Finally, what I had prayed for was coming to pass!

Quite a few years ago I had asked God to be given the chance to see and hold my first grandchild in my arms and I had lived for this moment!

Danny and Lynn were extremely excited and all they wished for was a healthy baby, so did I and gave a thanks to God that years ago I had not succumbed to the temptation of committing suicide!

Victor's birthday was a week after mine and I always reminded my sons to call their father, no matter what had happened between us he would always be their dad and I knew they loved and worried about him. He was also extremely excited about this child that was coming!

My birthday was followed by Lynn's birthday and then Kristin's, we got together with Danny and Carlos and celebrated in a restaurant of their choice. We talked, exchanged gifts, took pictures and they usually took off to spend the remaining of the day together with their mates.

Kristin was a Raiders fan, worked from home and loved Carlos dearly! Lynn was a bit quieter than Kristin and was studying to be a nurse. We had something in common, just like me she loved her parents and siblings, loved to decorate and lost a brother at a young age…

Mother's Day came around I was surprised to receive flowers from both my sons with cards! We had lunch out and spent time talking and reminiscing about our lives, I was so happy that my son's had both learned on their own how to appreciate and respect women!

I also got a gift for Lynn for Mother's Day since she was going to be a mother for the first time! I shared this happy news with my friends at work, they congratulated me and remarked what a young grandma I was going to be!

CHAPTER 121

Staying healthy and got propositioned!

*M*any times, I was asked how I stayed young looking, I just told them "I make sure to eat correctly, exercise and take care of my skin." Since steams were out of the question because of the covid outbreak, I now made sure that after a warm shower I used a face mask, my favorite was "Seibella" exfoliating mask from Melaleuca derived from Vitamin C…. among a couple of others. I had managed even while tightening the belt to still buy a few of my favorite products because I knew they were worth it! Among those the Crème to Powder foundation, the mint floss and my favorite…the Gold Bar...

Something amazing had also happened! I found out that I now was able to use regular products off the market to clean my home and use some perfumes to my liking! This worked for my benefit since I could not afford to buy all natural products for me or for my home….

I did find out that the more organic foods you ate and the more natural products you used the better your skin looked! Unfortunately, we all love high fat foods and sweets…. but they can also affect how you look!

One of things I had learned to do was to shop around for cheaper groceries and clothing, I tried different clothing stores and because of how small I was I had a really hard time finding pants and tops to fit me … by accident one day I found Savers and got hooked…They had donations from people all the time with extremely good clothes and what I really liked was that the styling of clothing was different! I actually found tops and pants that fitted me, even jewelry that I liked and specials on certain days!

Shopping at this store also gave me a chance to clean up my closet and receive an extra 20% off on anything I bought! When I got home, I hung the clothes in my closet for a day or so…washed them and then wore them.

When shopping at any store I always wore my mask, my glasses and gloves for protection, there were many people out there that touched everything with their hands, did not wear gloves and then touched their faces! Worse of all small children! I even thought that cashiers should use gloves while helping customers purchase their products for their own safety. I did see that on certain stores but not all of them! I also made sure to always have a disinfecting wipe on my hands so that I could clean my gloves often….

I was extremely surprised one day when a woman at Savers stopped me to tell me "You are the first person I see doing what I'm doing." I looked at her and just like me, she was wearing a mask, glasses and gloves! She shared with me that she was also afraid to use her hands while shopping anywhere because you never knew who could be sick! I told her that I also used an antibacterial wipe very often…. carried it with me and gave her one for her to try, she asked me right away where I got them from and I gave her the information…

My own mother if she had been alive during this epidemic would have to change something that she had been stuck on doing. This habit going back to the islands of Acores was to blow her nose and place the handkerchief or wipe back in her pocket to be used again! We were all advised that it was essential to use a wipe once and then throw it away…

What I found interesting was that because of the use of the mask I stopped using a lip liner and lipstick and the small cracks I had above my lips disappeared! It made me wonder if the lip liner or the lipstick used often could actually bring on those cracks! Probably the biggest protection we had against covid and all the variants was the use of masks!

Hum! I wonder if I could be right!

I also got a pleasant surprise one Sunday when I was shopping at Savers looking for a good movie (very reasonably priced), I had a guy approach me to ask me if I was interested in remodeling my kitchen cabinets and showed me his card, I took it because I always liked helping people and then realized this was a way for him to approach me! He started asking me personal questions and asked me to go out with him! He was not bad looking at all, I looked at him and said, "Do you realize that I'm old enough to be your mother?" He said "No way! I'm in my late 40's and you are around that age bracket!" I took off my mask and looked at him and he said "So? I still say that you around my age!" I finally had to tell him that I was in my early 60's, soon to be a grandma and he surprised me by telling me that he still wanted to take me out! Persistent as he was, I still declined politely but went home with a smile on my face!

When I got home and shared this with Danny, he also surprised me by asking me "So, mom, was he at least good looking?" we laughed together and I told him that yes, he wasn't bad looking but I didn't want to date anyone that was just a bit older than Carlos!

CHAPTER 122

Adjusting to Vegas and a wonderful surprise!

Adjusting to Vegas took time! I had been thru enough changes to know that in every state or country you lived in there were pluses and minuses!

One minus was having to drive my Acura around without using the A/C! I couldn't afford for the car to start leaking again!

Another plus was that the cost of living that was better than California and no State Tax!

Another adjustment was the sandstorms! That took a while for me to get used to and the alarms for flooding in certain parts of the city (mainly near the strip). Since we had bought our home away from that area…. we were fairly safe…

What I couldn't believe was all the palm trees around! Flowers and vegetation were still able to survive in the Las Vegas climate! The climate here was warmer and drier to live in but not difficult to adjust to….

I was surprised to see how many people from other states (including California) were living in Vegas, especially from the Mexican culture! Many times, while shopping I had my ears open just in case I heard someone speak my language.

July 4th was celebrated at our home with a barbecue done by both of my sons and a firework display that could be seen thru our glass door!

These were moments that I treasured with them…. just like I had done thru out my life we always finished by taking pictures on every Holiday!

We had an event coming up that I never experienced before and that was a Gender Reveal on July 17th for the baby, Danny and I were hoping for a girl!

Me especially because I hadn't been able to have one! Danny also wanted to have that wish come true for me and once the gender of the baby was revealed at the park we were both ecstatic! We hugged each other and took pictures, come home to eat dinner and Lynn ended up with a table full of gifts!

The next Monday at work I could hardly wait to tell my friends that the baby was a girl! They of course congratulated me and I could hardly wait for the day that I would be able to hold my first grandchild!

August of 2021 was also the year that the Pfizer vaccines came out and many people rushed to get vaccinated because they were fed up with having to use masks and other restrictions, I on the other hand was extremely cautious! I had been warned years ago because of my condition to stay away from vaccines and I knew I still suffered from leaky gut…so I decided to stay still for a while and observe…

My oldest son was also cautious about vaccines sense he believed he had been stricken with covid twice and was immune from it. He still used his mask and took precautions at work, his wife because she had health problems decided to get vaccinated. On the other hand, Lynn had it to protect herself and her baby, Danny decided to get vaccinated to protect them both. Lynn and Danny also worked for a Department Store so they were exposed to customer's every day. Jing (Lynn's friend that lived with us) had the vaccine and had a big reaction to it! She got extremely sick that night and could hardly make it up the stairs to go to her room! That made me afraid for myself!

I still had allergies to certain foods (I had noticed that even with certain Filipino foods we had on Holidays) and was afraid of my reaction to it!

I reacted to foods in a big way…even something as a TV dinner made with natural chicken and capers! I loved it and had it for dinner but that morning when I woke up I had ringing in my left ear and could not go back to sleep!

I actually did research on the ingredients but could not make myself have the vaccine! Believe me I wanted to especially because we had a baby coming but when I was almost at the point of making an appointment someone I knew at work would get sick after being vaccinated!

Even at work I encountered people that didn't not believe in the vaccines! One of them was one of my friends, Ann that worked for payroll… she kept to herself in her room and was also extremely stubborn! Many times, I would catch her in the bathroom or walking around the office not wearing a mask and I would have to remind her that she needed to take extra precautions because after all people were still getting sick even after being vaccinated….

That September I called my cousin Saozinha in Portugal for her birthday and to ask her how the covid pandemic was there and she shared with me that they were placing pressure on people to get vaccinated! She refused and so did most of her family, she had lost her husband to cancer and still had two grown sons and two sisters around, I asked her why she didn't want to get vaccinated and she told me "I have been observing how many people have negative reactions to the vaccines, including one young man that lost the function of his legs after he was vaccinated." She asked me if I had been vaccinated and I just told her "No, I have been too afraid of the side effects and have not made up my mind!"

She told me that they took precautions there like we did here by using masks and avoiding large gatherings, exactly what I did! That made me feel better, we had never lost our closeness…. she still was like a sister to me!

Much like me she believed in prayer and was by far the best cousin anyone could ask for! Our mother's had even given us the same first name and it was funny how much we had in common!

CHAPTER 123

A baby shower and a new position!

*M*eanwhile we got ready for my granddaughter's shower that had been scheduled for October 23rd, we all worked hard, cleaned our home and got food prepared. Kristin and Carlos bought their favorite dishes to share with us and I made some of mine including a Portuguese dessert that I used to make for them as kids, Angel food cupcakes with strawberries and a sour cream mixture topped with whip cream on top!

They decorated the back yard with a table for the cake and gifts and placed tables and chairs for everyone to sit and enjoy the wonderful foods that had been prepared with a lot of love for a child that was very much wished for!

We had music playing and some people stayed to dance a bit of karaoke! It turned out to be a great party and Danny and Lynn asked Carlos to be the baby's godfather.... a role he accepted with great joy!

The next big event would be the birth of a child that was already loved even before being born...

I kept my routine at work, used my precautions for covid as usual, stayed away from gym's and developed a workout routine. Right after I got off work once I got home.... I parked my car, changed my shoes, got my weights and walked around the neighborhood.... stretched using lamp posts and once done, changed my shoes again, took my laxative and went home to fix dinner. I liked the fact that just like in California people didn't ask what you were doing instead sometimes I had people say out loud to me "Good for you! Good job!"

I told Danny one day that I must look like some kind of bug out there! I used a mask, sunglasses and a hood to protect me from the sun and the wind, Danny was just like me! Sometimes in life we have to do something different if in the long run it's for our benefit…. he just shrugged and smiled at me!

Sometimes being different doesn't necessarily mean that you are strange! What I found strange was that I was never questioned why I worked out this way!

This routine that I had developed helped with the Caproyl mixture quite a bit not only with constipation but also helped to bring out hidden candida! When walking there were times I could hear my ear unclog and clicking sounds from my joints! It was like my body liked this type of exercise even more than the gym! I marveled how much better my bowel movements had become! Every time I tried a new treatment, I ended up going back to Caproyl because of constipation and toxicity…also because I believed that Caproyl had something in it that had protected me from covid so far…

The toxicity also could be eliminated by using a warm shower the next day!

At work we started to slow down and when I noticed this I reached out to Jeff and asked him to keep an eye open for another opportunity for me within the company somewhere, he immediately told me "Of course I will, I will keep you posted." I had learned to trust him, he was the type of person that liked to help anyone in need! He came to work one day and out of the blue shared with all of us in our small office that he had done something that we should all do to protect our homes! He advised us to contact the County Clerk's Office and request a Homestead Declaration Form, fill it out and have it notarized anywhere! I knew good advice when I heard it and immediately took action! Downloaded the form, filled it out and Danny and I took it to the Bank to have it notarized! Within a few weeks we received the form back stamped and we each kept a copy...

At work I kept on being teased by a supervisor, every time he passed by my desk, he would tell me that I deserved a better position and I thanked him for his belief in me! It wasn't too long after that Jeff called me into his office to let me know that he had spoken to Alex the Post Closing Manager and that they had a position in the Post Closing Department that they knew I would be perfect for! I was extremely happy! I loved this company and the friends that I had made there and this meant that my job would be assured!

I had to brief David on everything that I was doing and cleaned out my desk, I really felt for him, this young man was already overwhelmed by work and now had more work to do!

My move to next department was an easy one! They already had a desk prepared for me next to Haylie's (she and I had met in the bathroom), she proved to be a fountain of information! The training I received from her was instrumental in making me a success at work! She was extremely patient which proved to be beneficial because once I looked at what I had to be trained on I actually cringed! What helped me was my determination to succeed and their belief in me! Alex actually told me "We choose you because you happen to be very detail oriented and were very highly recommended, so we truly believe that you are going to get this sooner than you expect!"

I would be trained by two people, Haylie and Dante and each had a different approach at training! Where Haylie was patient and calm, Dante was fast at training and always stressed out! My approach to learning something new was to take lots of notes and then review them after everyone was gone…. with Haylie I was able to look at my notes and review them in case I missed something…. with Dante…. I could only watch him because it irritated him to no end when I looked at my notes while he was showing me how he did his job! This habit of mine was to add to my notes in case I had missed something…

455

Of all things to happen we were told to prepare to move! There had been talks about moving before because our building was too big for all the people that were working there…. some people had been eliminated, others worked from home and others worked 3 days at home and another 2 at the office.

My boss stopped my training and requested that I helped him clean up all the office cabinets that contained loan folders in alphabetical order. We needed to update them before the movers were ready to take them to our new office location in Town Square near the airport!

For me this was also now a longer distance to travel with an older car, I would have to pass the strip every day and without being able to use the A/C!

Where once it had taken me 15 to 20 minutes to get to work now it would take me between 30 to 45 minutes! It seemed that my life had always been about adapting to changes every year! Life unfortunately never stayed the same! All we can do is learn how to cope with the changes and go with the flow….

CHAPTER 124

Adapting to a new position and a new place…

We got everything packed and ready…. over the weekend the movers grabbed everything including our stuff from our desks and took it to our new location. By the time Monday came around when we got to our new location all our computers and personal stuff were already set up on each individual desk!

Some of us liked the new location, some did not! Some had been used to a bigger and fancier place, others like me had a longer commute but after a while we all started to adjust! Once settled I had to get re-trained by Haylie and Dante, I found that hands on experience works best…, submitting smaller house loans and then send them to different warehouses banks became an easy task for me! What I wasn't expecting was that they wanted me to learn how to assemble, upload missing docs and submit Federal Loans worth millions of dollars to warehouse banks once they were approved!

Was I intimidated? You bet! Once the sheet-sheet of how to submit these loans was printed and given to me I looked at it and thought "Oh, my God! How in the world am I going to keep all this information in my head?" Haylie probably knew that I was overwhelmed and put me at ease! She told me to take it one step at the time and once everybody left for the day to read and re-read not only the instructions but also my own personal notes, advice I took to heart and paid off big time!

After a while I was able to understand what I was doing and my manager become my biggest supporter! He would have weekly meetings with us and we were encouraged to discuss any issues we had with him, he was also our biggest cheerleader!

I never forget the day that I finally got it! I was able one Friday by myself to submit a huge amount of loans and send e-mails to everyone that I needed to! When I left for the day.... I got in my car and gave myself a high-five!!

We should never quit something because we consider it "Too difficult! "There is always a way!!"

It's funny how small our world can be! At work I was introduced to Laura, a young woman that was very outgoing… once I shared with her that I had two sons and told her where Danny worked, she immediately said "Wow, I remember Danny! I worked for the same company a few years back! I was heavier but I remember that he was very quiet but a very hard-working young man!" We become friends and she also trained me on uploading documents into our system, I also was introduced to Jackie… an older woman that absolutely loved to work but had problems with her vision. The It-tech had changed the text on her computer to make it easier for her to read but many times we caught her using a magnifying glass! She had a very outgoing personality and we became friends. I found out that one of her favorite foods was chestnuts (Portuguese people absolutely loved them) and she loved to read! That had become very hard for her due to her vision problems…. in the end she finally had to go to an eye specialist and had a cornea operation that kept her off work for quite a while! We all missed her and we knew she didn't want to give up her job and retire…

One afternoon after work as I walked towards my car (3rd floor-top level) and saw a big plane go right over the parking lot, I had the hugest grin on my face you ever saw! It wasn't because I loved the planes! It was because I realized that years ago if I had been given the opportunity to work in a place like this with planes flying over the building every so often out of fear, I wouldn't have taken the job! I told myself that day "You have come a long way baby!"

I just felt lucky to still have a job even with covid around! Many times, when I was on my way home or shopping and saw homeless individuals, my heart would go out to them… especially the veterans! I had been in that situation and when I prayed, I always included them! I come out with a special prayer just for them "That those that had been given an opportunity to change their lives, that they take it and use it for their benefit." Just like years ago I had been given the opportunity to change my life and had taken advantage of it!

You had to be a pretty strong individual in the first place to live in Vegas! There were way too many temptations around! For women and for men! Adult entertainment, a huge number of restaurants and gambling machines everywhere!

I was out shopping at Albertson's one afternoon…. Had just finished my shopping, looked to my right, saw a few slot machines and decided to try my luck! I decided to invest $20 dollars on one of my favorites "The Poker machine" I probably played for about 10 minutes and the money was gone! From that day forward I avoided the slot machines anywhere! I worked way too hard to waste my money! I was glad that both my sons felt the same way!

From that day forward I did my groceries and looked the other way…

CHAPTER 125

Good advice and the birth
of a very special child!

At work because of all the work that I was doing on the computer I realized that I needed to get new glasses! Sometimes when we arrange for an appointment with someone you can end up with information that you did not expect! I found an extremely good Optometrist close to my home and had an eye exam… he even took pictures of the inside of my eyes, sat with me and discussed what he had seen! I was amazed that they could see early on if a person had diabetes, high cholesterol or macular degeneration! I was very happy to hear from the doctor himself that I had no signs of any of these illnesses and when I asked him how to prevent macular degeneration…. he told me to try to eat lots of deep green leafy vegetables every day and then prescribed a couple of eyeglasses for me.

Adjusting to new glasses was something else! I actually had to go back to the eye doctor a couple of times! My eyes had gotten used to a certain prescription from glasses bought at Walgreens, I tried to use the new glasses at work, they weren't clear enough for me to do my work, so I ended up making another appointment this time with the office manager and found some useful information just by sharing some of my personal thoughts with her! I looked around and saw that just about everyone was wearing masks and we started discussing covid…

I shared with her that I was afraid of vaccines because of my food allergies and was surprised to find out from her that her own sister had been
vaccinated and had nothing but health problems one after the other!

She told me "It all depends on each individual but if you feel unsure,
I wouldn't do it! We are all different…after what happened to my sister,
I cannot recommend it to everyone!" She adjusted my glasses and when
I got into my car…I was amazed of what I had just found out!

Sometimes it's good to open your heart to someone!

Besides this usual information I also got some glasses to use at night
while driving that were one of the best gifts anyone could have given me…

In life there are always unexpected changes and we also found out
that Jing was moving out! She had been with Danny and Lynn for a
while and I actually liked her quite a lot! She was funny and outgoing
and whenever we had a Holiday or a Birthday coming up, she would
be the one we called to prepare great Filipino food! I found out that
just like my ex-husband she loved to play dominoes and was quite
good at it! She would my granddaughter's godmother and she absolutely loved kids!

Danny made me so proud as a father to be! He had pictures taken
of himself and Lynn while she was pregnant and you could see how
happy he was of becoming a new father!

And then what we had been waiting for finally happened! Bella was
born on November 27th, 2021, at a nearby Hospital!

Danny had kept in contact with me since the night before and I
stayed awake just to make sure everything was fine with the birth, he
texted me at 10.46PM with a picture of our baby and with these words
"Mom, your granddaughter is finally here!" When I saw her picture, I
was amazed, happy, thrilled! You name it! Most of all happy that she
was healthy and strong!

The next morning, I got in my car with a balloon, a gift for the baby,
for Lynn and one for Danny!

Danny met me at the parking lot…. I placed my mask on and we
headed to the elevator, when we entered Lynn's room…. Bella was

laying on a hospital container…. I gave them their gifts and proceeded to take my first look at my granddaughter! I was so moved! My son asked me to sit down and placed Bella in my arms to have a picture taken! As I looked down at my granddaughter my first thought was "I received what I prayed for years ago, to be alive to hold my first grand-daughter or grandson in my arms!"

My son totally amazed me! Because both mother and daughter had to stay in the Hospital for 48hours he decided to stay with them and never left their sight!

This was something his father would never have done! Being the typical male…. for both of my sons I was left by myself in the care of nurses until it was time to go home, he was there the day of their birth and on the day that I was ready to leave with the baby to go home and that was it!

CHAPTER 126

The Holidays this year included a beautiful little girl!

They finally came home and as we prepared for Christmas… I told Danny "We both got the best present we could have asked for Christmas! What do you think?" He agreed! Danny knew how much the birth of this child meant to me and we both wished that she would take after my mother and end up with blue eyes!

We prepared for Christmas at home and at work! At work it was always fun, people loved Christmas and it seemed that it always brought out the best in people! My friends were happy that I finally had a grand-daughter and one of my best friend's Ann actually surprised me by buying a baby gift for Bella!

Before Christmas we took a family picture with baby Bella dressed in black and red and sent it to a few family members and friends.

To my surprise I also found the former pastor of our church and decided to re-instate our friendship, he and his wife had moved quite far so our communication was mainly done by e-mail but I was glad that I had found a friend that meant so much to me! I sent them a family picture of all of us and he couldn't believe how Danny had grown…. he had been in his teen's when he had last seen him!

I bought a bassinet for Bella and my ex-husband sent money to Danny for him to buy her a stroller, we were all thrilled to have this little bundle of joy around!

That Christmas day we took a family picture with both my sons and Bella and since this Christmas was a special one for all of us…. I made two desserts that my sons loved…. a Portuguese Flan and an Orange Jell-O Cake.

The holidays proved to be wonderful for all of us even with covid around! We had managed to stay safe and healthy and had received a gift from Heaven!

Not everyone was that lucky! At work a few people had that gotten sick with covid! One of them was my friend Haylie! She had taken time off to go on a trip at Christmas time, while at the airport got infected with covid and had to work from home for a few days. Our Executive Assistant after getting vaccinated got extremely sick and was out for a while!

I prayed constantly that instead of vaccines and masks that God intervened and eliminated this illness with all the variants completely out of this planet that He had created! We were all suffering even by watching people that we cared for getting sick! What really worried me was our elderly and younger generation!

I wondered! Does anyone pray anymore!

When New Year's Eve came around…. we once again decided to celebrate it at home with Filipino food and other dishes, by far this turned out to be a wonderful New Year's Eve for all of us to remember!

One of the things that had not changed about me was my caring for other individuals. Sometimes we have a chance to observe a pattern on someone and are afraid to speak up and we shouldn't! It's up to the individual if he listens or not but you on the other hand feel that you have done what is right!

Also, for me it meant keeping my promise to God…to always help those in need…. even when I felt uncomfortable doing it!

I had been observing Dante at work, he was diabetic and always stressed out!

He would blow a fuse occasionally and sometimes I would see him bow is head down and I could see stress all over him! I told him one day "Dante, don't be like my father! He cared so much for his job that he didn't take his blood pressure medicine the way he was supposed to… it made him dizzy! In the long run, he ended up with a heart attack and a year later a stroke! For most companies you are just a number! Once you leave, they easily replace you." He nodded but I knew he wasn't ready to listen! That Christmas I got him some goofy socks and a plaque that said "Relax."

For my supervisor since he was a raiders fan, I got him a key chain and an oven mitt to use outside while barbecuing with the raider's logo, he loved it!

I always have been the type of person that observes people for a while, see what their likes and dislikes are before buying a gift for them…. this prevents you from giving a gift to someone that they don't need or like!

Even as a teenager at home I used this method….

CHAPTER 127

News from Acores and a very special birthday!

*A*fter the Holidays were over, my ex-husband got worse! He had waited to get a Balloon Heart Valve Surgery done on his heart and because of the expense had to wait for this procedure to be done in Lisbon, he finally found a way to have it done…. he had to wait a bit because he also contracted covid, recovered and flew to Lisbon to have the procedure done.

Unfortunately, after the Balloon procedure he got worse! They found out that his heart was not functioning correctly and placed a heart monitor on him…. It took quite a while for him to recover and to be able to fly back to Acores.

The kids kept in touch with him…they placed a video call to talk to their father and found out that he was recovering quite well… He made a comment that God didn't want mean people like him around! My sons wanted him to move to Vegas so that we could keep an eye on him… but he loved the Acores and had a woman watching over him, in the long run we had to respect his wishes!

When my birthday came around, my sons took me out as usual to a local restaurant and I received flowers and gift certificates from both… little did they know that for me the best gift of all was spending time with them!

That same night I was in bed already when Danny surprised me by knocking on my door with Bella! I was in my pajamas but I didn't care! My son placed Bella in my arms, gave me a red rose and captured Bella smiling in a picture that would touch anybody's heart!

The first time I baby sited my granddaughter I took pictures.... I placed her in a portable baby swing and watched our cat Bandit lay-down and quietly sit by us! I had lived for this moment!

Even Bandit had to adjust to our new addition in the family! Because he had been so attached to Danny that had carried him as a kitten on his shoulder, he had become a little jealous of the baby! I advised Danny to try to remember to pay attention to Bandit, I had gone thru this when I had Danny and Foxy had reacted to his presence in the house.... later Foxy had become Danny's best friend and protector!

I on the other hand started to get closer to Bandit, took on the responsibility of feeding him each morning, talked to him and found out that he was a very intelligent cat! I even knew when Danny left the house because he would stand by the door and meow!

CHAPTER 128

Adjustments and a very special Baptism...

*I*t seemed that adjustments and changes came around too often in my life, some were good and some not so good!

We started to experience a slowdown in our company due to the war between Russia and Ukraine that really affected the mortgage industry, my supervisor started to advise us to get further training in other positions so that we could become indispensable. Dante was helping one department while I started to help Rayna that was in charge of receiving all the loan documents that needed to be uploaded in our system, this was a job and half! Once all the documents were separated, we scanned them, uploaded them in our system and sent copies of the documents to each individual warehouse banks. Soon enough I knew enough to help her.... I become an expert on pulling missing loan documents and worked on a spreadsheet that was sent weekly to a Bank.

Our friend Jackie came back for a short while after her eye surgery and found out that she still had problems with the computer and had to make a very hard decision.... that was to retire! We loved having her around but understood that her health came first.... some of her co-workers got together and arranged for a retirement party. I bought her a small gift that included a key chain that had an engraved message "your work has meant something and you left an impact on all of us!"

We all hoped for this, to be able to leave an impact behind…One of the hardest decisions we all have to make, especially for those who have been working for a long time and enjoy it… is to make the decision to retire! She enjoyed her retirement party to the fullest but came back to see us often…. she missed us as much as we missed her!

One particular afternoon after just about everyone had left, Alex told me that he was leaving early and working from home the next day. I asked him if he was feeling ok and he surprised me by sharing with me that lately he had been experiencing anxiety while driving! This was a man that I would do anything for! He had become a close friend and was a man that cared a lot about other people, he also had taken care of his father until he passed away!

I did not hesitate and told him how Dr.Howard Liebgold had helped me years prior and told him " Alex, if you don't get a handle on this now, fears and anxiety can and will escalate." At my break time I looked up Dr. Howard Liebgold's book on Amazon and gave Alex the information via e-mail, he was very touched… This also gave me the opportunity to look up my friend and mentor and to my surprise he had passed away in 2013 at the age of 80! If anyone deserved Heaven, he did! He had helped so many individuals like me to re-start their lives without fear!

I cried that day for a man that had changed my life forever and that would be remembered by many people!

Our family was getting ready to have Bella baptized and we started to get everything ready to have the celebration done at home as usual, this time I made my homemade Spanish dip that my son's loved and was able to find "Pasteis de Nata" "Portuguese Tarts" in the freezer section at Trader Joe's.

Kristin came over to help decorate the inside of our home as well as the backyard, the table inside was beautifully decorated with Bella's cake and desserts. Once everything was ready Danny and I headed out together to St. Elizabeth Ann Seton Church and to pick up the roasted pork loin that a friend of his had prepared.

Danny and Lynn were pretty stressed out that day and unfortunately, we were running just a bit late! Lynn called to rush Danny to meet her and Bella at the church, sometimes smart phones are not the best things to have around! While he was on the phone, we encountered a crash on the freeway! All I had time to do was to alert my son quickly to avoid colliding with the other cars!

We could have gotten into a real serious crash that day! I told my son "Danny, sometimes when we are driving the best thing to do is to avoid answering the phone…. unless it's a life-or-death situation."

Bella was baptized on May1st of 2021 along with other children…. I placed on my granddaughter's neck a small little necklace with a small cross with her initials and asked God for this child of ours to be forever blessed!

Carlos and Kristin were already there, Jing and some of Danny's and Lynn's friends, it was time for us to approach the priest that would perform the ceremony and pour Holy water over Bella's head. I looked at Kristin and she was looking at me and I whispered to her "I find myself very blessed today! At one point in my life, I was so sick that I never thought that I would be alive to see this day!" She knew what I meant and squeezed my hand…

We took wonderful pictures inside the church and set out to have a late lunch at home that had been prepared with a lot of love by everyone…It turned out to be a beautiful day for all of us, one experience that no one would ever forget!

CHAPTER 130

Mother's Day and a shock that I was not expecting!

Mother's Day was also special for all of us! Lynn and I had something to celebrate this year! We went out to lunch and both my sons gave me flowers as usual! I took pictures of the flowers that I had received and marveled how both of my sons had turned out to be such thoughtful and respectful human beings after all we had gone thru!

I was at work for a couple of weeks when a group of us got the shock of our lives! We received an e-mail that was sent to a group of people requesting that we attend a video conference that morning that was extremely important! We were curious of course but not prepared for what we heard that morning!

The people that were selected to hear the video conference that morning were notified that within 2 weeks they would receive their final check! The excuse we heard was that due to the slowdown in the mortgage industry positions were being eliminated! I was worried and so was Dante! We were both in charge of submitting loans daily, I was in charge of submitting the larger loans and wondered how one individual was going to be able to submit them all!

We were also notified that we would be sent a final package thru the mail!

Dante was furious and our supervisor was not around that morning for us to ask him any questions, when he finally showed up, he informed us that he had not been notified of all these changes! When we asked him who to contact with any questions…. he referred us to HR. I didn't believe in delaying anything and in acting…...especially regarding income! I had rent coming up!

I found someone in HR that was an immense help, she informed me that this was a laid-off and that on our last day, June 3rd we would be able to file for E.D.D. She also helped me to revise my resume on my spare time, I shared this information with Dante but he was still too angry to listen to anybody! His anger was also due that he had been notified that he could not get paid for his remaining vacation! He had a vacation scheduled for September with his family…. they were actually going to visit Portugal among other countries! He told me that he had enough 401K to help him financially but he was still extremely angry!

Dante came and sat by me and vented… I looked straight at him and told him, "Dante, this is your perfect opportunity to finally spend time with your family! As you told me before you have enough money, you will also be able to file for E.D.D…why not enjoy the vacation you been waiting for!"

"Remember, you also told me that your daughter has been really worried about you because of your stress level and how it's affecting your blood pressure!"

In Portugal we have a saying "A males que vem por bem!" "Blessing in disguise." After our little conversation he was a bit calmer and thanked me for the advice…. But was still upset that he was losing his vacation pay! That I couldn't help him with!

Maybe this blessing in disguise also came for me! I was experiencing problems with the speedometer in my car, it would go from 65 to 0 and sometimes would get stuck on 0! This was something that would have to be fixed in the near future….

I spoke to Alex regarding the laid-off, he advised me to keep an eye open for another job opportunity within our company and told me where to look. I started to look for a position as a Junior Loan Assistant and e-mailed a couple of supervisors but unfortunately the positions had already been filled!

My supervisor really liked the way I worked and shared with me that if it was up to him…. he would never let me go! He also told me that I would be receiving a letter of recommendation from the Vice-President of Post-Closing to take with me, I was never one to quit on anything and happened to really like my job and the people that I worked with… so I e-mailed the Vice-President of Post-Closing, included my own supervisor on this e-mail and offered to work for the company making less money in order to keep my position.

That same day I received an answer back from the Vice-President to let me know that unfortunately…. they could not fulfill my request because my position was being eliminated!

Imagine how I felt! I was 64 and half! Really close to retirement age and having to start looking for work once again!

The last two weeks at my company were by far the saddest I ever experienced! Some people were too angry to feel sad! I decided to clean up as much as possible instead…. I found out from Alex that he was going to be the one handling all the loan processing and the last week I spent there I helped him to get together all the forms needed to submit the loans. We were also told to try to submit our claim to E.D.D on the last day, some of us were able to do it! I didn't have the time because Alex and I were busy trying to get all the forms ready so that all the loans could be submitted. I knew I had the time to submit the claim…. I had a little money coming from 401k to help me until I started to receive my income from E.D.D….

Before I left on my last day Alex and I had a conversation…. I reminded him of my father and told him "Alex, please be careful with your blood pressure! No job is worth risking your health and keep on reading Dr.Liebgold's book when you have a chance to help you manage anxiety."

I could tell he was touched that I was thinking about him at this time and I reminded him "Alex, you and Jeff believed in me when I first got here from California, both of you were ever so patient in training me to work for this company! I was treated with respect and kindness, I believe in giving back what is received! I will miss you both!"

In the end I got a hug from my two supervisors with a promise that if I ever needed a reference, they would be there to give me one! I also received a call from the Vice-President of Post-Closing to wish me well and to let me know if I ever needed a verbal reference from her for any position that she would be more than willing to give me one!

That afternoon I said goodbye to some of the friends I had made, got in my car with my belongings (without an escort) and as I got in my car…. I looked back at the company that I would certainly miss with all my heart, held back my tears and remembered that I had read somewhere "That God never closes one door without opening another." But there would never be another company like this one…of that I was sure of….

CHAPTER 131

From a working woman to a writer!

When I got home that afternoon instead of feeling sorry for myself, I got my weights out of my car and did my workout routine as usual! Just a bit harder! Once done…. I went to my room placed all my stuff that I had at work in my closet and thought with sadness "Here we go again! I'm so tired of being placed in this position and so tired of having to start over again!"

As I prepared my dinner that night my son totally surprised me by looking at me and said "Mom, don't worry about it, I know you have enough experience to get a job anywhere… but this could be your opportunity to finish your book."

Little did he know that he had placed a seed in my heart! I was no longer discouraged…. after that weekend was over… I developed a new routine.

So, life once again had changed for me! It's hard in the beginning to go from a working woman to a writer but I decided to give it a try!

In the morning I dedicated myself to look for work and answer e-mails, for the first time in years, I opened my word document that had all my previous writing of what I had been thru as well as my family and realized that my story needed to be told! I knew at that point that I wanted to leave a legacy behind for my children!

I set out the next few days to file for Unemployment which turned out to be an experience in itself! Everything was different from California filling! It took a lot of tries, including contacting a former co-worker of mine that helped me quite a bit! Finally, I was able to get a hold of someone on E.D.D that helped me to start a claim!

My mornings now were very different and took some adjusting! I made sure to look for work each day, once that was done, dedicated the time remaining to writing! I did research to verify information for my book and looked at family pictures to remember time and events…

One of my first priorities each morning in order to feel that I was still part of society was to always make sure that when I sat in front of my laptop…I had my hair done and my makeup on! Not only did it make me feel more confident in myself but I also wanted my sons to know that their mother had pride in the way she looked…I believed that no matter what you should always dress for success!

Working or not working… you never know once you step outside who remembers you and tries to follow your example!

After lunch I always found a way of going outside, even to a small store just to buy a few things… once done, parked my car…. took my daily walk as usual and came back to fix my dinner….

I learned soon enough from experience not to shop by impulse! This could affect your finances… looking in my refrigerator and cupboards before shopping prevented overspending. Being unemployed also meant tightening the belt a bit until I was either able to get a job or retire…

Once dinner was over with, cleaned up, watched a bit of TV and went to sleep. The going outside each day was essential to get some air! Walking was also essential for me to prevent constipation….so was eating correctly! Both helped me to be as cleared minded as possible to write! Writing as wonderful as it can be for writers can also keep you feel isolated and in your own world! You need to mingle with people every day…it also gives you a much-needed time off and helps to clear your thinking…

Another time off for me was Saturdays to do my laundry, clean my bathroom, my own room and do my groceries for the week, Saturday was the day that I rewarded myself by watching a movie of my choice on TV…

Along with a daily routine there has to be time to spend with family!

Carlos's birthday came around and we decided to meet at a Mexican restaurant, I went in Danny's car and met Carlos and Kristin at the restaurant. We ordered our food, played around with Bella and took pictures… the servers came over to sing Happy Birthday to him and we all shared a small piece of dessert, for me what made these celebrations so special was spending the time with them… It wasn't the food or going out…I loved being around my sons!!

Once done we stood outside talking and Carlos approached me to ask me how I was doing since I been laid-off, I shared with him what kind of routine I was now following and was surprised when I heard him say "Mom, you know this maybe the opportunity to finally retire and finish your book." To say the least I was surprised that he still remembered that I had a book to finish.!

It made me wonder…why suddenly both my sons were encouraging me to write instead of going back to work!

CHAPTER 132

Looking for work/versus retirement…

*M*y son and I also discussed the covid outbreak, I shared with him that even though things had gotten better around us I still used my mask everywhere and took precautions. Carlos confided in me that he also took precautions, I worried about him because he was working in an environment where they had customer's in and out all day but he also knew how to protect himself…

As a mother you tend to worry about your children no matter their age… this was something my own mother had shared with me and that I had found to be very true!

From my past training with Phoboease classes I knew this worry could not go overboard…there had to be a healthy balance so that you also allowed your children to become adults and live their own lives!

Danny's birthday came the next month…. we did the same, went out for lunch together and as usual had fun as a family, I was very proud of my sons, they had grown into incredible gentlemen…

For me this this was a reinforcement that I had done a good job as a parent!

My search for work continued of course but it wasn't easy to find a job near where I lived because of my car issues… I found that a lot of jobs were requiring experience that I didn't have and many of them not willing to train!

I continued my writing and called Social Security to check what my options were, I didn't want to lose my unemployment or get less retirement income for applying too early. I found a person that was extremely helpful and told me that I would not lose my unemployment benefits but also told me to apply later in the year, closer to my birthday. It's always good not to act on impulse on anything that could have a negative effect on your life later on…

Bella had just turned 9 months when as I prepared dinner for myself, I looked at Danny and Bella sitting on the couch and saw Bella pulling on his ear! Danny instead of getting upset, smiled and was teasing her back!

Tears came to my eyes at this scene and I told Danny "Danny aren't you glad that you did not succumb to depression years ago in California but came here instead? Look of what you would have missed!" He nodded in agreement, he knew what I meant and I told him "The same goes for me Danny." We both would have missed the gift of a very special child!"

Father's Day came around and I wanted to make it special for Danny, I shopped around for a great gift for him and for Carlos, what I did for one son I always did for the other. Carlos was alone that weekend, Kristin had taken the kids to Disneyland for that weekend and I called Carlos to tell him to come and pickup his gift.

My sons also called their father to wish him a Happy Father's Day individually! This made me so proud of them…. no matter what he would always be their father…

Danny placed him on a video call whenever he called him and if I was around, he always included me on the call, I can't tell you what an effect seeing him sitting on a recliner, looking older did to me! I felt sorry for him because this was not the Victor that I remembered! He did not resemble at all the man that had twirled me around the dance floor on a very special New Year's Eve night!

He surprised me by telling me that day that just like me he was single again and gotten rid of someone that had been living with him!

He said that he was better off! I asked him "Who is watching over you?" He said that he had a cleaning lady that came around to help him out, Danny also hoped of going to see him in Portugal the following year…. I prayed that this man that had been a part of my life for so many years would still have a long time left to spend with his sons and his first granddaughter!

CHAPTER 133

Don't forget those that helped you along the way...

$\mathcal{I}$ have always been the type of person that doesn't forget about past relationships or friends left behind…...one was Alex… my former supervisor. We had developed a great friendship and one morning I woke up thinking about him, because I have always been prone to premonitions, I called him that afternoon to check how he was and found out that he was now overwhelmed with work! Most of the personnel had been let go and he was now dealing with submitting all the loans! He also shared with me that on his last checkup his blood pressure had been up enough to be given a small dose of blood pressure medicine…. once again, I reminded him of my father. He thanked me for that and shared with me that because of all the overtime and working on the weekends he now had less time to spend with his bride! I was amazed that he also had contracted covid after being vaccinated and was once again back at work!

He said to me "Mary, you know if things improve here at work, you will be the first one that I will call to come back!" I had a response ready for him "Alex, I didn't call you to ask you for a job! I called you because I was concerned about you! I don't forget my friends just because I'm not nearby! For some reason I woke up thinking about you and wanted to check it you are ok."

I almost felt like he was smiling on the other end…. and when we hung up, he sounded a lot more upbeat! Sometimes knowing someone cares for you can change that person's day!

I continued my routine each morning of looking for work and writing… one September morning while reading what I had written about my father's illness I held back my tears and thought "I must publish this book, not so much for me but in their memory…. so that they are not forgotten!"

One day while at a grocery store, I heard in the background one of my favorite songs from Meghan Trainor "Like I'm Gonna Lose You." For me this song had a special meaning about loving someone while you can before you lose them, every time I heard this song it made me cry for all my loved ones that I lost…my father, my mother, my grandmother and my brother's…

This song can make us realize that none of us know how long we have with our family, that each moment should be treasured as if it was the last and to keep in touch with those left behind…

When September 27th came around as usual, I called my cousin Saozinha to wish her a happy birthday and to check on her, this was the first time that I shared with my cousin that I had been writing an autobiography and planned to publish it…. she was excited for me and told me that years prior she also had started one!

We had been in contact thru out the years but there were many things that I had hidden from her and everyone else that now would be revealed, I shared with her some of them, including having to do soliciting at one point to survive.

She was surprised to say the least and I explained to her that I had hidden many things not because I was ashamed but because I didn't want to embarrass my family…

She was excited for me that I decided to write a book about my life and I knew that with my cousin there was no judgement!!

CHAPTER 134

Still confronting fears and going forward!

*A*s far as treatment for candida, I had increased my treatment to see a bit more results while using caproyl and started to experience headaches and dizziness! Instead of getting scared I looked up the side effects from caproyl and found that sometimes you can experience these plus other symptoms...I increased my protein in my diet and vitamin C but I was still experiencing the dizziness especially at night! So, I decided as a precaution (due to my family history) to find a store nearby that had a blood pressure machine... Believe it or not I went to 3 or 4 stores and none of them were working!

In California most of the CVS Pharmacies had one that was available to the public, it was a good thing that I had brought with me my own blood pressure machine! I checked to see if it needed batteries and after replacing them, I took my blood pressure in the morning and found it at a normal 122-73 with my pulse @ 71!

I shared with Danny what had taken to finally get my blood pressure checked and he told me "Mom, you don't have anything to worry about! Look how healthy you eat and how you exercise every day! I told him "Danny, remember Dr.Liebgold's class? He always said, confront the fear by doing what you fear so that the fear is not allowed to escalate." He nodded in agreement...

To confront worry or fear there is nothing better than to find a way to put your fears to rest! What actually helped the dizziness go away was to have a couple of good bowel movements, exercise and drink plenty of water! I did some further research and found out that to help with side effects warm showers also helped a lot!

Sometimes we can see someone else confront fear without expecting it even out on the street! I happened to be stopped by a traffic light one afternoon when out of the corner of my eye I saw a homeless person on a wheelchair struggle with one arm to cross the street, he was so frustrated that he slapped his arm with his other hand!

My heart was going out to him, remembering how my father had struggled with his wheelchair and had slapped his arm around after his stroke! I had the strongest impulse to go and help him! Just as I was getting ready to turn my car around… he amazed me by maneuvering his wheelchair backwards and crossed the street regardless of the traffic!

People can sometimes surprise you by their will to live or to be independent!

I also decided to contact a friend of mine, Jim Amos, a man that had been a blessing to me and had changed my life by believing in me, I shared with him that I was thinking of publishing a book about my life and my reasons behind it…. I could tell that he was happy to hear from me and was extremely excited about my decision!

We went over how I had met him and his wife, he told me that he totally believed that him showing up the way He did was God's intervention! He also told me that he had my latest picture that I had sent him of me, my sons and Bella on top of his desk!

He had showed it to a woman at work that thought that I was not for real when he hired me and totally surprised her! He said something very important to me that day "Your story gave me the motivation to help someone else."

Now I had confirmation that my story could very well change someone else's life or motivate someone to help another human being!

It was funny that same weekend as I left Savers with a purchase, an older woman approached me on a wheelchair asking me for money, I shared with her that I had been in the same position years ago and asked her what her name was…

She told me her name was Marty, I looked at her very seriously and said "Marty, pray for your circumstances to change like I did, when the opportunity arises take it and let it change your life!"

She said she would and that night I prayed for her, unfortunately you never know who is serious about changing their lives or not! All you can do is give them the best advice and hope they take it…

I also seen for myself people you give advice to that pretended to listen but unfortunately are addicted to their lifestyle…I was not one of them…

Sometimes being without family or someone that you care about can keep you stuck in the same situation, loneliness can also be addictive…

Not for me, my children and Bella were my motivation for living…

CHAPTER 135

Bella's 1ˢᵗ Birthday and something I wasn't expecting!

*B*ella's birthday was coming up…she would be a year old in November…little did she know what a gift she had been for me! When I looked into Bella's blue eyes and saw her smile back at me….it made my life worth living!

I also got the surprise of my life by finding out in November of 2022 that my ex-husband Victor had decided to move to Vegas to live with my oldest son!

I realized that I was actually happy that he would be around his sons and have all the help and support that he needed…I knew from what I had seen my father go thru after a stroke that the patient is better off being around family….

He was set to arrive at the end of November and his oldest sister would be travelling with him…I was looking forward of seeing them both but at the same time afraid of my reaction on seeing the man that had been the love of my life after a stroke!

I knew life for him would never be the same and I wished with all my heart that the same Victor that I had loved could have remained the same!

On Thanksgiving Day, I asked Danny to take a picture of me and Bella as we were getting ready to celebrate her birthday… I wanted to have a picture of both of us to place on a picture frame…

Thanksgiving Day was spent at Lynn's family and as usual a lot of fun! A big spread of food and extremely friendly people that always made anyone feel welcome!

Everyone was captivated by Bella and took turns holding her and taking pictures…

After Thanksgiving we started to get ready for Bella's 1st birthday party…this meant a lot of decorating and cooking, we had quite a few people coming, unfortunately her grandfather could not be here on time because of the Holiday travel but I knew he was going to be crazy about Bella!

I watched as Bella took her first steps and my heart was full of love for a child that was already showing signs of being very smart and observant like her grandmother!

Everyone was captivated by her, she ended up with a whole bunch of gifts and a lot of attention!

I was amazed when Jodie, the child that Carlos and Kristin had been taking care of walked in to give me a hug! No longer looking like a child, she was 11 years old going on 14! She was really pretty and smart and when I looked at her, I remembered what had happened to me years ago because of looking older than I was…I looked at Jodie and told her "Jodie, please be careful when walking anywhere, even to school! You look older than 11 and you are also very pretty… I also matured early and years ago while delivering a skirt for my mom I was assaulted from behind by an older man and my father who was waiting for me almost killed the guy!"

She told me that she always thought that things like that would never happen to her and I told her "Jodie, absolutely wrong! As a young woman this can happen to anyone! There are a lot of child abusers out there! Always be on the lookout for anyone that stops you on the street!"

I could tell she was really listening and when I went to the kitchen, she followed me and hugged me…this child that was now turning into a young woman had always been close to me and had a very special place in my heart!

After the cake was cut and the gifts opened quite a few people left and Bella had been treated like a princess on her birthday!

CHAPTER 136

A family reunion must waited for...

*V*ictor finally arrived suffering from quite a bit of jet leg due to the long trip, his sister stayed for an extra day and then went back home, I would have liked to have seen her but that was not to be...

Carlos and Danny arranged for us to meet at Round Table in Lake Mead on a Saturday afternoon, I arrived a bit earlier with a small gift of seasonings to give my oldest son so that they could season his meals with a bit more flavor.

When I saw Victor came in with my oldest son my first thought was how much older he looked and when I saw him walk towards us he was walking a bit crooked...tall as before and smiling at me...

We sat across from each other and after a brief hug and while waiting for our food we engaged in conversation, he was anxious to share with me his experience with his stroke, he told me that life in the Acores was not the same.... how he had managed by himself and of his fears after the stroke...

When I asked him how he was taking care of himself, he told me that he was still walking... but if he walked too much...then he would get bad leg cramps and shared with me how his vision had been affected by the stroke.

I looked straight at him and asked him "So, Victor how are you really doing?"

He dropped his gaze and said "Existing. Not really living."

I didn't like that comment at all and told him "Victor, that sounds like depression to me and you have much to live for now! For example, your son's that worried a lot about you and wanted you here and a brand-new granddaughter." He shook his head...understanding what I was saying...

Carlos came by our table, I shared with my son the statement that I had just heard from his father about "just existing" and asked him to please set up an appointment with a heart doctor as soon as possible. I turned to Victor and told him in plain English "If you even try to give up on us, I will kick your butt." He smiled at that and I was glad that he was among family...

Once outside Carlos came behind me, placed his arm around my shoulders and asked me "Mom...Dad needs a friend, do you mind calling him once in a while or having him call you?" Of course, I agreed I knew how depression had affected my father after his stroke and wanted my son's father to be around for many years to come... I also insisted that he call a doctor for an appointment asap and to watch his diet carefully...

As I was getting in my car Victor turned to me and said "Are you still mad at me?" I turned around and replied "If I was mad at you, do you think I would be helping you?" He smiled and walked towards Carlos's car...I believe in a better mood...

Once inside my car I was able to reflect on our meeting and realized with sadness that my feelings towards him had changed...he no longer made my pulse race... now I just felt tenderness and the urge to help because after all he was my son's father...

Carlos brought his father to come and see me and to pick up a few groceries I had bought for him...as soon as I saw Victor enter thru the door just by looking at him the way he was now made me wish for the Victor that I once knew...

I worried about his state of mind, he still spoke about "just existing" he worried about the weather in the summer in Vegas and spoke about going back to Acores, when Carlos and I asked him who did he have to go back to, he said "friends."

He also had referred to the "Casa de Repouso" in Acores "Convalescent Home" and I reminded him of what had happened to my father and mother in one of these so called "Convalescent Homes" and he agreed that he didn't like them either, his mother had been placed on one and he taken her out two days after!!

My son and I both reminded him that there was nothing like family and that we were here to help him in anyway and that he was not alone now...He smiled and nodded, I had the feeling that he also suffered from depression due to the stroke and was feeling quite alone...

When Victor called, I answered because I didn't want him feeling alone while Carlos was working and Kristin was working on her computer, I knew that life away from Acores could be very hard for him, it was an adjustment I knew would take time to get used to....

CHAPTER 137

Holidays, a very special gift and finally following my dreams!

We prepared for our Christmas that this year would include Victor…I did my Christmas shopping and actually found a warm blanket from Portugal to give him and plenty of gifts for everyone…including a very special granddaughter!

For Christmas Eve we met at Carlos house, I took with me not only my gifts but also rice pudding and chestnuts, we took pictures as a family and had lunch together. Victor surprised me by giving me pictures that he had of our kids and an old Portuguese Bible with a dedication from my father, from the date of one of the marks inside the small bible from a saint, dated 1966, I must have been just about 8 years old!

This touched my heart more than any other gift, for me it was like holding a very special book that my father had read and believed in…. I tried not to cry in front of anyone and wondered besides Victor who had it before, due to the stroke he didn't remember how he had acquired it…

While looking at the kids' pictures, we shared happy memories of watching our kids grow up, laughed at the silly ones and Victor and I heard some things that our kids had tried to hide from us while growing up, including Danny that had driven my car as a teenager without a Driver's License!

After our lunch and gift exchange I had to make a quick stop at Trader Joes and Victor asked to go with me, we spoke about our family and friends…

We stopped by my house, met with Danny and Lynn and took a few more pictures, went to Lynn's uncle's house to share dinner together and I was glad that he was among family for the Holidays!

After dinner I took him back to Carlos's house and went back home, I knew Victor missed the connection with his family and I was glad that my son's had their father close by as they wished to celebrate this very special Christmas…

He asked me if it was going to take two months to see me again and I told him not to fret that New Year's Eve was just a week away and that I was just a phone call away…

I didn't want to go any further with him because I knew he would not change, he actually asked me where all my money had gone and I had to remind him that at one point I was doing my treatments and Danny's including all other expenses…

He would never understand because he hadn't been in my shoes…

I finally had made up my mind to retire and work part-time so that my writing career could continue…it was time to follow my dreams!

As I prepared to publish this book, I realized something very important! In the beginning I had prayed for God to give me a chance to live long enough to see my first grandchild and I was able to! I also realized the importance of this book was also to be able to change someone else's life…

I finally realized what I prayed for had come to pass…to be alive, close to my son's and have a granddaughter that I was now able to hold in my arms and after all I had survived!!

Just before Christmas I got to see my granddaughter take her first steps in our kitchen using her brand-new shoes with a smile from ear to ear! My heart swelled up with love for a little girl named Bella….

It was not easy hiding from my family the fact that along with looking for work I was also finishing the book that was almost forgotten, I wanted to surprise them all and leave a legacy behind for my family….

After all the miracle had been accomplished…. I had lived long enough to see the birth of my first grandchild, to hold her and love her…this from a woman that at one point had given up making plans for the future!

Miracles do happen!!

Notes

*T*his book is dedicated first and foremost to our Heavenly Father and His Son that came to my rescue when I needed help desperately and step by step showed me the way to heal.

Second to a family too stubborn to listen but too loved to be forgotten!

Especially to my father and mother and a note to anyone that will read this book "If I had to do it all over again…I would! Just to have them with me."

If I had my family in front of me, I wish I could ask them each one personally, "Do you think I could love you any less just because you didn't listen to me?"

This answer would be a definite "No" After all it's all about Unconditional Love in every sense of the word…

I hope as you read my story that you can manage to visualize certain passages on this book like I did! I found myself crying many times missing my family and the times we spent together! My hope for you the reader is that just maybe what I went thru can help you in some way and help you change your life for the better…like my family should have done…

I was listening to the radio one night and heard a song that made me cry! The words on this song is how I feel about writing this book "Words is all I have to take your heart away" and maybe to change your life!

A final Note: The picture on the front of this book is me and Bella at Christmas time and the Doves around us are there in honor of Lady of Fatima and the miracle that happened in Thornton, CA.

The pictures on the back of the book are treasured memories from a family that was never forgotten…

** Some people's names have been changed to protect their identities.

Acknowledgments

Dr. Gabrielle Francis – The Herban Alchemist
Dr. Jeri L. Heyman – Herbal Answers, Inc.
Dr. Steven Whiting, Ph.D. -The Institute of Nutritional Science
Dr. Howard Liebgold M.D – Phobease Classes
Jim Meyer – Christian Minister and friend
Jim Amos – The man that gave me a second chance in life.
Ken Sarnoski – Extended Stay America
Toastmasters, CA -Public Speaking
Cardinale Way Acura – Great Customer Service
My E-mail address is -ladyoffaith5000@sbcglobal.net.

Personal Training Success Story
Mary Lima

BEFORE   AFTER

My name is Mary Connie S. Lima and I would like to share with you how I went from a size 22 to a size 6/7, losing over 120 lbs. in the process. It all started in 1999, after having to deal with the death of seven family members and all of their illnesses. During that time, I took on the role of caregiver and it was not until after everyone was gone that I realized how much of a tole it had taken on me. I got a wake up call when my own health started to deteriorate. I was physically and emotionally ill with constant thoughts of suicide. I kept seeing doctor after doctor, but continued to feel worse. I later found out that I had a serious illness and my life was on the line. It had become apparent that i needed to start taking better care of myself, so I took on the responsibility of finding the resources I needed to achieve that goal. I finally stood up for myself and stopped feeling sorry. I realized this journey back to health included not only my physical well being, but also a spiritual growth since healing involves both. When my doctor wanted to give me medication for everything under the sun, I refused. I told her that I wanted to take charge of my life and come back after I made the necessary changes. I started at the library by doing research on which foods I should be eating to achieve my goal as well as which foods I needed to avoid. I switched my diet to organic foods, and avoided all unhealthy carbs along with sugar. To start exercising , I joined Curves where the pounds started coming off little by little. After working out for a while and doing well, I hit a plateau and became very frustrated. All of a sudden, everything I was doing was not producing the results I was looking for. So, I decided to join 24 Hour Fitness and that is where all of the hard work started to pay off. I started by walking and running on the treadmill, 24 cycle classes, weights, and finishing with the steam room. I found that I had to keep switching my routine in order to get rid of the stubborn pounds. I believe the key ingredient to my success was persistence and hard work - they both really paid off! All I have to say to anyone that is facing illnesses or weight problems is to refuse to wallow in misery and take charge of your life. The effort is worth the trouble. Your life is worth it!

Speak to a Personal Trainer about your goals today or

506

Ingram Content Group UK Ltd.
Milton Keynes UK
UKHW020938200423
420413UK00011B/50